W9-DJA-059

National
Educational
Technology
Standards for Teachers

Preparing Teachers to Use Technology

iste

National Educational Technology Standards for Teachers
Preparing Teachers to Use Technology

Document Development Director and Editor
M. G. (Peggy) Kelly

Editor
Anita McAnear

Director of Publishing
Jean Marie Hall

Acquisitions Editor
Mathew Manweller

Copy Editor
Lynne Ertle

Book Publishing Project Manager
Tracy Cozzens

Data and Communications Manager
Diannah Anavir

Cover Design
Katherine Getta, Getta Graphic Design

Book Design and Layout
Katherine Getta, Getta Graphic Design

Production
Kim McGovern

Administrative Assistant
Pam Calegari

International Society for Technology in Education (ISTE)
480 Charnelton Street
Eugene, OR 97401-2626
Order Desk: 800.336.5191
Order Fax: 541.302.3778
Customer Service: orders@iste.org
Books and Courseware: books@iste.org
World Wide Web: www.iste.org

First Edition
ISBN 1-56484-173-1
Library of Congress Control Number: 200197951

Acknowledgments

No document of this size can be completed without the assistance of a team of people.

Thanks go to the NETS for Teachers Writing Team for contributing to the activities section, for being willing to put their work out for public scrutiny, and for being flexible in working with the ambiguity of developing a unique lesson-plan format.

Thanks to my special friends on the NETS Leadership Team and ISTE Accreditation Committee who are always there, always contributing, always willing to participate in another crazy adventure in creativity.

A heartfelt thank you to Kathy Matthew and her group at Louisiana Tech University as well as Juanita Guerin for collecting additional stories of how university faculty instruction has been changed by participation in the QUEST Project, another PT[3] grant.

Thanks to Jeri Carroll, Wichita State University, for being on call to fill in miscellaneous details in lessons and for being a master of finding appropriate Web resources. Jeri has the critical eye for consistency and detail that was needed when my brain was fried.

Special thanks to my colleagues at California State University, San Marcos, who piloted lessons and shared their own special brand of teaching, especially Laura Wendling, Kathy Norman, Gib Stuve, and David Whitehorse.

A unique thank you to the students in the El Camino High School Choral Program and their director, George Bridgewater, for letting me use them as photo subjects and follow their high school learning experiences over the past four years. Thanks also to the students at Casita Center, Crestview Elementary, and Solana Santa Fe School for letting me take pictures and share in their learning.

An extraordinary thank you to Jean Hall, Anita McAnear, and the rest of the ISTE staff. With the tremendous number of people contributing to this book, it could have been a logistical nightmare had it not been for their assistance. I sincerely thank Jean for educating me on the whys and hows of production, for monitoring the schedule, and for being a good friend in the process. I value Anita's creative and analytical mind, depth of understanding of the field of educational technology, and ability to ask tough questions in a collegial, inquisitive manner while becoming another good friend. Jean and Anita, I am sorry for the gray hair this project produced, but we had a good time anyway.

This book would not have its distinctive look and feel without the genius of graphic designer Katherine Getta. I have not met another designer with such impeccable taste and a wonderful sense of humor.

And a last—but never least—thank you, Lajeane Thomas, for being the sounding board and last stop for manuscript feedback before submission. Lajeane double-checked the accuracy of names, was always sensitive to the needs of the NETS Partners and Contributors, and was the watchdog for project-related information that must be absolutely correct. Her insights and word tweaking added a finishing touch.

M. G. (Peggy) Kelly
Co-Director, ISTE NETS Project

Contents

v

Preface

Amid the worst set of thunder and electrical storms in Pittsburgh history, 52 dedicated educators flew into the airport to be bussed to Wheeling, West Virginia, to spend a week at NASA's Classroom of the Future (COTF) on the campus of Wheeling Jesuit University. In spite of a rough but almost comedic start, this National Educational Technology Standards (NETS) Writing Team worked for a week in the clear but humid weather to collaboratively develop the lessons that make up a large part of this book.

Selected from a national pool of nominees and volunteers, the writing team included teachers at all levels, technology coordinators, school administrators, state level administrators, curriculum association representatives, and many teacher educators. The curriculum association representatives were named by each of the subject area professional associations to ensure that standards for their curriculum were addressed appropriately in the lessons. Each writing team member brought a unique set of experiences to the discussion that contributed to making the outcome a wonderful experience for the participants and what we think is a rich volume of resources.

From the early morning until late in the evening, small groups worked in the computer labs or clustered in alcoves talking and debating, and made extensive use of the facilities provided by the Center for Educational Technologies, of which NASA's Classroom of the Future is a part. The staff of the center as well as many online consultants provided outstanding and timely feedback as the lessons developed.

The NETS Leadership Team, comprising members of the International Society for Technology in Education (ISTE) Standards and Accreditation Committee, ISTE staff, and staff from COTF, met every evening to debrief the day's experiences and set goals for the next day. Those evening meetings produced a unique lesson plan format designed specifically for university faculty and raised issues about the realities of implementing technology in teacher education in ways that were not in the literature. Those meetings not only brought clarity to issues being debated in the curriculum teams but also consensus to the ideas you see in this book.

Each participant in the writing meeting contributed as active members of two teams: a curriculum team and a program team. Curriculum teams, such as foundations, English language arts, mathematics, and science, spanned the P–12 levels with pairs of team members specifically responsible for the P–2, 3–5, 6–8, and 9–12 curriculum. Each team writer also participated in a program team: early childhood, elementary, middle school, and secondary. Every activity developed for this book was presented to both the curriculum and the program teams for review and revision.

In reality, a book can be only just so big. What started as a proposed 250-page book would have been well over 500 pages if all the activities developed were included. Through a yearlong process of review and testing, the activities were reduced to two lessons in each curriculum section for each program area. To the writers we apologize for not being able to include every wonderful idea, and to the reader we apologize for having a volume that is still quite long. But we feel the content presented is a rich and powerful resource for implementing technology throughout teacher preparation programs.

M. G. (Peggy) Kelly
Document Development Director and Editor

Lajeane Thomas
NETS Project Director

Introduction

The NETS Project

The NETS Project was initiated by ISTE's Accreditation and Professional Standards Committee. ISTE has emerged as a recognized leader among professional organizations for educators involved with technology. ISTE's mission is to promote appropriate uses of technology to support and improve learning, teaching, and administration. Its members are leaders in educational technology, including teachers, technology coordinators, education administrators, and teacher educators. ISTE supports all subject area disciplines by providing publications, conferences, online resources, and services that help educators combine the knowledge and skills of their teaching fields with the application of technologies to improve learning and teaching.

The primary goal of the NETS Project is to enable stakeholders in P–12 education to develop national standards for the educational uses of technology that facilitate school improvement in the United States. The NETS Project developed the standards for students and teachers that are highlighted in this book. The NETS Project also facilitated the Technology Standards for School Administrators (TSSA) Project in developing standards to guide educational leaders in recognizing and addressing the essential conditions for effective use of technology to support P–12 education.

This book was developed under ISTE's Preparing Tomorrow's Teachers to Use Technology (PT³) grant awarded by the U.S. Department of Education. With the strong and generous support of the project partners, contributors, and curriculum liaisons, the NETS Project continues to provide guidance in implementing the effective use of technology in teaching and learning.

Preparing Teachers to Use Technology

Developing a set of standards that has a broad base of consensus has never been touted as an easy task. But even more difficult is to create a set of real examples of how the standards play out in practice. The purpose of this book is to provide university faculty (and those engaged in staff development) a set of possibilities.

This book is not designed to be examples of the integration of "cutting edge" technologies. Rather, it is designed to use technologies that have been around awhile, are often already used by some members of the faculty, and are considered general tools.

This book is not designed to cover the entire teacher preparation curriculum. Rather, the examples follow the general pattern of teacher education with a huge caveat that the examples were never meant to be all-encompassing, only a jumping-off point.

This book is not designed to be a prescription for how to implement the standards. Rather, it is designed to make the faculty, administration, supporting school districts, and general university community think about how the whole picture of technology use for teaching and learning should take place. The implementation of technology into a teacher preparation program is best developed collaboratively with all the key players at the table.

This book is not designed to provide perfect lessons. Only the faculty member can decide what are perfect lessons and implementation strategies. Rather, the book, especially the lessons in Section 2, is designed to help faculty members understand what implementation might look like, to provide a framework or starting point in a lesson or topic, and to encourage faculty members to use all their intellectual and creative license to make the experience appropriate for the teacher candidates.

What Is in This Book

The book is designed around the four profiles highlighted in the NETS for Teachers document. The profiles were developed to help entities training teachers to interpret how the six standards can be implemented throughout the teacher candidate's program.

SECTION 1—The first section contains chapters on the standards, setting the stage for technology use, general models for implementation, and the first profile, General Preparation. Included in the first chapter are both the teacher and student standards and profiles in a condensed, easy-to-read format. This section contains explanatory information on what is meant by the essential conditions and how they can be interpreted. Additional information on general strategies is provided as a backdrop to implementing the standards across the university setting. The first profile, General Preparation, concludes this section by discussing ways that technology-rich experiences should be provided for teacher candidates and all students as they complete their academic discipline studies.

SECTION 2—The decision to organize the activities, or lesson plans, by program rather than academic discipline was a tough decision by the writers. In the end, it was the consensus that programs must look at the entirety of offerings and experiences for teacher candidates. Because faculty should collaborate and consult with peers to present a coordinated program, having all the activities together encourages looking outside a single discipline. However, individual faculty members are encouraged to take the book apart and regroup the lessons by content area when necessary. Most often, faculty teach across programs and frequently within the one or two disciplines. Therefore, the chapters are organized by educational foundations, early childhood, elementary, middle school, and secondary education programs.

SECTION 3—Within this section are chapters on student teaching/internship and first-year teaching profiles as well as assessment. Because the university and the public school share the responsibility, these areas support each other. The chapters are designed to provide a set of recommendations and examples of how to look at a novice teacher's development in the use of technology. Each chapter can be excerpted to use with supervisors, master teachers, and others who are supporting the new teacher. To acknowledge that that school classroom is an extension of the university setting, you will not find detailed activities in these sections. Many of the experiences gained in professional preparation coursework will be modified and used during this time period. Many of the professional preparation activities in Section 2 can be used for staff development. For this reason and because supporting first-year teachers may be part of the staff development efforts of the school district, Section 3 also has a chapter on staff development using the NETS for Teachers.

APPENDIXES—The appendixes provide a set of resources that support the activities in the book. It is always difficult to garner all the national standards documents in one location. Therefore, in addition to text copies of the NETS for Teachers, the NETS for Students and a condensed form of the standards for English language arts, mathematics, science, social studies, and early childhood are included for reference.

Throughout the activities, reference is made to assessment and the use of generic rubrics. Included in the appendixes is a collection of rubrics that be used across technology-rich projects. It is anticipated that the user will modify these rubrics to include the content specific criteria associated with the specific situation.

Also included in the appendixes are a sample software evaluation form, a sample Web site evaluation form, a list of software and Web site resources, a glossary of terms, and credits for the many individuals who contributed to this project.

Please check the ISTE Web site at **www.iste.org** for an electronic form of this book as well as other NETS materials supporting technology in education.

Creating a Foundation for Technology Use

- Establishing National Educational Technology Standards for Teachers

- Setting the Stage for Technology Use

- Using Model Strategies for Integrating Technology into Teaching

- Integrating Technology in General Education

Establishing National Educational Technology Standards for Teachers

To live, learn, and work successfully in an increasingly complex and information-rich society, students and teachers must use technology effectively. Within a sound educational setting, technology can enable students to become:

▶ *Capable information technology users*

▶ *Information seekers, analyzers, and evaluators*

▶ *Problem solvers and decision makers*

▶ *Creative and effective users of productivity tools*

▶ *Communicators, collaborators, publishers, and producers*

▶ *Informed, responsible, and contributing citizens*

Through the ongoing use of technology in the schooling process, students are empowered to achieve important technology capabilities. The key individual in helping students develop those capabilities is the classroom teacher. The teacher is responsible for establishing the classroom environment and preparing the learning opportunities that facilitate students' use of technology to learn, communicate, and develop knowledge products. Consequently, it is critical that all classroom teachers are prepared to provide their students with these opportunities. Both professional development programs for teachers currently in the classroom and preparation programs for future teachers must provide technology-rich experiences throughout all aspects of the training programs. Standards and resources within this document provide guidelines for all teachers but specifically for planning teacher education programs that will prepare teachers to play an essential role in producing technology-capable students.

Today's classroom teachers must be prepared to provide technology-supported learning opportunities for their students. Being prepared to use technology and knowing how that technology can support student learning must become integral skills in every teacher's professional repertoire.

Teachers must be prepared to empower students with the advantages technology can bring. Schools and classrooms, both real and virtual, must have teachers who are equipped with technology resources and skills and who can effectively teach the necessary subject matter content while incorporating technology concepts and skills. Real-world connections, primary source material, and sophisticated data-gathering and analysis tools are only a few of the resources that enable teachers to provide heretofore unimaginable opportunities for conceptual understanding.

Traditional educational practices no longer provide prospective teachers with all the necessary skills for teaching students, who must be able to survive economically in today's workplace. Teachers must teach students to apply strategies for solving problems and to use appropriate tools for learning, collaborating, and communicating. The following chart lists characteristics representing traditional approaches to learning and corresponding strategies often associated with new learning environments for P–12 students. These new learning environments should also be established in teacher preparation programs.

ESTABLISHING NEW LEARNING ENVIRONMENTS

Incorporating New Strategies

Traditional Learning Environments	⟶	New Learning Environments
Teacher-centered instruction	⟶	Student-centered learning
Single-sense stimulation	⟶	Multisensory stimulation
Single-path progression	⟶	Multipath progression
Single media	⟶	Multimedia
Isolated work	⟶	Collaborative work
Information delivery	⟶	Information exchange
Passive learning	⟶	Active/exploratory/inquiry-based learning
Factual, knowledge-based learning	⟶	Critical thinking and informed decision-making
Reactive response	⟶	Proactive/planned action
Isolated, artificial context	⟶	Authentic, real-world context

To provide a sense of what teachers must prepare students to be able to do, the following pages list the standards and performance indicators for students at specified grade ranges. Each profile of performance indicators builds on the prior list of competencies. Teachers must be able to create learning experiences that enable students to achieve these competencies in a meaningful way.

The technology standards for students are divided into six broad categories. Standards within each category are to be introduced, reinforced, and mastered by students. These categories provide a framework for linking performance indicators found within the Profiles for Technology-Literate Students to the standards. Teachers can use these standards and profiles as guidelines for planning technology-based activities in which students achieve success in learning, communication, and life skills.

TECHNOLOGY STANDARDS FOR STUDENTS

1. Basic operations and concepts

▶ Students demonstrate a sound understanding of the nature and operation of technology systems.

▶ Students are proficient in the use of technology.

2. Social, ethical, and human issues

▶ Students understand the ethical, cultural, and societal issues related to technology.

▶ Students practice responsible use of technology systems, information, and software.

▶ Students develop positive attitudes toward technology uses that support lifelong learning, collaboration, personal pursuits, and productivity.

Profiles for Technology-Literate Students

GRADES PK–2
Prior to completion of Grade 2, students will:

1. Use input devices (e.g., mouse, keyboard, remote control) and output devices (e.g., monitor, printer) to successfully operate computers, VCRs, audiotapes, and other technologies. (1)

2. Use a variety of media and technology resources for directed and independent learning activities. (1, 3)

3. Communicate about technology using developmentally appropriate and accurate terminology. (1)

4. Use developmentally appropriate multimedia resources (e.g., interactive books, educational software, elementary multimedia encyclopedias) to support learning. (1)

5. Work cooperatively and collaboratively with peers, family members, and others when using technology in the classroom. (2)

6. Demonstrate positive social and ethical behaviors when using technology. (2)

7. Practice responsible use of technology systems and software. (2)

8. Create developmentally appropriate multimedia products with support from teachers, family members, or student partners. (3)

9. Use technology resources (e.g., puzzles, logical thinking programs, writing tools, digital cameras, drawing tools) for problem solving, communication, and illustration of thoughts, ideas, and stories. (3, 4, 5, 6)

10. Gather information and communicate with others using telecommunications, with support from teachers, family members, or student partners. (4)

GRADES 3–5
Prior to completion of Grade 5, students will:

1. Use keyboards and other common input and output devices (including adaptive devices when necessary) efficiently and effectively. (1)

2. Discuss common uses of technology in daily life and the advantages and disadvantages those uses provide. (1, 2)

3. Discuss basic issues related to responsible use of technology and information and describe personal consequences of inappropriate use. (2)

4. Use general purpose productivity tools and peripherals to support personal productivity, remediate skill deficits, and facilitate learning throughout the curriculum. (3)

5. Use technology tools (e.g., multimedia authoring, presentation, Web tools, digital cameras, scanners) for individual and collaborative writing, communication, and publishing activities to create knowledge products for audiences inside and outside the classroom. (3, 4)

6. Use telecommunications efficiently and effectively to access remote information, communicate with others in support of direct and independent learning, and pursue personal interests. (4)

7. Use telecommunications and online resources (e.g., e-mail, online discussions, Web environments) to participate in collaborative problem-solving activities for the purpose of developing solutions or products for audiences inside and outside the classroom. (4, 5)

8. Use technology resources (e.g., calculators, data collection probes, videos, educational software) for problem solving, self-directed learning, and extended learning activities. (5, 6)

9. Determine when technology is useful and select the appropriate tool(s) and technology resources to address a variety of tasks and problems. (5, 6)

10. Evaluate the accuracy, relevance, appropriateness, comprehensiveness, and bias of electronic information sources. (6)

GRADES 6–8

Prior to completion of Grade 8, students will:

1. Apply strategies for identifying and solving routine hardware and software problems that occur during everyday use. (1)

2. Demonstrate knowledge of current changes in information technologies and the effect those changes have on the workplace and society. (2)

3. Exhibit legal and ethical behaviors when using information and technology, and discuss consequences of misuse. (2)

4. Use content-specific tools, software, and simulations (e.g., environmental probes, graphing calculators, exploratory environments, Web tools) to support learning and research. (3, 5)

5. Apply productivity/multimedia tools and peripherals to support personal productivity, group collaboration, and learning throughout the curriculum. (3, 6)

6. Design, develop, publish, and present products (e.g., Web pages, videotapes) using technology resources that demonstrate and communicate curriculum concepts to audiences inside and outside the classroom. (4, 5, 6)

7. Collaborate with peers, experts, and others using telecommunications and collaborative tools to investigate curriculum-related problems, issues, and information, and to develop solutions or products for audiences inside and outside the classroom. (4, 5)

8. Select and use appropriate tools and technology resources to accomplish a variety of tasks and solve problems. (5, 6)

9. Demonstrate an understanding of concepts underlying hardware, software, and connectivity, and of practical applications to learning and problem solving. (1, 6)

10. Research and evaluate the accuracy, relevance, appropriateness, comprehensiveness, and bias of electronic information sources concerning real-world problems. (2, 5, 6)

GRADES 9–12

Prior to completion of Grade 12, students will:

1. Identify capabilities and limitations of contemporary and emerging technology resources and assess the potential of these systems and services to address personal, lifelong learning, and workplace needs. (2)

2. Make informed choices among technology systems, resources, and services. (1, 2)

3. Analyze advantages and disadvantages of widespread use and reliance on technology in the workplace and in society as a whole. (2)

4. Demonstrate and advocate for legal and ethical behaviors among peers, family, and community regarding the use of technology and information. (2)

5. Use technology tools and resources for managing and communicating personal/professional information (e.g., finances, schedules, addresses, purchases, correspondence). (3, 4)

6. Evaluate technology-based options, including distance and distributed education, for lifelong learning. (5)

7. Routinely and efficiently use online information resources to meet needs for collaboration, research, publications, communications, and productivity. (4, 5, 6)

8. Select and apply technology tools for research, information analysis, problem solving, and decision making in content learning. (4, 5)

9. Investigate and apply expert systems, intelligent agents, and simulations in real-world situations. (3, 5, 6)

10. Collaborate with peers, experts, and others to contribute to a content-related knowledge base by using technology to compile, synthesize, produce, and disseminate information, models, and other creative works. (4, 5, 6)

3. Technology productivity tools

▶ Students use technology tools to enhance learning, increase productivity, and promote creativity.

▶ Students use productivity tools to collaborate in constructing technology-enhanced models, preparing publications, and producing other creative works.

4. Technology communications tools

▶ Students use telecommunications to collaborate, publish, and interact with peers, experts, and other audiences.

▶ Students use a variety of media and formats to communicate information and ideas effectively to multiple audiences.

5. Technology research tools

▶ Students use technology to locate, evaluate, and collect information from a variety of sources.

▶ Students use technology tools to process data and report results.

▶ Students evaluate and select new information resources and technological innovations based on the appropriateness to specific tasks.

6. Technology problem-solving and decision-making tools

▶ Students use technology resources for solving problems and making informed decisions.

▶ Students employ technology in the development of strategies for solving problems in the real world.

Technology Standards and Performance Indicators for Teachers

Building on the NETS for Students, the ISTE NETS for Teachers (NETS•T), which focus on preservice teacher education, define the fundamental concepts, knowledge, skills, and attitudes for applying technology in educational settings. All candidates seeking certification or endorsements in teacher preparation should meet these educational technology standards. It is the responsibility of faculty across the university and at cooperating schools to provide opportunities for teacher candidates to meet these standards.

Performance indicators for each standard provide specific outcomes to be measured when developing a set of assessment tools.

The six standards areas with performance indicators on the facing page are designed to be general enough to be customized to fit state, university, or district guidelines and yet specific enough to define the scope of the topic. The standards and the performance indicators also provide guidelines for teachers currently in the classroom.

THE EVOLUTION OF ISTE TECHNOLOGY STANDARDS

ISTE Technology Standards for Teachers have provided a framework for implementing technology in teaching and learning that has been widely used in universities, state departments of education, and school districts across the nation. This document includes the third revision in the evolutionary development of the standards.

1993

First Edition—ISTE Technology Standards for All Teachers adopted, 13 indicators

1997

Second Edition—ISTE Technology Standards for All Teachers, 18 indicators organized into the following three categories:

1. Basic Computer/Technology Operations and Concepts
2. Personal and Professional Use of Technology
3. Application of Technology in Instruction

2000

For standards to continue to be useful, changes in the standards topics and organization must reflect alignment with the ISTE NETS for Students (NETS•S), research on teaching and learning with technology, and advances in technology. The NETS for Teachers are designed to address what teachers should know about and be able to do with technology in order to prepare their students to meet the ISTE NETS for Students.

The third edition, modeled upon the NETS•S, expands the three previous categories into six categories. These include dividing the Application of Technology in Instruction category into the areas of planning, implementing, and assessing, while adding a category on the social, ethical, legal, and human issues related to technology use.

Third Edition—ISTE NETS•T, 23 indicators organized into the following six categories:

I. Technology Operations and Concepts
II. Planning and Designing Learning Environments and Experiences
III. Teaching, Learning, and the Curriculum
IV. Assessment and Evaluation
V. Productivity and Professional Practice
VI. Social, Ethical, Legal, and Human Issues

ISTE NETS AND PERFORMANCE INDICATORS FOR TEACHERS

All classroom teachers should be prepared to meet the following standards and performance indicators.

I. TECHNOLOGY OPERATIONS AND CONCEPTS

Teachers demonstrate a sound understanding of technology operations and concepts. Teachers:

A. demonstrate introductory knowledge, skills, and understanding of concepts related to technology (as described in the ISTE NETS for Students).

B. demonstrate continual growth in technology knowledge and skills to stay abreast of current and emerging technologies.

II. PLANNING AND DESIGNING LEARNING ENVIRONMENTS AND EXPERIENCES

Teachers plan and design effective learning environments and experiences supported by technology. Teachers:

A. design developmentally appropriate learning opportunities that apply technology-enhanced instructional strategies to support the diverse needs of learners.

B. apply current research on teaching and learning with technology when planning learning environments and experiences.

C. identify and locate technology resources and evaluate them for accuracy and suitability.

D. plan for the management of technology resources within the context of learning activities.

E. plan strategies to manage student learning in a technology-enhanced environment.

III. TEACHING, LEARNING, AND THE CURRICULUM

Teachers implement curriculum plans that include methods and strategies for applying technology to maximize student learning. Teachers:

A. facilitate technology-enhanced experiences that address content standards and student technology standards.

B. use technology to support learner-centered strategies that address the diverse needs of students.

C. apply technology to develop students' higher-order skills and creativity.

D. manage student learning activities in a technology-enhanced environment.

IV. ASSESSMENT AND EVALUATION

Teachers apply technology to facilitate a variety of effective assessment and evaluation strategies. Teachers:

A. apply technology in assessing student learning of subject matter using a variety of assessment techniques.

B. use technology resources to collect and analyze data, interpret results, and communicate findings to improve instructional practice and maximize student learning.

C. apply multiple methods of evaluation to determine students' appropriate use of technology resources for learning, communication, and productivity.

V. PRODUCTIVITY AND PROFESSIONAL PRACTICE

Teachers use technology to enhance their productivity and professional practice. Teachers:

A. use technology resources to engage in ongoing professional development and lifelong learning.

B. continually evaluate and reflect on professional practice to make informed decisions regarding the use of technology in support of student learning.

C. apply technology to increase productivity.

D. use technology to communicate and collaborate with peers, parents, and the larger community in order to nurture student learning.

VI. SOCIAL, ETHICAL, LEGAL, AND HUMAN ISSUES

Teachers understand the social, ethical, legal, and human issues surrounding the use of technology in PK–12 schools and apply that understanding in practice. Teachers:

A. model and teach legal and ethical practice related to technology use.

B. apply technology resources to enable and empower learners with diverse backgrounds, characteristics, and abilities.

C. identify and use technology resources that affirm diversity.

D. promote safe and healthy use of technology resources.

E. facilitate equitable access to technology resources for all students.

Technology Performance Profiles for Teacher Preparation

Today's teacher preparation programs provide a variety of alternative paths to initial licensure. They address economic conditions, the needs of prospective teachers, and the demands of employing school districts. Regardless of the configuration of the program, all teachers must have opportunities for experiences that prepare them to meet technology standards. The existence of many types of programs virtually ensures that there will be no one method for providing learning experiences to meet these standards.

The Technology Performance Profiles for Teacher Preparation suggest ways programs can incrementally examine how well candidates meet the standards. The profiles correspond to four phases in the typical preparation of a teacher. The profiles are not meant to be prescriptive or lock step; they are specifically designed to be fluid in providing guidelines for programs to create a set of benchmarks in planning and assessment that align with unique program design.

The four profiles relating to each environment are defined as the General Preparation Performance Profile, Professional Education Performance Profile, Student Teaching/Internship Performance Profile, and First-Year Teaching Performance Profile.

▶ GENERAL PREPARATION PERFORMANCE PROFILE

Candidates may be in their major or minor course of study. They may be at the lower division level or may have received skill development through on-the-job training, obtaining a degree or experience in a nontraditional program. Typically, the university arts and sciences areas provide the experiences defined in this profile. Programs may have multiple ways for candidates to demonstrate that they are able to perform the tasks that go beyond the classroom setting. Upon completion of the general preparation component of their programs, prospective teachers should be able to meet the competencies described in this profile.

▶ PROFESSIONAL PREPARATION PERFORMANCE PROFILE

Candidates have been admitted to a professional core of courses or experiences taught by the school or college of education or professional education faculty. Experiences in this profile are part of professional education coursework that may also include integrated fieldwork. The school or college of education or professional development school is typically responsible for preservice teachers having the experiences described in this profile. Prior to the culminating student teaching or internship experience, prospective teachers should be able to meet the competencies described in this profile.

▶ STUDENT TEACHING/INTERNSHIP PERFORMANCE PROFILE

Candidates have completed or are finalizing their professional education coursework and assigned to classrooms where they are completing their final student teaching or intern teaching experience with extensive time spent with students. These individuals will obtain their initial licensure or credential required for a teaching job at the completion of this phase of their education. They are being supervised by a mentor or master teacher on a consistent basis. Upon completion of the culminating student teaching or internship experience, and at the point of initial licensure, teachers should meet the competencies described in this profile.

▶ FIRST-YEAR TEACHING PERFORMANCE PROFILE

Teachers have completed their formal teacher preparation program and are in their first year of independent teaching. They are typically in control of their own classroom and are under contract with a school district. Teachers at this stage, as with any teacher in the building, are supervised by their school administrator. The novice teacher may be part of a beginning teacher support program and may be receiving coaching and mentoring. Upon completion of the first year of teaching, teachers should meet the competencies described in this profile.

HOW TO READ THE PERFORMANCE PROFILES

Example:

Performance tasks indicating progress

Roman numerals identify standards met by each profile indicator

Standard category

Standard

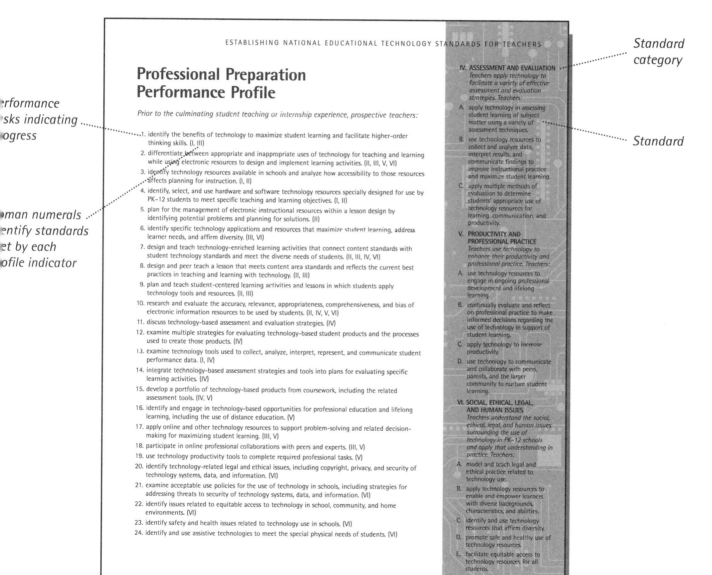

ESTABLISHING NATIONAL EDUCATIONAL TECHNOLOGY STANDARDS FOR TEACHERS

Professional Preparation Performance Profile

Prior to the culminating student teaching or internship experience, prospective teachers:

1. identify the benefits of technology to maximize student learning and facilitate higher-order thinking skills. (I, III)
2. differentiate between appropriate and inappropriate uses of technology for teaching and learning while using electronic resources to design and implement learning activities. (II, III, V, VI)
3. identify technology resources available in schools and analyze how accessibility to those resources affects planning for instruction. (I, II)
4. identify, select, and use hardware and software technology resources specially designed for use by PK–12 students to meet specific teaching and learning objectives. (I, II)
5. plan for the management of electronic instructional resources within a lesson design by identifying potential problems and planning for solutions. (II)
6. identify specific technology applications and resources that maximize student learning, address learner needs, and affirm diversity. (III, VI)
7. design and teach technology-enriched learning activities that connect content standards with student technology standards and meet the diverse needs of students. (II, III, IV, VI)
8. design and peer teach a lesson that meets content area standards and reflects the current best practices in teaching and learning with technology. (II, III)
9. plan and teach student-centered learning activities and lessons in which students apply technology tools and resources. (II, III)
10. research and evaluate the accuracy, relevance, appropriateness, comprehensiveness, and bias of electronic information resources to be used by students. (II, IV, V, VI)
11. discuss technology-based assessment and evaluation strategies. (IV)
12. examine multiple strategies for evaluating technology-based student products and the processes used to create those products. (IV)
13. examine technology tools used to collect, analyze, interpret, represent, and communicate student performance data. (I, IV)
14. integrate technology-based assessment strategies and tools into plans for evaluating specific learning activities. (IV)
15. develop a portfolio of technology-based products from coursework, including the related assessment tools. (IV, V)
16. identify and engage in technology-based opportunities for professional education and lifelong learning, including the use of distance education. (V)
17. apply online and other technology resources to support problem-solving and related decision-making for maximizing student learning. (III, V)
18. participate in online professional collaborations with peers and experts. (III, V)
19. use technology productivity tools to complete required professional tasks. (V)
20. identify technology-related legal and ethical issues, including copyright, privacy, and security of technology systems, data, and information. (VI)
21. examine acceptable use policies for the use of technology in schools, including strategies for addressing threats to security of technology systems, data, and information. (VI)
22. identify issues related to equitable access to technology in school, community, and home environments. (VI)
23. identify safety and health issues related to technology use in schools. (VI)
24. identify and use assistive technologies to meet the special physical needs of students. (VI)

IV. ASSESSMENT AND EVALUATION
Teachers apply technology to facilitate a variety of effective assessment and evaluation strategies. Teachers:

A. apply technology in assessing student learning of subject matter using a variety of assessment techniques.

B. use technology resources to collect and analyze data, interpret results, and communicate findings to improve instructional practice and maximize student learning.

C. apply multiple methods of evaluation to determine students' appropriate use of technology resources for learning, communication, and productivity.

V. PRODUCTIVITY AND PROFESSIONAL PRACTICE
Teachers use technology to enhance their productivity and professional practice. Teachers:

A. use technology resources to engage in ongoing professional development and lifelong learning.

B. continually evaluate and reflect on professional practice to make informed decisions regarding the use of technology in support of student learning.

C. apply technology to increase productivity.

D. use technology to communicate and collaborate with peers, parents, and the larger community to nurture student learning.

VI. SOCIAL, ETHICAL, LEGAL, AND HUMAN ISSUES
Teachers understand the social, ethical, legal, and human issues surrounding the use of technology in PK–12 schools and apply that understanding in practice. Teachers:

A. model and teach legal and ethical practice related to technology use.

B. apply technology resources to enable and empower learners with diverse backgrounds, characteristics, and abilities.

C. identify and use technology resources that affirm diversity.

D. promote safe and healthy use of technology resources.

E. facilitate equitable access to technology resources for all students.

TECHNOLOGY STANDARDS FOR TEACHERS

I. TECHNOLOGY OPERATIONS AND CONCEPTS

Teachers demonstrate a sound understanding of technology operations and concepts. Teachers:

A. demonstrate introductory knowledge, skills, and understanding of concepts related to technology (as described in the ISTE NETS for Students).

B. demonstrate continual growth in technology knowledge and skills to stay abreast of current and emerging technologies.

II. PLANNING AND DESIGNING LEARNING ENVIRONMENTS AND EXPERIENCES

Teachers plan and design effective learning environments and experiences supported by technology. Teachers:

A. design developmentally appropriate learning opportunities that apply technology-enhanced instructional strategies to support the diverse needs of learners.

B. apply current research on teaching and learning with technology when planning learning environments and experiences.

C. identify and locate technology resources and evaluate them for accuracy and suitability.

D. plan for the management of technology resources within the context of learning activities.

E. plan strategies to manage student learning in a technology-enhanced environment.

III. TEACHING, LEARNING, AND THE CURRICULUM

Teachers implement curriculum plans that include methods and strategies for applying technology to maximize student learning. Teachers:

A. facilitate technology-enhanced experiences that address content standards and student technology standards.

B. use technology to support learner-centered strategies that address the diverse needs of students.

C. apply technology to develop students' higher-order skills and creativity.

D. manage student learning activities in a technology-enhanced environment.

General Preparation Performance Profile

Upon completion of the general preparation component of their program, prospective teachers:

1. demonstrate a sound understanding of the nature and operation of technology systems. (I)*

2. demonstrate proficiency in the use of common input and output devices; solve routine hardware and software problems; and make informed choices about technology systems, resources, and services. (I)*

3. use technology tools and information resources to increase productivity, promote creativity, and facilitate academic learning. (I, III, IV, V)

4. use content-specific tools (e.g., software, simulation, environmental probes, graphing calculators, exploratory environments, Web tools) to support learning and research. (I, III, V)*

5. use technology resources to facilitate higher order and complex thinking skills, including problem solving, critical thinking, informed decision-making, knowledge construction, and creativity. (I, III, V)*

6. collaborate in constructing technology-enhanced models, preparing publications, and producing other creative works using productivity tools. (I, V)*

7. use technology to locate, evaluate, and collect information from a variety of sources. (I, IV, V)*

8. use technology tools to process data and report results. (I, III, IV, V)*

9. use technology in the development of strategies for solving problems in the real world. (I, III, V)*

10. observe and experience the use of technology in their major field of study. (III, V)

11. use technology tools and resources for managing and communicating information (e.g., finances, schedules, addresses, purchases, correspondence). (I, V)*

12. evaluate and select new information resources and technological innovations based on their appropriateness to specific tasks. (I, III, IV, V)*

13. use a variety of media and formats, including telecommunications, to collaborate, publish, and interact with peers, experts, and other audiences. (I, V)*

14. demonstrate an understanding of the legal, ethical, cultural, and societal issues related to technology. (VI)*

15. exhibit positive attitudes toward technology uses that support lifelong learning, collaboration, personal pursuits, and productivity. (V, VI)*

16. discuss diversity issues related to electronic media. (I, VI)

17. discuss the health and safety issues related to technology use. (VI)

* Adapted from the ISTE NETS for Students.

Professional Preparation Performance Profile

Prior to the culminating student teaching or internship experience, prospective teachers:

1. identify the benefits of technology to maximize student learning and facilitate higher-order thinking skills. (I, III)

2. differentiate between appropriate and inappropriate uses of technology for teaching and learning while using electronic resources to design and implement learning activities. (II, III, V, VI)

3. identify technology resources available in schools and analyze how accessibility to those resources affects planning for instruction. (I, II)

4. identify, select, and use hardware and software technology resources specially designed for use by PK–12 students to meet specific teaching and learning objectives. (I, II)

5. plan for the management of electronic instructional resources within a lesson design by identifying potential problems and planning for solutions. (II)

6. identify specific technology applications and resources that maximize student learning, address learner needs, and affirm diversity. (III, VI)

7. design and teach technology-enriched learning activities that connect content standards with student technology standards and meet the diverse needs of students. (II, III, IV, VI)

8. design and peer teach a lesson that meets content area standards and reflects the current best practices in teaching and learning with technology. (II, III)

9. plan and teach student-centered learning activities and lessons in which students apply technology tools and resources. (II, III)

10. research and evaluate the accuracy, relevance, appropriateness, comprehensiveness, and bias of electronic information resources to be used by students. (II, IV, V, VI)

11. discuss technology-based assessment and evaluation strategies. (IV)

12. examine multiple strategies for evaluating technology-based student products and the processes used to create those products. (IV)

13. examine technology tools used to collect, analyze, interpret, represent, and communicate student performance data. (I, IV)

14. integrate technology-based assessment strategies and tools into plans for evaluating specific learning activities. (IV)

15. develop a portfolio of technology-based products from coursework, including the related assessment tools. (IV, V)

16. identify and engage in technology-based opportunities for professional education and lifelong learning, including the use of distance education. (V)

17. apply online and other technology resources to support problem solving and related decision making for maximizing student learning. (III, V)

18. participate in online professional collaborations with peers and experts. (III, V)

19. use technology productivity tools to complete required professional tasks. (V)

20. identify technology-related legal and ethical issues, including copyright, privacy, and security of technology systems, data, and information. (VI)

21. examine acceptable use policies for the use of technology in schools, including strategies for addressing threats to security of technology systems, data, and information. (VI)

22. identify issues related to equitable access to technology in school, community, and home environments. (VI)

23. identify safety and health issues related to technology use in schools. (VI)

24. identify and use assistive technologies to meet the special physical needs of students. (VI)

IV. ASSESSMENT AND EVALUATION
Teachers apply technology to facilitate a variety of effective assessment and evaluation strategies. Teachers:

A. apply technology in assessing student learning of subject matter using a variety of assessment techniques.

B. use technology resources to collect and analyze data, interpret results, and communicate findings to improve instructional practice and maximize student learning.

C. apply multiple methods of evaluation to determine students' appropriate use of technology resources for learning, communication, and productivity.

V. PRODUCTIVITY AND PROFESSIONAL PRACTICE
Teachers use technology to enhance their productivity and professional practice. Teachers:

A. use technology resources to engage in ongoing professional development and lifelong learning.

B. continually evaluate and reflect on professional practice to make informed decisions regarding the use of technology in support of student learning.

C. apply technology to increase productivity.

D. use technology to communicate and collaborate with peers, parents, and the larger community to nurture student learning.

VI. SOCIAL, ETHICAL, LEGAL, AND HUMAN ISSUES
Teachers understand the social, ethical, legal, and human issues surrounding the use of technology in PK–12 schools and apply that understanding in practice. Teachers:

A. model and teach legal and ethical practice related to technology use.

B. apply technology resources to enable and empower learners with diverse backgrounds, characteristics, and abilities.

C. identify and use technology resources that affirm diversity.

D. promote safe and healthy use of technology resources.

E. facilitate equitable access to technology resources for all students.

TECHNOLOGY STANDARDS FOR TEACHERS

I. TECHNOLOGY OPERATIONS AND CONCEPTS

Teachers demonstrate a sound understanding of technology operations and concepts. Teachers:

A. demonstrate introductory knowledge, skills, and understanding of concepts related to technology (as described in the ISTE NETSfor Students).

B. demonstrate continual growth in technology knowledge and skills to stay abreast of current and emerging technologies.

II. PLANNING AND DESIGNING LEARNING ENVIRONMENTS AND EXPERIENCES

Teachers plan and design effective learning environments and experiences supported by technology. Teachers:

A. design developmentally appropriate learning opportunities that apply technology-enhanced instructional strategies to support the diverse needs of learners.

B. apply current research on teaching and learning with technology when planning learning environments and experiences.

C. identify and locate technology resources and evaluate them for accuracy and suitability.

D. plan for the management of technology resources within the context of learning activities.

E. plan strategies to manage student learning in a technology-enhanced environment.

III. TEACHING, LEARNING, AND THE CURRICULUM

Teachers implement curriculum plans that include methods and strategies for applying technology to maximize student learning. Teachers:

A. facilitate technology-enhanced experiences that address content standards and student technology standards.

B. use technology to support learner-centered strategies that address the diverse needs of students.

C. apply technology to develop students' higher-order skills and creativity.

D. manage student learning activities in a technology-enhanced environment.

Student Teaching/Internship Performance Profile

Upon completion of the culminating student teaching or internship experience, and at the point of initial licensure, teachers:

1. apply troubleshooting strategies for solving routine hardware and software problems that occur in the classroom. (I)

2. identify, evaluate, and select specific technology resources available at the school site and district level to support a coherent lesson sequence. (II, III)

3. design, manage, and facilitate learning experiences using technology that affirms diversity and provides equitable access to resources. (II, VI)

4. create and implement a well-organized plan to manage available technology resources, provide equitable access for all students, and enhance learning outcomes. (II, III)

5. design and facilitate learning experiences that use assistive technologies to meet the special physical needs of students. (II, III)

6. design and teach a coherent sequence of learning activities that integrates appropriate use of technology resources to enhance student academic achievement and technology proficiency by connecting district, state, and national curriculum standards with student technology standards (as defined in the ISTE NETS for Students). (II, III)

7. design, implement, and assess learner-centered lessons that are based on the current best practices on teaching and learning with technology and that engage, motivate, and encourage self-directed student learning. (II, III, IV, V)

8. guide collaborative learning activities in which students use technology resources to solve authentic problems in the subject area(s). (III)

9. develop and use criteria for ongoing assessment of technology-based student products and the processes used to create those products. (IV)

10. design an evaluation plan that applies multiple measures and flexible assessment strategies to determine students' technology proficiency and content area learning. (IV)

11. use multiple measures to analyze instructional practices that employ technology to improve planning, instruction, and management. (II, III, IV)

12. apply technology productivity tools and resources to collect, analyze, and interpret data and to report results to parents and students. (III, IV)

13. select and apply suitable productivity tools to complete educational and professional tasks. (II, III, V)

14. model safe and responsible use of technology and develop classroom procedures to implement school and district technology acceptable use policies and data security plans. (V, VI)

15. participate in online professional collaboration with peers and experts as part of a personally designed plan, based on self-assessment, for professional growth in technology. (V)

First–Year Teaching Performance Profile

Upon completion of the first year of teaching, teachers:

1. assess the availability of technology resources at the school site, plan activities that integrate available resources, and develop a method for obtaining the additional necessary software and hardware to support the specific learning needs of students in the classroom. (I, II, IV)

2. make appropriate choices about technology systems, resources, and services that are aligned with district and state standards. (I, II)

3. arrange equitable access to appropriate technology resources that enable students to engage successfully in learning activities across subject/content areas and grade levels. (II, III, VI)

4. engage in ongoing planning of lesson sequences that effectively integrate technology resources and are consistent with current best practices for integrating the learning of subject matter and student technology standards (as defined in the ISTE NETS for Students). (II, III)

5. plan and implement technology-based learning activities that promote student engagement in analysis, synthesis, interpretation, and creation of original products. (II, III)

6. plan for, implement, and evaluate the management of student use of technology resources as part of classroom operations and in specialized instructional situations. (I, II, III, IV)

7. implement a variety of instructional technology strategies and grouping strategies (e.g., whole group, collaborative, individualized, and learner centered) that include appropriate embedded assessment for meeting the diverse needs of learners. (III, IV)

8. facilitate student access to school and community resources that provide technological and discipline-specific expertise. (III)

9. teach students methods and strategies to assess the validity and reliability of information gathered through technological means. (II, IV)

10. recognize students' talents in the use of technology and provide them with opportunities to share their expertise with their teachers, peers, and others. (II, III, V)

11. guide students in applying self- and peer-assessment tools to critique student-created technology products and the process used to create those products. (IV)

12. facilitate students' use of technology that addresses their social needs and cultural identity and promotes their interaction with the global community. (III, VI)

13. use results from assessment measures (e.g., learner profiles, computer-based testing, electronic portfolios) to improve instructional planning, management, and implementation of learning strategies. (II, IV)

14. use technology tools to collect, analyze, interpret, represent, and communicate data (student performance and other information) for the purposes of instructional planning and school improvement. (IV)

15. use technology resources to facilitate communications with parents or guardians of students. (V)

16. identify capabilities and limitations of current and emerging technology resources and assess the potential of these systems and services to address personal, lifelong learning, and workplace needs. (I, IV, V)

17. participate in technology-based collaboration as part of continual and comprehensive professional growth to stay abreast of new and emerging technology resources that support enhanced learning for PK–12 students. (V)

18. demonstrate and advocate for legal and ethical behaviors among students, colleagues, and community members regarding the use of technology and information. (V, VI)

19. enforce classroom procedures that guide students' safe and healthy use of technology and that comply with legal and professional responsibilities for students needing assistive technologies. (VI)

20. advocate for equal access to technology for all students in their schools, communities, and homes. (VI)

21. implement procedures consistent with district and school policies that protect the privacy and security of student data and information. (VI)

IV. ASSESSMENT AND EVALUATION

Teachers apply technology to facilitate a variety of effective assessment and evaluation strategies. Teachers:

A. apply technology in assessing student learning of subject matter using a variety of assessment techniques.

B. use technology resources to collect and analyze data, interpret results, and communicate findings to improve instructional practice and maximize student learning.

C. apply multiple methods of evaluation to determine students' appropriate use of technology resources for learning, communication, and productivity.

V. PRODUCTIVITY AND PROFESSIONAL PRACTICE

Teachers use technology to enhance their productivity and professional practice. Teachers:

A. use technology resources to engage in ongoing professional development and lifelong learning.

B. continually evaluate and reflect on professional practice to make informed decisions regarding the use of technology in support of student learning.

C. apply technology to increase productivity.

D. use technology to communicate and collaborate with peers, parents, and the larger community to nurture student learning.

VI. SOCIAL, ETHICAL, LEGAL, AND HUMAN ISSUES

Teachers understand the social, ethical, legal, and human issues surrounding the use of technology in PK–12 schools and apply that understanding in practice. Teachers:

A. model and teach legal and ethical practice related to technology use.

B. apply technology resources to enable and empower learners with diverse backgrounds, characteristics, and abilities.

C. identify and use technology resources that affirm diversity.

D. promote safe and healthy use of technology resources.

E. facilitate equitable access to technology resources for all students.

ISTE NETS Essential Conditions for Teacher Preparation

As with the implementation of NETS for Students, a combination of essential conditions is required for teachers to create learning environments conducive to powerful uses of technology.

The most effective learning environments meld traditional approaches and new approaches to facilitate learning of relevant content while addressing individual needs. For these new learning environments to develop, certain prerequisite factors or essential conditions must be present in every phase of an aspiring teacher's education—in the university's general education programs, in the chosen major, in teacher preparation programs, and at the school sites hosting student teachers and interns. First-year teachers cannot be expected to put into practice what they have learned about how to use technology without the presence of these essential conditions in their new job environment. Policy decisions supporting technology use greatly affect a new teacher's ability to apply technology effectively.

Because there are many avenues to becoming a teacher, the standards address a wide variety of teacher preparation program designs. In the context of university-based programs, teacher preparation must be viewed as a university-wide responsibility. Prospective teachers must experience and observe effective uses of technology in their general education and major coursework. School and college of education coursework must consistently model exemplary pedagogy that integrates the use of technology for learning content with methods for working with P–12 students.

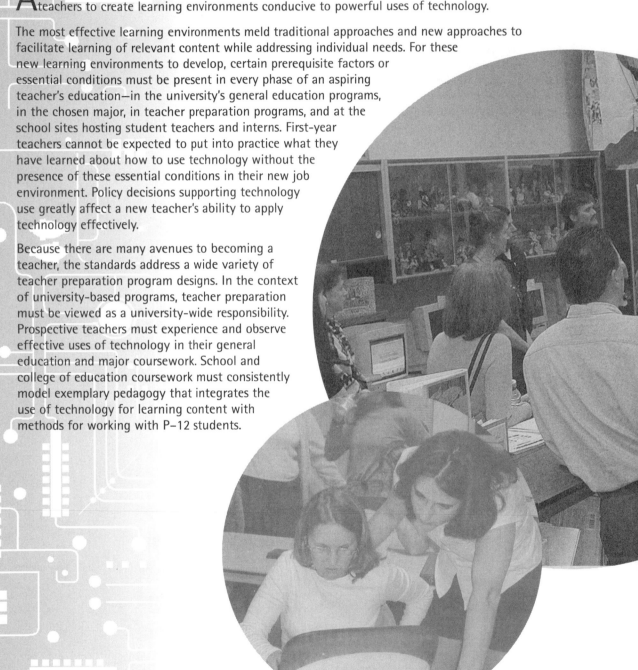

In school-based programs, candidates must continually observe and participate in the effective modeling of technology use for both their own learning and the teaching of their students. Technology must become an integral part of the teaching and learning process in every setting supporting the preparation of teachers.

The following elements should be in place at the university, the college or school of education, and the school site.

▶ Shared vision

▶ Access

▶ Skilled educators

▶ Professional development

▶ Technical assistance

▶ Content standards and curriculum resources

▶ Student-centered teaching

▶ Assessment

▶ Community support

▶ Support policies

The chart on the following page indicates how these essential conditions can be interpreted for each of the profiles in a teacher education program.

Essential Conditions for Implementing NETS for Teachers

GENERAL PREPARATION	PROFESSIONAL PREPARATION
SHARED VISION—There is proactive leadership and administrative support from the entire system.	
University leaders share a vision for technology use in all appropriate courses and content areas.	The professional education administration and faculty share a vision for technology use to support new modes of teaching and learning.
ACCESS—Educators have access to current technologies, software, and telecommunications networks.	
Access to current technologies, software, and telecommunications networks is provided for all students and faculty both inside and outside the classroom.	Access to current technologies, software, and telecommunications networks is provided for teacher education faculty classes, and field including sites, technology-enhanced classrooms that model environments for facilitating a variety of collaborative learning strategie
SKILLED EDUCATORS—Educators are skilled in the use of technology for learning.	
Faculty teaching general education and major courses are knowledgeable about and model appropriate use of technology in their disciplines.	Teacher education faculty are skilled in using technology systems and software appropriate to their subject area specialty and model effective use as part of the coursework.
PROFESSIONAL DEVELOPMENT—Educators have consistent access to professional development in support of technology use in teaching and learning.	
University faculty and students are provided with opportunities for technology skill development and reward structures that recognize the application of technology in teaching, learning, and faculty collaboration.	Personnel in teacher education and field experience sites are provided with ongoing professional development.
TECHNICAL ASSISTANCE—Educators have technical assistance for maintaining and using the technology.	
Timely technical assistance is available for all faculty to ensure consistent, reliable functioning of technology resources.	Technical assistance for teacher education faculty and students is readily accessible and includes expertise in the use of technology resources for teaching and learning in P–12 settings.
CONTENT STANDARDS AND CURRICULUM RESOURCES—Educators are knowledgeable in their subject matter and current in the content standard	
Prospective teachers have knowledge in the subject area(s) they intend to teach.	Technology-based curriculum resources that address subject matter content standards and support teaching, learning, and productivity are available to teacher candidates.
STUDENT-CENTERED TEACHING—Teaching in all settings encompasses student-centered approaches to learning.	
University faculty incorporate student-centered approaches to learning (e.g., active, cooperative, and project-based learning).	Teacher education faculty and professional teaching staff model student-centered approaches to instruction in education coursework and field experiences.
ASSESSMENT—There is continuous assessment of the effectiveness of technology for learning.	
University faculty and support staff assess the effectiveness of technology for learning to examine educational outcomes and inform procurement, policy, and curriculum decisions.	Teacher education faculty and professional teaching staff model the integration of teaching and assessment to measure the effectiveness of technology-supported teaching strategies.
COMMUNITY SUPPORT—The community and school partners provide expertise, support, and resources.	
Prospective teachers experience technology use in real-world settings related to their general education and courses in their majors.	Teacher preparation programs provide teacher candidates with opportunities to participate in field experiences at partner schools whe technology integration is modeled.
SUPPORT POLICIES—School and university policies, financing, and reward structures are in place to support technology in learning.	
University faculty are provided with resources for meeting subject area needs and with reward structures that recognize the application of technology in teaching, learning, and faculty collaboration.	Policies associated with accreditation, standards, budget allocations, an personnel decisions in teacher education programs and field experience sites support technology integration. Retention, tenure, promotion, and merit policies reward innovative uses of technology by faculty with their students.

STUDENT TEACHING/ INTERNSHIP	FIRST-YEAR TEACHING
...niversity personnel and teachers and school administrators at the ...ooperating school site share a vision for technology use in the classroom.	Schools, districts, and universities share a vision for supporting new teachers in their use of technology in the classroom.
...ccess to current technologies, software, and telecommunications networks ...provided for student teachers/interns and their master ...eachers/mentors/supervisors in the classroom and professional work areas.	Access to current technologies, software, and telecommunications networks is provided for new teachers for classroom and professional use, including access beyond the school day.
...laster (cooperating/supervising) teachers and university supervisors model ...echnology use that facilitates students' meeting the ISTE NETS for Students.	Peers and administrators are skilled users of technology for teaching and school management.
...ooperating/master teachers and supervisors of student teachers/interns are ...eadily provided with professional development in applications of technology ...teaching.	Faculty has continuous access to a variety of professional development opportunities in several delivery modes, with time to take advantage of the offerings.
...field-experience settings, technical assistance is on-site to ensure ...eliability of technology resources.	Technical assistance for faculty and staff is timely, onsite, and includes mentoring to enhance skills in managing classroom software and hardware resources.
...eaching methodologies in their discipline. ...echnology-based curriculum resources that are appropriate in meeting the ...ontent standards in teaching areas and grade ranges are available to ...eacher candidates at the student/intern site.	The school district provides professional development opportunities related to local policies and content standards and the technology-based resources to support the new teacher's efforts to address those standards.
...pportunities to implement a variety of technology-enhanced, student-...entered learning activities are provided for teacher candidates/interns.	Faculty routinely use student-centered approaches to learning to facilitate student use of technology.
...ooperating/master teachers work with student teachers/interns to assess ...he effectiveness of student learning and of technology in supporting that ...earning.	The district and school site support the classroom teacher in the assessment of learning outcomes for technology-supported activities to inform planning, teaching, and further assessment.
...tudent teachers/interns teach in partner schools where technology ...ntegration is modeled and supported.	Schools provide beginning teachers with connections to the community and models of effective use of local and other resources.
...tudent teaching/internships are located at sites where administrative ...olicies support and reward the use of technology.	School induction-year policies, budget allocations, and mentoring assignments support the first-year teacher's use of technology. Hiring practices include policies regarding technology skills of prospective hires.

This chart provides guidelines for the NETS for Teachers essential conditions that should be in place for each phase in the teacher preparation process to support effective use of technology to improve learning, communication, and productivity.

Setting the Stage for Technology Use

As discussed in the previous chapter, standards for teachers and technology leaders are critical to the development of new learning environments for the integration of technology. Equally necessary are

- establishing the underlying conditions for supporting educational environments with technology,
- adhering to national accreditation standards,
- preparing educational leaders,
- assessing and evaluating technology effectiveness, and
- sustaining progress through professional development.

These elements are necessary to provide a supporting environment and high probability of successful, self-sustaining implementation of the NETS for Teachers. This chapter explores these elements to emphasize the need to examine and put in place or improve these essential conditions to the maximum extent possible.

Essential Conditions for Preparation of New Teachers

As educational entities have worked to implement the NETS, barriers have been identified that prevent or restrict successful implementation. In public forums and through electronic communications, educators have expressed frustration by stating, "I am having problems implementing the standards because..." This comment is followed by a list of conditions found to be common across the nation. Thus, the ISTE NETS Leadership and Writing Teams distilled the comments into a list of essential conditions necessary for creating learning environments conducive to powerful uses of technology. The chart of essential conditions on pages 18-19 lists, defines, and provides descriptions of the essential conditions and how they can be addressed in environments common to teacher preparation programs.

SHARED VISION

Defined as the presence of proactive leadership and administrative support, shared vision means that the commitment to technology is systemic. From the leadership to the grounds personnel, there is an understanding of, commitment to, and sense of advocacy for facilitating the implementation of technology across all entities on the campus and the school site. When the implementation of a technology initiative is problematic, a major reason often cited is a breakdown in the common understanding of the institution's goals among those who hold the decision-making power. These situations can occur over something as simple as unlocking the door to a lab or as complex as having the support for a technology line item in the budget. Facilitating the integration of technology may require a change in policy or rules, and the decision-maker has to be willing to look at the situation, forge some type of compromise or exception, and see that it is communicated. The collaborative environment necessary to creating a shared vision is also needed to sustain that vision if creative and beneficial uses of technology are to take place.

ACCESS

The fact that educators need access to current technologies, software, and telecommunications networks seems simple enough. However, this access must be consistent across all of the environments necessary for the preparation of a teacher. Funding for technology and emphasis on technology in institutions across the country varies from those universities that have long supported technology-intensive academic areas, to schools that have just begun to garner technology support. Those institutions with scarce resources and limited human capacity for managing technology often exhibit an environment with access to technology that is sporadic, at best. Courses providing content background to the college of education and the collaborating school sites that support candidates and new teachers in the classrooms must provide consistent access to technology regardless of the institution's focus and funding source.

Additionally, access to technology should be appropriate to the subject areas being studied, from word processors and Internet access in English classrooms to technology labs and electronic microscopes for science labs. Access must be in the classroom as well as lab settings, and provisions must be made for special populations. The technology should be accessible immediately when technology provides the best route to the information or tools needed by teacher candidates, teachers, and students. Furthermore, university model classrooms are important for mirroring effective strategies for using technology in the P–12 environment. The model classrooms should include at least an instructor's station with a presentation system and four to six stations for candidates. Candidates need to see and experience models that demonstrate the kind of access desired in the P–12 classroom.

In addition to the access in their coursework, candidates must have technology access in their student teaching environments and in their classrooms during the induction year and beyond. Without such, there will be limited opportunity to observe or participate in the active use of technology with students and to use communication tools for mentoring or staying connected with parents.

SKILLED EDUCATORS

The educators who work with teacher candidates at all levels must be skilled in the use of technology for learning. They must be able to apply technology in the presentation and administration of their coursework and facilitate the appropriate use of technology by their teacher candidates. From the first course taken as a freshman through collaborative work at the school site, teacher candidates should participate with and observe their mentors' effective use of technology. The skilled educator models and demonstrates techniques for managing the technology in the classroom and for communicating outside the classroom through other electronic means.

PROFESSIONAL DEVELOPMENT

It is only a snapshot in time when it is said that the educators who work with teacher candidates are skilled in the use of technology. Maintaining those skills involves consistent access to professional development as the technology is constantly changing. Opportunities for professional development should be available to university faculty and P–12 faculty and administrators who participate in the preparation of teachers. Selection criteria for venues and delivery mechanisms should take into account issues of time, location, distance, credit options, and so on. Professional development is not a one-time event. It should be focused on the needs of the faculty member, teacher, or administrator and sustained through coaching and periodic updates.

TECHNICAL ASSISTANCE

What happens if the hardware or software doesn't work? Educators require technical assistance for maintaining and using the technology. The focus of the faculty member, teacher, and teacher candidate should be on the teaching and learning; the focus should be not on maintaining, repairing, and trouble-shooting the technology beyond a set of basic trouble-shooting skills. When the technology does not function well, a learning opportunity is lost and faculty frustration grows. Technical assistance in a timely manner is imperative if faculty and candidates are to feel confident that they can plan for the use of technology in the course of their teaching and learning. Because of the many ways technical assistance can be obtained, from asking peers or student assistants to making use of an around-the-clock help desk, there can be no excuses for the lack of assistance.

CONTENT STANDARDS AND CURRICULUM RESOURCES

Educators must be knowledgeable in their subject matter and current in the content standards and teaching methodologies of their discipline. Teacher candidates must learn to use technology in powerful, meaningful ways in the context of teaching content. Technology brings resources from the real world relevant to subject area content, provides tools for analyzing and synthesizing data and presenting knowledge, and conveys content and processes through a variety of media and formats. Teacher candidates should learn to use technology in ways that support attaining the content standards as well as the NETS for Students and Teachers.

STUDENT-CENTERED TEACHING

Teaching in all settings should encompass student-centered approaches to learning. Technology should not be used only as a tool for demonstration, such as an electronic overhead projector. Student use of technology should be integral to the learning process. Student-centered approaches to learning dictate that students become the source for identifying problems to be investigated. Students and teacher candidates must have opportunities to identify problems, collect and analyze data, draw conclusions, and convey results using electronic tools to accomplish each task. Faculty should model the use of the technology in such a way as to communicate the usefulness and appropriateness of technology for learning collaboration, acquisition of resources, analysis and synthesis, and presentation or publication.

ASSESSMENT

In addition to assessing teaching and student outcomes, institutions should continually assess the effectiveness of technology for learning throughout all teacher preparation environments. The data obtained from this continual assessment

- inform the effectiveness of learning strategies applied,
- ensure that the vision for technology use maintains the appropriate direction,
- pinpoint potential problems, and
- provide information for altering policies and instructional strategies and acquiring resources.

With a continuous stream of data, changes necessary over time and those necessary because of technology innovation will become apparent. The information resulting from the examination of assessment data will provide ongoing guidance for decision making.

COMMUNITY SUPPORT

The visioning process includes the community and school partners who are able to provide expertise, support, and resources to extend and advise on technology implementation. The community must see that the use of technology in teaching and learning is a valuable tool for prospective teachers and their students, and must be willing to advocate for support within homes and in the political environment from the school board room to the state house.

SUPPORT POLICIES

School and university policies, financing, and reward structures must be in place to support technology in learning. Policies can either support or become barriers to the implementation of technology. As new policies are developed, decision-makers must consider how the policies affect the access and acquisition of technology as well as instruction. Some major barriers to the use of technology center on the expectations of faculty regarding incentives and reward structures. The expectation for the use of technology must cut across all subject areas and teacher preparation contexts so that faculty and teacher candidates can be assured that their work will be celebrated, valued, and rewarded.

Policies related to technical assistance should support the use of technology and not obstruct it. For example, although firewalls are essential in the university environment, there are ways to have dial-up and remote access while maintaining the security of campus servers. Likewise, school level access to the Internet poses threats to the control of the P–12 students' exposure to unwanted images and information. School systems must investigate options for controlling access to various Internet sites while maintaining an environment of exploration and inquiry.

CONCLUSION

The chart on pages 18–19 specifically addresses issues related to each of the above essential conditions for each of the four environments that support the preparation of teachers: General Preparation, Professional Preparation, Student Teaching/Internship, and First-Year Teaching. Recognition of the essential conditions underscores the shared responsibility for preparing teachers among the university, teacher education unit, and P–12 educational environments. Educators have a professional responsibility to advocate for all of the essential conditions in all four environments. In examining the elements of the chart horizontally, note that a particular essential condition takes on a different meaning as the environmental context changes. These conditions are important regardless of the environment or phase of a teacher's development.

Institutions can use the chart as a self-study device to examine their current conditions as part of a technology implementation plan. For example, members of a college of education might examine the General Preparation column to look at what conditions exist in the university where their prospective students receive their background education. Like the CEO Forum StaR Chart (**www.ceoforum.org**), a rubric can be created for each of the profiles as part of the self-evaluation. Because the organization, process, and partners involved in the preparation of teachers vary widely, the exact progression of a rubric is not defined in this book. To develop that rubric, entities responsible for teacher preparation should collaborate on a self-evaluation that looks across the development process and outlines the weaknesses, processes for addressing the weaknesses, and target evidence that validates a condition has been met.

For the environment in which the General Preparation Performance Profile is being addressed, a sample chart to guide the assessment of essential conditions in a teacher preparation program is provided below.

General Preparation Performance Profile

Example of Completed Assessment of Meeting Essential Conditions.

ESSENTIAL CONDITION	DEFINITION	GENERAL PREPARATION	WEAKNESS/PLAN FOR ADDRESSING*	EXAMPLE EVIDENCE
Shared Vision	There is proactive leadership and administrative support from the entire system.	University leaders share a vision for technology use in all appropriate courses and content areas.		Vision statement Technology-use plan List of outcomes of implementation committee
Access	Educators have access to current technologies, software, and telecommunication networks.	Access to current technologies, software, and telecommunication networks is provided for all students and faculty both inside and outside the classroom.		Favorable student/computer ratio Student lease/buy programs 24 hour access to lab(s) Access for all university classrooms Faculty access to student data Off-campus access to networks for all
Skilled Educators	Educators are skilled in the use of technology for learning.	Faculty teaching general education and major courses are knowledgeable about and model the appropriate use of technology in their disciplines.		Syllabi review Course Web sites on servers with critical review and usage data Data on faculty requests and response Job description on posted faculty openings
Professional Development	Educators have consistent access to professional development in support of technology use in teaching and learning.	University faculty and students are provided with opportunities for technology skill development and reward structures that recognize the application of technology in teaching, learning, and faculty collaboration.		List of technology offerings Evaluation plan/results for technology offerings Travel requests for off-campus professional development Effect of experiences of the professional development offerings they attended
Technical Assistance	Educators have technical assistance for maintaining and using the technology.	Timely technical assistance is available to ensure consistent, reliable functioning of technology resources.		Budget line item for assistance services Response time data Evaluation of quality of service data Ongoing needs assessment plan/data

ESSENTIAL CONDITION	DEFINITION	GENERAL PREPARATION	WEAKNESS/PLAN FOR ADDRESSING*	EXAMPLE EVIDENCE
Content Standards and Curriculum Resources	Educators are knowledgeable in their subject matter and current in the content standards and teaching methodologies in their discipline.	Prospective teachers have knowledge in the subject areas they plan to teach.		Syllabi review Student evaluations Comparison review of major coursework with standards of professional society
Student-Centered Teaching	Teaching in all settings encompasses student-centered approaches to learning.	University faculty incorporate student-centered approaches to learning (e.g., active, cooperative, and project-based learning).		Syllabi review Student evaluations Peer evaluations
Assessment	There is continual assessment of the effectiveness of technology for learning.	University faculty and support staff assess the effectiveness of technology for learning to examine educational outcomes and inform procurement, policy, and curriculum decisions.		Assessment policies Procurement of hardware and software records Assessment of testing instrument results Student outcomes assessment Curriculum decisions
Community Support	The community and school partners provide expertise, support, and resources.	Prospective teachers experience technology use in real-world settings related to their general education and courses in their major.		Service learning experiences Field trips Part-time job opportunities
Support Policies	School and university policies, financing, and reward structures are in place to support technology in learning.	University faculty are provided with resources for meeting subject area needs and with reward structures that recognize the application of technology in teaching, learning, and faculty collaboration.		Retention, tenure, and promotion (RTP) policies Outcomes of RTP decisions Procurement of hardware and software records Awards programs with outcomes Grant programs with outcomes

*To be completed by university self-study

This table is only an example of how an assessment of meeting the essential conditions for the General Preparation Performance Profile might be conducted. Completion of the chart gives the university a starting point for a dialogue about fully supporting all elements in the institution for sustaining the effective use of technology. Meeting the above essential conditions for the General Preparation Performance Profile is not only good for prospective teachers, but for *all* students.

National Accreditation Standards for Teacher Preparation

The ISTE affiliation with the National Council for Accreditation of Teacher Education (NCATE) has resulted in strong accreditation guidelines for technology in teacher preparation as well as programs specializing in educational technology. Guidelines are also in place for the requirements for the integration of technology throughout teacher preparation programs as required by the new NCATE 2000 unit standards, adopted in May 2000. Each unit, or college of education, seeking initial accreditation is required to submit its conceptual framework outlining the philosophical and pedagogical underpinnings of the program as a precondition for establishing eligibility for NCATE accreditation. The framework provides direction for programs, courses, teaching, candidate performance, scholarship, service, and unit accountability. In addition to providing evidence on how the standards are met, the unit's document includes an overview of the conceptual framework in the preliminary section of the institutional report.

Board of examiner teams, who conduct the on-campus institutional accreditation visit, examine the conceptual framework of the teacher preparation unit. The conceptual framework developed by the institution bases its description on six defined indicators specified in the NCATE 2000 standards. One of the six indicators solicits a description of the university's commitment to technology in its overall program. The indicator states:

"Commitment to Technology. The unit's conceptual framework(s) reflects the unit's commitment to preparing candidates who are able to use educational technology to help all students learn; it also provides a conceptual understanding of how knowledge, skills, and dispositions related to educational and information technology are integrated throughout the curriculum, instruction, field experiences, clinical practice, assessments, and evaluations" (NCATE, 2001, p. 12–13).

Other indicators include shared vision, coherence, professional commitments and dispositions, commitment to diversity, and candidate proficiencies aligned with professional and state standards. (NCATE, 2001, p. 13).

All universities seeking accreditation must verify their commitment to technology within their conceptual framework. Many universities are making plans to reference the new ISTE NETS for Teachers in their descriptions supporting the technology commitment portion of their conceptual framework.

In addition to the clear identification of the unit's commitment to technology in the conceptual framework, the NCATE unit standards include further specific technology requirements. The following NCATE 2000 standards and elements include specific reference, supporting explanation, and rubrics related to integration of technology.

Technology References in the NCATE 2000 Standards*

NCATE 2000 STANDARDS	ELEMENT	TARGET RUBRIC
I. CANDIDATE PERFORMANCE STANDARD 1: CANDIDATE KNOWLEDGE, SKILLS, AND DISPOSITIONS	Professional Knowledge and Skills for Other School Personnel	Candidates have an in-depth understanding of professional knowledge in their fields as delineated in professional, state, and institutional standards. They collect and analyze data related to their work, reflect on their practice, and use research and technology to support and improve student learning.
STANDARD 2: ASSESSMENT SYSTEM AND EVALUATION	Assessment System	The unit, with the involvement of its professional community, is implementing an assessment system that reflects the conceptual framework(s) and incorporates candidate proficiencies outlined in professional and state standards. The unit continually examines the validity and utility of the data produced through assessments and makes

NCATE 2000 STANDARDS	ELEMENT	TARGET RUBRIC
		modifications to keep abreast of changes in assessment technology and in professional standards. Decisions about candidate performance are based on multiple assessments made at multiple points before program completion. Data show the strong relationship of performance assessments to candidate success. The unit conducts thorough studies to establish fairness, accuracy, and consistency of its performance assessment procedures. It also makes changes in its practices consistent with the results of these studies.
	Data Collection, Analysis, and Evaluation	The unit is implementing its assessment system and providing regular and comprehensive data on program quality, unit operations, and candidate performance at each stage of a program, including the first years of practice. Data from candidates, graduates, faculty, and other members of the professional community are based on multiple assessments from both internal and external sources. Data are regularly and systematically compiled, summarized, analyzed, and reported publicly for the purpose of improving candidate performance, program quality, and unit operations. The unit is developing and testing different information technologies to improve its assessment system.
II. UNIT CAPACITY STANDARD 3: FIELD EXPERIENCES AND CLINICAL PRACTICE	Design, Implementation, and Evaluation of Field Experiences and Clinical Practice	Field experiences allow candidates to apply and reflect on their content, professional, and pedagogical knowledge, skills, and dispositions in a variety of settings with students and adults. Both field experiences and clinical practice extend the unit's conceptual framework(s) into practice through modeling by clinical faculty and well-designed opportunities to learn through doing. During clinical practice, candidate learning is integrated into the school program and into teaching practice. Candidates observe and are observed by others. They continually interact with teachers, college/university supervisors, and other interns about their practice. They reflect on and can justify their own practice. Candidates are members of instructional teams in the school and are active participants in professional decisions. They are involved in a variety of school-based activities directed at the improvement of teaching and learning, including the use of information technologies. Candidates collect data on student learning, analyze the data, reflect on their work, and develop strategies for improving learning.
		Clinical faculty are accomplished school professionals who are jointly selected by the unit and partnering schools. Clinical faculty are selected and prepared for their roles as mentors and supervisors and demonstrate the skills, knowledge, and dispositions of highly accomplished school professionals.
STANDARD 5: FACULTY QUALIFICATIONS, PERFORMANCE, AND DEVELOPMENT	Modeling Best Professional Practices in Teaching	Faculty have an in-depth understanding of their fields and are teacher scholars who integrate what is known about their content fields, teaching, and learning in their own instructional practice. They exhibit intellectual vitality in their sensitivity to critical issues. Teaching by the professional education faculty reflects the unit's conceptual framework(s); incorporates appropriate performance assessments; and integrates diversity and technology throughout coursework, field experiences, and clinical practices. Faculty value candidates' learning and adjust instruction appropriately to enhance candidate learning. They understand assessment technology, use multiple forms of assessments in determining their effectiveness, and use the data to improve their practice. Many of the unit faculty are recognized as outstanding teachers by candidates and peers across campus and in schools.
STANDARD 6: UNIT GOVERNANCE AND RESOURCES	Unit Personnel	Workload policies and practices permit and encourage faculty not only to be engaged in a wide range of professional activities, including teaching, scholarship, assessment, advisement, work in schools, and service, but also to professionally contribute on a community, state, regional, or national basis.

NCATE 2000 STANDARDS	ELEMENT	TARGET RUBRIC
		Formal policies and procedures have been established to include online course delivery in determining faculty load. The unit's use of part-time faculty and of graduate teaching assistants is purposeful and employed to strengthen programs, including the preparation of teaching assistants. Clinical faculty are included in the unit as valued colleagues in preparing educators. Unit provision of support personnel significantly enhances the effectiveness of faculty in their teaching and mentoring of candidates. The unit supports professional development activities that engage faculty in dialogue and skill development related to emerging theories and practices.
	Unit Facilities	The unit has outstanding facilities on campus and with partner schools to support candidates in meeting standards. Facilities support the most recent developments in technology that allow faculty to model the use of technology and candidates to practice its use for instructional purposes.
	Unit Resources including Technology	The unit aggressively and successfully secures resources to support high-quality and exemplary programs and projects to ensure that candidates meet standards. The development of and implementation of the unit's assessment system is well-funded. The unit serves as an information technology resource in education beyond the education programs—to the institution, community, and other institutions. Faculty and candidates have access to exemplary library, curricular, and/or electronic information resources that serve not only the unit but also a broader constituency.

*NCATE, 2001, p. 14–41

Preparation of Educational Technology Leaders

The opportunities for effecting widespread change in our educational system have grown exponentially in the last few years. The circle of experts necessary to lead the efforts surrounding integration of technology throughout America's educational system is ever widening. With billions of dollars invested in technology in both P–12 and higher education, the need for leaders prepared to address the myriad of issues surrounding the integration of technology in our educational system has reached crisis proportions. The technical and educational needs to take advantage of the opportunities for learning that technology can bring to our educational system have outgrown the pool of educational leaders to guide the effort.

The ISTE Accreditation and Professional Standards Committee has developed accreditation standards for teacher preparation programs in educational computing and technology. These specialization guidelines have been adopted by NCATE and are currently being used in evaluating teacher preparation programs for accreditation.

Adopted in October 2001, ISTE/NCATE accreditation standards for programs in educational computing and technology include:

• The ISTE/NCATE Educational Computing and Technology Facilitation initial endorsement program, which is designed to prepare building/campus-level technology facilitators who will exhibit knowledge, skills, and dispositions equipping them to teach technology applications; demonstrate effective use of technology to support student learning of content; and provide professional development, mentoring, and basic technical assistance for other teachers in their efforts to apply technology to support student learning.

• The ISTE/NCATE Educational Computing and Technology Leadership advanced program, which is designed to prepare candidates to serve as educational computing and technology directors, coordinators, or specialists, equipping them with special preparation in computing systems, facilities planning and management, instructional program development, staff development, and other advanced applications of technology to support student learning and assessment. It is also geared toward preparing candidates to serve in technology-related leadership positions at district, regional, and/or state levels.

• The ISTE/NCATE Educational Computing and Technology Secondary Computer Science Education initial endorsement and degree programs, which are designed to prepare secondary teachers of computer science.

The current version of the specialty area standards for these areas can be obtained at **www.ncate.org** or **www.iste.org.**

As noted in the essential conditions, the existence of a shared vision with support from the multiple levels of an organization points to the need for standards for administrators. Currently, ISTE is an integral part of the Technology Standards for School Administrators (TSSA) Collaborative. For universities to work collaboratively with school districts on appropriate field placements and new teachers to be supported in their new position, school administrators must understand and support the use of technology at all levels. The TSSA Collaborative has developed standards for school administrators that include the levels of superintendent, site administrator, and district level program director. ISTE has adopted the TSSA standards as a part of its National Educational Technology Standards (NETS) for Administrators. To obtain a full copy of the current standards, visit **www.iste.org** and navigate to ISTE NETS for Administrators.

Assessment and Evaluation of Technology Effectiveness

A critical issue in implementing any set of standards is identifying a useful, accurate, and appropriate assessment system for measuring progress toward meeting the standards. Initial models, tools, and resources for development of assessments for teacher preparation candidates and programs are included in the Section 3 chapter, "Assessment of Educational Technology Competence." As implementation of the standards with attention to the profiles takes place, it is important to consider the assessment issues in the development of any plan. Among the common questions that continue to plague educators are: How do you know what you did is effective? What is the effect on candidate/student achievement?

An appropriate assessment system should not only evaluate effectiveness across all dimensions, but also evaluate the outcomes of student/candidates learning. The system should be an integral part of an overall assessment system that considers all the variables that contribute to the data collected. Effective use of technology is an important element that is subject to a wide set of variables.

Future activities of ISTE will address the development of a comprehensive and systemic assessment system. The resulting system will assist teacher preparation programs and professional development programs to document their success in preparing teachers to use technology effectively.

Sustaining Progress through Professional Development

Section 2 contains model learning activities for general preparation, professional preparation, and each grade range (early childhood education, elementary education, middle school education, and secondary education) for use throughout the preparation programs for teachers. Each learning activity integrates technology with content that would likely be encountered in the teacher preparation program and includes a variety of ways of assessing candidate outcomes.

The learning activities in Section 2 may be easily adapted to professional development settings for experienced teachers. While the activities are outlined in terms of the preparation of new teachers, many of the activities model classroom practice. As experienced teachers participate in professional development activities designed to enhance their use of technology in teaching and learning, they too need to be actively involved in their own learning in the same way as P–12 students and teacher candidates.

It has long been proven that effective professional development must be sustained, ongoing, and supported. The activities in Section 2 can easily be re-purposed for professional development programs designed as part of a content area enhancement or a specific grade-range program.

For example, professional development focusing on improving mathematics achievement can draw from the mathematics activities within each of the major sections. Likewise, a program targeting early childhood education teachers can easily utilize the activities in the early childhood education section.

Additionally, as new technologies emerge, professional development programs often need to be quickly developed to find ways to prompt experienced teachers to draw on their vast expertise to envision new ways of using what is available. By experiencing some of the activities and conducting a study of the lesson through reflecting on the curriculum, experienced teachers naturally begin to brainstorm creative ways to extend and modify the original activity to fit the new circumstances.

Reference

National Council for Accreditation of Teacher Education. (2001). *Professional standards for the accreditation of schools, colleges, and departments of education.* Washington, DC: NCATE.

M. G. (Peggy) Kelly is a professor of education at California State University, San Marcos, and co-director of the ISTE NETS Project.

Lajeane Thomas is a professor of education at Louisiana Tech University, director of the ISTE NETS Project, and chair of the ISTE Standards and Accreditation Committee.

Using Model Strategies for Integrating Technology into Teaching

In an effort to implement the NETS for Teachers across the university, many methods and strategies have been identified. As with many teaching strategies, there are common methods in using technology that can be applied across various academic disciplines and grade levels. Having a set of generic models and strategies that are multipurpose in application assists teacher candidates in quickly developing technology-rich lessons for their fieldwork. This set can be continuously modified as experience in teaching increases through their student teaching.

This chapter provides an overview of proven effective models and strategies for the following:

- **Web-based lessons**
  WebQuests
  CyberGuides
  Filamentality

- **Multimedia presentations**

- **Telecomputing projects**

- **Online discussions**

Most of the examples have online reference sites for further explanation and additional examples. Many of the activities in this book use versions of the models described in this section.

Web-Based Lessons

WEBQUESTS

http://edweb.sdsu.edu/webquest/webquest.html

A WebQuest is an inquiry-oriented activity in which most or all of the information used by learners is drawn from the Web. WebQuests are designed to use learners' time well; to focus on using information rather than looking for it; and to support learners' thinking at the levels of analysis, synthesis, and evaluation. Developed by Bernie Dodge with Tom March at San Diego State University, the WebQuest model has been effectively applied to all levels of education, from elementary to postgraduate study.

The Model

The Internet offers teachers a wealth of information and resources for use in supporting curriculum-based experiences. Teachers often search the Web for hours and become frustrated with the quantity of resources and the time needed to actually identify the best sites to use with students in a lesson for a particular unit. If turned loose on the Web, students (and teacher candidates) can often have the same experience. In an effort to focus student learning and limit the time needed for a specific search, the WebQuest model provides teachers an option of reviewing and selecting Web-based lessons structured in a lesson-type format.

Note: The following is from the WebQuest site,
http://edweb.sdsu.edu/people/bdodge/webquest/buildingblocks.html

INTRODUCTION
The purpose of the Introduction section of a WebQuest is twofold. First, it should orient the learner as to what is coming. Second, it should raise some interest for the learner through a variety of means.

TASK
The Task block in a WebQuest is a description of what the learner should have done at the end of the exercise. It could be a product, like a HyperStudio stack or PowerPoint presentation, or it might be a verbal act, such as being able to explain a specific topic. For example, "MexQuake" (**http://students.itec.sfsu.edu/edt628/ mexquake/earthquakers.html**), by Edith Kelly and Ryen Partin, ends in a newpaper account and videotaped newscast in Spanish.

PROCESS
The Process block in a WebQuest is where the teacher suggests the steps that learners should go through in completing the task. It may include strategies for dividing the task into subtasks, descriptions of roles to be played, or perspectives to be taken by each learner. The instructor can also use this place to provide learning advice and interpersonal process advice, such as how to conduct a brainstorming session. The Process description should be relatively short and clear. For example, Week 1 of Cheryl Rondestvedt's "Ocean Pollution/Solution" unit (**http://edweb.sdsu.edu/triton/PollSol/Week1.html**) involves students doing a lot of activities, but the steps are clearly specified. Note that in this case, the resources needed are embedded within the steps rather than separately listed.

RESOURCES
The Resources block in a WebQuest is a list of Web pages the instructor has located that will help the learner accomplish the task. The resources are preselected so that learners can focus their attention on the topic rather than surfing aimlessly. It's important to note that resources for the students are not restricted to those found on the Web. For example, the "Investigating Archaeotype" WebQuest (**http://edweb.sdsu.edu/Courses/EDTEC596/ WebQuest1.html**), involved a wide range of resources, including an audioconference with a distant expert, a videoconference with a not-so-distant teacher, a videotape, the hard copy of an evaluation report, and a number of Web pages. There's no reason that a WebQuest might not include textbooks, audiotapes, and face-to-face interaction with other people among the resources.

Very often, it makes sense to divide the list of resources so that some are examined by everyone in the class, while others are read by subsets of learners who are playing a specific role or taking a particular perspective. For example, in "Avoid It Like the Plague" (**http://students.itec.sfsu.edu/edt628/ascendedone/ plaguell.html**), by Tommy Lee, all students look at three sites to give them a basic grounding in the Black Plague. Then, depending on the role they are playing, they make use of an additional two Web sites. By giving separate data sources to learners, you ensure the interdependence of the group and give the learners an incentive to teach each other what they've learned.

EVALUATION
Since the Evaluation block has been only recently added to the model, there aren't many examples of this component to point to. In the "San Diego-Biarritz Comparison Unit" (**http://edweb.sdsu.edu/triton/SDBiarritz/SDBiarritzUnit.html**), by Susanne Hirsch, Janice Thiel developed a rubric for evaluating the Web pages created in French by the students.

The rubric examines six different aspects of the student product and establishes four benchmarks for each aspect. It's intended to be printed out and given to the evaluators, who could be teachers, parents, or peers. Evaluation rubrics will take a different form depending on the kind of task given to the learner.

CONCLUSION

The Conclusion section of a WebQuest provides an opportunity to summarize the experience, to encourage reflection about the process, to extend and generalize what was learned, or some combination of these. It's not a critically important piece, but it rounds out the document and provides readers with a sense of closure.

One good use for the Conclusion section is to suggest questions that a teacher might use in whole class discussion to debrief a lesson. In "The 1960s Museum" (http://school.discovery.com/schrockguide/museum/webquest.html), for example, Kathy Schrock asks learners to think about the sites they had visited and discern any biases represented at those sites. She also asks the learners to predict the reaction their own creations will receive once posted on the Web.

This model encourages teachers to create new activities and adapt already successful ones to take advantage of the power of the Web for their students. Because the model does not specify length of lesson, these lessons can be a short WebQuest (one to three days) or a long WebQuest (one week to one month).

Example

The social studies curriculum for grades K–4 contains investigations into relationships in our world. Topics include weather, life cycle, and communities in both science and social science. One WebQuest, hosted on the Pacific Bell Knowledge Network site, asks students to look at these relationships and aspects of life on our planet. The "Big Wide World WebQuest" (www.kn.pacbell.com/wired/bww/index.html) uses a rubric appropriate for students at this age level. However, most students in K–1 grades would not be ready to explore all of the activities; teacher candidates or faculty may want to select a few activities that target their curriculum specifically. Some faculty and teachers in Grade 4 have chosen to include all the areas, reviewing foundation knowledge and adding more depth to student understanding of these relationships.

As an example, one activity relating to language arts in the "Big Wide World WebQuest" asks students in Grades K–1 to link to International Symbols or hear animal sounds while looking at a picture of the animal. Students in third or fourth grade explore heroes of the world under the section entitled "People."

Online Samples

The WebQuest site offers the opportunity to search a database collection for specific topics. Everything is here, from world hunger to planning a trip to Canada, current issues, core literature, and even physical education topics. The WebQuest teaching strategy is an excellent framework for teacher candidates designing technology-rich experiences for students. As teachers, they can share their ideas with other educators by submitting their WebQuest lesson to the database.

This site also has the potential to engage candidates in critical analysis of WebQuests so they might develop Web-based lessons of their own with an eye toward learning outcomes. There is a WebQuest on a WebQuest. This site provides the experience of going through a WebQuest by exploring what a WebQuest is: **http://edweb.sdsu.edu/webquest/webquestwebquest.html**

By the end of the activity, learners know enough about the model to be able to answer the following questions: (1) Which two of the example WebQuests examined are considered to be examples of effective instruction? Why? (2) Which two examples need considerable revision? Why?

Other developers of Web-based lessons have offered similar models or versions of WebQuests. An example is MiniQuests from Illinois (**www.biopoint.com/wq2/Welcome.html**), sponsored by Internet Innovations, Inc. These Web-based activities include scenario, task, and product, simplifying the structure into these three steps.

Resources

WEB SITES
The WebQuest Page: **http://edweb.sdsu.edu/webquest/webquest.html**

WebQuest Collections: **http://edweb.sdsu.edu/webquest/webquest_collections.htm (collections)**

MAGAZINE ARTICLES
Dodge, B. (2001). FOCUS—Five rules for writing a great WebQuest. *Learning & Leading with Technology, 28*(8), 6–9, 58.

Peterson, C., & Koeck, D. (2001). When students create their own WebQuests. *Learning & Leading with Technology, 29*(1), 6–9.

Yoder, M. (1999). The student WebQuest—A productive and thought-provoking use of the Internet. *Learning & Leading with Technology, 26*(7), 10–15, 52.

CYBERGUIDES

www.sdcoe.k12.ca.us/score/cyberguide.html

A CyberGuide is a supplementary, standards-based, Web-delivered unit of instruction centered on core works of literature. CyberGuides provide a quick supplementary set of activities for students (and teacher candidates) as they explore specific pieces of literature.

The Model

Each CyberGuide contains a student and teacher edition, identified targeted standards, a description of the task and a process by which it may be completed, teacher-selected Web sites, and an assessment rubric. The teacher's guide includes an overview of the activities, suggestions from the author, and a library of links provided to students in the activities. The student guides include activity directions written in a format appropriate for the age and reading ability of the students. The Cyberguide Web page contains a list of sites organized by grade level clusters, K–3, 4–6, 6–8, and 9–12.

Example

An example of a CyberGuide for intermediate grades is "Dragonwings," by Laurence Yep (**www.sdcoe.k12.ca.us/score/drag/dragtg.html**). During this unit, students use the Internet to investigate and write a descriptive paragraph of San Francisco's Chinatown in 1903, read a firsthand account of the 1906 earthquake, and trace the route of a group of Chinese orphan girls from their home in Chinatown to safety in San Anselmo. Students may also research and prepare an earthquake safety checklist for their own homes and discuss how relationships with elders influence their own knowledge about their heritage. And because the definition of the dragon and the emergence of flight at the time can spark a discussion about the history of flight, students can investigate how a plane flies at the National Air and Space Museum, prepare a class demonstration of one of the principles of flight, and take a simulated flight on an early Wright brothers plane. Each of these activities is self-contained, and the classroom teacher may select any or all for a class to do.

FILAMENTALITY

www.kn.pacbell.com/wired/fil/index.html

The Filamentality name is derived from the way the teacher can combine the "filaments" of the Web with a learner's "mentality." The Filamentality site provides templates and resources that allow educators to create their own Internet-based activity or search for one that has been created by others and adapt it. There are several formats and helpful hints. The entire tutorial is offered at the beginner level.

Teachers who create an activity are empowered by the personalized product and feel secure because it is password protected and immediately available on a server for their use with students. This experience motivates teachers to explore Web-based lessons for their students as an interactive learning experience.

Many teacher candidates find it easy to create experiences beyond the limitations of Filamentality. Adding graphics or creating a new format is not difficult. Changes can be easily saved and edited with any text editor, word processor, or Web-authoring tool (Adobe PageMill, Claris HomePage, Microsoft FrontPage, etc.). Teachers and teacher candidates can ask for their activity to be hosted on the university or district server or use it offline at their classroom computers. Opened from a saved file, the Internet links still work to access the sites referenced in the Web activities.

The Model

www.kn.pacbell.com/wired/fil/index.html

The main Filamentality menu provides resources for creating or searching for an activity with the desired focus. Support is built-in through Mentality Tips, which guide the user along the way to creating a Web-based activity that can be shared with others without knowledge of HTML, Web servers, or the www-dot jargon.

Templates provide a step-by-step process in creating an Internet activity in one of the following formats:

Note: The following is from the Filamentality Web site.

HOTLIST	This is a Web page with hot buttons linking to Web sites that the creator of the page has felt are most useful for the topic. This saves the user, or learner, the time searching endlessly for information and focuses the search. See "China on the Net," a collection of Web sites that focus on various aspects of China (**www.kn.pacbell.com/wired/China/hotlist.html**).
SCRAPBOOK	If learners already have a general understanding of the subject they are studying (i.e., they've done some preliminary learning in class or with traditional resources), their first Web-based activity could be the exploration of a "Multimedia Scrapbook." Here learners dig through a collection of Internet sites organized around specific categories, such as, photographs, maps, stories, facts, quotations, sound clips, videos, virtual reality tours, and so on. Learners use the Multimedia Scrapbook to find aspects of the broader topic that they feel are important. For an example, see "Democracy Online in America" (**www.kn.pacbell.com/wired/ democracy/scrapbook.html**)
HUNT	When it's time to develop solid knowledge on a subject, teachers and students can create "Treasure Hunts." The basic strategy here is to find Web pages that hold information (text, graphics, sound, video, etc.) essential to understanding the given topic. First, gather 10–15 links. Remember, these are the exact pages students should go to for information, not the top page of a huge Web site. Don't expect students to find the needle in a cyberstack. After gathering these links, Filamentality prompts the teacher to pose one key question for each Web resource that has been linked to. If the teacher doesn't want to use all collected links, that's fine. Filamentality will take care of that.
	A smartly designed Treasure Hunt can go far beyond finding unrelated nuggets of knowledge. By choosing questions that define the scope or parameters of the topic, when the students discover the answers they are tapping into a deeper vein of thought, one that now stakes out the dimensions or schema of the domain

being studied. Finally, by including a culminating "Big Question," students can synthesize what they have learned and shape it into a broader understanding of the big picture. For an example, see "Black History: Past to Present" (www.kn.pacbell.com/wired/BHM/hunt.html).

SUBJECT SAMPLER
In a Subject Sampler, learners are presented with a smaller number (maybe half a dozen) of intriguing Web sites organized around a main topic. What makes this a particularly effective way to engage student buy-in is that the selected Web sites each offer something interesting to do, read, or see. Additionally, students are asked to respond to the Web-based activities from a personal perspective. Rather than uncover hard knowledge (as they do in a Treasure Hunt), students are asked for their perspectives on topics, comparisons to experiences they've had, interpretations of artworks or data, and so on. Thus, more important than the right answer is that students are invited to join the community of learners surrounding the topic to see that their views are valued in this context. Use a Subject Sampler when the goal is to make students feel connected to the topic and that the subject matter matters.

Resources

WEB SITES
www.kn.pacbell.com/wired/fil/index.html

www.kn.pacbell.com/wired/fil/beyond.html (Access this site for an activity to post on your own server.)

http://coefm.sdsu.edu/edfirst/filregister/ (Access this site to search the Filamentality Register.)

Multimedia Presentations

Multimedia combines media objects such as text, graphics, video, animation, and sound to represent and convey information. In the course of designing, planning, and producing a multimedia product, students can acquire new knowledge and skills through a method of teaching and learning that often is project-based.

The Model

Many teachers have found that students are motivated to learn when they can use technology to present the results of a research project or activity. The multimedia presentation contains content but the messages are conveyed by the student's selection of the media. The teacher candidate can look at examples of projects and lessons at Internet sites housing collections of student samples.

Exemplary project-based learning with multimedia is

- anchored in core curriculum,
- multidisciplinary,
- demonstrates sustained effort over time,
- promotes student decision making,
- supports collaborative groupwork,
- exhibits a real-world connection,
- utilizes systematic assessment, both along the way and for the end product, and
- employs multimedia as a communication tool.

As new forms of multimedia are explored and bandwidth increases, the types of projects become more complex. HyperStudio and other multimedia-authoring tools are used to link and branch screens, making them interactive and layered with information, with photos, scanned images, movies, and text. Students and candidates can easily narrate their project using a microphone. PowerPoint and other slideshow programs add tools for developing sequenced screens including all the elements of multimedia. Publishing multimedia products over the Internet provides that added dimension of having student works viewed by a distant audience. It is well recognized that the quality of student work increases markedly when they realize their work will be viewed by others outside of school.

Models of multimedia presentations include:

- Creating a Web page or site

- Developing a branching hypermedia stack

- Using PowerPoint or other mutimedia tool to create a computer presentation

- Editing digital video to create a computer-generated movie

CyberFair

Publishing a Web site is a rewarding experience for classrooms. The Global Schoolhouse (now part of Lightspan.com) organized several contests for students that provided rich multimedia experiences for project-based learning using the Web.

CyberFair is an annual contest that involves students with the community through collaborations with local leaders, businesses, special populations, environmental awareness, local music and art collections, and historical landmarks. These projects

- engage students,

- support standards-based coursework,

- connect students to their local communities,

- increase real-world, transferable skills,

- involve students in peer evaluation, and

- teach students education technology skills.

"Historical Landmarks of Escondido" (**http://cyberfair.gsn.org/berhman/Page1.html**) is a CyberFair example involving third-grade students as historians reporting local history documented through interviews and research with the community.

Students at Southampton Middle School in Virginia (**http://cyberfair.gsn.org/smsflood/index.html**) document a disaster and a community's efforts to rebuild and survive. The project title, Hurricane Floyd— Disaster in Motion in Southeast Virginia, demonstrates that students can focus on real situations that center the learning in a real-world context.

ThinkQuest

The ThinkQuest model (**www.thinkquest.org/**) provides opportunities for students (Grades 4 through12), to collaborate on Web projects. Projects are hosted in a searchable library at the ThinkQuest Web site. Teachers and learners can explore a multitude of topics. Students in Hong Kong created a project called Genetic Engineering of Agriculture (**http://library.thinkquest.org/C005206/**). This site includes music, animation, and text covering topics from defining genetic engineering to exploring pros and cons of this area of science. Students in Australia created another ThinkQuest project called The Contemporary Art Experience (**http://library.thinkquest.org/26183/**). The project gives students the opportunity to analyze artworks and to learn from the interpretations of others.

Multimedia and Copyright

For educational use, many copyright issues fall under the Fair Use clause. Teachers can use the fair use criteria to decide when use of materials in multimedia is appropriate. Criteria for judgment include that the use is for nonprofit; that the amount copied is minimal and not significant; and that no intent is made to replace the original—only to make it more accessible. Fair use is restricted to educational institutions. If the project is to be released outside the classroom in any way—published on the Web or in a school newsletter, broadcast outside the classroom, and so on—then fair use no longer applies. The teacher or student must have written permission for any copyrighted material, indeed for any material not created by the teacher or student. You can't go wrong by always getting permission.

Resources

WEB SITES FOR MORE INFORMATION
Copyright and Fair Use, Stanford University Libraries: **http://fairuse.standford.edu/**

U.S. Copyright Office Study on Distance Education: **www.loc.gov/copyright/disted/**

Fair Use Guidelines for Educational Multimedia: **www.libraries.psu.edu/mtss/fairuse/guidelinedoc.html**

University of Iowa Copyright Considerations: **http://twist.lib.uiowa.edu/resources/fairuse/index.html**

WEB SITE FOR SAMPLE PERMISSION FORMS
Midlink magazine: **www.ncsu.edu/midlink/permission.html**

WEB SITE FOR CITING REFERENCES
Online Writing Lab, Purdue University:
http://owl.english.purdue.edu/handouts/research/r_mla.html#Works-Cited

Telecomputing Projects

Telecomputing projects are Internet-enriched learning activities that often involve students in one location collaborating with students or adults in one or more other locations. They may share, among other things,

- experiences,
- beliefs,
- data,
- information,
- problem-solving strategies, and
- products they have developed or the joint development of products.

Telecomputing tools include e-mail, electronic mailing lists, electronic bulletin boards, discussion groups, Web browsers, real-time chatting, and audio- and videoconferencing. Online resources include Web sites and interactive environments, and remotely operated robotic devices.

The Model

Judi Harris at the University of Texas at Austin has been doing telecomputing with students since 1981 and has researched and studied telecomputing projects since 1987. She has identified two types of Internet-enriched learning activities: telecollaboration and teleresearch. Both types are often present in the same project. Each of these areas focuses on particular learning processes, which she further divides into activity structures and purposes that facilitate curriculum development.

Telecollaboration projects focus on at least one of three primary learning processes: interpersonal exchange, information collection and analysis, and problem solving. Here is a list of the activity structures for each process of telecollaboration (Harris, 1998):

- **Interpersonal Exchange**
    - Keypals
    - Global Classrooms
    - Electronic Appearances
    - Telementoring
    - Question-and-Answer Activities
    - Impersonations

- **Information Collection and Analysis**
    - Information Exchanges
    - Database Creation
    - Electronic Publishing
    - Telefieldtrips
    - Pooled Data Analysis

- **Problem Solving**
    - Information Searches
    - Peer Feedback Activities
    - Parallel Problem-Solving
    - Sequential Creations
    - Telepresent Problem-Solving
    - Simulations
    - Social Action Projects

Most telecollaborative projects incorporate some elements of teleresearch. Teleresearch is distinguished by a variety of activity purposes rather than structures. These purposes are to

- practice information-seeking skills,

- become informed about a topic of inquiry and/or answer a question,

- review multiple perspectives on an issue,

- generate data needed to explore a topic,

- solve authentic problems, and

- publish synthesized and/or critiqued information overviews for other students to use (Harris, 1998).

Harris has also developed a curriculum design process for curriculum-based telecollaboration. Here are her steps to design and carry out telecollaborative projects (Harris, 1998):

- Choose the curriculum-related goals

- Choose the activity's structure

- Explore examples of other online projects

- Determine the details of your project

- Invite telecollaborators

- Form the telecollaborative group

- Communicate!

- Create closure

To help make the curriculum design decisions while considering content knowledge and processes, Harris suggests that teachers think about what they want students to do to build understanding while engaged in the learning activities. She has identified the following student action sequences evident in telecomputing projects that teachers have created and used successfully in their classrooms (Harris, 1999):

- **Correspond:** Prepare a communication locally and send it to others. They respond, and the process continues.

- **Compete:** Register to participate, then do an activity locally. Submit completed work by a deadline and receive feedback.

- **Comprehend:** Locate online resources, then make primarily local use of them.

- **Collect, Share, and Compare:** Create something locally and add it to a group of similarly created works, combined to form a centrally located collection.

- **Chain:** Do an activity locally, create records of that activity, and send something on so that the next group can do something similar.

- **Come Along:** Shadow others as they travel either physically or cognitively, perhaps communicating briefly in the process.

- **Collaborate:** Work with remotely located others to realize a common goal.

In any telecollaborative or teleresearch project, therefore, there are one or more activity structures, teleresearch purposes, and action sequences working together that describe the plan and its implementation in the classroom (Harris, 1999).

Harris has developed these ideas over the years through her Mining the Internet column in *The Computing Teacher*, now renamed *Learning & Leading with Technology*, published by ISTE. In 1998, she wrote *Virtual Architecture—Designing and Directing Curriculum-Based Telecomputing*. (The second edition of *Virtual Architecture* is due out in 2002.) She continues to develop her ideas in Mining the Internet and through the Guest Expert column in the *Classroom Connect* newsletter.

Resources

Virtual Architecture's Web Home: **http://ccwf.cc.utexas.edu/~jbharris/Virtual-Architecture/index.html**

Harris, J. (1997). Content and intent shape function—Designs for Web-based educational telecomputing activities (10 ways that Web sites can function to support curriculum-based educational projects). *Learning & Leading with Technology, 24*(5), 17–20.

Sample Curriculum-Based K–12 Educational Telecomputing Project Pages, Classified by Page Functions: **http://ccwf.cc.utexas.edu/~jbharris/form-follows-function/**

The Electronic Emissary Project's WebCenter: **http://emissary.ots.utexas.edu/emissary/index.html**

Teachers can search an index of more than 800 projects at the Internet Projects Registry **(http://gsh.lightspan.com/pr/index.cfm)**. Listings include grade level, date, curriculum area, technology used, and complexity of project. This "one stop shop" database of projects contains descriptions of projects from reputable organizations such as I*EARN, IECC, NASA, GLOBE, Academy One, TIES, and TENET.

References

Harris, J. (1998). *Virtual architecture—Designing and directing curriculum-based telecomputing*. Eugene, Oregon: ISTE.

Harris, J. (1999). "I know what we're doing but how do we do it?"—Action sequences for curriculum-based telecomputing. *Learning & Leading with Technology, 26*(6), 42–44.

Online Discussions

With the growth of infrastructure around the world comes the ability to access others through remote connections. Students and teacher candidates can connect to experts and peers through a variety of formats such as chat rooms, electronic bulletin boards, and e-mail. What makes communicating online unique is that it offers participants freedom to send and receive information efficiently during varying time frames from diverse geographic locations. Communication can occur asynchronously, that is, not at the same time, which allows periods of time for reflection or to compensate for varying time zones. In real-time online communication, as in chat groups, the communication is synchronous and provides immediate feedback for reinforcement and understanding.

The Model

The model for online environments has been explored by several organizations. The structure includes environments for sharing information using e-mail, chat, and threaded discussions. It is important to set up protocols for communication and management. For example, when students post in a threaded discussion, they should consider how they can contribute to, enhance, or expand on knowledge with each posting. These environments can easily become nonproductive and disorganized without careful planning and consideration.

Experience tells us that group organization and working procedures take longer to develop online. It is critical to establish procedures early for contributing, posting, monitoring, and assessing. Online discussions can be moderated or unmoderated. In a moderated discussion, the instructor facilitates the discussion by initiating the discussion topic; organizing the forum around calendar or class requirements; matching discussion topics to class activities and curriculum; establishing expectations for participation; and categorizing, clustering, and summarizing student postings.

It is helpful to post topics in advance and agree on rules for the conduct of the chat. For example, pose a series of questions for students to think about before posting responses online. Or have them respond to something they have experienced or read about and compare that with readings that occur in class. Not all students respond well to the same approaches to discussion. To address diversity within an online group, be aware of cultural patterns as well as personal learning styles. How questions are framed can make a big difference to learner success. It may help to require a minimum number of postings.

Examples

One online environment for professional development, Tapped In, is the online workplace of an international community of education professionals. The educators involved include K–12 teachers and librarians, professional development staff, teacher education faculty and students, and researchers. They participate in professional development programs and informal collaborative activities with colleagues.

An example of a project that uses online communications models is NASA Quest: Farming in Space, **http://quest.arc.nasa.gov/ltc/farming/farming.html**. Students and teachers participating in the Farming in Space investigation observe, share information, and develop research questions for experiments. Students and teachers are encouraged to share their questions and results with others by

participating in online chats, by e-mailing the ISS Challenge team, and by publishing findings on school Web sites. NASA researchers and International Space Station payload specialists answer questions and share project results.

There are commercial programs targeted at supporting online environments in higher education and the classroom setting. Blackboard.com is a Web site resource that powers e-Learning in the academic marketplace of schools, colleges, universities, and many organizations on the Internet today. This Web resource allows the posting of class materials, chat and threaded discussions with password protection. Another example of these models is found in WebCT software used by some educational institutions.

Resources

Tapped In: **www.tappedin.org/**

Blackboard: **www.blackboard.com**

WebCT: **www.webct.com/**

Beaudin, B. (1999, November). Keeping online asynchronous discussion on topic. *The Journal of Asynchronous Learning Networks* [Online serial], *3*(2). Available: **www.aln.org/alnweb/journal/ Vol3_issue2/beaudin.htm**

Winiecki, D. (1999, March). Keeping the thread: Adapting conversational practice to help distance students and instructors manage discussions in an asynchronous learning network. *Deosnews* [Online serial], *9*(2). Available: **www.ed.psu.edu/acsde/deos/deosnews/deosnews9_2asp**

Katherine Hayden is coordinator for ILAST (Improving Learning for All Students through Technology) and is president of San Diego Computer Using Educators Organization. She teaches the technology course required for a teaching credential at California State University, San Marcos.

Joan Hanor is an associate professor at California State University, San Marcos. She is director of ILAST, a consortium providing professional development in educational technology to K–12 teachers and administrators.

Integrating Technology in General Education

Higher education is on a path of change (in some cases a forced path) regarding teaching and learning at the post-secondary level. Institutions that ignore the potential for technology in teaching and learning will be left behind as students raised in a digital world enter the university with expectations of an interactive, e-learning culture. Students are driving the change in higher education just as they did in the K–12 environment and at a speed that is challenging faculty and the traditional structures of the university.

The NETS for Teachers General Preparation Performance Profile is targeted at the courses and experiences teacher candidates have in both their general education coursework and academic major and minor preparation. A common concern in examining the quality of teachers is the depth of the academic preparation they receive prior to their study of pedagogy and correlated field experience. This concern reinforces the notion that teacher preparation is a university-wide responsibility.

The concern over technology experiences in the academic major and general education coursework is similar to the concern over preparation to use technology in teaching and learning. The statements in the General Preparation Performance Profile target the depth of technology experience teacher candidates should have prior to professional preparation. Prior to entering professional preparation, teacher candidates use technology as an integral part of the learning process in the specialized way that their academic field requires as they increase their conceptual understanding of complex topics. These experiences using technology provide another dimension to the academic preparation of the teacher candidate; the experiences can translate into a deeper understanding of the field as well as an understanding of how to use technology in working with their own students. These experiences are for all university students, not just teacher candidates.

Some teacher preparation programs have large numbers of candidates who are second career students, having received their undergraduate education elsewhere and, typically, years before entering teacher preparation. The focus of this chapter, however, is on the undergraduate, non-college of education experience. The special case of the second career and re-entry student is unique to the institutional setting and requires unique solutions.

Essential Conditions

If the expectation of the entire university is to prepare teacher candidates effectively to use technology in every aspect of their education at the institution, then, as with the college of education, there are essential conditions that must be met to enable faculty and support staff to make it happen. The support structure must be present from a university- and community-wide shared vision of the importance and long-range plan for technology implementation to effective support policies that promote innovative faculty and student work.

The Teaching, Learning, and Technology Group (**www.tltgroup.org**), a nonprofit affiliate of the American Association of Higher Education, has as its mission the "improve [ment] of teaching and learning by making more thoughtful use of information technology." The TLT Group is unique in its work to assist universities in making use of resources from a collaborative point of view to

- invent and support new teaching roles to match new learning needs and find ways to use technology to support these new linkages;

- improve internal communication and collaboration, especially in support of the institution's instructional mission;

- focus personal and institutional resources on shared goals to improve education;

- develop environments in which it is safe to take the risks needed to improve teaching and learning in times of constant, accelerating change; and

- identify and continue to support the institution's fundamental values and educational goals while embracing new technology options.

The initiatives of the TLT Group, such as the Roundtable Forum developed in collaboration with other institutions of higher education, work to holistically examine resources, talents, and internal goals of the institution to determine ways that the use of technology can help meet the teaching and learning goals. This organized effort causes participating institutions to coordinate all academic and support areas of the institutions to look at the use of technology as a way to improve instruction. Thus, these institutions avoid bowing to pressure and using resources in an indiscriminate manner.

Because teaching and learning is fundamentally different in a university that coordinates and targets the use of technology, emerging technologies are assessed by the degree to which they support the learning goals of the institution. For example, wireless technology offers teaching and learning options that are just beginning to be realized.

"A nomadic learning environment" is what Jessica DeCerce calls the effects of the campus commitment to a wireless technology at SUNY Morrisville. The campus instituted a wireless technology program as a way of increasing accessibility to technology-based resources. Students are able to meet in groups without being tethered to the campus technology lab.

As anticipated, students do not have to wait for office hours to obtain an answer to a question. The availability of the technology has opened the lines of communication between faculty and students as e-mail queries can be answered much more quickly. Office hours are no longer as necessary as in the past (DeCerce, 2001). As students and faculty explore the pedagogical implications of ubiquitous wireless technology—how faculty make assignments, where class meets, expectations for group interaction, and so on—teaching and learning at SUNY Morrisville is changing.

Technology Integration—What Does It Mean?

More than using PowerPoint as a delivery tool or WebCT to host course materials, the integration of technology in teaching and learning promises powerful tools for both teachers and learners. The use of technology is a natural, seamless act of selecting the right tool for the learning task. The culture created by having powerful tools accessible to teachers and learners is one in which the lines between teacher and learner are blurred as professors recognize that they can no longer be the fountain of all information and direct all learning. The notion of facilitating learning, fostering self-motivated, self-regulated learning with multifaceted assessment and accountability, permeates the university.

This ideal learning environment does not happen instantaneously in any setting. Faculty, regardless of their years in the classroom, must begin somewhere. Graduate students desiring to be professors are expected to know how to use technology in their field but may have no experience in using technology as a tool for teaching. They must begin somewhere to acquire this knowledge and experience. In all the options for using technology in teaching and learning, there is a starting point for faculty members and graduate students that is commensurate with their experience and comfort level.

Beginning Somewhere

The starting place can be as simple as developing the skill to move overhead transparencies to electronic slides or learning to create a course Web site. When faculty members become comfortable with the use of technology and allow students to assist, provide feedback, and offer new ways of doing things, an e-learning type of culture emerges.

First Steps

A 30-year veteran of the university classroom had been struggling with the overhead projector transparencies for years. With the assistance of a workshop sponsored by the Faculty Development Center, he learned how to scan images, enter the text of his old overheads into the computer, update the material, and create new presentations. It took two years, but after the process of digitizing and improving his overheads, he made the transition to using PowerPoint as a presentation tool. He commented to the Faculty Development Center staff that now he can update or change his presentation right before class as opposed to having to run another overhead transparency.

THE SYLLABUS

The syllabus is a good place to start as it represents the contract between the professor and the student. It is often the most underdeveloped piece of writing a professor generates. In an era of assessment and accountability, the syllabus can provide both the cognitive map for the student and the qualitative anchor for assessment criteria. In the process of posting the course syllabus online, the faculty member is provided with an opportunity to think more deeply about the syllabus and to provide resources and readings directly to students. A Web-based syllabus can have hot buttons that take students immediately to documents and readings, creating a one-stop location for course resources. Students can always "find" the course syllabus, and money from the faculty duplication budget is saved.

At a minimum, an online course syllabus should contain course information, instructor information, course descriptions, goals and objectives, readings, instructional methods, a calendar, classroom policies with links to university policies, grading criteria and standards, assignments tied to calendar dates, and available support services.

CLASS WEB SITE

The typical reaction of faculty to producing a course Web site is that it takes a large investment in time. This is true. That investment, however, diminishes with assistance from the university computing services or the faculty development center, or with the use of Web site creation software such as FrontPage or Claris Home Page. Whatever the support systems available, the investment in time is worth the later saving of time and enhancement of course resources. Benefits include accessibility to course resources 24 hours a day, 7 days a week. Enhancements to the course Web site include audio, video, threaded discussions, automated e-mail to the instructor, and bulletin boards. Faculty can address the multiple learning styles of students and encourage even the less overt students to participate. Additionally, the outside of class interaction sparked by the Web site discussion increases the quality of interaction inside of class and supports the development of a learning community based on the course content.

More sophisticated enhancements to a course Web site include:

- A place for students to post their work with opportunities for peers to respond or comment results in an audience other than the professor for students. The quality of work displayed can be significantly higher than if the student perceives that only the professor will scrutinize the product.

- Posted PowerPoint notes or other class materials can become valuable study aids for students. This enables the students to download the presentation and review the content when preparing for course assessments.

- Posting electronic quizzes on the Web site as a means of checking for understanding enables students to check their own progress in the course. This can be coupled with the posting of project scoring rubrics, sample student work, and other resources for helping students understand the expectations of the assignments given in class.

- An interactive calendar can provide students with another way to connect to the assignment sheets, resources, and other information necessary to keep up in class.

COURSE MANAGEMENT SOFTWARE

Using commercially produced course design and management software is another approach to using technology as a tool in the university classroom. Web CT and Blackboard are two common Web-based course packages that offer customization, file management, communication tools, assessment tools, and general course management. These tools are not a course Web site as originally conceived (National Education Association, 2001). Rather, these tools provide a common standard for the university to support faculty in including some of the online course management functions they desire.

Distance Learning

Web-based courses have created an understandable stir in the higher education community. Some perceive the use of online courses as the definition of integrating technology into teaching learning. While online teaching provides a unique experience for students, it does not represent the integration of technology into teaching. (Unless discipline-specific technology use is also integrated into the coursework, it merely acts as a delivery system.) Faculty concerns about intellectual property rights, teaching load, and redefined faculty responsibilities are very real issues that need to be resolved. The students' and university administrations' push for "anytime/anywhere" learning is part of the discussion of what is and is not appropriate use of the online learning environment to meet the objectives of a given course. There are no canned answers.

In terms of meeting the NETS for Teachers General Preparation Performance Profile guidelines, online learning is an experience that teacher candidates should have in their preparation. The use of online learning will continue to evolve. Teacher candidates must have a frame of reference for participating in the discussion as they consider their own students and their own teaching opportunities.

Faculty Development Models

What the education community has learned about staff development at the K–12 level applies to faculty at the university level. Single meeting workshops are not effective. Change requires sustained faculty development over time with support as defined by the situation. The Preparing Tomorrow's Teachers to Use Technology (PT³) grants program, funded by the U.S. Department of Education, has supported various configurations of professional development at the university level. Some of the reportedly successful models include:

- **Technology Tuesdays**—These are workshops of short duration on specific topics that become an expected part of the weekly schedule. The topics are defined by a faculty survey, with many topics covered in installments.

- **Mentors**—Mentoring programs that allow the faculty member to define the mentor they are most comfortable with are the most successful. Some faculty prefer to have a graduate student at their elbow as they learn new techniques, while others prefer to learn from a colleague who is already implementing the technique in the classroom. The flexibility and consistent checking on progress and needs are reportedly motivating faculty to take risks with technology in areas they would not have ordinarily considered.

- **Model Classrooms**—A model classroom is created as a staff development center where pedagogy and classroom organizational strategies that have proven successful with students are modeled. Faculty members learn various technologies and then apply them in their teaching.

- **Collaboration with K–12**—Vertical teams of arts and science faculty, college of education faculty, and K–12 teachers explore, develop, and support one another in the development of technology experiences for students K–16.

- **Service Learning**—As a well-known pedagogy, service learning is used as students work with faculty teams to explore how technology can enhance their learning. Students collaborate with faculty in developing course materials and experiences.

Sustained, ongoing professional development at the university level is an essential condition that cannot be overlooked. University faculty development programs in collaboration with the unit providing technology services must communicate with one another to provide the consistent level of training and opportunities for innovation that will continuously move the institution along in supporting teaching and learning with technology.

Discipline Area Examples

Movement along a continuum of technology use takes many forms. As with other portions of this volume, examples of technology integration are not necessarily at the "bleeding edge." Rather they are examples of what faculty are already doing that provide ideas of places to start. The following stories are composites of many stories gathered from faculty across the country.

A biology professor observed the science educators at the college of education using the large microscope to have 5-year-olds look at their hands, faces, and feet. The enthusiasm of the children along with their astute observations about the similarities and differences in the surface of the skin caused the professor to consider how technology could be used in biology lab sessions. After exploring possibilities of obtaining additional electronic microscopes, computer stations, and Vernier ProLab probes, he consulted with the college of education staff about the effective organization of a model classroom within the lab. Using the learning center organization, the model lab can now handle many specialized stations using a rotation model. Now all biology students are required to digitize images of their specimens, import the image into their lab report, and either print or post their lab report on the class Web site. The professor is working with biotech firms in the area to provide the appropriate experiences for students to prepare them for work with local projects.

Another biology course followed elementary and secondary students on the Internet as they participated in adding data to the GLOBE (Global Learning and Observations to Benefit the Environment) database. Students measured soil and water quality using detailed collection protocols for measuring the characteristics of their local environment. The university students examined the database of information contributed from around the world and made generalizations from what they found. They were able to monitor the elementary and secondary students participating in scheduled Web chats with the scientists who depended on the accuracy of the information for their research. This experience broke the perception that only skilled scientists can collect high-quality data.

A human ecology professor attended a faculty development session on using technology in teaching and learning. He found a cohort of other faculty who were interested in creating an interdisciplinary course using technology tools as a common thread with the theme of human development and change—psychologically, physically, intellectually, and so on—over time. This collaborative has spawned requests for electronic collaboration tools that the university had not yet explored at the undergraduate level.

A chemistry professor developed a series of WebQuests for her students. (See previous chapter for more information on WebQuests.) Rather than giving the material and Web sites in class, she posts the WebQuest on the course Web site for students to obtain background understanding of concepts they may have forgotten or never fully grasped in their high school coursework. A colleague at a local high school tests the WebQuests with her students at the end of each unit of study to validate that they have the prerequisite understandings that the university is expecting from high school graduates.

A professor of elementary genetics discovered the Australian Academy of Sciences Web site, on which there was a discussion of gene technology. After mentioning the Web site to his class, he discovered that some of his students not only accessed the Web site on their own but found links and other related Web sites that enriched the discussion of the next class period. Because his classroom had a computer and a connection that allowed him to get on the Web while in class, he allowed his students to take the class on a tour of the related Web sites. The class learned of more resources available, and the professor was able to provide an impromptu lesson on evaluating the sources of information, as not all information on the Web is accurate.

MATHEMATICS

In an effort to make the use of technology seamless as students progress from the local high schools to the university classrooms, professors are working with high school teachers to learn about the technology they are using in class. The state of California has generously funded high schools under the Digital High School grant programs, which provide schools with the opportunity to connect to the Internet and develop technology-rich opportunities for students. Through this grant, some mathematics departments have purchased technology such as class sets of graphing calculators and Geometer's Sketchpad software for access by all students. Some departments are experimenting with handheld devices such as PDAs in which cartridges can be inserted that hold the software for use at home. University faculty members have worked collaboratively with the high school faculty to share ideas related to technology implementation. They have also helped talented students take university courses and talented high school teachers become adjunct faculty for the mathematics department.

ENGLISH

A children's literature class uses Brøderbund's Living Books series to explore the potential stories within the stories of hallmark children's literature. Because the CD-ROMs containing the books are modestly priced and available in local computer stores, the professor has discovered that students who are planning to become teachers often buy the software themselves along with the book to use in lessons later. An additional outgrowth of using the library of Living Books has been the students' realization that when toggling between languages in presenting the story, the role of the pictures changes. They have become aware of how much children learn about the storyline through the pictures and clues in the inflection of the language even when the story is read in a different language.

A senior-level writing seminar class mentors high school students through a service learning project that pairs each university student with a high school student as a writing coach. Using electronic mail, the university student's responsibility is to respond to the writing with probing questions. It is explicitly not the intent to have the university student edit the high school student's writing. The university class spends time diagnosing their mentees' difficulties in writing and formulating questions that promote self-analysis of the identified issues. The technology keeps the identification of the students anonymous and provides mutually beneficial experiences for both groups.

HEALTH/PE

A kinesiology professor has his students wear a SportBrain pedometer to measure how much exercise they are getting during the semester. The device synchronizes through a cradle connected to a computer and downloads the information onto a Web site. The Web site software analyzes the data in conjunction with each day's entry and calculates calories burned over the time period of the class. As a result of the experience, students state that they become very aware of which activities burn more calories than others. Additional comments center around lifestyle changes in activity habits.

SOCIAL SCIENCES

A freshman interdisciplinary general education program begins the first semester with activities that require students to access the Web for resources to answer thematic questions. The primary objectives of the activities are to present an overview of the course and to teach the students how to evaluate and appropriately use and cite Web resources. As an example, students learn about the Strategian Web site, a "Guide to Quality Information—Biology, Chemistry, Computer Science, Mathematics, Medicine, Physics, and Psychology" (www.strategian.com), as one site where a synopsis of an article can be found with links to the full text of the article.

HISTORY

A history professor has created WebQuests on the major controversial issues in his course. He assigns the WebQuests to be completed by a specified time for presentation in class. Over time, he has discovered that the students who are anticipating enrolling in his course begin working on the WebQuests a semester in advance. One student commented, "In what other class can I access the course material in advance and take my time to digest the assignment so I know I can do well on it without the usual time constraints?"

A history course on immigration accesses primary source data off the Internet including databases of immigrants from Sweden, Ireland, and other countries where students' ancestors originated. Additional information was found at the American Family Immigration History Center, Ellis Island (www.ellisisland.org), which discusses the years and backgrounds of those who immigrated to the U.S. and how immigration patterns affected the political and economic environment as well as internal migration patterns, and urban and economic development.

The same history professor utilizes Tom Snyder Production's Timeliner software to keep track of events as they are uncovered in the research. The software provides a visual representation of the events in both a close up and telescopic form. Using the overhead projection system in the classroom, the time line can be brought up and amended at any time during the class discussion.

GEOGRAPHY

Geographic Information Systems (GIS) is a method to visualize, manipulate, analyze, and display spatial data. GIS creates "Smart Maps" that overlay database information on the map. The ability of GIS to combine data from many sources enables the geography classes to assemble maps that help answer questions in a problem-based learning environment. The university students use Global Positioning Systems (GPS) to place accurate local points on a map. They combine remote sensing data obtained from the Internet with aerial photography to create a complex picture. Used in an ecology class, the GIS with the GPS provides students with the ability to collect important field data from the area and contribute it to the growing database of information for tracking changes in the environment over time.

POLITICAL SCIENCE

A political science professor visited a professional development school classroom and observed students using Tom Snyder's Decisions, Decisions: On the Campaign Trail simulation software. He was not only impressed by the sophisticated concepts covered in the simulation but also with the group work and interaction. As a result, he uses the simulation in his political science course with some modifications to fit his objectives.

In the context of discussing the Constitution and the Bill of Rights, a political science professor has his students complete an activity that tests the privacy of information available on the Web. He begins by having students research their own names to see what kind of information is available about themselves using the usual search engines of Excite (www.excite.com), FAST (www.alltheweb.com), Google (www.google.com), AltaVista (www.altavista.com), and The Big Hub (www.thebighub.com). He then asks them to use Deja (www.deja.com) to find any use of their name in a newsgroup posting. Additional searches he prescribes are Think Direct Marketing (www.thinkdirectmarketing.com), which offers a reverse address search for students to test their own address. Switchboard.com offers the same information but also includes phone numbers. Because many states post bankruptcies and other information on Web sites, he challenges students to test the limits of the state reporting devices to find other personal information sources. This information provides a complex debate on what information should be accessible and to whom.

Assessment of NETS for Teachers in General Preparation

Many universities have developed agreements with regional educational agencies requiring that incoming students fulfill a computer competency requirement either upon entry or within the first few semesters at the university. This requirement ensures that lower division general education faculty can make valid assumptions about the skills of their students as they create assignments. To complete the assessment requirements of the General Preparation Performance Profile, universities must go beyond basic technology competency skills and examine the technology experiences provided for students across the curriculum. The combination of technology literacy and academic discipline experience creates a backdrop for teacher candidates to apply what they know to their teaching.

The "Assessment of Educational Technology Competence" chapter in Section 3 outlines a Candidate Readiness Benchmark for university students ready to enter professional preparation. This entry-level assessment should occur at the end of the General Preparation, or upon entry into the teacher education program. The assessment should provide information to the candidate about what skills will be required for use in the teacher education program and information to the teacher education program about what skills candidates are lacking to be prepared for entry. The university must provide multiple means for teacher candidates to demonstrate competency in meeting the entry-level requirements as well as multiple ways to address identified weaknesses.

Summary of Recommendations

As P–12 and post-secondary experiences become less separated by artificial barriers of student age and geography due to access to technology tools, so too will the lines between teacher and learner become blurred. Tomorrow's general education students will likely bring low-cost learning tools to class in a backpack and will expect to use wireless technology to access resources within the classroom. The professor who is able to adjust instruction to take advantage of students' natural curiosity and the vast amount of information instantaneously available in class will make the intellectual class discourse more student-centered and, likely, more stimulating than it is today.

The following is a summary of recommendations for the general preparation phase of teacher candidates.

1. Universities must coordinate the implementation of technology use for teaching and learning across the campus. This includes issues of access as well as organized, balanced curriculum mapping of technology competencies.

2. Ubiquitous access to non-tethered technology should be available to all students across the campus.

3. All students must have e-mail and Internet access to university technology-based resources as a consequence of enrollment in the institution regardless of geographic location.

4. Faculty development programs cannot be a "one-size-fits-all" design. The program must be flexible, provide multiple approaches, and vary in starting points.

5. Every student should have an online learning experience as part of general preparation.

6. Faculty must have access to technology resources in the classroom.

References

DeCerce, J. (2001). Broadband. *T.H.E. Journal, 28*(8), 26–27.

National Education Association. (2001, January). Course Web sites: Are they worth the effort? *NEA Higher Education Advocate Online* [Online serial]. Available: **www.nea.org/he**.

M. G. (Peggy) Kelly is a professor of education at California State University, San Marcos, and co-director of the ISTE NETS Project.

Lajeane Thomas is a professor of education at Louisiana Tech University, director of the ISTE NETS Project, and chair of the ISTE Standards and Accreditation Committee.

Integrating Technology in Professional Preparation

Introduction

The standards and essential conditions discussed in Section 1 provide the content and supporting requirements for the integration of technology in teacher preparation programs. This section focuses on model learning activities that portray how the standards can be met through classroom examples. Each learning activity integrates technology with content that would likely be encountered in the teacher preparation program and includes a variety of ways of assessing learning outcomes.

Like the stages of development associated with learning, the stages of integrating technology into classroom instruction at the university level are beginning to emerge in the descriptive literature. A proliferation of articles purports to provide models of effective use of technology in teaching and learning. The articles cover online courses, distance learning technologies, packaged online software such as Blackboard and WebCT, and presentation software such as PowerPoint. These are uses of technology as delivery mechanisms. These tools are powerful but do not necessarily represent effective use of technology to promote deep understanding of content.

The focus of this section is to move beyond the professor's use of a presentation tool to a teacher candidate's experience in learning with technology as a tool and creating experiences for students to use technology as a learning tool. Rather than having the technology completely in the hands of the teacher, thus supporting old habits of teaching, this section places technology into the hands of learners, moving the learning environment to one that is learner centered and inquiry oriented. (See the graphic on new learning environments in Section 1, under "Establishing National Educational Technology Standards for Teachers.")

Limitations and No Limits

Section 2 provides teacher education faculty with examples of ways to integrate technology into their teaching. It is not the purpose of this section to provide a set of "bleeding edge" examples of technology use. Rather, most of the software and hardware cited in the activities are easily obtained or already present in most colleges and universities.

As with any set of examples, it is expected that faculty will review the activities with a critical eye to modify and adjust the method and content to meet the needs of their teacher candidates and program. It is the faculty member's knowledge of the subject areas and experience in working with students and teacher candidates that will provide the necessary modifications of the activities. It has never been the intention of the writers that faculty would implement the activities exactly as written.

The expectation of infused creativity and personalization extends to the intended subject area of the activities. Although an activity may be written for the English language arts, for example, the method used in the activity may be re-purposed for a science or social studies methods course. Faculty should take the time to review many activities for ideas that fit individual and programmatic circumstances. Limiting a review to a specific area of study would be limiting the possibilities of technology integration.

Assessment Is Everywhere

As briefly discussed in Section 1 and more thoroughly in Section 3, assessment in teacher preparation is an area of concern both in terms of how the concept of assessment is approached with teacher candidates and how the candidates and programs are assessed in an outcomes and standards-based environment. It is with this backdrop of a high-pressured environment that the writers and NETS Leadership Team made the decision to depart from presenting a consistent means of assessing the activities.

The activities contained in this section purposefully include a variety of scoring rubrics and means of assessing teacher candidate work. Some activities include fully developed rubrics divided by the criteria to be assessed. Other activities include partially completed rubrics with the intention of having candidates participate in the completion of the rubric as part of the activity. A few activities include a table of accountability that aligns the standards listed at the top of the activity with the elements of the activity and associated processes and products. This last type of assessment table validates that the activity addresses the standards as stated.

The scoring rubrics provided also vary in their construction and emphasis. The scoring scale varies from a three, four, five, or six point scale. Some rubrics have checklists associated with criteria that are assessed as either present or not present in the product. Other rubrics have generalized statements holistically describing the criteria at each level, while still others separate the criteria into a grid format. Finally, some activities refer to a generic set of rubrics found in Appendix C that can be applied to any culminating project, such as a multimedia presentation, oral report, Web site development, reflective journal entry, and so on

Mentoring Everyone

Some activities seem quite simple while others involve multiple days and multiple technologies. In any case, the success of implementing any of the activities is not only dependent on meeting the essential conditions as outlined in Section 1, but is equally dependent on the degree to which faculty mentor one another, share experiences, and collaboratively address the needs of teacher candidates. Like the public school classroom, the university classroom is no longer a place of isolation, even for the professor. Setting aside traditional issues of peer assessment, faculty must take the time to assist one another in reworking in-class and online experiences for teacher candidates.

Thinking that the mere addition of a few activities that are technology-rich will meet the call for technology in teacher preparation is shortsighted. The integration of technology into the teacher education program in a systematic, organized, strategic manner will fundamentally change the teaching and learning in the classroom and beyond. This fundamental change will require that faculty work together, mentor one another, and openly discuss the issues at hand. Colleges of education that have created a culture of isolation and independence will find that the use of collaboration and interdependence will foster new and stimulating conversations centered on the core function of the college—that of teaching and learning.

Organization of This Section

This section is organized by commonly found departments or programs in a college of education. Learning activities are provided for

- foundations courses,
- early childhood education programs,
- elementary education programs,
- middle school education programs, and
- secondary education programs.

The activities clustered in the foundations section are those that cross the boundaries of licensure programs. The experiences vary from beginning to organize for technology-based portfolios to the study of educational psychology. The foundations section contains a wide range of options that are in no way all-encompassing of the concepts covered in typical educational foundations curricula. Like the other sections, the activities are a beginning for thinking differently about how technology can support learning within the coursework.

The activities in the remainder of the section are program-oriented. Each section is divided into the content areas of English language arts, mathematics, science, and social studies.

Noticeably absent in the list is a section entitled "Curriculum" or "Learning and Instruction". It was the consensus of the writers and NETS Leadership Team that the activities found in various program areas would be used in the typical curriculum or learning and instruction course as needed.

Design of an Activity

At first glance, you might expect the lessons for university faculty members to be written in the same format as is often taught to teacher candidates, for example, the seven-step lesson plan, the five-step lesson plan, an into-through-and-beyond instructional model, and so on. The collection of activity writers, NETS Leadership Team, and activity reviewers all expressed concern that the traditional lesson plan would not get at the issues that university faculty are concerned about—active engagement of adults while covering content in a tightly packed program of coursework. The format used for these activities was derived over the development and feedback cycle of this project. It began as the format used in Japanese schools when using the technique of "lesson studies," and evolved into what you see in the following pages.

The layout of the activities is designed to help the faculty member or staff developer to see what the expectations are of both the instructor and the teacher candidate. Reading down a single column will provide only a glimpse of the action that is taking place. It is recommended that faculty examine both down and across the columns for each section to obtain a full view of what is expected.

Each lesson is introduced with a Subject, Topic, Profile, and Abstract. Other sections are:

Standards—States both the applicable NETS for Teachers and content standards.

Lesson Description

> **Teacher Prep Faculty—**Lists chronologically what the instructor should be doing. This section is designed for active teaching.

> **Teacher Candidates—**Outlines the expectations of teacher candidates as the activity takes place. This column provides a check on how involved the candidates should be in the lesson.

> **Faculty Notes—**Contains suggestions, cautions, and alternative ideas for completing the activity.

Assessment—Varies in the activities. The variation is purposeful in providing the user with a variety of ways to look at the assessment of technology-rich activities.

Tools and Resources—Does not include basic resources such as a computer. This section includes resources that should be available to make the activity successful. Additional resources and information about locating resources are in Appendix E.

Credits—Names and contact information for members of the writing team who took primary responsibility for the activity.

Comments/Stories—Comments and anecdotes from a variety of sources and those who piloted the activities.

Learning Activity from Elementary Education Program
Subject Area: Social Studies
Lesson Title: Oral History

Stage of teacher preparation addressed by learning activity

Contains directions for the faculty member on how to organize the activity and the sequence of events

Provides specific directions to the teacher candidate to ensure they are actively involved

List of NETS•T and curricular standards covered by the learning activity

Provides tips and alternative ideas to the faculty member

Ideas for assessing teacher candidate learning

Name and contact information for activity writer(s)

Stories or advice from the writer(s)

Tools and resources to support the learning activity

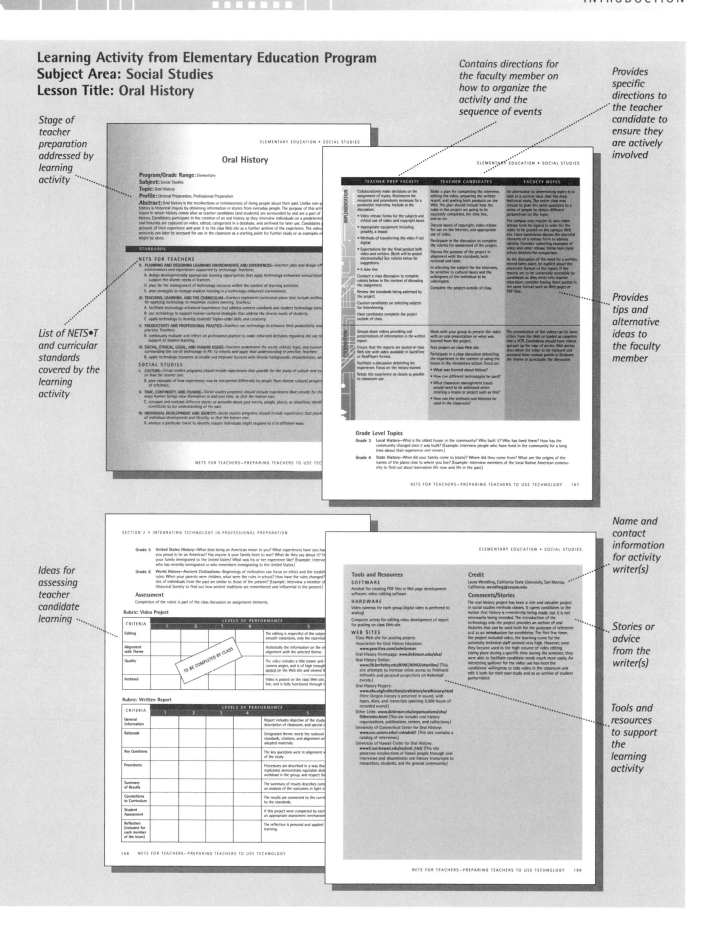

Educational Foundations

- Introduction
- Achieving Equitable Access in and out of School
- Analyzing Legal, Moral, and Ethical Dilemmas
- Becoming a Digital Packrat
- Discovering Multiple Ways of Knowing
- Exploring Cultural Differences
- Grouping Students for Learning

Educational Foundations

Introduction

At the heart of all study of education is a set of foundations courses that provide the basis for understanding schools of the past, present, and future. Regardless of the names of the courses within the various types of programs, the disciplines covered include the history, philosophy, sociology, and politics associated with education. The specific topics of study might include the history and future of education, various philosophies of education or the schools of thought, culture and multicultural issues, school governance and finance, school law, and school reform. Other courses that also provide a base for classroom culture are the study of human growth and development, educational psychology, learning and evaluation, and special education. Additionally, at some institutions, notions of curriculum design and management are also included as foundations. All of these topics provide opportunities for critical thinking and reflection.

In addition to the study of associated content, teacher candidates can use technology tools and technology-based products to increase knowledge and productivity within the foundations courses. Rather than taking a multiple-choice test over various philosophies of education, candidates can design school mission statements and technology-generated brochures that highlight a school representing a particular school of thought. Development of an online personal growth plan, similar to an IEP, can document understanding of both special education content and technology skills. Courses can be offered online. Candidates can participate in online study groups. Electronic portfolio entries can help to document candidate learning within the foundations area. In fact, candidates can "use technology productivity tools to complete [many] required professional tasks" associated with their coursework (see Section 1, "Establishing National Educational Technology Standards for Teachers.")

ACTIVITIES

The following activities were designed for the purpose of connecting the foundations and educational psychology curriculum with technology:

Achieving Equitable Access in and out of School

Creating, giving, and analyzing a simple survey instrument to determine the technological resources that are readily available to students in their homes allow candidates to reflect on how technology access affects their planning and teaching.

Analyzing Legal, Moral, and Ethical Dilemmas

By participating in a short modeling exercise and then deeply researching a topic introduced by vignettes, candidates explore legal and ethical dilemmas that K–12 educators may confront in educational environments.

Becoming a Digital Packrat

Developing an electronic portfolio can meet several critical needs including detailing NCATE unit performance assessment and reporting requirements, documenting candidate professional growth, and listing K–12 student achievement of content standards. This activity is intended to be one of the first lessons in a teacher education program to provide candidates with an organizing framework for an electronic portfolio to be kept throughout the program.

Discovering Multiple Ways of Knowing

Exploring major figures in educational philosophy helps prospective teachers begin to think about their own philosophy of education and how that might affect instructional decisions they will make. Various technology tools are used in conjunction with demonstrating the theory of multiple intelligences to communicate information about this philosopher.

Exploring Cultural Differences

In addition to increasing their awareness of the diverse elements of the local community by locating, evaluating, and collecting demographic information about a local community and its schools, the candidates use electronic formats to communicate the information to their peers and potentially to an external audience.

Grouping Students for Learning

As a part of learning about the various ways of grouping students for instruction, candidates experience how various groupings of computers are used in the classroom. Candidates explore various grouping strategies and the effect of each on learning.

Achieving Equitable Access in and out of School

Subject: Foundations

Topic: Legal and Ethical Concerns, Equitable Access

Profile: Professional Preparation

Abstract: The teacher candidates create a simple survey instrument to determine the technological resources that are readily available to students in their homes. The candidates provide a rationale as to how each resource on the survey can be used to foster learning. The data gathered from these surveys is used to create graphs and charts indicating those resources most often available. Candidates reflect on how the information obtained from the survey might affect their planning for learning activities of the students surveyed. When needed, candidates write a letter to a community organization explaining the results of the survey and describing the role the organization might play in expanding learning resources for the community.

Note: This activity requires access to a classroom and the ability to administer a survey to children. Ensure that university and district guidelines regarding collecting information from children, privacy issues (although this survey is anonymous), and the use of human subjects have been consulted.

STANDARDS

NETS FOR TEACHERS

I. **TECHNOLOGY OPERATIONS AND CONCEPTS**—*Teachers demonstrate a sound understanding of technology operations and concepts. Teachers:*

    A. demonstrate introductory knowledge, skills, and understanding of concepts related to technology (as described in the ISTE NETS for Students).

    B. demonstrate continual growth in technology knowledge and skills to stay abreast of current and emerging technologies.

II. **PLANNING AND DESIGNING LEARNING ENVIRONMENTS AND EXPERIENCES**—*Teachers plan and design effective learning environments and experiences supported by technology. Teachers:*

    A. design developmentally appropriate learning opportunities that apply technology-enhanced instructional strategies to support the diverse needs of learners.

VI. **SOCIAL, ETHICAL, LEGAL, AND HUMAN ISSUES**—*Teachers understand the social, ethical, legal, and human issues surrounding the use of technology in PK–12 schools and apply that understanding in practice. Teachers:*

    E. facilitate equitable access to technology resources for all students.

Lesson Description

	TEACHER PREP FACULTY	TEACHER CANDIDATES	FACULTY NOTES
PREPARATION	Prepare a simple anonymous survey to assess the technology available in each teacher candidate's home. Include a list of technologies, a blank for "other," and a couple of questions.		Create the survey with the notion that it will be given to the candidates to model how the larger survey is to be done and what the possibilities are.
INTRODUCTION	Have the candidates fill out the survey individually to determine the kind of technological resources that are available in their homes. Work in class to score and chart the results. Facilitate the discussion of the conclusions that can be made from the survey. Review access and a class Digital Divide. Insist that the candidates critique the questions in terms of meeting the objective of the survey.	Fill out technology surveys in class. Develop conclusions based on the information obtained in the survey. Discuss the results in terms of the variability of access by peers. Find solution to a class Digital Divide. Critique the questions used in terms of readministering the questionnaire to students.	This survey provides the class with information about the technology resources available to the class as a whole, but also provides the instructor with information about the assumptions that can be made about student access. Questions may be added about how often or easy it is for candidates to access university technology resources. This information may cause some restructuring of class assignments to meet student access restrictions.

TEACHER PREP FACULTY	TEACHER CANDIDATES	FACULTY NOTES
IMPLEMENTATION Facilitate a discussion of the educational importance of each technology prevalent in candidates' homes. Divide candidates into groups. Assign each group to a class of students. Have groups develop a survey for students. The survey should assess the technological resources that are available in each of their students' homes, providing enough information on which to make instructional decisions. Check the surveys before candidates give them in assigned classrooms. Have candidates pool and organize their data by grade or age level, depending on classroom access. Have them enter the data into a spreadsheet or graphing program for analysis and presentation. Assign groups the task of making a multimedia presentation on the results of their data. Prior to completing the assignment, develop a rubric, either with or without the candidates, for how the presentations will be assessed and the important components of the project. Share and discuss the rubric with the candidates to clarify expectations. Elements of the rubric should at least include content (quality of survey, analysis of results, and recommendations for instructional planning based on results) and presentation. (See the "Multimedia Presentation" rubric in Appendix C.)	Participate in a discussion of the educational importance of each technology present in candidates' homes. In groups, create a survey instrument to be used in determining which technological resources are readily available to students in their homes. Allow the faculty member to check the survey before administering it. Each member of the group administers a survey to a classroom of students. Pool the data from all the classrooms or break it out by grade or age level depending on the classroom access, before analyzing the data. Enter the data into a spreadsheet or graphing program and select an appropriate graph format for presentation. In the presentation, be prepared to provide • a rationale for the questions, • the conclusions, and • recommendations for home-related assignments.	The groups can be organized by subtopic to develop the survey. For example, the computer group may develop questions on the type, capacity, Internet access, and peripherals available. The VCR group may want to ask questions about where the VCR is located and what household restrictions are imposed for access. Because the candidates may have classroom access that varies by grade levels, encourage them to think about how student developmental levels may cause the access to some technologies to vary. Depending on the type of program the candidates are enrolled in, the assignment can be modified to require analysis of the data in terms of teaching a specific subject area or discipline. Groups could be arranged by targeted credential or discipline. For example, how can access to VCRs enhance the teaching of the visual arts? What resources could be provided that would make teaching specific concepts easier and more connected to the home?
CULMINATION Schedule the presentations and ensure the appropriate technology is available. Evaluate the presentations using the collaboratively developed rubric. Guided Reflection: What did you learn from this activity? How will you use what you have learned in your own classroom? Encourage candidates to develop a letter to a community organization suggesting ways to remedy inequitable access using the data obtained.	Give a group multimedia presentation of the results of the survey. Reflect on what you learned and how you can use what you learned in your own classrooms. Develop a community plan that identifies strategies to assist in locating technological learning resources to facilitate more equitable access to technology resources for all students.	Consider posting the groups' results on the class Web site. When serious access issues arise in the data, encourage candidates to develop plans for remedying the inequities. You may find that some candidates will become very discouraged about the lack of technology in some locations. Empower candidates to search for ways to change the inequities.

Assessment

The following table clearly indicates how standards, performance indicators, and artifacts from candidates are connected for the purposes of assessment and documenting achievement of the standards. Consult the "Multimedia Presentation" rubric in Appendix C.

Table: Connecting Standards and Artifacts for Assessment

STANDARDS	PERFORMANCE INDICATORS	ASSESSMENT (Processes and Products)
NETS for Teachers I. Technology Operations and Concepts—Teachers demonstrate a sound understanding of technology operations and concepts.	Teachers: A. demonstrate introductory knowledge, skills, and understanding of concepts related to technology.	Candidates create a report that identifies how the data produced will affect their planning for further instruction. Candidates produce a draft of a letter to a community organization explaining the data collected and describing the role this organization might play in expanding learning resources for the community.
	B. demonstrate continual growth in technology knowledge and skills to stay abreast of current and emerging technologies.	Results of survey will identify access to emerging technologies. Candidates demonstrate growth in knowledge through analysis of survey results as compared with their own access given during the class session.
NETS for Teachers II. Planning and Designing Learning Environments and Experiences—Teachers plan and design effective learning environments and experiences supported by technology.	Teachers: A. design developmentally appropriate learning opportunities that apply technology-enhanced instructional strategies to support the diverse needs of learners.	Analysis provided of student data should reflect modifications in how to work with technology in the classroom and what alternative assignments can be given to take advantage of the technology available.
NETS for Teachers VI. Social, Ethical, Legal, and Human Issues—Teachers understand the social, ethical, legal, and human issues surrounding the use of technology in PK–12 schools and apply that understanding in practice.	Teachers: E. facilitate equitable access to technology resources for all students.	Candidates present a plan for equitable access in the classroom as well as suggestions for equitable access outside the classroom.

Rubric: Equitable Access

CRITERIA	LEVELS OF PERFORMANCE			
	1	2	3	4
Survey	Questions are written.	Questions are written and are sensitive to various families.	Purpose is given for survey. Questions are written and are sensitive to various families.	Purpose is given for survey. Directions for taking survey are complete. Questions are written and are sensitive to various families.
Graph	Data are reported.	Data are reported in graph form.	Data are reported in graph form and are compared with other data.	The graph for reporting results shows creative and innovative use of graphing software.
Recommendations for Instructional Planning	Recommendations are given.	Recommendations are given, sensitive to the needs of families.	Recommendations are given, sensitive to the needs of students, teachers, and families.	Creative and innovative ways are recommended, appropriate for the level and needs of students.
Letter	Letter is written.	Letter contains data and request for technology resources.	Letter contains data and request for technology, and is sensitive to needs of diversity.	All of previous levels are present, but the letter is also passionate.

Tools and Resources

HARDWARE AND SOFTWARE

Computer with Internet connectivity

Presentation hardware and software

WEB SITES

Access community, school, and government sites as needed.

Closing the Digital Divide: **www.digitaldivide.gov/** (Presents information about efforts to provide all Americans with access information technologies that are crucial to their economic growth and personal advancement.)

Diversity—Issues and Responses: **www.cde.ca.gov/iasa/diversity.html** (Information and resources are provided here to help you learn how diversity can become a resource for enrichment rather than a source of conflict and divisiveness.)

Internet Access and Content for Urban Schools and Communities: **http://ericweb.tc.columbia.edu/ digests/dig157.html** (An October 2000 monograph on the Digital Divide with sections on the Extent of Computer Use in Communities, Computer and Internet Access in Schools, The Value of Internet Content for Underserved Communities, and Policies to Increase Access.)

Recent Statistics (2000 Census) on the Digital Divide: **www.ntia.doc.gov/ntiahome/fttn00/chartscontents. html**

Credits

Michael Jordan, California State University, Fresno, California, **michaelj@csufresno.edu**

Gib Stuve, California State University, San Marcos, California, **gibstuve@home.com**

Comments/Stories

This activity could also be extended to both student teaching and first-year teaching. It is important that candidates develop methods of gathering data about prospective students to include information of a demographic nature. This information may then provide valuable insights into planning and preparation for teaching these students.

Analyzing Legal, Moral, and Ethical Dilemmas

Subject: Foundations

Topic: Legal and Ethical Issues of Teaching

Profile: Professional Preparation, Student Teaching/Internship, First-Year Teaching

Abstract: First by participating in a short modeling exercise and then by deeply researching a topic introduced by vignettes, teacher candidates explore legal and ethical dilemmas that K–12 educators may confront in educational environments. Using a "jigsaw" approach, dyads or small groups analyze the issues raised in a vignette and search for credible legal resources on the Internet. The research teams synthesize the information, propose possible solutions for class discussion, and share their solutions and advice using electronic media. As a culminating activity, heterogeneous groups of candidates compare various codes of professional conduct with outcomes from vignette research and discussion. The groups may revise an existing code or create a new one.

Note: Categories of dilemmas and sample vignettes appear at the end of this activity.

STANDARDS

NETS FOR TEACHERS

V. PRODUCTIVITY AND PROFESSIONAL PRACTICE—*Teachers use technology to enhance their productivity and professional practice. Teachers:*

A. use technology resources to engage in ongoing professional development and lifelong learning.

VI. SOCIAL, ETHICAL, LEGAL, AND HUMAN ISSUES—*Teachers understand the social, ethical, legal, and human issues surrounding the use of technology in PK–12 schools and apply that understanding in practice. Teachers:*

A. model and teach legal and ethical practice related to technology use.

D. promote safe and healthy use of technology resources.

Lesson Description

	TEACHER PREP FACULTY	TEACHER CANDIDATES	FACULTY NOTES
PREPARATION	Assign teacher candidates to research the difference between legal, ethical, and moral issues. Have candidates bring at least one issue and/or review the list of possible issue categories and select one or more of the sample vignettes provided at the end of this lesson. Or write one of your own. Create a handout with the directions for the activity and vignettes candidates will be using and/or post on the class Web site. Decide whether to use or modify the assessment rubric located in the assessment section of this lesson. Gather sample codes of conduct or professional codes of ethics. (See Web sites in Tools and Resources.)	Before class, research the difference between legal, ethical, and moral issues. Search an online dictionary for definitions of ethics in general, professional ethics, and the distinction between moral, ethical, and legal dilemmas. Bring at least one issue a teacher might face with respect to using technology in the classroom that presents a dilemma.	Check the media for current local or regional issues that school districts may have encountered recently. Often a call to a district technology coordinator will reveal some of the current legal, ethical, and moral concerns. The culminating activity includes the comparison of entries to a code of conduct or professional code of ethics. In addition to using the national documents, locate the district and state codes for substitution or later comparison. Using local district information raises the interest of the candidates as they progress to student teaching.
INTRODUCTION	**Modeling** Ask candidates to describe an ethical or legal issue surrounding technology use or media that has been featured in recent news. Organize candidates into dyads or small groups to generate the issues that are evident in the vignette or dilemma and to	In a whole class setting, participate in the discussion by providing examples of legal and ethical issues in the news. Share opinions and advice. In small groups, discuss at least one of the dilemmas presented. Come to a consensus on recommendations for resolution of the issue. Determine whether the decisions	Check for candidates' understanding of the relationship among legal issues, ethical issues, and their role as educational professionals. For additional practice, work together in small groups to provide a response to a single dilemma: determine the issues, who is affected, possible solutions, and the

TEACHER PREP FACULTY	TEACHER CANDIDATES	FACULTY NOTES

INTRODUCTION

develop a set of recommendations for what should be done in this situation.

Ask candidates whether their recommendations were based on care, rules, or justice and see if they can explain why. Require them to justify each answer shared.

Once candidates have become engaged in the topic, provide examples of the distinction between concepts of legality and ethics or have candidates search an online dictionary for those definitions. Several connections appear at the Kid's Search Tools Web site (see Tools and Resources).

Display at least one code of professional conduct listed in the resources as a comparison with solutions shared by groups. Encourage candidates to look for alignment between their advice and the code.

were care-based, rules-based, or justice-based.

Reflect on the solutions proposed in terms of alignment with the models of professional conduct for educators as defined by the institution, state, and country.

outcomes for each, and make a recommendation for a solution. Candidates provide reasons for their decisions.

As candidates continue working on group assignments, periodically check on whether they feel their decisions are care-based, rules-based, or justice-based.

IMPLEMENTATION

Divide the candidates into groups, ensuring that both the number of groups and the number of candidates in each group are the same. Thus, the jigsaw nature of the culminating activity can occur with representatives from each group.

Assign each group one of the vignettes below or others that are relevant to the region. Provide the vignettes and details of the research project (handout) and post them on the class Web site.

Facilitate the collaborative development of a rubric to assess the upcoming research project defined below. At the conclusion of class, post the rubric on the class Web site. Possible rubric categories are included in the Assessment section of this lesson.

Research
In small groups, direct the candidates to break down the dilemma into component parts to determine what the central issue is, who is affected, what possible solutions there are, what the short-term and long-term effects are of each, and propose a solution.

Have candidates research credible resources on the vignette issues. Direct them to propose a solution in writing based on two or more resources.

In vignette groups, discuss the relationship of the introductory dilemmas to the research assignment.

Participate in the development of a scoring rubric for the research project described.

Read the vignettes and use a search engine or previously selected Web sites to find and analyze:

- The central issue
- Who is affected (victims)
- Solution options
- Short- and long-term effects of possible solutions
- Legal issues
- Relationship to code of ethics/conduct

Research information from law and other credible resources on the issues featured in the vignette dilemma.

Synthesize the information and propose a solution (in writing) to the dilemma. Solutions should include at least two or more reliable or credible resources.

The development of an assessment rubric should follow some previous experience in developing rubrics. If assessment rubrics have not been discussed prior to this time, develop your own rubric asking for candidate input. Share with candidates your thinking on how the rubric was developed.

Often candidates confuse recommendations for process and criteria for assessment.

Be clear about what is expected in the presentations and what process you suggest in obtaining the information. By consulting the rubric, candidates will know how they are being assessed.

Consider having groups post their finding on the class Web site for common access to the information. Set a posting date for the information. The optimum posting date may be the date that the presentations are due. The availability of this information can enrich the conversation during the jigsaw if the groups have access to the Internet.

	TEACHER PREP FACULTY	TEACHER CANDIDATES	FACULTY NOTES
CULMINATION	**Listen and Assess** Facilitate the summarizing and discussing of the findings from the vignettes. If technology is being used for the presentation, include a second rubric on the effective use of technology (see "Multimedia Presentation" rubric in Appendix C). As a concluding activity, use a jigsaw approach of reshuffling the candidates into new groups with representative members from each research team. Have the groups discuss a set of professional standards in light of the presentations made. Each group can then compose an entirely new code of ethics/conduct or revise one that is presented. Facilitate groups reporting how the codes of ethics/conduct deal with the issues brought forth in the dilemmas.	Present the findings to the class. Rearrange yourselves in heterogeneous jigsaw groups to discuss the outcomes of the research related to a set of professional teaching standards. What conclusion can be made? Present oral reports to the whole group.	When comparing the result of the research on the vignettes, candidates may be surprised at the difference between a professional code of conduct and the law. Encourage candidates to identify elements that seem to be missing as well as discuss those that seem strong or ambiguous. The option is proposed that groups compose a code of ethics/conduct of their own based on their research. An alternative is to revise an existing code of ethics/conduct to reflect their learning. The latter provides the added benefit of having the candidates become very aware of the details of a code of ethics/conduct. Composing a code of ethics/conduct places candidates in a creative role and often results in very serious conversations about what ethics is and how it is conveyed in writing to apply to multiple situations.

Assessment

Rubric: Legal and Ethical Issues Associated with Technology Use

CRITERIA	LEVELS OF PERFORMANCE		
	EXCEEDS EXPECTATIONS 3	MEETS EXPECTATIONS 2	BELOW EXPECTATIONS 1
Two or more "credible" sources to support the proposed solution			
Depth of response			
Accuracy of practical advice to peers and colleagues			
Inclusion of the most current and past legal history of the selected dilemma			
Alignment of candidates' proposed solutions with the models of professional conduct for educators as defined by the institution, state, and country			

Tools and Resources

SOFTWARE

Internet browser required. Depending upon the format of the "proposed solutions," faculty should choose which software tool or tools candidates might use to create and present their solutions. Possible software tools could include Web editor, presentation software, e-mail, class discussion lists, and word processors.

HARDWARE

At least one computer with an Internet connection for every group of students

WEB SITES

Codes of Conduct

AFT Code of Ethics (1971):
www.aft.org/history/histdocs/code.html

Ethics for Union Teachers (1942):
www.aft.org/history/histdocs/kuenzli.html

National Association for the Education of Young Children Code of Ethical Conduct:
www.naeyc.org/resources/position_statements/ pseth98.htm

National Education Association Code of Ethics of the Education Profession: **www.nea.org/aboutnea/code.htm**

Ethics Sites

A Process for Identifying and Solving Ethical Dilemmas:
http://duke.usask.ca/~vonbaeye/gsr985/1.2.htm

Legal Sites

Center for Law and Education: **www.cleweb.org**

Federal and State Legislation:
http://bailiwick.lib.uiowa.edu/ge/legmenu.html

Federal Statutes and Regulations:
www.aristotle.net/~hantley/hiedlegl/statutes/overview. htm

Legal Essays (Indexed by Subject):
www.law.cam.ac.uk/essays/educat.htm

Search Sites

Computer Professionals for Social Responsibility:
www.cpsr.org/ (Search this site for ethical, legal, and social issues surrounding technology.)

Kid's Search Tools: **www.rcls.org/ksearch.htm** (Several dictionary and encyclopedia search engines are linked here.)

REFERENCE TEXT

Kidder, R. M., & Born, P. L. (1998). Resolving ethical dilemmas in the classroom. *Educational Leadership, 56*(4), 38–41.

Extensions for Other Profiles

Student Teaching: During student teaching or a senior capstone seminar, candidates review the policies of the district in which they are student teaching regarding legal and ethical issues including professional conduct. They compare the policies with the proposed solutions to the sample dilemmas.

First-Year Teacher: In first-year mentoring sessions, encourage the early career teachers to become familiar with school and district policies so that they can enforce classroom procedures that guide students' safe and healthy use of technology and that comply with legal and professional responsibilities for students needing assistive technology. Encourage these teachers to develop and maintain connections with their university or college methods faculty, who can serve as resources to guide them through ethical and legal dilemmas they are facing. Encourage them also to keep bookmarks or favorite Web sites that provide legal information on these issues.

Categories and Related Dilemmas

- Free speech
    - Yahoo/Nazi literature controversy in France
    - Pornography on the Web
- Intellectual property rights
    - Copyright
    - Copying
    - Plagiarism
    - Fair use
    - Public domain/works for hire/derivative works
- Abuse and exploitation
    - Stalking, online predators
    - Pornography
    - Netiquette
    - Commercially sponsored educational resources
- Obligation to employer—off-task Internet use; obligation of school in off-task student Internet use
- Privacy
    - e-mail
    - Discussion forums—releasing account information in opposition to expectations of anonymity
- Security of technology systems, data, and information

Sample Vignettes

Obligation to Employer: It is discovered that a teacher is using the Internet to track her stock portfolio during her "planning period." Is this a legal issue or an ethical issue? If so, in what way? Would it make a difference if the teacher uses her own computer? Does the issue change if the teacher only monitors the stock market, but does not act on the information until her lunch break?

Obligation to Employer: All employees in the school district have e-mail accounts. The district encourages use of this technology to work toward a goal of a "paperless" school. The Teacher's Association uses the e-mail to urge a "job action" to get a salary settlement. Is this a breach of any legal or ethical issue or obligation to the employer? As a student teacher in the district, what action should you take?

Free Speech: A student club, "Kids for Christ," uses the school LAN to advertise their meetings and religious philosophy. Some students object. Is this a violation of any "free speech" issues? If so, what is the law and how might this be resolved?

Privacy: The director of the technology for a school or school district uses her position to review e-mail of two employees she suspects are involved in an affair. What laws (if any) have been violated and what ethical issues are raised? Should anyone be disciplined? How can this be prevented, or can it?

Ownership—Copying Music: The local high school is in the second week of presenting "Godspell" to sellout crowds of students and parents. The son of the president of the local board of education has a lead role. You discover the music used in the play was downloaded illegally. What actions should you take as the school district technology coordinator?

Ethical Conduct: One of the student mentors who works with faculty in your school is attending a training session that you are conducting. She doesn't seem to be paying attention to the training and as you pass by her computer you see games and other sites that are not at all related to the training. After the break, you remind students once again that they have already signed a fair use policy that doesn't allow noninstructional use of the computers in the school lab. The student mentor, who is quite bright and proficient and who needs the money provided by this job, continues the exploration of game sites. Later in the day, the tech coordinator searches the history of the sites used most recently and finds that there are not only games, but pornographic sites in the history. Only the one student mentor has used this computer today. What are the legal and ethical issues involved? As the faculty member responsible for student mentors, what should you do?

Credits

Margaret Merlyn Ropp, Michigan Virtual University, Lansing, Michigan, **megropp@mivu.org**

Gib Stuve, California State University, San Marcos, California, **gibstuve@home.com**

Comments/Stories

The exploration of the vignettes at first seems comical to the candidates. In one respect, they usually don't believe that anyone would be faced with some of the dilemmas outlined until a brief session of "I know someone who..." gets underway. The discussion then gets down to the issues of how to handle the situation. Although there are many good acceptable use policies (AUPs) already in schools, not every school has one. In those cases, the code of ethics/conduct usually provides guidance. Introducing the AUPs of the area school districts will provide an additional dimension to the conversation.

Becoming a Digital Packrat

Subject: Foundations

Topic: Assessment, Becoming a Reflective Practitioner

Profile: Professional Preparation, Student Teaching/Internship, First-Year Teaching

Abstract: Developing an electronic portfolio can meet several critical needs, including detailing NCATE unit performance assessment and reporting requirements, documenting teacher candidate professional growth, and listing K–12 student achievement of content standards. Electronic portfolios can use the same digital artifacts to document a candidate's achievement of multiple standards for various audiences. In this lesson, candidates learn to collect their work in a digital format and learn how to store the data for easy retrieval.

The concept of portfolio development should be introduced early in a foundations class to establish the expectations that candidates will maintain an electronic portfolio throughout their Professional Preparation program. From that initial introduction, candidates become a "digital packrat" so that they can easily access the information. Candidates set up a record-keeping system (a database or spreadsheet) with fields (or columns) for name of file, date, course, standards addressed (if known), and reflection on the artifact. Candidates use their record-keeping system to keep track of all their files, as well as to record their reflections on their work.

The assessment chapter in Section 3 contains a more detailed description of the electronic portfolio and its role in supporting learning and assessment in the teacher education program.

STANDARDS

NETS FOR TEACHERS

I. **TECHNOLOGY OPERATIONS AND CONCEPTS—***Teachers demonstrate a sound understanding of technology operations and concepts. Teachers:*

   A. demonstrate introductory knowledge, skills, and understanding of concepts related to technology (as described in the ISTE NETS for Students).

IV. **ASSESSMENT AND EVALUATION—***Teachers apply technology to facilitate a variety of effective assessment and evaluation strategies. Teachers:*

   B. use technology resources to collect and analyze data, interpret results, and communicate findings to improve instructional practice and maximize student learning.

V. **PRODUCTIVITY AND PROFESSIONAL PRACTICE—***Teachers use technology to enhance their productivity and professional practice. Teachers:*

   B: continually evaluate and reflect on professional practice to make informed decisions regarding the use of technology in support of student learning.

   C. apply technology to increase productivity.

Note 1: This activity requires candidates to each have access to a computer during the class time. The activity can be adjusted for whole class demonstration followed by individual independent work. However, it is most successful when the candidates are able to begin the setup of their portfolio system while in class.

Note 2: This activity assumes that candidates have met the competencies outlined in the General Preparation Performance Profile. Specifically, candidates should have a working knowledge of the development of a database.

Lesson Description

	TEACHER PREP FACULTY	TEACHER CANDIDATES	FACULTY NOTES
PREPARATION	Since this activity is best completed in a lab or with access to laptops, check on equipment access and instruct teacher candidates where to meet for class. Select a piece of your own professional work to use for demonstration purposes. Instruct the candidates to bring a digital artifact from prior coursework that might eventually be included in a portfolio.	Carefully select a piece of prior work in digital format that has potential for inclusion in a portfolio. This may come from a class you are currently taking or one that is completed.	The digital portfolio can become documentation for accreditation if candidates save their portfolios on the school's server. Refer candidates who have poor technology skills to resources on campus for additional training.

	TEACHER PREP FACULTY	TEACHER CANDIDATES	FACULTY NOTES
INTRODUCTION	Introduce the concept of portfolios and how they can be used to demonstrate professional growth and accomplishment. Have candidates brainstorm potential uses for portfolios in the classroom. Show how the portfolio will be used in the teacher preparation program and coursework by showing sample portfolios that have been developed as a model. Have candidates list essential attributes. If appropriate, access recent graduate portfolios or have graduates come to class and show their portfolios.	Brainstorm uses for portfolios in general. Discuss the advantages of maintaining a portfolio electronically. Make a list of the attributes of the portfolios observed that seem essential for cataloging the works.	The chapter "Assessment of Educational Technology Competence" in Section 3 contains a more complete rationale for the many uses of an electronic portfolio. There are also Web sites that identify the concept and provide many examples. Suggest advantages for electronic portfolios including availability for job interviews, maximum portability, easy editing for future uses, and empowerment. This is a powerful tool for lifelong professional development.
IMPLEMENTATION	Have candidates search the Web for digital portfolios. Show different tools for maintaining data or files used for the portfolio (database and spreadsheet). Set up a database with the fields the same as the essential attributes identified during the introductory session. As a beginning step, use the standards or benchmarks for completion of the teacher preparation program as the choices for the standards field. Using your own work, model how to enter the information about the work into the spreadsheet and/or database. Create a reflection for the sample work emphasizing the importance of the reflection in meeting specific as well as general criteria. Save the file on a disk. If possible, demonstrate how to save the file on a server that the candidate can maintain throughout the program. Reinforce the need to make backup copies of all entries. Review how to store work for eventual use in a formal portfolio, including options for free Internet-based storage Web sites.	Do a search for Web sites to examine different types of digital portfolios. Brainstorm ideas to maintain an organizational structure of the work produced throughout the teacher education program. Identify the pieces of information that need to be gathered. Set up a database with the fields that seem to be essential attributes. Create a reflection about the artifact brought to class. Record the reason for the selection and the rationale for how this selection fits a given criteria identified as an element of the portfolio. Enter the data and the reflections on the work into the working portfolio and save to disk.	The process of developing an electronic portfolio based on the ISTE standards is more fully described in Section 3. **Note:** This activity is introduced at the beginning of an entire process of electronic portfolio development. A system, including technical support, should be in place to support both faculty and candidates as they progress through the program.
CULMINATION	Show a former candidate's database supporting the electronic portfolio. Reiterate the need to keep the work organized and cataloged. Discuss the importance of the portfolio for professional development. Have candidates discuss the variety of items that can become part of the portfolio. Remind the candidates to maintain the database when they finish a document/artifact and save it in their folder on the server or on an Internet-based storage Web site.	Reexamine the fields selected for organizing artifacts. Brainstorm other course and noncourse artifacts that can be used for the portfolio.	Plan to revisit this record-keeping system along with the artifacts and associated reflections at strategic points during the class and as a regular event in the teacher education program.

Extension of Lesson

This lesson begins the process of developing an electronic portfolio for candidates. In later classes, show candidates how to scan in documents, photographs, and other artifacts. Show how to convert documents into a digital format. Use the process of constructing an electronic portfolio to build hands-on technology skills. Show how to use a variety of tools to create electronic portfolios, including five different levels of e-portfolio development depending on the level of technology skills of the portfolio developer.

Rubric: Levels of E-Portfolio Development

0	All documents are in paper format. Some portfolio data may be stored on videotape.
1	All documents are in digital file formats, using word processing or other commonly used software, and stored in electronic folders on a hard drive, floppy disk, or LAN server. Some word processors allow hyperlinks.
2	Portfolio data are entered into a structured format, such as a database or HyperStudio template or slideshow (such as PowerPoint or AppleWorks) and stored on a hard drive, Zip, floppy disk, or LAN.
3	Documents are translated into Portable Document Format (PDF) with hyperlinks between standards, artifacts, and reflections using Adobe Acrobat. They are stored on a hard drive, Zip, Jaz, CD-R/W, or LAN server.
4	Documents are translated into HTML, complete with hyperlinks between standards, artifacts, and reflections, using a Web-authoring program and posted to a Web server.
5	Portfolio is organized with a multimedia-authoring program, incorporating digital sound and video, and converted to digital format and pressed to CD-R/W or posted to the Web in streaming format.

Assessment

The list below refers to the information that should be provided for each artifact. This rubric can be used as an assessment of the activity outlined above or as a check sheet to ensure that each portfolio element has the necessary information to maintain an organized structure.

Rubric: Electronic Portfolio Development

Database/Spreadsheet Entries Include:			
	Artifact name (and any related files)		
	Date completed		
	Course where artifact was created		
	Type of file (slideshow, word processing, JPEG, etc.)		

CRITERIA	LEVELS OF PERFORMANCE		
	DEVELOPING 1	ADEQUATE 2	THOROUGH 3
Database or spreadsheet structure	Fields constructed and named	Information entered into appropriate field	Creative and innovate use of the database or spreadsheet
Connection to standards	Little or no connection to any standards	At least one standard area is identified	Identification of application to multiple standards
Description of artifact	Little or no description	Basic description of the artifact and what was learned	In-depth description of artifact and how it is evidence of achieving identified standards
Level of teacher candidate reflection	Focus on personal feelings about the experience	Focus on personal feelings and the skills that are needed for planning and teaching	Focus on personal feelings, what candidates learned, what they still have to learn, and how the experience will affect them as a teacher

Tools and Resources

SOFTWARE

Database or spreadsheet; portfolio development software to complete e-portfolio

HARDWARE

Computer, scanner, storage media (CD-ROM, floppy disks, Zip disks)

WEB SITES

Using Technology to Support Alternative Assessment and Electronic Portfolios:
http://transition.alaska.edu/www/portfolios.html

See bibliography at:
http://transition.alaska.edu/www/portfolios/
bibliography.html

Additional bibliographic information is listed at:
http://electronicportfolios.com/portfolios/
bibliography.html

Credit

Helen Barrett, University of Alaska, Anchorage, Alaska,
afhcb@uaa.alaska.edu

Comments/Stories

Faculty members could model for candidates the process they go through to develop their own electronic teaching portfolio for promotion and tenure. One such process is described in detail in the proceedings of the 2001 conference of the Society for Information Technology and Teacher Education (SITE) and published on the author's Web site at http://electronicportfolios.com/portfolios/
SITE2001.pdf.

Discovering Multiple Ways of Knowing

Subject: Foundations

Topic: Philosophy/History of Education

Profile: Professional Preparation

Abstract: Exploring the major figures in educational philosophy and history helps teacher candidates begin to think about their own philosophy of education and how that might affect the kinds of instructional decisions they will make. Organized in small groups, candidates first research an educational theorist such as constructivists, e.g. Dewey, Brunner, or Vygotsky. Then they discuss and organize the key information about this individual and how his or her theories might be applied in schooling. The groups then use what they have learned about multiple intelligences to communicate about the educational theorist in such a way as to appeal to a particular intelligence. Technology tools are particularly useful in communicating information in ways appropriate to a variety of intelligence. As an outcome of this experience, candidates will be exposed to the breadth of theories and will experience learning in multiple modes that address the various intelligences.

STANDARDS

NETS FOR TEACHERS

I. TECHNOLOGY OPERATIONS AND CONCEPTS—*Teachers demonstrate a sound understanding of technology operations and concepts. Teachers:*

   B. demonstrate continual growth in technology knowledge and skills to stay abreast of current and emerging technologies.

III. TEACHING, LEARNING, AND THE CURRICULUM—*Teachers implement curriculum plans that include methods and strategies for applying technology to maximize student learning. Teachers:*

   B. use technology to support learner-centered strategies that address the diverse needs of students.

   C. apply technology to develop students' higher-order skills and creativity.

   D. manage student learning activities in a technology-enhanced environment.

Lesson Description

	TEACHER PREP FACULTY	TEACHER CANDIDATES	FACULTY NOTES
PREPARATION	Have the class complete the study of multiple intelligence theory prior to beginning this activity. Point the teacher candidates to original source materials (written, Web, and video/CD-ROM resources) related to the philosophers to be explored. Relevant Web pages are given in Tools and Resources.	Read background material and develop an initial knowledge base related to educational philosophers.	Be sure to provide time for candidate research. This project is best done in small, three to five person groups. Through collaborative work, candidates will develop additional insight into the philosopher. This assignment may be a modification of an existing assignment on studying an educational philosophy.
INTRODUCTION	Explain the assignment to the candidates: "In this class you will be asked to research an educational philosopher and choose a type of intelligence in which you will communicate your findings." Form groups to cover each of the philosophers desired. As the groups select or are assigned a topic, have them each randomly select a learning style/intelligence through which to structure their multimedia presentation. Check that all the intelligences are going to be covered. Have candidates organize their research and presentation strategies.	Meet in small groups to plan research. Brainstorm ways the research can be completed, taking into account access to technology-based resources, time available, status meetings, and a general work plan. Begin thinking of ways to present the information from the research in a way that is appropriate for the intelligence selected.	You might want to provide a template of essential facts to include for each theorist or philosopher such as beliefs about learning, the historical context in which they worked, how their philosophy might look if applied in a school or classroom, and important books or writings. Rather than have each group focus on one intelligence, an alternative organization is to require that each group address each of the intelligences as they design their presentation. This organization is beneficial for the learning of each group, but it may be difficult to schedule equipment and avoid repetition of techniques.

	TEACHER PREP FACULTY	TEACHER CANDIDATES	FACULTY NOTES
INTRODUCTION			Focusing on one learning style/intelligence can be difficult for some groups. Encourage the groups to highlight one intelligence but use others to ensure a comprehensible presentation
IMPLEMENTATION	Decide who (peers and/or instructor) assesses the presentations. Develop a rubric to guide candidates in terms of expected outcomes. A sample is provided in the Assessment section of this lesson. Have candidates collect information on philosophers and choose a presentation method that exemplifies the chosen intelligence. Let candidates know that after their presentations, they will need to turn in their assigned part of the group work on the theorist or philosopher and a written reflection addressing these questions: • What did you learn about multiple intelligences? • How did you learn this information? • Why did your group choose the technology it did? • How might you apply this in your own classroom in the future? Help candidates select technologies that support the chosen type of intelligence.	Participate in the development of a scoring rubric of the required elements outlined in the assignment. Collaboratively locate the key information on the philosophers. Develop a song, dance, diagram, painting, and so on— whatever method exemplifies the assigned or chosen intelligence. Use an appropriate technology to record or archive the presentation or as an active example of how the intelligence can be used through the technology. Post a digital archive on the class Web site.	To design a multimedia presentation about an educational philosopher, candidates may do one of the following: • Use draw tools (spatial/visual intelligence) • Create a play and videotape it (linguistic/kinesthetic) • Write a newsletter from the time and point of view of the philosopher (linguistic) • Create a PowerPoint presentation in which several philosophers interact (interpersonal intelligence) • Draw a picture or illustrated cartoon (visual) • Write a song (musical) Using each of the intelligences for a presentation supports a wide range of technology uses, from tape recorders to computers to video camcorders. Act as a facilitator as candidates investigate, research, select technologies, and design presentations.
CULMINATION	Schedule the presentations. Facilitate the predetermined assessment process (instructor or peers). Have candidates post a digital archive on the class Web site. As an introduction to a follow-up assignment, model the use of a graphic organizer software program to map an educational theory or philosophy. Assign candidates the creation of a map of their own emerging teaching philosophy based on what they have learned.	Present multimedia, multiple intelligence presentations. Participate in a peer- and self-assessment process as assigned by instructor. Hand in the research that was your part of the group work and the written reflection. Use a concept-mapping tool to develop a graphic representation of your own emerging educational philosophy.	The presentation represents an appropriate digital item for inclusion in a digital portfolio. Encourage candidates to think graphically about their philosophy. For example, important philosophers could be made into large circles and placed near the center of a graphical chart, while those who are less important may occupy smaller circles. The uniqueness of each map should be valued in the same way a candidate's beliefs should ground her or his growth as a professional. The maps can provide an interesting point of discussion for later topics in the course. Candidates may want to periodically revise their map as their teacher preparation program progresses.

Assessment

Rubric: Multimedia Multiple Intelligence Presentations on Educational Theorists

CRITERIA	LEVELS OF PERFORMANCE			
	4	3	2	1
Content	Content is correct. Content compares and contrasts various authors' views.	Content is correct. Multiple perspectives are not given.	Content is mostly free from error.	Content is riddled with errors that must be corrected.
Resources	Excellent use is made of a rich variety of current and original resources.	Multiple resources are used. Facts are given.	Limited number of resources are present.	Presentation uses only text and/or one resource.
Presentation	Creative and inventive use is made of focus, instruction, and audience engagement.	Presentation is clear and focused, objectives clear, audience engaged.	Presentation is focused, objectives clear, little audience engagement.	Presentation is loosely focused, objectives unclear.
Technology Use	Technology is integrated appropriately throughout presentation to enhance effectiveness of lesson and learning of audience.	Technology is integrated into the presentation to improve the quality of presentation or learning.	Technology used for the presentation seems contrived.	The technology is only basic overheads, chalkboard, or VCR.
Concept Map (Uniqueness of each map is to be valued.)	Map is creative and innovative and meets previous criteria.	Map is complete. Candidates see the connectedness of different parts.	Map is complete with few labels and minimal connections.	Candidates complete map.

Note: Rubric modified from Making Connections: Lesson Plan Rubric: **www.lcet.doe.state.la.us/connections**.

Rubric: Level of Reflection

3 — Clear evidence that the candidate can critically assess his or her own beliefs and actions and has considered salient issues in examining classroom practices

2 — Some evidence that the candidate is able to assess the educational implications and consequences of teaching decisions and actions

1 — Candidate focuses on personal feelings about the experience. Little questioning of teaching objectives

Tools and Resources

SOFTWARE AND HARDWARE

A wide variety of available software and hardware may be used in this activity.

WEB SITES

General Reference

Britannica Online: **www.britannica.com/**

Multiple Intelligence

The Key School: **www.ips.k12.in.us/mskey/**

Multiple Intelligences Schools: **http://pzweb.harvard.edu/Research/MISchool.htm**

Multiple Intelligence Theory: **www.harding.edu/~cbr/midemo/mifirst.html**

Multiple Intelligences: Theory and Practice in the K–12 Classroom: **www.indiana.edu/~eric_reclieo/bibs/multiple.html**

Project Zero: **http://pzweb.harvard.edu/Research/MISchool.htm**

Philosophies and Theories

Constructivist Theorists: **http://curriculum.calstatela.edu/faculty/psparks/theorists/501const.htm**

Five Educational Philosophies: **http://edweb.sdsu.edu/people/LShaw/F95syll/philos/phintro.html**

From Essentialism to Constructivism: **www.agora.qc.ca/textes/feenberg.html**

History of Progressivism:
www.ils.nwu.edu/~e_for_e/nodes/NODE-86-pg.html

John-Paul Sartre on Existentialism Is a Humanism:
http://members.aol.com/DonJohnR/Philosophy/
S_Human.html

Operant Conditioning and Behaviorism—An Historical
Outline: www.biozentrum.uniwuerzburg.de/genetics/
behavior/learning/behaviorism.html

Perennialism and Essentialism:
www.westga.edu/~jdbutler/ClassNotes/philosophy.html

Philosophy Resources on the Internet:
http://12.6.109.229/Main/MainPers.asp

Jerome Bruner

Jerome Bruner: www.gwu.edu/~tip/bruner.html

Jerome Bruner:
http://leda.calstatela.edu/faculty/psparks/theorists/
501brune.htm

John Dewey

Center for Dewey Studies: www.siu.edu/~deweyctr/

Democracy and Education (1938):
www.ilt.columbia.edu/academic/texts/dewey/d_e/
contents.html

Maria Montessori

Montessori: www2.msstate.edu/~ksc2/montesorri.htm

Montessori Online: www.montessori.org/

Jean Piaget

Jean Piaget Society: www.piaget.org/

Lev Vygotsky

Vygotsky Internet Archive:
www.marxists.org/archive/vygotsky/

REFERENCE TEXTS

Bruner, J. (1960). *The process of education.* Cambridge, MA: Harvard University Press.

Bruner, J. (1966). *Toward a theory of instruction.* Cambridge, MA: Harvard University Press.

Dewey, J. (1897). *My pedagogic creed* [Pamphlet]. Battle Creek, MI: Kellogg & Co.

Gardner, H. (1993). *The unschooled mind: How children think and how schools should teach.* New York: Basic Books.

Haggarty, B. (1995). *Nurturing intelligences.* Boston: Addison-Wesley.

Piaget, J. (1929). *The child's conception of the world.* New York: Harcourt, Brace Jovanovich.

Piaget, J. (1970). *The science of education and the psychology of the child.* New York: Grossman.

Vam der Veer, R., & Valsiner, J. (Eds.). (1994). *The Vygotsky reader.* Cambridge, MA: Blackwell.

Vygotsky, L. S. (1978). *Mind in society: The development of higher psychological processes.* Cambridge, MA: Harvard University Press.

Extension for Other Profiles

A group of candidates can be assigned the task of designing a newsletter as if it were written at the time of the theorist or philosopher. Candidates can gather pictures from the Web site of the philosopher, the place he or she lived, and the times. For example, a newsletter from the Dewey Foundation might invite the reader to a debate on the value of progressive education. A Montessori Missive might invite educators to observe street children learning in the new school designed for them by Montessori.

Credit

Karin Wiburg, New Mexico State University, Las Cruces, New Mexico, kwiburg@nmsu.edu

Comments/Stories

In working with this activity with a variety of teachers, many have stated that the presentations focusing on a specific intelligence really became quite comical. Some candidates selected an intelligence that they were not strong in to be able to explore that method of learning for themselves. The groups became quite creative, which provided stories and tidbits for class teasing later. But months later, even as a little teasing went on, it was apparent that they used the teasing as a way to show just how much they remembered about the tenets of a given philosophy.

Exploring Cultural Differences

Subject: Foundations

Topic: Cultural Diversity

Profile: Professional Preparation

Abstract: This activity is designed to increase teacher candidates' awareness of the diverse populations in the local community. Individuals or pairs locate, evaluate, and collect demographic data about a local community and its schools from a variety of sources. Then they specifically collect demographic data about a cultural group in the community that is different from their own. Following the research, candidates attend a public function of the group being studied. After participation in the function, candidates reflect on their feelings and observations as they interacted with the community group. As part of their personal analysis, candidates share their learning as to how this awareness affects their classroom instruction. Multimedia and other electronic formats are used to effectively communicate the information and ideas to their peers and, potentially, to an external audience.

STANDARDS

NETS FOR TEACHERS

I. **TECHNOLOGY OPERATIONS AND CONCEPTS**—*Teachers demonstrate a sound understanding of technology operations and concepts. Teachers:*

   A. demonstrate introductory knowledge, skills, and understanding of concepts related to technology (as described in the ISTE NETS for Students).

II. **PLANNING AND DESIGNING LEARNING ENVIRONMENTS AND EXPERIENCES**—*Teachers plan and design effective learning environments and experiences supported by technology. Teachers:*

   B. apply current research on teaching and learning with technology when planning learning environments and experiences.

   C. identify and locate technology resources and evaluate them for accuracy and suitability.

   E. plan strategies to manage student learning in a technology-enhanced environment.

IV. **ASSESSMENT AND EVALUATION**—*Teachers apply technology to facilitate a variety of effective assessment and evaluation strategies. Teachers:*

   B. use technology resources to collect and analyze data, interpret results, and communicate findings to improve instructional practice and maximize student learning.

VI. **SOCIAL, ETHICAL, LEGAL, AND HUMAN ISSUES**—*Teachers understand the social, ethical, legal, and human issues surrounding the use of technology in PK–12 schools and apply that understanding in practice. Teachers:*

   B. apply technology resources to enable and empower learners with diverse backgrounds, characteristics, and abilities.

   C. identify and use technology resources that affirm diversity.

Lesson Description

	TEACHER PREP FACULTY	TEACHER CANDIDATES	FACULTY NOTES
PREPARATION	Assign teacher candidates background reading. Research several Web sites from areas where candidates are likely to be assigned. Include schools, school districts, local government, chambers of commerce, and local businesses. Additional information on student populations could be acquired from state educational agencies. Have candidates list the cultural influences in their region. Determine how the final projects will be stored for eventual sharing with others. Options to consider are capturing presentations on a class Web site, a class CD-ROM, a video, and so on.	Complete assigned readings focusing on the effects of the presence of diverse cultures in the classroom. Make a tentative list of the cultural influences present in the region that may affect classroom practice.	Often candidates focus on what differences are visually apparent, failing to distinguish between racial, ethnic, and cultural differences. As you prepare candidates for class, encourage them to think beyond the obvious, including other variables such as gender, ability, age, size, religion, socio-economic status (SES), homelessness, and so on. Be sure to allow enough time for candidates to complete the final project/presentation because they will need to attend a public event and would likely prefer choices in selecting public events if possible.

	TEACHER PREP FACULTY	TEACHER CANDIDATES	FACULTY NOTES
INTRODUCTION	Introduce the activity by giving a brief overview of the demographic makeup of the local community. Lead a discussion on the information. Encourage candidates to locate other sources of information on the specific communities identified in the demographic studies.	Listen carefully to the presentation about the demographics of the local community. Discuss: • What cultures can be identified based on the demographic information? • Are there other cultures in the region that are not identified in a demographic study? • Consider the differences in information provided. Are the demographics of the region changing? In what way and why? • What types of data would be helpful in preparing to teach in that community? Identify various sources to examine that could contain demographic data about a local community and its schools. Try to identify other sources of information on the cultures of this region. Locate and investigate at least three Web sites that provide pertinent demographic data. Locate, evaluate, and collect information from these sources.	Use demographic information from a variety of sources including both school and community data. The presentation of the demographic information can be done in statistical form, void of visual cues other than graphs and charts. As an introduction to the use of a multimedia presentation on the cultures listed, weave in ways the cultures could be presented that highlight the richness of the cultures and their differences. Media to consider are video, audio, digital still images, historical images obtained from Web sites (with appropriate citations), and so on.
IMPLEMENTATION	Assign candidates, individually or in pairs, the exploration of various cultural groups. Be sure all the cultural elements of the region are covered in the class presentations to come. Discuss the type of appropriate public events that would gain insight into the culture. Provide guidance on how to collect observational data at such events. Have candidates gather information from the Web about specific cultural groups. Be explicit about the expected elements of the research and digital multimedia presentations. At a minimum, include the following elements: • Statistical information—demographics, educational history, school performance data • Geographical information on where they reside • Origin of cultural group • Local history • Values/characteristics • Effect on classroom practice • Written reflection Encourage candidates to clarify and add other elements that they consider would benefit their own understanding of the culture being presented.	Participate in a discussion about the types of public events that would provide insights into a particular culture. Locate Web sites to gather information about the culture and cultural origins of the group being researched. If the group has roots in a specific country or region, find background information about the group, especially information relating to attitudes and values of education, expectations of schooling, and student behavior. Following the research, plan the kind of images and data that need to be obtained. Attend a public function of the group chosen or assigned to research. Collect data, images, and video, being sensitive to the beliefs and preferences of the participants. Record reflections, feelings, and observations from the event as data for the upcoming presentation. Prepare a digital multimedia presentation for peers and potentially for other educational groups based on the research and experience. Obtain Web-based and other media to further illustrate the culture. As the presentation is being developed, keep in mind the means of final storage—posting to a Web site, burning a class CD, or whatever means has been decided.	The effectiveness of this activity is dependent on prior coursework and experiences in multicultural settings. It is imperative that candidates research beyond the level of the typical dress, holidays, and food orientation. Encourage candidates to look into issues of child-rearing and values that influence how children and their parents perceive the notion of schooling, predominant learning styles, and so on. Reinforce the notion of teachers needing to take responsibility for their own professional growth by examining what is necessary to learn about the cultures being presented. Participation in the adjustment of the scoring rubrics is an important exercise in demonstrating the alignment between the learning goals and what is assessed and how it is assessed.

	TEACHER PREP FACULTY	TEACHER CANDIDATES	FACULTY NOTES
IMPLEMENTATION	Propose the rubrics listed below for evaluation of the presentations. With candidates, adjust the rubrics to be in alignment with expectations based on the conversation above. Discuss with candidates the means for final storage.		
CULMINATION	Schedule presentations. Facilitate a discussion about the similarities and differences in the cultures presented. Questions might include: • How can you accommodate the various cultures in your classroom? • Do you see any cultural clashes that could cause difficulties between students? How do you handle that in the classroom? • What are the differences between the attitudes toward school and learning that may affect planning for instruction and relationships with families? Assess and debrief presentations and communicate results. Facilitate archiving presentations on a class Web site, a CD, or other storage medium.	In presentations, use a variety of media and formats to communicate information including how this research might affect teaching in the classroom. Include personal insights as a result of the experience. Actively participate in the discussion of all presentations while carefully considering how what is being shared influences personal perceptions as well as classroom practice. Archive presentation on a class Web site or by another means outlined by instructor. Also, save a copy for your own personal use.	Following the presentations—the richness of the discussion of the similarities and differences in the cultures is an important element not to overlook. Candidates need to thoughtfully consider how their classroom practices can inadvertently offend some students and discourage their participation in schooling. The presentations are an appropriate artifact for a digital portfolio.

Assessment

Assessing Multimedia Presentation

See "Multimedia Presentation" rubric in Appendix C.

Assessing Presentation Content

Use the scoring rubric created in class. Ensure that the candidate-created scoring rubric includes four to five constructs/concepts/content areas and at least three levels of performance. For example, the rubric created in class could contain the following elements with the criteria for each level of the performance levels determined by the candidates:

Rubric: Exploring Cultural Differences

CONSTRUCTS/CONCEPTS/CONTENT	LEVELS OF PERFORMANCE		
	1	2	3
A. Statistical information			
B. Geographical information on where located			
C. Origin of cultural group			
D. Local history			
E. Values/characteristics		IN CLASS DISCUSSION, COMPLETE PERFORMANCE DESCRIPTIONS FOR EACH CRITERIA	
F. Event attended			
G. Effect of learning on classroom practice			
H. Other			

Rubric: Written Reflection

 Clear evidence that the candidate can critically assess his or her own beliefs and actions and has considered salient issues in examining classroom practices

 Some evidence that the candidate is able to assess the educational implications and consequences of teaching decisions and actions

 Candidate focuses on personal feelings about the experience. Little questioning of teaching objectives

Tools and Resources

HARDWARE

In addition to computer access, a variety of image capturing hardware such as digital cameras, digital video/video cameras, tape recorders, and scanners

SOFTWARE

Presentation, multimedia authoring, Internet browser, video editing, sound recording

WEB SITES

Access local and state community, school, government sites as needed.

Bilingual Education: The Controversy:
www.pdkintl.org/kappan/krot9805.htm

Diversity: Issues and Responses:
www.cde.ca.gov/iasa/diversity.html (Information and resources are provided here to explore how diversity can become a resource for enrichment rather than a source of conflict and divisiveness.)

Equity Center: **www.nwrel.org/cnorse/index.html**

Hall of Multiculturalism:
www.tenet.edu/academia/multi.html (Links to resources of several cultural groups appear at this site.)

Immigration and Naturalization Service:
www.ins.usdoj.gov/graphics/index.htm

Multicultural Education and Ethnic Groups: Selected Resources:
www.library.csustan.edu/lboyer/tmp/multicu.htm

Multicultural Pavilion:
http://curry.edschool.virginia.edu/curry/centers/multicultural/

Poverty Related Links:
www.ssc.wisc.edu/irp/povlinks.htm#Poverty (An extensive number of links are located at this site.)

U.S. Census Bureau Home Page: **www.census.gov**

REFERENCE TEXT

Rocap, K. (Ed.). (1998). *Virtual power: Technology, education, and community.* Long Beach, CA: Pacific Southwest Regional Technology in Education Consortium.

Credits

Michael Jordan, California State University, Fresno, California, **michaelj@csufresno.edu**

Gib Stuve, California State University, San Marcos, California, **gibstuve@home.com**

Comments/Stories

One of the important aspects of this activity is spending time within the culture being studied. Candidates who enter into the activity with an idea of just attending a church service for an hour or observing in a neighborhood short-change the experience by failing to interact with individuals from a culture other than their own. For many candidates, this is an eye-opening experience of immersing themselves in the thoughts and experiences of people different from themselves. Issues of prejudice emerge early in the experience. Some candidates are reluctant to share their original perceptions as they come to realize how unfounded and ignorant the perceptions are.

The multimedia presentations not only serve to share the insights, but have provided a basis for other presentations after leaving teacher preparation. Candidates have continually commented on how valuable it was to have done significant research on a cultural group from which they have students in their classroom. For some, it has provided the basis for a faculty or paraprofessional inservice presentation. The importance of the discussion of the effect on teaching and learning in the classroom cannot be overemphasized.

Grouping Students for Learning

Subject: Foundations

Topic: Grouping Strategies, Managing Computers in Classrooms

Profile: Professional Preparation

Abstract: As a part of learning about the various ways of grouping students for instruction, teacher candidates experience how various groupings of computers are used in the classroom, whether it is a single computer, a small group of computers, a computer for every student, or a computer lab. Candidates explore various grouping strategies (independent learning, small group learning, cooperative learning, and whole group instruction) and the effect of each on learning. In conjunction with other methods courses, candidates create lesson plans that reflect appropriate grouping strategies for the concepts being taught and available technology. The lessons can be assessed by both methods faculty and foundations faculty for methodology and content. Ideas included are:

One computer in a classroom

- Teacher or student presentations

- Teacher or student presentations in conjunction with electronic whiteboard

- One station in a set of learning stations set up for small groups of students to rotate through for research, analysis, and communication

- Individual or small group research (sign-up sheet—timed work)

Small numbers of computers

- Small groups at each computer

- Individuals at each computer at specific assigned times during the day

- Stations of technology equipment designed to handle sets of three students

- A computer station or center into which students are rotated during learning centers

Individual computers or a lab setting

- Individual, independent work assigned in the classroom but carried out in the lab

- Whole group instruction

- Collaborative groups with preassigned tasks working toward a group project

STANDARDS

NETS FOR TEACHERS

I. TECHNOLOGY OPERATIONS AND CONCEPTS—*Teachers demonstrate a sound understanding of technology operations and concepts. Teachers:*

   A. demonstrate introductory knowledge, skills, and understanding of concepts related to technology (as described in the ISTE NETS for Students).

II. PLANNING AND DESIGNING LEARNING ENVIRONMENTS AND EXPERIENCES—*Teachers plan and design effective learning environments and experiences supported by technology. Teachers:*

   A. design developmentally appropriate learning opportunities that apply technology-enhanced instructional strategies to support the diverse needs of learners.

   C. identify and locate technology resources and evaluate them for accuracy and suitability.

   D. plan for the management of technology resources within the context of learning activities.

   E. plan strategies to manage student learning in a technology-enhanced environment.

III. TEACHING, LEARNING, AND THE CURRICULUM—*Teachers implement curriculum plans that include methods and strategies for applying technology to maximize student learning. Teachers:*

   B. use technology to support learner-centered strategies that address the diverse needs of students.

   D. manage student learning activities in a technology-enhanced environment.

Lesson Description

	TEACHER PREP FACULTY	TEACHER CANDIDATES	FACULTY NOTES
PREPARATION	Assign readings and prepare a multimedia presentation of the content of the readings about grouping strategies. Set up five computers for the teacher candidates to use during the latter part of this assignment. Schedule the computer lab for the final part of this assignment. Assign and collect lesson plan formats from the various disciplines represented by the candidates in the class.	Read the chapter information about various grouping strategies in classrooms or various learning strategies associated with independent learning, small group instruction, cooperative learning, and whole group instruction. Think about a topic to do as a peer teaching lesson or one that is appropriate for methods and/or student teaching.	Because foundations courses are often open to all candidates enrolled in teacher preparation, it is important to assess the class on their area and level of teaching, for example, elementary, secondary, specific discipline, and so on. To make this assignment relevant to candidates, attempt to organize them in groups that will provide a forum for relevant discussion.
INTRODUCTION	**One Computer** Model the use of one computer, presenting the information from the text about grouping or another relevant subject in a multimedia presentation. Make the PowerPoint presentation available for candidates to download either before or after the lesson from the class Web site.	Take notes on the information in a traditional whole class structure or with a print copy of the outline from the multimedia presentation. Download the PowerPoint presentation before or after the lesson.	Note that the subject of the presentation is not specified. Use content that is relevant to the course. At the conclusion of the lesson, debrief not only the content but also the effectiveness of the technology as a tool. The use of a class Web site will significantly enhance the distribution of materials to candidates.
IMPLEMENTATION	**Few Computers/Collaborative Groups** Divide the candidates into grade level and/or subject area groups. The number of groups will be determined by the number (four to six) of computers you have set aside for this assignment. Assign the following tasks: • Decide on a topic and/or the subject matter for the lesson you are to design. • Search the Web for three lesson plans that integrate technology with instruction. • Keep a list of the activities and the various ways technology is used in each. • Compare and contrast the various grouping strategies suggested by the authors of the lessons with those learned in class. • Assess the appropriateness of the strategy. Make suggestions for improvement. **Lab Setting/Independent Task** Independently or in pairs, have candidates use the information to design one lesson plan showing how they would modify the lesson depending on whether they had one computer in the classroom, five computers, computers for every student in the classroom, or a fully equipped computer lab. Have candidates develop a rubric to evaluate the work of individuals or pairs.	Work with a small group on one computer to locate at least three lesson plans on the Web that integrate technology and that focus on the topic or subject chosen following the steps outlined by the instructor. Analyze the appropriateness of the grouping strategies used in the lesson according to criteria developed in class or provided by the instructor. Compare and contrast the various grouping strategies suggested by the authors of these lessons. Individually or in groups of two, write one technology-rich lesson plan that is revised three ways using: • 1 computer • 5 computers • 25 computers in the room • 25 computers in a lab Participate in a group discussion to develop a rubric to assess the individual's or pair's work.	The use of the four to six computers in a traditional classroom can be managed in one of several ways: • A mobile cart of wireless computers • Asking five candidates to bring their laptops to class on the specified day, or • Having the tech staff move five computer stations into the methods classroom. However, the classroom must have the capacity for the computers to access the Internet. For universities instituting a required laptop program, ensure that no more than five laptops are accessible. An alternative to having candidates write their own lesson plan is to give them the option of pulling one they think is particularly good off the Internet. They can then alter that lesson plan to fit the various configurations of computers outlined in the assignment.

TEACHER PREP FACULTY	TEACHER CANDIDATES	FACULTY NOTES
CULMINATION Arrange candidates into grade or subject area groups to share versions of the lesson. Focus the discussion around the appropriateness of the group strategy for the objectives outlined in the lesson. Conclude the discussion by eliciting a set of generalizations about grouping strategies, meeting various cognitive and affective objectives, and the use of the various numbers of computers that might be available in schools. Have candidates post the lesson version with the most appropriate grouping strategy on the class Web site.	Analyze the lessons shared, making generalizations about grouping strategies and lesson design. Reflect on the experience by answering the question "How can you translate this experience to what you might do in your future classroom?" Post the most appropriate lessons on the class Web site.	The strength of this activity lies in the debriefing of the experience about making judgments about lesson design. Encourage candidates to debate the issues of effective use of the technology within the context of the content being covered. There should be varying opinions that spur the discussion. The posting of the lesson on a class Web site often causes candidates to rewrite and rethink their submission. Posting work for view by classmates raises the writing quality as they are writing for an unknown audience.

Assessment

Assessment of this activity can be done on a variety of levels. Below are three rubrics to consider when having candidates collaboratively develop an assessment rubric for various aspects of the activity. For the first rubric, have candidates collaboratively define the elements in the levels of performance further, prior to doing the assignment.

Rubric: Modified Lesson Plan

CRITERIA	LEVELS OF PERFORMANCE			
	COMPLETE EVIDENCE 4	PARTIAL EVIDENCE 3	MINIMAL EVIDENCE 2	NO EVIDENCE 1
Lesson plan is screened for appropriateness.				
Lesson plan is modified from the one listed in a Web resource.				
Lesson uses various grouping strategies for instruction.				
Lesson is modified for use with one, several, and many computers.				
Technology is integrated into the lesson.				
The lesson has all required parts.				

Rubric: Lesson Plan Integrating Technology

CRITERIA	LEVELS OF PERFORMANCE			
	COMPLETE EVIDENCE 4	PARTIAL EVIDENCE 3	MINIMAL EVIDENCE 2	NO EVIDENCE 1
The lesson does not provide for any technology-connected activities or technology is mentioned only superficially.				
Technology-connected learning activities are contrived or limited to enrichment or extension activities.				
Technology is integrated into the lesson to improve the quality of the work and presentation.				
A variety of technology is integrated appropriately throughout the lesson in a manner that enhances the effectiveness of the lesson and student learning.				

Note: Rubric modified from www.lcet.doe.state.la.us/connections.

Rubric: Cooperation/Responsibility

CRITERIA	LEVELS OF PERFORMANCE			
	1	2	3	4
Fulfills Team Role's Duties	Does not perform any duties of assigned team role	Performs very few of the duties of assigned team role	Performs nearly all duties of assigned team role	Performs all duties of assigned team role
Shares Equally	Always relies on others to do the work	Rarely does the assigned work—often needs reminding	Usually does the assigned work—rarely needs reminding	Always does the assigned work without having to be reminded

Note: Rubric modified from http://projects.edtech.sandi.net/morse/oceanhealth/rubrics/collrubric.html.

Tools and Resources

SOFTWARE

Internet, word processing

HARDWARE

Computers—one for presentation, four to six for use with small groups, a computer lab, printer

WEB SITES

Integrate the Internet into the Classroom

Integrate the Internet into the Classroom:
www.cln.org/integrating.html

Kiko WebQuest Showcase:
www.kiko.com/wqst/showcase.jsp

Memphis City Schools: www.memphisschools.k12.tn.us/admin/tlapages/web_que.htm

Using the Internet and WebQuests

The Power of the Internet for Learning: Final Report of Web-Based Education Commission:
www.ed.gov/offices/AC/WBEC/FinalReport/

Science Centered WebQuests:
http://horizon.nmsu.edu/ddl/ddllessongrid.html

Spartanburg WebQuests:
www.spa3.k12.sc.us/WebQuests.html

WebQuests: www.macomb.k12.mi.us/wq/webqindx.htm

WebQuests by Graduate Students of Bernie Dodge:
www.lfelem.lfc.edu/tech/DuBose/webquest/wq.html

WebQuests and Resources for Teachers:
www.davison.k12.mi.us/academic/hewitt14.htm

Lesson Plans

Apple Learning Interchange Units of Practice (most subjects and levels): http://ali.apple.com/ali/ (Click on Units of Practice.)

Blue Web'N: www.kn.pacbell.com/wired/bluewebn/

Education World Teacher Lesson Plans:
www.education-world.com/a_tsl/

HPR*TEC TrackStar (Social Studies, Language Arts, Math, and Science): http://trackstar.hprtec.org/

Innovative Classroom Lesson Plans:
www.iste.org./news/dec_08_mastersearch.html

Kathy Schrock's Guide for Educators: Teaching Tools:
http://school.discovery.com/schrockguide/edtools.html

Laptop Learning Challenge:
www.nsta.org/programs/laptop/teach.htm

Lightspan.com Online Learning for School and Home:
www.lightspan.com/

Microsoft in Education Resources:
www.microsoft.com/Education/lesson/default.asp

SEIR*TEC Lesson Plans:
www.seirtec.org/k12/lessons.html

Computers in Classrooms

D & W's Computers in the Classroom:
www.ametro.net/~teachers/classroom_computers.html

Episcopal High School Wireless Network:
www.nortelnetworks.com/products/02/studies/3258.html

Infrastructure:
www.netdaycompass.org/categories.cfm?category_id=2

Model Technology Classroom:
www.edb.utexas.edu/coe/technology/techclassroom.html

Scientific American on the Future of Computing:
www.sciam.com/featureart/featarch99.html

Wired Classroom: www.nea.org/cet/wired/

Wired Versus Wireless—Technology in School Computer Networks:
www.designshare.com/Research/Wired/Wired1.htm

Extensions for Other Profiles

Student Teaching: During the first weeks of student teaching, candidates can inventory the technology equipment available to them in their classroom and school. Discussion can occur in student teaching seminars about how lessons can be configured or reconfigured to fit available technology.

First-Year Teaching: During the first weeks of teaching, candidates can inventory the technology equipment available to them in their classroom and school and figure out how to configure or reconfigure lessons to fit available technology.

Credits

Lola Franks, Wooster Ohio City Schools, Wooster, Ohio, lfranks@bright.net

Jeri Carroll, Wichita State University, Wichita, Kansas, jeri.carroll@wichita.edu

Comments/Stories

In my classroom I have an electronic super cart, which I usually use for presentations. It is connected to the Internet. During an activity in my Introduction to Education class one day, I set up five areas of the classroom where candidates had different activities to do in small groups. One of the stations included only one computer. Here candidates were to access school Web sites to find the mission statement and pictures of the schools they had been observing for the past 10 weeks. Most of their written assignments had told me that there was at least one computer in each classroom, but they seldom had seen it in use. During the debriefing after all stations had been completed, one candidate said, "I never realized that students could actually use the one computer in the classroom."

Technology in Early Childhood Education Programs

- Introduction

- English Language Arts
    - Cloze and Choral Reading Connections
    - Creating a Literacy-Rich Learning Environment

- Mathematics
    - Mother Nature Pattern Maker
    - What Does Place Value Look Like?

- Science
    - ABCs of Magnetism
    - A Closer Look

- Social Studies
    - Where Do I Live?
    - Why Am I Special?

TECHNOLOGY IN
Early Childhood Education Programs

Introduction

Perhaps the most controversial age group in which to promote the use of technology in teaching and learning is very young children. The popular press continues to carry stories in which kindergarteners and first graders are described as automatons chained to computers or bleary-eyed preschoolers are said to have muscles atrophied from lack of movement. As teachers and parents, we know that although young children are enamored by the technology, social and physical development in the early years along with intellectual development play critical roles in child development.

The NETS for Teachers and Students convey a very strong philosophical perspective that technology is a tool among many in a teacher's repertoire of teaching tools. Young children must explore, play, inquire, socialize, and test situations as they mature. Technology can provide an environment for creativity and expression, a focal point for socialization, sharing, discussion, and so on. It is acknowledged that the use of technology often increases small motor coordination, but that is not reason enough to use technology nor will it take the place of a wild run through the playground chasing a friend. The judicious, appropriate use of technology supports the intellectual, social, and physical development when coupled with other well-recognized elements of a rich early learning environment.

ACTIVITIES

The activities in this section are designed to provide the university faculty member in the early childhood program with ideas and choices of how to use technology in the classroom as a replacement for similar activities already part of the methods courses. Some of the activities are designed for teacher candidates to learn a teaching method, while others are designed to have the faculty member model appropriate pedagogy as the candidates are learners in the classroom. In each situation, it is the faculty member's use of manipulative, active, inquiry-based supporting experiences that provide a model learning experience for teacher candidates of very young children. To meet the complex needs of the early childhood curriculum the activities include:

Cloze and Choral Reading Connections (English Language Arts)

Cloze and choral reading are used in early learning to develop literacy skills. This lesson is taught as a model lesson using concept-mapping software as well as Web resources to obtain background literature.

Creating a Literacy-Rich Learning Environment (English Language Arts)

Teacher candidates use a jigsaw method to learn about the various aspects of a balanced literacy-rich environment. They then create an ideal environment for an early childhood classroom.

Mother Nature Pattern Maker (Mathematics)

Using digital media, teacher candidates explore the notion of patterning as it is found in nature. They create a similar lesson for early education students.

What Does Place Value Look Like? (Mathematics)

In this lesson, teacher candidates have experiences with models for one-, two-, and three-digit numbers, using both physical materials and technology tools. The emphasis in the lesson is building models that support conceptual understanding.

ABCs of Magnetism (Science)

This inquiry lesson focuses on what is magnetic and what is not. Using technology tools as a reporting and sharing mechanism, teacher candidates are tasked with the job of finding objects in the environment that are magnetic beginning with each letter of the alphabet.

A Closer Look (Science)

Sorting and classifying objects by attributes enable teacher candidates to investigate how young children explore various science concepts. Technology is used to capture images, display results, and report findings.

Where Do I Live? (Social Studies)

Using digital maps and other resources, teacher candidates make a map of a neighborhood that can be used in class and as the basis for developing a similar lesson.

Why Am I Special? (Social Studies)

Teacher candidates use online resources to explore attributes of their own personality. The lesson is used as a basis for creating a similar lesson for young children, highlighting the uniqueness of individuals.

Cloze and Choral Reading Connections

Program/Grade Range: Early Childhood

Subject: English Language Arts

Topic: Decoding and Word Recognition Strategies

Profile: Professional Preparation, Student Teaching/Internship

Abstract: Two of the most effective early reading teaching strategies are "cloze exercises" and "choral reading." Both of these strategies are used in this model lesson to provide teacher candidates with experience using these techniques. Visual display and concept-mapping technologies are used to facilitate the activities of the model lesson. Additionally, Web-based research is used to provide basic resources for the lesson.

STANDARDS

NETS FOR TEACHERS

II. PLANNING AND DESIGNING LEARNING ENVIRONMENTS AND EXPERIENCES—*Teachers plan and design effective learning environments and experiences supported by technology. Teachers:*

A. design developmentally appropriate learning opportunities that apply technology-enhanced instructional strategies to support the diverse needs of learners.

B. apply current research on teaching and learning with technology when planning learning environments and experiences.

E. plan strategies to manage student learning in a technology-enhanced environment.

III. TEACHING, LEARNING, AND THE CURRICULUM—*Teachers implement curriculum plans that include methods and strategies for applying technology to maximize candidate learning. Teachers:*

A. facilitate technology-enhanced experiences that address content standards and student technology standards.

C. apply technology to develop students' higher-order skills and creativity.

D. manage student learning activities in a technology-enhanced environment.

ENGLISH LANGUAGE ARTS

3. Students apply a wide range of strategies to comprehend, interpret, evaluate, and appreciate texts. They draw on their prior experience, their interactions with other readers and writers, their knowledge of word meaning and of other texts, their word identification strategies, and the understanding of textual features (e.g., sound-letter correspondence, sentence structure, context, and graphics).

Lesson Description

	TEACHER PREP FACULTY	TEACHER CANDIDATES	FACULTY NOTES
PREPARATION	Assign the following two research questions to teacher candidates along with a required online reading. Have candidates visually represent their research findings in a brainstorming web. 1. "What is the role research indicates that 'phonemic awareness' plays in early reading?" 2. "What strategies does research indicate good readers use to decode unfamiliar words in print?" Identify literature resources to be used for the cloze exercise during class (Shel Silverstein's "Sick" from *Where the Sidewalk Ends*). Create an electronic copy of the poem for electronic display, citing the source. For the model cloze strategy lesson, select the words for omission using a word-count	Prior to class research the following questions: 1. "What is the role research indicates that 'phonemic awareness' plays in early reading?" 2. "What strategies does research indicate good readers use to decode unfamiliar words in print?" Visually represent your research findings in a brainstorming web prior to the class meeting.	Required Online Reading: *Phonemic Awareness: What Does It Mean?* by Kerry Hempenstall. For the URL see Tools and Resources. Suggestions for brainstorming webs are found at the Web site listed in Tools and Resources. To obtain an electronic copy of the Shel Silverstein poem, go to the Ask Jeeves Web site, **www.ask.com**. The poem can also be easily found from the kids' portion of the Ask Jeeves Web site. Going through the process of locating an electronic copy of a poem is a brief demonstration you may want to do at the end of the lesson for the candidates' reference.

	TEACHER PREP FACULTY	TEACHER CANDIDATES	FACULTY NOTES
PREPARATION	formula, such as every fifth word or every other word. Decide what the purpose of the model lesson is: If the purpose is to assess candidates' knowledge of the topic or their abilities to use semantic cues, delete content words that carry meaning, such as nouns, main verbs, adjectives, and adverbs. To assess candidates' use of syntactic cues, delete some conjunctions, prepositions, and auxiliary words.		
INTRODUCTION	**Strategies**—Use the think-pair-share cooperative learning strategy to begin discussion and then move to groups of four using the think-pair-square method. Facilitate the discussion of the reading by recording the candidates' points using the Rapid Fire feature of Inspiration software. Identify the purpose of the model lesson to come. Relate the purpose to the use of the cloze technique.	In class, use the think-pair-share and think-pair-square techniques to discuss and identify the strategies that each pair (and then each square) has in common. Each square comes to consensus on the list of strategies.	You may choose think-pair-share, think-pair-square, or the jigsaw method for cooperative learning discussions. Descriptions of these teaching strategies are found at the Web site called Three Common Cooperative Learning Structures. For the URL, see Tools and Resources.
IMPLEMENTATION	**Cloze Exercise**—Using a projection system, introduce an oral cloze exercise using Shel Silverstein's "Sick," from *Where the Sidewalk Ends*. Use the shared reading technique to read through the poem completely. Position each group at one computer. Use the shared reading while candidates take turns recording couplets from the poem into a word processor. As they are reading and recording, encourage them to insert the missing words. Have candidates identify and electronically color-code rhyming pairs. Model an all-candidates' response by giving a thumbs-up as classmates correctly identify pairs. **Choral Reading**—Introduce a choral reading exercise of Verna Aardema's *Bringing the Rain to Kapiti Plain*. Use a projection system and the directions and prompts from the Web site. Return to Shel Silverstein's poem. Discuss how the poem can be read in a choral manner. Complete a choral reading of it according to suggestions made by candidates. Debrief the model lesson. Focus the discussion on the benefits of the technique used, identification of situations in which it would be most appropriate, and types of learners for whom the technique is particularly applicable.	Participate in the model lesson in a dual role—as the learner and as a critical observer of how the technique enhances learning to read. Use "shared reading" to orally read the poem. In groups, record the poem in text as it is read. Insert the missing words as the reading and recording take place. Use the highlight function or the word processing program to color highlight each unique set of rhyming words. Participate in all-response questions. In groups of four, participate in a choral reading activity of *Bringing the Rain to Kapiti Plain*. Relate background research on choral reading to the choral reading of Shel Silverstein's "Sick." Participate in the debriefing discussion of the two techniques—cloze and choral reading.	For an extension idea for the "Sick" activity, see Giggle Poetry: Sick (a poetry lesson for kids who love Shel Silverstein's poetry), by Bruce Lansky, at the Web site listed in Tools and Resources. Additional information on the shared reading strategy is found at the Shared Reading: An Effective Instructional Model Web site, listed in Tools and Resources. Additional information on the cloze procedure that could be a required reading or projected during class is found at the Cloze Procedure Web site, listed in Tools and Resources. The technique of recording the words with a word processor as they are read or reread taps into the kinesthetic style of some learners. Hearing and typing (feeling) the words can connect meaning, thus assisting with completing the missing words. A choral reading exercise is found at the Web site called Choral Reading: Bringing the Rain to Kapiti Plain, by Verna Aardema, listed in Tools and Resources. Additional information on choral reading that could be a required reading or a project during class is found at Choral Reading Method Web site, listed in Tools and Resources.

TEACHER PREP FACULTY	TEACHER CANDIDATES	FACULTY NOTES
Group candidates into writing teams of three to complete a mini-lesson on any subject or literature selection using these techniques. Collaboratively develop a rubric for critiquing mini-lessons and the quality of posting on a class Web site according to assignment elements (see rubric below). Facilitate presentation of mini-lessons. Review with candidates how to post the lesson plan on the class Web site. Encourage candidates to revise the lesson following a critique. Collect peer assessment forms. Have candidates record a journal entry or e-mail reflection of the experience.	Participate in the development or refinement of a scoring rubric. Equitably divide responsibilities for development of mini-lesson. Present mini-lesson to class and share written mini-lesson on using cloze exercises and choral reading with entire class using projection system. Post lesson on Web site after reviewing peer critiques. Turn in peer assessment of observation of other groups. Record in a journal a reflection of the experience and insights, or e-mail the reflection to instructor after class as a homework assignment.	Consider videotaping candidates as they teach their mini-lesson. This tape can be used as an artifact for an electronic portfolio and/or as a means of critiquing teaching techniques and delivery.

(Side label: CULMINATION)

Assessment

Rubric: Mini-Lesson

CRITERIA	LEVELS OF PERFORMANCE		
	BELOW EXPECTATIONS 1	MEETS EXPECTATIONS 2	EXCEEDS EXPECTATIONS 3
Objectives	Vague in focus	Clearly stated	Clearly stated and aligned with state and national standards
Teaching Strategies	Teaching strategies are weak in focus, appropriateness, and structure.	Cloze procedure and choral reading methods are structured with clear connections to lesson purpose.	Excellent use is made of cloze technique and choral reading and is sequenced well with subject integration.
Technology Integration	Ineffective use, or inappropriate use of technology	Appropriate use of technology	Presentation and materials used were visually motivating and technology was infused throughout lesson in an appropriate and effective manner.
Assessment	Performance-based project did not correlate to objectives.	Performance-based project was similar to objectives.	Performance-based project clearly met all objectives.
Reflection	Note: A sample "Written Reflection" rubric is available in Appendix C.		

Tools and Resources

SOFTWARE

Concept-mapping software, word processing programs or simpletext

HARDWARE

Demonstration station in classroom, small group setting (approximately one computer to four candidates) or a lab setting and one projector system

WEB SITES

Brainstorming Webs: **www.graphic.org/brainst.html**

Choral Reading: Bringing the Rain to Kapiti Plain, by Verna Aardema: **www.teacherlink.usu.edu/Tlresources/longterm/ LessonPlans/africa/monhan/choralreading.htm**

Choral Reading Method: **www.d21.k12.il.us/dept_instr/langarts/parentinfo/ choral_rdg.html**

Cloze Procedure: **www.sasked.gov.sk.ca/docs/ela/ ela_cloz.html**

Giggle Poetry: Sick (A Poetry Lesson for Kids Who Love Shel Silverstein's Poetry), by Bruce Lansky: **www.gigglepoetry.com/sick.html**

Phonemic Awareness: What Does It Mean?: **www.educationnews.org/phonemic_awareness_what _does_it_.htm**

Shared Reading: An Effective Instructional Model: **www.cduplace.com/rdg/res/literacy/em_lit4.html**

Shel Silverstein's "Sick": **www.ezy.net/~quix/sick.html**

Three Common Cooperative Learning Structures: **www.dal.ca/~oidt/taguide/ ThreeCommonCooperativeLearningStructures.html**

REFERENCE TEXTS

Aardema, V. (1981). *Bringing the rain to Kapiti Plain: A Nandi tale.* New York: Dial.

Silverstein, S. (1974). *Where the sidewalk ends.* New York: Harper Collins.

Credits

Amy Massey Vessel, Louisiana Tech University, Ruston, Louisiana, **avessel@latech.edu**

Dara Feldman, The Literacy through Technology Initiative, Kensington, Maryland, **darafeldman@hotmail.com**

Comments/Stories

Think-Pair-Square is similar to Think-Pair-Share. Students first discuss problem-solving strategies in pairs and then in groups of fours. Students are given time to think about the question and then form groups of four. Two pairs of two students gather, each pair working to solve the problem. They then reassemble as four and compare answers and methodologies. If one student pair is unable to solve the problem, the other student pair can often explain its answer and methodology. Finally, if the problem posed does not have a "right" answer, the two student pairs can combine their results and generate a more comprehensive answer.

The first response from candidates is usually amazement at how easy it was to obtain the poem "Sick" and prepare the cloze exercise. Although the series of events is complex in this activity, candidates seem to better understand how one piece of poetry or literature can be accessed using multiple techniques to target the many kinds of learners in the classroom. Turning the lesson back to using the choral reading with the "Sick" poem brings the activity to full-circle in the discussion of techniques. Although candidates seem to resist creating another mini-lesson, the application of what was learned in class seems to find its way into the candidate teaching and internship experiences in a much more connected way than if the mini-lesson were not assigned.

Creating a Literacy-Rich Learning Environment

Program/Grade Range: Early Childhood

Subject: English Language Arts

Topic: Six Areas of the Language Arts

Profile: Professional Preparation

Abstract: A literacy-rich environment is composed of carefully orchestrated experiences in reading, writing, speaking, listening, viewing, and visually representing ideas and understandings. In this lesson, teacher candidates use a jigsaw method to learn about the six areas of the language arts. As an outcome, candidates develop and describe their vision of a literacy-rich environment for their classroom. In the process of the lesson, the faculty member models the following strategies that candidates will be expected to incorporate into lessons with students: a KWHL chart (Know, Want to know, How to find out, and what was Learned), cooperative learning, self-reflection, formative/summative assessment, graphical organization, and a multimedia presentation.

STANDARDS

NETS FOR TEACHERS

III. TEACHING, LEARNING, AND THE CURRICULUM—*Teachers implement curriculum plans that include methods and strategies for applying technology to maximize student learning. Teachers:*

  A. facilitate technology-enhanced experiences that address content standards and student technology standards.

  B. use technology to support learner-centered strategies that address the diverse needs of students.

  C. apply technology to develop students' higher-order skills and creativity.

IV. ASSESSMENT AND EVALUATION—*Teachers apply technology to facilitate a variety of effective assessment and evaluation strategies. Teachers:*

  A. apply technology in assessing student learning of subject matter using a variety of assessment techniques.

ENGLISH LANGUAGE ARTS

12. Students use spoken, written, and visual language to accomplish their own purposes (e.g., for learning, enjoyment, persuasion, and the exchange of information).

Lesson Description

	TEACHER PREP FACULTY	TEACHER CANDIDATES	FACULTY NOTES
PREPARATION	Be sure teacher candidates have had exposure to • KWHL, • the six areas of the language arts, • meeting the diverse needs of learners, including variations of learning styles, and • how technology enhances learning. Create a KWHL template in a table format in your word processor. Post it on a class Web site or send it as an attachment in an e-mail to the class. Assign candidates to reflect on the six areas of the language arts while creating the KW portion of the chart on literacy-rich, technology-enhanced learning environments. Review the candidates' KW submissions (sent prior to class using e-mail) and use this information to identify gaps and commonalities in candidates' K and W.	Review and reflect on the six areas of language arts (reading, writing, speaking, listening, viewing, and visually representing) including how technology enhances each. Complete the K and W parts of the KWHL document to answer the question "Taking into account diverse learning styles, what does a literacy-rich, technology-enhanced environment look like in an early childhood classroom?" Consider activities, materials, and equipment. Record • what you know (K) and • what you want to know (W). E-mail the partially completed template to your instructor. Bring the original to class.	In prompting the candidates to prepare for this activity, remind them • that the four traditional areas of language arts have been expanded to six (adding "viewing" and "visual representation"—see Tompkins [1998]), and • to use the Internet to locate lesson plans, activities, equipment, software, materials, and the latest research and promising practices. See Web sites in Tools and Resources. For those classes that do not have class level access, develop a visual of the template during class for candidates to replicate. To reduce the number of e-mail submissions, consider having small groups collaborate on the K and W portions of the chart. Although each group can submit one chart, each candidate should record an individual reflection.

	TEACHER PREP FACULTY	TEACHER CANDIDATES	FACULTY NOTES
PREPARATION	Save the KW portion of the KWHL documents as informal preassessment data. Have candidates bring their original documents to class.		An alternative strategy to identifying gaps and commonalities is to summarize all the K and W submissions on the table prior to the class meeting. Use the table to assist students in identifying the gaps and commonalities. See the KWHL Web site for additional information.
INTRODUCTION	Display a blank KWHL document for recording during the discussion. Guide the discussion on what candidates already know about literacy-rich learning environments and what they want to know, highlighting research on areas of the language arts as they emerge. Guide candidates to identify missing essential ELA areas and technology applications based on an analysis of e-mail data.	Share what you recorded on the "know" and "want to know" portions of the chart. As the discussion is in progress, modify your KWHL document as an ongoing reflection of learning.	The KWHL document is in an electronic table format. Using a projection system, the electronic recording of the discussion enables candidates to see the active nature of the exercise. For ease of facilitating the discussion, consider having a candidate do the recording.
IMPLEMENTATION	Using what they learned from the discussion and current readings, guide candidates to develop a description of their ideal classroom, based on current research about learning environments. Break candidates into six expert groups, each of which is assigned an area of the language arts. Remind the groups to complete the H portion of the KWHL chart as they engage in the following tasks. Have expert groups • develop an oral presentation addressing how the assigned language arts area is a vital part of a literacy-rich early childhood environment, including how technology enhances the area, and • prepare a summary to post on the class Web site. Facilitate the development of a rubric for assessing both the oral presentations and written summaries. Schedule groups to present their findings at the next class session. Following the presentations, regroup the class into heterogeneous groups composed of one person from each of the six areas. Have the groups • brainstorm the elements (activities, materials, and equipment) of a literacy-rich, early childhood classroom, including appropriate uses of technology, and • briefly outline an example that includes all six ELA areas.	During discussion, take notes on elements of an ideal early childhood classroom environment that includes technology. Become a part of a group that is assigned an area of the language arts in which to become an expert. With the group, brainstorm how to become experts in the assigned areas of the language arts including how technology supports the area. Complete the H (how to learn) portion of the KWHL chart. Contribute to the development of a rubric for assessing both the oral presentations and written summaries. Create a work plan for increasing the group's knowledge. Assign tasks for developing the oral presentation and for posting the printed findings on the class Web site. Orally present the findings to the class on ideas for classroom implementation of assigned language arts area. In heterogeneous groups, review as an expert the essential elements of your area. Ask clarifying questions of peers as they share their area of expertise. Participate with the group in the development of a literacy-rich, technology-enhanced learning environment. Consider activities, materials, and equipment. Share your group's experience with the class.	See the jigsaw method Web site for additional information (in Tools and Resources). Emphasize to candidates that this is an intentionally very open-ended set of activities to allow their creativity in completing the task. Examples for the completed projects might be a visual representation using KidPix, video/iMovie, Inspiration web, and so on, or the printout from an electronic whiteboard. Consider including an element of peer assessment at the conclusion of the group presentations of each area of the language arts. If used, be sure to include elements of collaboration, that is, the ability of the groups to work well together, the equity of work, learning from others, and so on. Include the quality of the Web posting in the assessment.

	TEACHER PREP FACULTY	TEACHER CANDIDATES	FACULTY NOTES
IMPLEMENTATION	Have groups briefly share their plan. Assign each candidate the development and description of a complete literacy-rich, technology-enhanced learning environment for an early childhood classroom. Facilitate the development of a rubric to be applied to the completed projects. (See sample below.)	Based on group presentations, select a particular age/grade level and create a description of a literacy-rich, technology-enhanced learning environment for that level.	
CULMINATION	Facilitate the presentations to the class. Assess presentations using a rubric based on the sample below. Have candidates complete the KWHL chart and e-mail them to you. Read completed KWHLs of candidates and provide constructive feedback. Use the data as a post-assessment.	Present learning environments to class. At the conclusion of listening to all the presentations, complete KWHL chart. Send completed KWHL chart to professor electronically.	Consider having the class peer-assess the presentations. Consider one or more of the following: • Virtual tour of a literacy-rich environment • Videoconference with a kindergarten or first-grade teacher • Digital slideshow of several classrooms • Visitation of teachers to the university to share how they set up their classrooms • Class field trip to a school to visit several classrooms Save the preassessment KW portion of the chart as well as the complete KWHL chart as evidence of candidate learning for NCATE review.

Assessment

Rubric: Understanding of the Six ELA Areas

CRITERIA	LEVELS OF PERFORMANCE			
	1	2	3	4
Literacy Content	Addresses few of the six ELA areas	Addresses some of the six ELA areas with moderate understanding	Addresses all of the six ELA areas with moderate understanding	Includes all six ELA areas and demonstrates a deep understanding of their role in the early childhood classroom
Learning Environment	Learning environment is not adapted to learners	Learning environment shows some adaptation to learner needs	Learning environment shows significant adaptation to learner needs	Learning environment is learner centered and responsive to individual as well as group needs
Examples of Activities, Materials, and Equipment	Contains few examples and no rationale for example selection	Contains some examples for each area with some rationales	Contains five examples for each area with minimal rationale for all examples	Contains a rich set of examples (more than five) with rationales and demonstrates an understanding of the way they work together to promote and support learning
Technology Enhancements	Uses at least one technology per area—not always appropriate for the developmental level of the learners	Includes two uses of technology per area, somewhat appropriate for the developmental level of the learners	Includes three uses of technology per area, mostly appropriate for the developmental level of the learners	Includes at least three creative uses of technology per area, each of which are appropriate for the developmental level of the learners
Diversity	Learner diversity not addressed	Learner diversity addressed minimally	Several dimensions of learner diversity addressed	Multiple dimensions of learner diversity addressed creatively

Tools and Resources

SOFTWARE

Word processing, concept mapping or graphics, presentation

HARDWARE

Demonstration station in the classroom with word processing software, student access to presentation hardware

WEB SITES

The Jigsaw Method: **www.jigsawhelper.org/**

The KWHL Graphic Organizer:
www.graphic.org/kwhl.html

REFERENCE TEXT

Tompkins, G. E. (1998). *Language arts*. Upper Saddle River, NJ: Prentice Hall.

Credits

Amy Massey Vessel, Louisiana Tech University, Ruston, Louisiana, **avessel@latech.edu**

Dara Feldman, The Literacy Through Technology Initiative, Kensington, Maryland, **darafeldman@hotmail.com**

Comments/Stories

This activity provides an opportunity to use candidate work in advance of class to make the quality of the class time much more valuable. It takes a little organization to handle the e-mail and quickly review the results to be able to set up for the next class. The first time, the volume of e-mail was too high to handle so a sample was taken. The next few times, the e-mail volume lessened considerably, with students collaborating on their responses. An additional feature of this lesson is the creative ways candidates developed their presentations. As the activity is now a mainstay of the class, students are aware of the expectations and seem to plan ahead on using the technology in innovative ways.

Mother Nature Pattern Maker

Program/Grade Range: Early Childhood

Subject: Mathematics

Topic: Early Algebra—Patterns

Profile: Professional Preparation

Abstract: The ability to perceive patterns is central to mathematical understanding and enhances the ability to develop conceptual thinking. This lesson is designed to heighten teacher candidates' awareness of naturally occurring (and man-made patterns) in the environment and to help them learn how to support their students in developing skill in describing patterns in mathematical terms. The teacher development goals are to play the role of a K–2 student in collecting images from nature using digital capture tools. Candidates then sort them by increasingly more complex sets of attributes and consider the importance of framing well-designed questions to lead student thinking. It asks participants to explore learner interaction with the tasks and to design a similar lesson for a specific student population with differing needs. The lesson also includes opportunities to discuss strategies for selecting and using appropriate technology and to match them to student activity.

STANDARDS

NETS FOR TEACHERS

II. PLANNING AND DESIGNING LEARNING ENVIRONMENTS AND EXPERIENCES—_Teachers plan and design effective learning environments and experiences supported by technology. Teachers:_

    C. identify and locate technology resources and evaluate them for accuracy and suitability.

    D. plan for the management of technology resources within the context of learning activities.

    E. plan strategies to manage student learning in a technology-enhanced environment.

III. TEACHING, LEARNING, AND THE CURRICULUM—_Teachers implement curriculum plans that include methods and strategies for applying technology to maximize student learning. Teachers:_

    C. apply technology to develop students' higher-order skills and creativity.

    D. manage student learning activities in a technology-enhanced environment.

V. PRODUCTIVITY AND PROFESSIONAL PRACTICE—_Teachers use technology to enhance their productivity and professional practice. Teachers:_

    B. continually evaluate and reflect on professional practice to make informed decisions regarding the use of technology in support of student learning.

    D. use technology to communicate and collaborate with peers, parents, and the larger community in order to nurture student learning.

VI. SOCIAL, ETHICAL, LEGAL, AND HUMAN ISSUES—_Teachers understand the social, ethical, legal, and human issues surrounding the use of technology in PK-12 schools and apply that understanding in practice. Teachers:_

    A. model and teach legal and ethical practice related to technology use.

MATHEMATICS

Standard 2: Algebra

Instructional programs from PK-12 should enable all students to—

- understand patterns, relations, and functions.

Standard 3: Geometry

Instructional programs from PK-12 should enable all students to—

- analyze characteristics and properties of two- and three-dimensional geometric shapes and develop mathematical arguments about geometric relationships.

Standard 7: Reasoning and Proof

Instructional programs from PK-12 should enable all students to—

- recognize reasoning and proof as fundamental aspects of mathematics.

Standard 8: Communication

Instructional programs from PK-12 should enable all students to—

- organize and consolidate their mathematical thinking through communication

EARLY CHILDHOOD PROFESSIONALS

2. Curriculum Development and Implementation

2.1. Plan and implement developmentally appropriate curriculum and instructional practices based on the knowledge of the individual children, the community, and the curriculum goals and content.

Lesson Description

	TEACHER PREP FACULTY	TEACHER CANDIDATES	FACULTY NOTES
PREPARATION	Review research on questioning techniques. Collect a variety of image capture tools: 35mm cameras, Polaroid cameras, still and video digital cameras, scanners, and the appropriate digitizing software. Assign teacher candidates the task of learning how to use the hardware and software. Ask candidates to search for or acquire digital images found in nature that illustrate patterns. Prepare 8–10 images from nature that candidates can sort. Choose a few printed images as well as digital. Develop a series of questions, some requiring lower-level thinking and some evoking higher-order thinking. For example: What shapes do you see in this image? How would you represent the pattern found on this leaf using just the numerals 0 and 1.	Learn to use the hardware and software associated with digital photography and video. Locate image libraries focusing on nature or patterns in nature.	Locate online tutorials for the candidates (check the Web sites for the companies producing the equipment) or schedule short training sessions in the computer lab to help them learn processes associated with digital photography. As an alternative, locate digital image libraries (Web sites, CD-ROM libraries) and use only those images.
INTRODUCTION	Explain the purposes of this lesson: (1) to examine the relative merits of various technologies for collecting digital images, (2) to facilitate through questioning an examination of properties and patterns in nature, and (3) to develop a lesson for young children focusing on these principles. Assign candidates to design a spreadsheet or table to monitor the relative merits of various technologies for collecting digital images. Assign candidates to collect a set of images. Bring three images to class to use for the introduction. It is best to get each from a different source so that issues of acquiring the images can be woven into the lesson. Display the set of model pictures. First, working independently, have candidates create a list of the properties and patterns in each picture. Have the candidates examine the pictures as a set to discover	Design a spreadsheet or table to monitor the relative merits of various technologies to include • the photo, • the digital media tools used, • the process used, • hardware, • software, • costs, and • comments, describing the positive and negative effects each has in relation to the student learning process. Take or gather a set of images from nature to sort and resort. List the properties of two to three single pictures. Note the shapes and patterns in these pictures. Share the results you found with a partner. Can you find more in each other's collection of pictures?	Consider altering the assignment by specifying a unique population of students and decide which technology tool may be most appropriate for their use. Alert candidates to the risk of copyright infringement. Be careful of scanning images from books and other printed materials without appropriate consent and citation. (See the Multimedia and Copyright section of "Using Model Strategies for Integrating Technology into Teaching" in Section 1.) Listen to candidate descriptions. Be alert for clear descriptions of criteria. Draw an analogy between the question asked and the type of response they might expect from learners. Conclude with best applications. Check for the following types of questions: recall, comprehension, analysis, evaluation, open, probing, direct, hypothetical, reflective, and closed.

	TEACHER PREP FACULTY	TEACHER CANDIDATES	FACULTY NOTES
INTRODUCTION	the commonalities in the patterns. In pairs, ask candidates to share the results. Record the words used to describe the commonalities (or future sorting criteria). Focus on the mathematical vocabulary used to describe their thinking. Brainstorm other criteria that they might not have initially found. Step outside of the mode of modeling the lesson by guiding the candidates in generating questions to elicit a variety of beginning level responses from K–2 students. Discuss the type of questions generated while referring back to prior experiences on questioning techniques.	Develop a list of questions to ask young children that will help them find properties and patterns in the pictures they have collected.	
IMPLEMENTATION	Place the partners into groups of six or so. Have the groups share the images they brought to class. Have the group determine the criteria for sorting. Lead the candidates in a discussion describing their thought processes for determining the sorting criteria and their questioning techniques for working with each other. Discuss the kinds of questions a teacher might ask to help young students generate conceptual knowledge about patterns. Lead candidates in discussing the kinds of questions to ask to support learners moving to the next level of thinking about their sorting properties and patterns. Back in their pairs, have candidates generate examples of two and three criteria to use for sorting (for example, striped and round) and model solution with pictures. Demonstrate the use of a Venn diagram to display the sorts (use large string circles to make the Venn diagram). Instruct groups to create their own Venn diagram. Have candidates generate a question to lead children to build this type of sort and/or resort. Bring candidates back together into groups and share results. Support candidates in comparing the types of questions asked and results obtained.	Share the pictures and the criteria for sorting in the larger group. Participate in discussions about thought processes and questioning techniques. Share sorting results. Develop a list of possible questions to use with young students. Sequence the types of questions by level. Develop scaffolding questions to move students to the next level of thinking. Shuffle the pictures and generate a second sorting with more than one characteristic in common. Use drawing tools to generate three to four overlapping circles to make a Venn diagram. Place pictures in the appropriate circles. Identify sorts. Generate questions to help students design the same or similar diagrams and/or sorts. Revise chart of key questioning techniques including useful phrases or words that can be used.	Consider using a drawing program, Inspiration, or an online Venn diagram generator. It might be possible to connect candidates' thought processes in resorting to Torrance's categories of creative thinking: Fluency, Flexibility, Originality, and Elaboration. (See the Creative Ideas Web site in Tools and Resources.) Try these types of questions: • A question that captures the essence of the phenomenon you are looking at. • A question whose answer isn't obvious and neither is how to get it. • A question that is clearly stated so that someone else would know how to answer it if they had the answer.
CULMINATION	Have candidates describe what they did in their own language and then in the language that young children might understand. What was the thinking process they used? What strategies did they use to make sense	Participate in discussion. Add to and revise the technology chart generated in the introductory step. Design a lesson plan appropriate for an expected student population based on the elements examined.	Extend the activity by having a group discussion about creating a rubric to evaluate their own work and then that of their students.

TEACHER PREP FACULTY	TEACHER CANDIDATES	FACULTY NOTES
CULMINATION of the pictures? Were there any surprises in their thinking? What are some of the key words or ways of phrasing questions that a teacher can use to build conceptual bridges for students? How can the manner in which questions are phrased support students to move to higher levels of thinking about mathematical concepts? What were the strengths and weaknesses of the technology used?	Write a reflective journal entry on your experience in learning about patterns and designing a lesson.	
Summarize the exercise of patterning in mathematics as it evolves with the samples collected.		
Have candidates revise their technology chart.		
Using a lesson plan format you provide, have candidates design a lesson plan appropriate for their expected student population based on this lesson.		
Assign candidates a reflective journal entry on their experience in sorting, drawing generalizations, and completing a lesson plan.		

Assessment

Rubric: Mother Nature Pattern Maker

CRITERIA	LEVELS OF PERFORMANCE		
	EXCELLENT 3	**ADEQUATE 2**	**UNSATISFACTORY 1**
Images	8-10 images are digitized. Images are clear, visually appealing and consistent in size, downloaded into the software program, and filed appropriately.	6-8 images are digitized and the images are clear. Some lack appeal and are not consistent in size. Some may not be filed appropriately.	Images are provided, but not digitized, are unclear, and may not be consistent in size. The candidate has not filed the images for future use.
Sorting of Images (Venn Diagram)	The Venn diagram is done using a computer program. All circles are appropriately labeled. All items are in the appropriate spots.	The Venn diagram might not be done with a computer program, some elements are inappropriately labeled or the items are not appropriately placed.	The Venn diagram is hand drawn, elements are not in appropriate places, parts are not labeled.
Questions	A hierarchical list of questions is provided with each type of question labeled. Scaffolding comments are provided between the levels.	A list of questions is provided, but the hierarchy is not appropriate and/or the scaffolding comments are inappropriate or absent.	A list of questions is provided, not related to young children, not sequenced, and no scaffolding is evident.
Lesson Plan	The lesson plan notes a specific student population, identifies appropriate resources, and defines an effective plan for managing the instruction and resources in exploring the curriculum and assessing student learning.	The lesson plan is mechanical in nature, providing an outcome, but there is no thought as to what the teacher does, what the student is required to do, and what the pitfalls and possibilities are.	The lesson plan does not specify student population, resources, or management.
Reflection/Journal	The focus is on personal feelings, skills needed for planning and teaching, and how they can use this experience with young students.	The focus is on personal feelings with some thought given to the skills needed for planning and teaching.	The focus of the reflection is on how they liked the lesson.

Tools and Resources

SOFTWARE

Software required to capture pictures from camera or scanner, if necessary; photo manipulation software, image CD-ROM software, or Internet browser and picture viewing software

HARDWARE

Printer; digital, video, or still cameras and accompanying hardware (e.g., scanner, video cards) necessary to pull pictures from the camera and print them

WEB SITES

Creative and Critical Thinking

Creative Ideas:
www.creativeideasforyou.com/creativity_testing.html

Critical Thinking on the Web:
www.philosophy.unimelb.edu.au/reason/critical/

Introduction to Creative Thinking:
www.vanguard.edu/rharris/crebook1.htm

Images

Kids Image Search Tools:
www.kidsclick.org/psearch.html

Patterns

Pattern Math Bag:
http://plato.acadiau.ca/courses/educ/reid/4173/
Mathbag/A–f/fieldsmathbag.html

Patterning and Algebra in the Primary Grades:
http://MathCentral.uregina.ca/RR/database/
RR.09.97/sauter1.html

Patterns: http://MathCentral.uregina.ca/RR/database/
RR.09.97/maeers7.html (This site has multiple links
to patterns of many kinds.)

Patterns Here, There, and Everywhere:
http://MathCentral.uregina.ca/RR/database/
RR.09.96/hanlin1.html

Questioning Strategies

Advanced Questioning Techniques:
www.petervenn.co.uk/adquest/adquest.html

Annotated Bibliography: Resources on Effective
Questioning for Teachers and Staff:
www.ael.org/rel/quilt/biblio.htm

Effective Classroom Questioning:
www.oir.uiuc.edu/did/booklets/question/question.html

Effective Techniques of Questioning:
http://tec.uno.edu/SS/TeachDevel/Questions/
EffectQuest.html

Improving Your Teaching through Effective Questioning
Techniques: www.aged.vt.edu/methods/que–skil.htm

Venn Diagrams

Venn Diagram: **www.venndiagram.com/**

REFERENCE TEXTS

Pengelly, H. (1992). *Making patterns.* New York: Scholastic.

Pluckrose, H. (1995). *Pattern (math counts).* Danbury, CT: Children's Press.

Extensions for Other Profiles

Candidates import digital images into a multimedia program and use the drawing tool to trace over each image to recreate the pattern.

Concept Mapping: Create concept maps of the various patterns and draw relationships.

There are a variety of activities using the following software: Introduction to Patterns and Creating Patterns from Shapes (Sunburst Technology), Exploring Tessellations (Tom Synder Productions).

Credits

Pamela Redmond, University of San Francisco, California, **predmond@usf.edu**

Virginia (Ginny) Keen, Bowling Green State University, Bowling Green, Ohio, **gkeen@bgnet.bgsu.edu**

James Wiebe, California State University, Los Angeles, **jwiebe@calstatela.edu**

Comments/Stories

Perhaps the hardest part of the lesson is getting candidates to look for images that show patterns to bring into class. Providing the Web sites listed in the Tools and Resources section shows them that sites already exist containing patterns that are quite useable. Some candidates have to be reminded how to capture images off a Web site for use in this activity. When demonstrating how to do this, invariably discussions about appropriate use of digital images, citation, and copyright become a valuable part of the conversation. Once the candidates see the images that are possible, they seem to see patterns everywhere and have no trouble launching into the activity.

What Does Place Value Look Like?

Program/Grade Range: Early Childhood

Subject: Mathematics

Topic: Number Sense—Place Value

Profile: Professional Preparation

Abstract: In this lesson, teacher candidates have experiences with models for one-, two-, and three-digit numbers, using both physical materials and technology tools. As an introduction, candidates are guided to an understanding of the concept of proportional models (such as base 10 blocks) and nonproportional models (such as colored chips representing 1s, 10s, etc.). Candidates consider the potential of concrete and digital models to meet the needs of various student learning styles and curriculum instructional requirements. In small groups, candidates collect information from a broad range of professional resources to support the analysis of a specific model's characteristics and how each model might influence children's ability to construct place value meaning. They discuss how this analysis can inform instructional decisions, first in small groups, and then with the whole class. Candidates expand their work to consider how various models support the extension to renaming numbers, a prerequisite for meaningful computational representation (e.g., 51 = 5 tens and 1 one = 4 tens and 11 ones).

STANDARDS

NETS FOR TEACHERS

II. PLANNING AND DESIGNING LEARNING ENVIRONMENTS AND EXPERIENCES—*Teachers plan and design effective learning environments and experiences supported by technology. Teachers:*

  C. identify and locate technology resources and evaluate them for accuracy and suitability.

VI. SOCIAL, ETHICAL, LEGAL, AND HUMAN ISSUES—*Teachers understand the social, ethical, legal, and human issues surrounding the use of technology in PK-12 schools and apply that understanding in practice. Teachers:*

  E. facilitate equitable access to technology resources for all students.

MATHEMATICS

Standard 1: Number and Operations

Instructional program from PK-12 should enable all students to—

- understand numbers, ways of representing numbers, relationships among numbers, and number systems.

Standard 10: Representation

Instructional programs from PK-12 should enable all students to—

- create and use representations to organize, record, and communicate mathematical ideas.
- select, apply, and translate among mathematical representations to solve problems.
- use representations to model and interpret physical, social, and mathematical phenomena.

EARLY CHILDHOOD PROFESSIONALS

2. Curriculum Development and Implementation

  2.1 Plan and implement developmentally appropriate curriculum and instructional practices based on knowledge of individual children, the community, and curriculum goals and content.

    2.1.5 Create, evaluate, and select developmentally appropriate materials, equipment, and environments.

    2.1.6 Evaluate and demonstrate appropriate use of technology with young children, including assistive technologies for children with disabilities.

Lesson Description

	TEACHER PREP FACULTY	TEACHER CANDIDATES	FACULTY NOTES
PREPARATION	Obtain examples of proportional models of place value such as base 10 blocks, Unifix cubes, and so on. Obtain examples of nonproportional models such as colored chips and coins (penny, dime, dollar). Examine the textbook to assign any necessary reading prior to the lesson. Obtain some of the software examples listed in Tools and Resources. Select materials for candidates to view. Examine support materials related to the use of place value software that is available locally or at the university curriculum resource center.	Complete reading assignment.	There are many examples of on-screen manipulative software. Try to select ones that are frequently available in the area in which candidates will be student teaching. If none are apparent, check the *2002 Educational Software Preview Guide* or Web sites of software publishers listed in Appendix E, Resources. As a preparatory assignment, consider asking candidates to search the Internet for place value related lessons and resources.
INTRODUCTION	Present the prepared examples of proportional and nonproportional models. Solicit additional examples of each from candidates. Go through each model asking candidates for a description and use. Tie in with previous work on learning styles, second language learners, and special needs students. Facilitate the candidates' ability to discriminate between proportional and nonproportional place value models.	Consider several examples of proportional and nonproportional models for base 10 numbers. Create a set of descriptors that discriminates proportional from nonproportional models.	This activity can be done in a computer lab setting as well as a regular classroom provided a projection system is available for whole class viewing of software. As you present, use both virtual and physical examples of place value models. Be sure to discuss the benefits and detriments of each type. For example: • Virtual • Helpful for students with limited mobility • Expense • Physical • Kinesthetic • Space • Noise
IMPLEMENTATION	Assign groups of two to four candidates one proportional and one nonproportional physical model to investigate as well as one electronic-based model. Ask candidates to analyze the potential for enhancing student learning of place value (one-, two-, and three-digit) using each representation. Encourage the use of a variety of resources to inform their research. Be sure to include electronic resources. Introduce the elements of the assignment. Have candidates prepare a presentation that: 1. Identifies the strengths and weaknesses of the models for the mathematical learning of young children 2. Evaluates the place value models for suitability for use by young children and children with special needs	Break into small groups of two to four. Become familiar with the proportional and nonproportional models assigned to the group. After discussing the assignment, participate in the development of a scoring rubric for comparing models. Prepare a presentation to educate peers on the particular models assigned and explain how you assigned scores for each. Participate in a discussion that focuses on the identification of the influences on instructional decision-making (such as age, grade, and physical, social, emotional, aesthetic, and cognitive development of the children) with regard to use of specific representational forms.	Observe groups to see if candidates are able to use each model to represent one-, two-, and three-digit numbers accurately. Emphasize the symbolic nature of some of the nonproportional models. Focus on appropriate models for developing student mathematical thinking. In addition to the criteria established by the class, be sure to include the groups' analyses of the two models studied by each group. It is common to find differing opinions on the value of the electronic manipulatives in comparison with the physical model. Concentrate on issues of learning styles and developmentally appropriate teaching.

	TEACHER PREP FACULTY	TEACHER CANDIDATES	FACULTY NOTES
IMPLEMENTATION	3. Compares the use of physical models with technology-based models 4. Makes recommendations for how to make models more accessible to children with disabilities and how instructional uses can be adjusted to children's learning styles and previous experiences Facilitate the development of a scoring rubric for comparing models. Have groups create a technology-based reporting instrument to record their findings. This can be done using a concept-mapping tool, word processor, presentation software, and so on. Coordinate groups to share their findings with the whole class. Lead the class in a discussion of place value models. Have candidates identify attributes that might constrain the use of a model or serve as distractions to young children as well as those that make each model attractive to young children. Record their findings.	Participate in a discussion focusing on identifying the aspects of a place value model that make it attractive to use with young children. Record. Create a technology-based reporting instrument that addresses the criteria of the assignment. Complete research and comparisons, and come to conclusions. Complete presentation.	
CULMINATION	Ask candidates to apply what they have learned to create a place value model that is appropriate for their own field-based teaching or observation placement. Have candidates make a reasoned argument for the appropriate use of their model, identifying the appropriate audience in an electronic journal.	Create, identify, or modify a model that can be used to enhance children's understanding of place value and the base 10 number system for your field experience. Include an explanation of when and for what children the model should be beneficial as well as the identification of those times when and for whom the model might not be as effective as an alternative. Record an argument in a reflective electronic journal supporting the model and justifying its use, especially in terms of its proportional or nonproportional nature.	Encourage candidates to create models that are culturally sensitive and appropriate to their students or the students in the region. Evaluate these models based on criteria that include the elements decided on by the class for the project rubric.

Assessment

The following table is appropriate for tracking how candidates are able to address the standards within the context of a course. Note that in this table, the specific performance indicators provided for the Professional Preparation Performance Profile are not addressed individually. Rather, the elements of the activity are used to justify meeting the standard, in general, with the applicable performance indicators listed as a group as they apply to the analysis of the physical materials and electronic tools for developing place value concepts.

Table: Tracking Standards Met within the Context of a Course

STANDARDS	PERFORMANCE INDICATORS	ASSESSMENT (Processes and Products)
NETS for Teachers II. Planning and Designing Learning Environments and Experiences—Teachers plan and design effective learning environments and experiences supported by technology.	Teachers: C. identify and locate technology resources and evaluate them for accuracy and suitability.	Candidates evaluate technology-based place value models for suitability for use by young children and children with special needs. Group reporting instrument includes analyses of all models studied by the group.

STANDARDS	PERFORMANCE INDICATORS	ASSESSMENT (Processes and Products)
Early Childhood Professionals 2. Curriculum Development and Implementation 2.1 Plan and implement developmentally appropriate curriculum and instructional practices based on knowledge of individual children, the community, and curriculum goals and content.	2.1.5 Create, evaluate, and select developmentally appropriate materials, equipment, and environments. 2.1.6 Evaluate and demonstrate appropriate use of technology with young children, including assistive technologies for children with disabilities.	Candidates make a reasoned argument for the appropriate use of their model, identifying the appropriate audience and validating the proportional/nonproportional nature. The argument is recorded in a journal.
NETS for Teachers VI. Social, Ethical, Legal, and Human Issues—Teachers understand the social, ethical, legal, and human issues surrounding the use of technology in PK–12 schools and apply those principles in practice.	Teachers: E. facilitate equitable access to technology resources for all students.	Candidates are able to create place value models using physical materials and technological tools that incorporate attributes to maximize their range of usability and accessibility.
Mathematics 1. Number and Operations	Instructional programs from PK–12 should enable all students to— 1. understand numbers, ways of representing numbers, relationships among numbers, and number systems.	Candidates correctly categorize and describe physical or visual representations of place value as proportional or nonproportional.
Mathematics 10. Representation	Instructional programs from PK–12 should enable all students to— 10. create and use representations to organize, record, and communicate mathematical ideas; select, apply, and translate among mathematical representations to solve problems; and use representations to model and interpret physical, social, and mathematical phenomena.	Class reporting instrument includes analysis of the various place value models.

Tools and Resources

SOFTWARE

MacCandy Factory: www-rohan.sdsu.edu/faculty/jbowers/macpics/intro.htm

Number and Number Sense CD—part of *Reconceptualizing Mathematics: Courseware for Elementary and Middle Grade Teachers*, prepared by the Center for Research in Mathematics and Science Education, San Diego State University. For more information, contact Judith Sowder by e-mail (jsowder@sciences.sdsu.edu), phone (619-594-1587), or at the following address:

Judith Sowder
Center for Research in Mathematics and Science Education
6475 Alvarado Road, Suite 206
San Diego, CA 92120

Axel's Whirled Math: Numbers and Equations (Great Wave) PreK–3

Easy Early Math CD (EME) 1–6

Grouping and Place Value CD (Sunburst) 1–3

Hands-On Math Volume I CD (Ventura) K–8

Math 1 & 2 CD (School Zone) PreK–2

Math 1 On-Track Software CD (School Zone) Grade 1

Math 2 On-Track Software CD (School Zone) Grade 2

Mathosaurus—Dinoset 3—Grade 2 (Micrograms) 2–4 or Mathosaurus Ages 7–9 CD (Micrograms) 2–4

Quarter-Mile Math: Grades K–3 CD (Barnum)

Splish Splash Math CD (Sunburst) 1–3

Unlocking Whole Numbers K–2 (the Learning Company)

Early Math (Sierra) ages 3–6

Mighty Math Carnival Countdown (Edmark) ages 5–7

Millie's Math House (Edmark Corp.) PreK–1

Interactive Math Journey (The Learning Company) Grades 1–4

Schoolhouse Rock: Math Rock (The Learning Company) Grades 1–6

HARDWARE

Minimum: one station with projection capability
Optimal: one station for each group of two

WEB SITES

Place Value

Place Value Chart: **www.mentalarithmetic.net/**

Place Value Game:
www.syvum.com/math/arithmetic/level1.html

Place Value Made Fun:
www.teachnet.com/lesson/math/matmon.html

REFERENCE TEXTS

Bowers, J. (1995). An alternative perspective for developing a mathematical microworld. *Proceedings of the CSCL* [Online]. Available: **wwwcscl95.indiana.edu/cscl95/bowers.html**.

Clements, D. (1999). *First experiences in science, mathematics, and technology—Young children and technology, a part of dialogue on early childhood science, mathematics, and technology education.* [Online]. Available: **www.project2061.org/newsinfo/earlychild/experience/clements.htm**.

Clements, D., & Sarama, J. (2000). Predicting pattern blocks on and off the computer. *Teaching Children Mathematics, 6*(7), 458–462.

Clements, D., & Swaminathan, S. (1995). *Technology and school change: New lamps for old?* [Online]. Available: **www.gse.buffalo.edu/org/buildingblocks/NewsLetters/Tech_and_School_DHC.htm**.

Education Development Center. (1992). *Exploring mathematics with manipulatives.* Boca Raton, FL: IBM.

International Society for Technology in Education. (2001). *2002 educational software preview guide.* Eugene, OR: ISTE.

Mankus, M. L. (2000). *Using virtual manipulatives on the Web to develop number sense:* [Online]. Available: **http://mason.gmu.edu/~mmankus/talks/nctm2000/nctmch00.htm**.

OTHER

Manipulatives like Cuisenaire rods, chips (three colors), base 10 materials, bean sticks, money (pennies, dimes, dollars), inch cubes

Credits

Virginia (Ginny) Keen, Bowling Green State University, Bowling Green, Ohio, **gkeen@bgnet.bgsu.edu**

Pamela Redmond, College of Notre Dame, Belmont, California, **Redmond@cnd.edu**

James Wiebe, California State University, Los Angeles, **jwiebe@calstatela.edu**

Comments/Stories

As with many learning opportunities, constraints have a way of altering the richness of the learning outcome. Time and technology access are the two constraints that have limited the in-class potential for this activity in my experience. Because candidates share little experience with many (most) of the physical and technological models, time is needed to familiarize them with the models prior to any professional analysis of the appropriateness of the place value representations.

While I have always included this type of background building on the use of physical models, incorporating the technology piece into regular in-class work requires easy access to the Internet and place value software. This access is limited. In addition, with the often uncooperative nature of technology, the activity must be thoroughly pretested before attempting so that precious class time is not eaten up by unrelated activities. I have opted for a pared-down version of this activity in which one presentation computer is used to access a few examples of place value modeling software. The class analyzes these models and compares their potential with that of physical and pictorial models.

ABCs of Magnetism

Program/Grade Range: Early Childhood, Elementary

Subject: Science

Topic: Magnets/Magnetism

Profile: Professional Preparation

Abstract: This interdisciplinary activity is both a modeling activity in the use of technology as a means of reporting an investigation as well as a scientific inquiry lesson focusing on the notion of what is magnetic and what is not. Following a classroom investigation of the attributes of objects that are magnetic, the teacher candidates are tasked with the job of finding objects that are magnetic that begin with a letter of the alphabet. In the investigation, candidates will also discover objects that begin with their assigned letter that are not magnetic. Slides are created for each letter of the alphabet showing those objects that are magnetic beginning with the given letter and also objects that are not magnetic beginning with the same letter. At the conclusion of the electronic slideshow, candidates list the conclusions about what makes an object magnetic. (Note: The development of a slideshow based on the alphabet—called the ABC Book—can be used with any curriculum area as well as most topics in science. Magnetism is used as an illustrative example.)

STANDARDS

NETS FOR TEACHERS

I. **TECHNOLOGY OPERATIONS AND CONCEPTS—***Teachers demonstrate a sound understanding of technology operations and concepts. Teachers:*

    A. demonstrate introductory knowledge, skills, and understanding of concepts related to technology (as described in the ISTE NETS for Students).

II. **PLANNING AND DESIGNING LEARNING ENVIRONMENTS AND EXPERIENCES—***Teachers plan and design effective learning environments and experiences supported by technology. Teachers:*

    D. plan for the management of technology resources within the context of learning activities.

    E. plan strategies to manage student learning in a technology-enhanced environment.

III. **TEACHING, LEARNING, AND THE CURRICULUM—***Teachers implement curriculum plans that include methods and strategies for applying technology to maximize student learning. Teachers:*

    A. facilitate technology-enhanced experiences that address content standards and student technology standards.

    B. use technology to support learner-centered strategies that address the diverse needs of students.

    C. apply technology to develop students' higher-order skills and creativity.

IV. **ASSESSMENT AND EVALUATION—***Teachers apply technology to facilitate a variety of effective assessment and evaluation strategies. Teachers:*

    A. apply technology in assessing student learning of subject matter using a variety of assessment techniques.

SCIENCE

Content Standard A: Science as inquiry

    A1. Abilities necessary to do scientific Inquiry

    A2. Understanding about scientific inquiry

Content Standard B: Physical Science

    B3. Light, heat, electricity, and magnetism

Lesson Description

TEACHER PREP FACULTY	TEACHER CANDIDATES	FACULTY NOTES
PREPARATION Be sure you have completed a lesson on the process of scientific inquiry before starting this one. Assign background material. Collect samples of common items that are magnetic and others that are not magnetic. Collect enough magnets for teacher candidates to share partner teams. Determine a common slideshow software to use as a standard for all candidate presentations. Create a "how to" sheet for the software selected. Duplicate storyboarding worksheets.	Review background material on magnetism and the scientific inquiry method.	Survey the schools in the area to determine which software is commonly used to create slideshows in the primary grade classrooms. In preparing for storyboarding the slideshow, look at the following Web sites for additional ideas (see Tools and Resources): • Kid Pix/HyperStudio Planning Sheet Slideshow Script • Mr. Reinhart's Classroom Conneaut Elementary You may choose to have candidates bring objects from home that are magnetic and some that are not.
INTRODUCTION Distribute the magnets to the candidates. Pose the question: How do you know an object or surface is magnetic? What are the properties to look for that help to determine whether a surface is magnetic? Distribute the objects. Have candidates hypothesize about which are magnetic and which are not. Insist on a rationale for each hypothesis.	Record a hypothesis on the properties of surfaces that are magnetic. Classify the objects given into those you consider to be magnetic and those you consider not to be magnetic. Be prepared to provide a rationale for your decision.	**Important Note:** Keep magnets away from electronic equipment and digital storage devices as they may cause damage. You may want to have a chart on the wall that lists the objects as they are tested—with columns for Magnetic and Not Magnetic.
IMPLEMENTATION Divide class into cooperative groups of four to six. Have groups test the objects with the magnets. Have candidates record their conclusions based on the limited experiment. For the purposes of recording the results, ask candidates to place the objects in alphabetical order separated in columns of Magnetic and Not Magnetic. Ask candidates to test additional objects from their purses, pockets, and so on that begin with a letter of the alphabet that has not been used, and classify the object in the correct column. Prompt candidates to adjust their conclusions of what is and is not magnetic based on the new information. Assign groups of candidates a range of letters of the alphabet to find other objects that begin with the unused letters. Groups should gather information from the investigations done in class that fall in their letter range as well as make plans for obtaining other objects outside of class for completion of the assignment.	In your group, test the objects with the magnets provided. Adjust your conclusion of how to determine whether an object is magnetic. Arrange the objects in alphabetical order. Classify the objects for each letter as magnetic or not magnetic. Retrieve several objects in your possession to test for magnetism. Add them to the alphabetical chart. Adjust the conclusions about what determines whether an object is magnetic. In the segment of the alphabet assigned to your group, gather the data from the class on the objects that have been determined to be magnetic and not magnetic. Using draw programs, Web images, or digital pictures, record the images in slides for your segment of the slideshow. At a minimum, create one slide for each letter of the alphabet. Create a work plan for completing the missing letters of the alphabet. At the conclusion of the investigation of objects beginning with the letter span	Classroom management issues will differ with how the project is structured in the K–2 classroom—individual project, whole class project, or small group project. See Reinhart Web site (URL is listed in Tools and Resources) to see how the project was carried out as a whole class project. Saving files will be a management issue, especially if you are having candidates add narration to each slide. The assessment process includes two parts: • process (observations) and • product (ABC Book). There are difficult letters in virtually every segment of the alphabet for which to find objects that are magnetic. It is possible that the slide created for the given letter will have examples of objects tested, all of which are not magnetic. Determine ahead of time whether one slide is allocated for each letter of the alphabet or whether more slides are going to be used—such as one slide for those objects that are magnetic followed by an

	TEACHER PREP FACULTY	TEACHER CANDIDATES	FACULTY NOTES
IMPLEMENTATION	Assign groups to practice their slide-making skills by creating slides for a predetermined number of letters that have already been tested with classroom supplied objects. A final slide should present a conclusion about magnetism. To prepare for assessment of the slideshow, create or have the candidates contribute to altering an existing rubric to meet the criteria for the assignment.	assigned, create an additional slide that captures the group's conclusions about the notion of magnetism using the questions posed. Participate in creating or altering a rubric to assess the slideshows.	additional slide of those objects that are not magnetic. The question may arise about the acceptability of obtaining Web images of objects that are magnetic but not tested. In the spirit of inquiry, you may want to limit the objects to only those that have been tested. Determine whether the class is going to peer-assess, self-assess, and so on in addition to instructor assessment.
CULMINATION	Have groups present their segments of the slideshow with their conclusions. (Blend sections of slideshow together into a single show or assign that task to candidates in advance of class.) Assess the presentations based on the rubric created above. Discuss the suitability of the rubric. Review slideshow. Discuss the attributes of magnetic objects and those that are not magnetic. Confer on how to reach all students. Have candidates complete a journal entry that reflects on their experience and extends it into answering the question "How can you translate this experience to what you might do in your future classroom?"	Share slideshow alphabet segment with class. Assess each other using the agreed upon rubrics. Discuss how to reach all students. Discuss how well the rubric covered the task. Complete a journal entry on how you can translate this experience to what you might do in your future classroom: What are the management issues and the technology issues with very young children? How can this activity be modified to fit other curriculum areas?	Have the scoring rubric available if groups are to peer-assess. Emphasize the issues of how to make the concept of magnetism accessible to special needs students and emerging English-speaking students. The topic of second language acquisition in the content area may be one that has specific importance in your region and should be addressed explicitly. This is especially important in light of using the technology to present student conceptual understanding in alternative ways. Extensions for use of the slideshow in the classroom: • Print out the slides to create a book. This would increase the need for a title slide. • Create a videotape of the slideshow using a computer with video out connected to a VCR. This works great to allow a student whose parents can't or don't make it to school to see the project. • Very young students may use the stamping tool on one slide as a way of introducing the items, testing and reinforcing the appearance of the letter.

Assessment

The following table is appropriate for tracking how candidates are able to address the standards within the context of a course. Note that in this table, the specific performance indicators provided for the Professional Preparation Performance Profile are not addressed individually. Rather, the elements of the activity are used to justify meeting the standard, in general, with the applicable performance indicators listed as a group as they apply to the development of an electronic ABC slideshow on magnetism.

Table: Tracking Standards Met within the Context of a Course

STANDARDS	PERFORMANCE INDICATORS	ASSESSMENT (Processes and Products)
NETS for Teachers I. Technology Operations and Concepts—Teachers demonstrate a sound understanding of technology operations and concepts.	Teachers: A. demonstrate introductory knowledge, skills, and understanding of concepts related to technology (as described in the ISTE NETS for Students).	Assess the degree to which candidates are able to: • Use the children's slideshow program • Import digital images Candidates should be able to divide the project work in an equitable fashion, working collaboratively to complete the finished product.
NETS for Teachers II. Planning and Designing Learning Environments and Experiences—Teachers plan and design effective learning environments and experiences supported by technology.	Teachers: D. plan for the management of technology resources within the context of learning activities.	In class discussion and journal writing, candidates should reflect on the issues necessary to complete the project with students. This includes issues of access to technology and file management.
	E. plan strategies to manage student learning in a technology-enhanced environment.	In class discussion and journal writing, candidates should reflect on how to ensure the technology-based reporting used in the slideshow enhances students' inquiry process.
NETS for Teachers III. Teaching, Learning and the Curriculum—Teachers implement curriculum plans that include methods and strategies for applying technology to maximize student learning.	Teachers: A. facilitate technology-enhanced experiences that address content standards and student technology standards.	Through the assessment of the group products, the rubric should address the accuracy of the conclusions about the classification of the magnetic and nonmagnetic objects and the rationale for determining magnetism.
	B. use technology to support learner-centered strategies that address the diverse needs of students.	Critique student discussion. Through the discussion and journal writing, assess how candidates address a range of student physical and learning difficulties as well as suggestions for appropriate solutions to meet the needs of all students.
	C. apply technology to develop students' higher-order skills and creativity.	Assess the conclusions in the slides for evidence of higher-order thinking.
NETS for Teachers IV. Assessment and Evaluation—Teachers apply technology to facilitate a variety of effective assessment and evaluation strategies.	Teachers: A. apply technology in assessing student learning of subject matter using a variety of assessment techniques.	Assess the quality of understanding displayed in the slideshow.
Science Content Standard A: Science as Inquiry	A1. Abilities necessary to do scientific inquiry A2. Understanding about scientific inquiry	Observe the use of inquiry in collecting the data, drawing conclusions, and revising conclusions based on additional data.
Science Content Standard B: Physical Science	B3. Light, heat, electricity, and magnetism	Assess the level of understanding of the concept of magnetism through the evidence provided in the slideshow.

Tools and Resources

SOFTWARE

KidPix Studio Deluxe, Inspiration (optional), whatever software may be necessary to get your images from the camera to the computer

HARDWARE

Digital camera

WEB SITES

Conneaut ABC Slideshow '99:
www.wcnet.org/~bgschool/Conneaut/Reinhart/ pastproj/index.html

KidPix/HyperStudio Planning Sheet Slideshow Script:
www.wcnet.org/~bgschool/Conneaut/Reinhart/ plansheet.html

Mr. Reinhart's Classroom Conneaut Elementary:
www.wcnet.org/~bgschool/Conneaut/Reinhart/ index.html

Credits

Paul Reinhart, Bowling Green Elementary School, Bowling Green, Ohio, **preinhart@bgcs.k12.oh.us**

Judi Mathis Johnson, ISTE and Lesley University, Powhatan, Virginia, **judimj@iste.org**

Comments/Stories

The activity often surprises a preservice teacher education class in just how much thinking it takes to find objects that begin with specific letters of the alphabet. Testing the objects becomes interesting as they strive to find at least one object for each letter. When moving into student teaching and first-year teaching, candidates have enjoyed having a completed slideshow to use with their own students as an example of what might be produced when focusing on scientific concepts. Moving the slideshow to videotape makes demonstrating the end product easy.

A Closer Look

Program/Grade Range: Early Childhood

Subject: Science

Topic: Properties of Objects and Materials

Profile: Professional Preparation

Abstract: This activity investigates the properties of objects and materials. Teacher candidates experience an activity appropriate for young students that engages in classification of objects according to like and unlike properties. Magnification devices, such as whole group projection and hand-held lenses, help facilitate data collection and analysis. After working in small groups to explore and classify objects, candidates identify objects in their environment that have similar properties. In the process of collecting data, candidates use digital cameras to capture the images, which are used as part of a presentation illustrating each property, combinations of two properties, and nonexamples.

STANDARDS

NETS FOR TEACHERS

II. PLANNING AND DESIGNING LEARNING ENVIRONMENTS AND EXPERIENCES— *Teachers plan and design effective learning environments and experiences supported by technology. Teachers:*

    A. design developmentally appropriate learning opportunities that apply technology-enhanced instructional strategies to support the diverse needs of learners.

    D. plan for the management of technology resources within the context of learning activities.

III. TEACHING, LEARNING, AND THE CURRICULUM— *Teachers implement curriculum plans that include methods and strategies for applying technology to maximize student learning. Teachers:*

    A. facilitate technology-enhanced experiences that address content standards and student technology standards.

    B. use technology to support learner-centered strategies that address the diverse needs of students.

    C. apply technology to develop students' higher-order skills and creativity.

IV. ASSESSMENT AND EVALUATION— *Teachers apply technology to facilitate a variety of effective assessment and evaluation strategies. Teachers:*

    A. apply technology in assessing student learning of subject matter using a variety of assessment techniques.

    B. use technology resources to collect and analyze data, interpret results, and communicate findings to improve instructional practice and maximize student learning.

SCIENCE

Content Standard A: Science as Inquiry

    A1. Abilities necessary to do scientific inquiry:

- Ask questions about objects, organisms, and events in the environment.
- Employ simple equipment and tools to gather data and extend the senses.
- Use data to construct a reasonable explanation.
- Communicate investigations and explanations.

Content Standard B: Physical Science

    B1. Properties of objects and materials

Lesson Description

	TEACHER PREP FACULTY	TEACHER CANDIDATES	FACULTY NOTES
PREPARATION	Have teacher candidates review digital camera use and multimedia presentation software, considering methods of efficient data and image storage and retrieval. Prepare packets of objects with various attributes or properties for small group work. Set up a magnification projection device for whole group viewing. Gather one magnifying glass for each candidate.	Review how to use a digital camera to capture images and how to use multimedia presentation software. Before coming to class, consider how to store images and other data in a way that makes retrieval efficient.	Packets may all be similar (each has one metal toy such as a jack, one piece of sponge, etc.) or packet contents may vary, but all have at least one common attribute, such as soft, hard, red, green, noisy, and so on.
INTRODUCTION	Review the concept of same and different using concrete models. Discuss how objects may initially appear the same but upon closer inspection have different attributes. Discuss how objects fit into a variety of categories.	Participate in a discussion with a focus on differentiating the objects and using appropriate language to describe thinking.	Periodically step outside the role of teacher to the role of coaching candidates into thinking through what they are experiencing so that they can replicate the lesson. Ask questions about managing the classroom, organizing the equipment, and ensuring a focus on student thinking.
IMPLEMENTATION	Break candidates into groups. Hand out packets of objects without a magnifying glass. Have candidates categorize the objects. Monitor candidate work; assess thought processes through questioning; encourage multiple categorizations. Lead large group discussion about their categorizations. Introduce objects that have more than one attribute. Monitor candidate work and assess through questioning. Lead large group discussion on the new categories assigned. Discuss new attributes that might be revealed when objects are viewed from a different perspective using magnification. Review outcome of activity: a presentation of the attributes of the items in the bag on one, two, and multiple dimensions. Present the rubric being used to evaluate the presentations. Modify the rubric based on the class discussion. (**Note:** In rubric below, concentrate on defining the expectations that are being assessed.) Demonstrate the use of a digital camera. Have candidates collect images from their environment that reflect single property, two or more properties, and nonexamples. Assign a presentation using the images that they collected.	In groups, examine objects without a magnifying glass. Categorize the objects using a single attribute. Rearrange to describe objects on a different attribute. Describe categorizations for each way of sorting. Sort the objects using two attributes. Explain why some objects are not included when sorted. Resort objects according to multiple attributes. Sort objects by a magnified attribute. Participate in the modification of the presentation rubric. Organize your group for efficient collection of the data and preparation of the presentation. Use camera to take digital images. Create a multimedia presentation to demonstrate the understanding of concepts and use of magnification to identify similarities and differences.	**Assessment Observation:** How well did they sort into categories? How many different categories are there? Do candidates understand inclusion and exclusion (or example and nonexample)? **Assessment Interview Questions:** • What are the two attributes of this collection? • Why is this object not a part of this category? • What are the new categories? Use the telephoto capabilities of the camera to hone in on the specific attributes being discussed. Digital cameras can be used easily in the early grades. Often the initial difficulty comes in assisting young students in being able to look through a hole (eye piece) to frame up their picture. Discuss how that skill might be developed. Discuss how the transfer of the digital images to the computer might be accomplished in an efficient way in the classroom.

CULMINATION	TEACHER PREP FACULTY	TEACHER CANDIDATES	FACULTY NOTES
	Have multimedia equipment available and ready for presentations. Debrief activity on usefulness in meeting science standards and logistic issues with the use of technology.	Show multimedia presentations to large group. Monitor time taken to put presentation together. Use this information to discuss how the activity would be modified for the classroom.	Use both a multimedia rubric and a science content assessment device. Encourage candidates to discuss the value of the technology in the completion of this activity. Concentrate on the ability of the digital camera to enable students to see and remember their thinking. Consider posting presentations on the class Web site.

Assessment

The rubric below is for assessing this lesson. It is structured to match the desired attribute in the task column with points assigned according to the degree to which the tasks have been met. A conversation must take place in class to define what is meant by "expectations" for each criteria. Note that the rubric is scored using points with totals recorded at the bottom of the table. Grades can, therefore, be assigned based on the points obtained.

Rubric: Categorizing Objects and Multimedia Presentation

TASKS	CATEGORIZING OBJECTS			
	APPROACHES EXPECTATIONS 1	MEETS EXPECTATIONS 2	EXCEEDS EXPECTATIONS 3	ITEM POINTS
Sorts into categories				
Includes appropriate number of categories				
Demonstrates understanding of categories				
Recategorizes with two attributes				
Uses magnifying lens correctly				
Sorts objects by magnified attribute				

TASKS	MULTIMEDIA PRESENTATION			
	APPROACHES EXPECTATIONS 1	MEETS EXPECTATIONS 2	EXCEEDS EXPECTATIONS 3	ITEM POINTS
Demonstrates appropriate use of digital camera				
Imports digital images into presentation				
Covers content of lesson				
Contains required number of slides				
Uses correct language mechanics				
Works cooperatively				
Communicates information effectively				
TOTAL				

Tools and Resources

SOFTWARE

Multimedia presentation software (HyperStudio, PowerPoint, KidPix slideshow, Claris slideshow)

HARDWARE

Computers, digital cameras (one for every five candidates), presentation system, magnification device

WEB SITES

U.S. Department of Education: Helping Your Child Learn Science:
www.ed.gov/pubs/parents/Science/Home.html
WonderNet:
www.acs.org/wondernet/activities/activities.html

REFERENCE TEXTS

Bryan, S. J., & Sharth, S. (2001). *Up close! Exploring nature with a magnifying glass.* Pleasantville, NY: Reader's Digest.

Carlson, A. E. (1986). *Under the magnifying glass.* Eatontown, NY: Parkwest Publications.

Ross, M. E. (1993). *The world of small: Nature explorations with a hand lens.* El Portal, CA: Yosemite Association.

VanCleve, J. (1993). *Janice VanCleave's microscopes and magnifying lenses: Mind-boggling chemistry and biology experiments you can turn into science fair projects.* New York: John Wiley & Sons.

OTHER

Packets of items to compare, magnifying glasses (one magnifying glass per group)

Credits

Carole Hruskocy, formerly with NASA Classroom of the Future, Wheeling, West Virginia, **carolehrus@aol.com**

Judi Mathis Johnson, ISTE and Lesley College, Powhatan, Virginia, **judimj@iste.org**

Louisiana Review Team:

Juanita Guerin, **jguerin@louisiana.edu**
Dolores Champagne, **djchampagne@louisiana.edu**
Sue Jackson, **sujax@louisiana.edu**
Gloria Hendrickson, **gloria@louisiana.edu**

Comments/Stories

An activity similar to this had originally been implemented without the use of the digital cameras. In the old version, candidates recorded the attributes of their objects by writing and drawing pictures. Although they were successful in the activity, they never seemed to look beyond the obvious. With the introduction of the digital camera, candidates want to use the magnifying glasses more as the camera can pick up some of the same level of detail. Candidates spend much more time looking closely at an object, asking deeply probing questions, and working hard to document their findings. What was once a short exercise of moderate success has become a very successful activity that is highly stimulating and motivating, with a high-level end product.

Where Do I Live?

Program/Grade Range: Early Childhood

Subject: Social Studies

Topic: Neighborhood Maps

Profile: Professional Preparation, Student Teaching/Internship, First-Year Teaching

Abstract: Teacher candidates participate in a social studies lesson that incorporates the use of a multimedia CD-ROM, a digital graphic organizer, digital cameras and images, and instructional tool software to maximize the young children's ability to construct physical maps of their neighborhood. Candidates will use the software presented in the model lesson to develop an original technology-enhanced lesson to be tested in their field placement.

STANDARDS

NETS FOR TEACHERS

II. PLANNING AND DESIGNING LEARNING ENVIRONMENTS AND EXPERIENCES—*Teachers plan and design effective learning environments and experiences supported by technology. Teachers:*

A. design developmentally appropriate learning opportunities that apply technology-enhanced instructional strategies to support the diverse needs of learners.

B. apply current research on teaching and learning with technology when planning learning environments and experiences.

D. plan for the management of technology resources within the context of learning activities.

E. plan strategies to manage student learning in a technology-enhanced environment.

SOCIAL STUDIES

III. PEOPLE, PLACES, AND ENVIRONMENTS—*Social studies program should include experiences that provide for the study of people, places, and environments, so that the learner can:*

A. construct and use mental maps of locales, regions, and the world that demonstrate understanding of relative location, direction, size, and shape.

B. interpret, use, and distinguish various representations of the earth such as maps, globes, and photographs.

C. use appropriate resources, data sources, and geographic tools such as atlases, databases, grid systems, charts, graphs, and maps to generate, manipulate, and interpret information.

Lesson Description

	TEACHER PREP FACULTY	TEACHER CANDIDATES	FACULTY NOTES
PREPARATION	Remind teacher candidates to review the information on developing scoring rubrics as they will participate in developing one for this lesson. A shell is provided at the end of this lesson.	Review information on developing scoring rubrics. Examine the rubric shell to become familiar with the expectations for this lesson.	Pointing candidates to professional standards on Web sites and focusing their attention on the objective for the activity ahead of time models
	Have candidates locate information about problem-based learning.	Locate information about problem-based learning. Read the information and be ready to share what you have learned in class.	• the use of the Internet as a resource and
	Point candidates to the National Council for the Social Studies (NCSS) Web site to review the targeted standards for the lesson: III. People, Places, and Environments, with possible connections to I. Culture and II. Time, Continuity, and Change.	Visit the National Council for the Social Studies (NCSS) Web site to review strands I, II, and III.	• teaching to the standards and clearly stated objectives.
	Select a school in the area to use for the model lesson. Have a group of candidates take digital pictures of landmarks in the school area.	Participate in taking a series of digital pictures of landmarks in the vicinity of a preselected area school.	This lesson allows the integration of technology and technology supported lessons into the typical learning environment.

TEACHER PREP FACULTY	TEACHER CANDIDATES	FACULTY NOTES
INTRODUCTION		
Provide a time at which preservice teachers develop a rationale for problem-based learning based on an authentic K–1 lesson problem: "Where Do I Live?"	Form small groups to discuss the elements of problem-based learning and how they relate to an authentic K–1 lesson problem: "Where Do I Live?"	Problem-based learning information is available on several Web sites noted in Tools and Resources.
Place the candidates in small groups. Use Inspiration software to brainstorm (use the Rapid Fire mode) and record answers to the question "Where Do I Live?"	Develop a rationale for the value of problem-based learning in early childhood education.	This introductory investigation can be done prior to class. Consider bringing the Web site up live in class to model how to locate targeted information on a Web site.
Introduce the social studies standards and performance expectations as the guide for core content knowledge to be developed in this lesson.	Work in small groups to review the Early Grades Student Performance Expectations of the NCSS strands I (Culture) and II (Time, Continuity, and Change), but especially focusing on strand III (People, Places, and Environments).	Encourage candidates to "discover" that the standards are written in such a way that related content knowledge is disseminated throughout various strands. For example, the problem "Where Do I Live?" can be addressed through the Performance Expectations in strands I, II, and III.
Have candidates label the elements of the resulting Inspiration/Kidspiration diagram with the social studies standards.	In small groups, brainstorm and record in Inspiration (Rapid Fire mode) answers to the question "Where Do I Live?"	
Have them make a list of performance expectations.	Label the elements of the resulting Inspiration/Kidspiration diagram with the social studies standards.	
	Use a word processor or change to outline view in Inspiration/Kidspiration to make a list of all Early Grades Student Performance Expectations that can be addressed as students construct knowledge to the lesson problem "Where Do I Live?"	
IMPLEMENTATION		
Model the development of a holistic rubric as a tool for planning and assessing student performance in response to the lesson standards.	Participate in the discussion of refining the holistic rubric designed to guide instruction and assess the lesson.	Depending on how much prior experience candidates have had with the development of rubrics, it may be necessary to set aside time to discuss the relationship among the development of assessment rubrics, teaching to standards, and meeting student technology standards.
Present a primary globe and a digital image of a physical map of the earth, from an electronic world atlas or the MapQuest Web site. Using the two models, set the scene for an inquiry lesson surrounding the question "Where Do I Live?" Use questions such as	Participate in a discussion on the similarities and differences between the maps, images, and models presented.	
	Log on to an electronic location finder such as MapQuest. Examine the site in terms of use by young children.	It may be necessary to provide a variety of student recording sheets that have been designed to assist teachers in collecting data to meet lesson standards.
• How is the globe the same as the physical map?	Use the MapQuest site to "zoom in" on the exact neighborhood of a school used for field placement. Print the neighborhood map.	Stress the importance of allowing the young child to construct knowledge in authentic, concrete ways. Technology can assist students in establishing a "connection" between the concrete, physical objects and a symbolic representation of the real, physical world.
• How is the globe different from the physical map?	Independently or in a small group, create a K–1 lesson that will encourage small groups of young children to collaborate on the construction of models of their neighborhood. The student groups will be given the task of developing	
• Which map is "real" and which one is a model?	• a floor map (plastic table cloth, blocks, and labels),	The instructor may need to demonstrate Internet search strategies that query for specific images. Example: Use Alta Vista, image: earth. The query will index images only.
Have candidates log on to the MapQuest Web site: www.MapQuest.com. Model the use of the MapQuest site to "zoom in" on a particular state, city, street, and street address.	• a bulletin board (using icons developed from the digital images from the area surrounding the school, which have been stored for use in this lesson), and	The lesson plan that is developed could be taught in candidates' field placement and assessed by peers, the classroom teacher, and/or the university supervisor using the candidate-developed rubric.
Divide candidates into cooperative groups. Assign groups to create "maps" of the neighborhood—moving from a concrete physical map (floor map) to a picture map (bulletin board) to an electronic template (Neighborhood Map Machine). Pass out materials. Have candidates begin the construction of the three types of maps.	• an electronic map (Neighborhood Map Machine).	
	As part of the lesson development, create a student rubric by embedding a table in a	

TEACHER PREP FACULTY	TEACHER CANDIDATES	FACULTY NOTES
IMPLEMENTATION Suspend the group work after enough time has passed for them to understand the issues in developing the type of map assigned to their group. (This usually takes 30–45 minutes.) Have candidates create a rubric for students. Assign individuals or pairs the task of creating a lesson plan for K–1 students that focuses on one of the three types of maps. Group the candidate pairs or individuals into threes such that all three types of lessons will eventually be developed to work in concert with one another. Using Inspiration or other concept-mapping software, brainstorm the important elements in the lesson plan. Have candidates compile Web sites that contain satellite images of Earth.	word processing document. The rubric should define the criteria that will be measured to assess the student learning outcomes. Construct data collection sheets to be used by K–1 students. The data collection sheets must be designed to engage the K–1 student in actively processing the information in response to teacher-guided questions. The data collection sheet must cause students to make observations and construct knowledge needed to meet the performance expectations. For your own reference, create a list of browser bookmark sites containing current satellite images of the Earth.	
CULMINATION Lead a discussion on the value of technology in creating learning environments in which young children can develop conceptual understandings of maps and globes. List the candidate responses in a large-screen word processing document (24-point size) to allow for a synthesis of the observations.	Contribute to a list of ways technology enhanced the process of "map making" and assisting young children in responding to the lesson problem "Where Do I Live?"	Consider posting the images from the area surrounding the school on a Web site so that the schools can use them for other purposes. Apple's online iTools (apple.org) will allow that posting.

Assessment

Rubric: "Where Do I Live?"

CRITERIA	LEVELS OF PERFORMANCE		
	APPROACHING EXPECTATIONS 1	MEETS EXPECTATIONS 2	EXCEEDS EXPECTATIONS 3
Map Building			
Distinguishes between map, primary globe, other globes, and satellite images			
Locates online mapping resources and bookmarks them			
Takes digital pictures to use in map building			
Uses information technology to create maps of a local neighborhood			
Uses instructional software to create maps of a local neighborhood			
Teaching the Lesson Includes			
Managing the environment for centers and technology use			
Purpose of the lesson			
Directions for completing the lesson			
Active monitoring of student progress			
Closure			

Tools and Resources

SOFTWARE

Tom Snyder's Neighborhood Map Machine; world atlas; word processing; Inspiration, Kidspiration, or concept-mapping software

HARDWARE

Multimedia computer, digital camera, scanner

WEB SITES

Social Studies

National Council for Social Studies (NCSS):
www.ncss.org

Maps

Geography with Matt Rosenberg:
http://geography.about.com

MapQuest Web site: **www.MapQuest.com**

U.S. Geological Survey Department of the Interior:
http://ask.usgs.gov/education.html

Problem-Based Learning

Learning Theory Funhouse: www.funderstanding.com.

Problem-Based Learning:
www.mcli.dist.maricopa.edu/pbl/

University of Guelph Teaching Support Services on Problem-Based Learning:
www.tss.uoguelph.ca/onlineres/pbl.htm

What Is Problem-Based Learning?:
http://edweb.sdsu.edu/clrit/learningtree/Ltree.html

REFERENCE TEXTS

Hartman, G. (1994). *As the roadrunner runs: A first book of maps.* New York: Macmillan.

Hartman, G. (1991). *As the crow flies: A first book of maps.* New York: Macmillan.

Credits

Beth Holmes, Columbus State University, Columbus, Georgia, **Holmes_Elizabeth@colstate.edu**

Pam Burish, Metropolitan Nashville Public Schools, Nashville, Tennessee, **pjburish@usa.net**

Comments/Stories

Going through the developmental sequence of looking at how maps can be perceived by young children provides the candidates with wonderful insight. This activity addresses various learning styles and points out to candidates deficits in their own experiences as well as once again reinforcing their own learning styles. Working together to create the lesson sequence seems to ensure that candidates share their lesson, justify how it is organized and assessed, and generally engage in a first-level professional collaboration activity that can be replicated at the school site.

Why Am I Special?

Program/Grade Range: Early Childhood

Subject: Social Studies

Topic: Individual Development and Identity

Profile: Professional Preparation, Student Teaching/Internship, First-Year Teaching

Abstract: Teacher candidates experience a model, technology-enhanced lesson to learn about the characteristics of their own personality. The lesson incorporates the use of database and spreadsheet software to explore factors that contribute to one's personal identity such as interests, capabilities, and perceptions. Candidates use the software presented in the model lesson to develop an original technology-enhanced lesson to be field-tested in the student teaching/internship setting. This activity can be easily coupled with an educational psychology session in a foundations course.

STANDARDS

NETS FOR TEACHERS

II. PLANNING AND DESIGNING LEARNING ENVIRONMENTS AND EXPERIENCES—*Teachers plan and design effective learning environments and experiences supported by technology. Teachers:*

  A. design developmentally appropriate learning opportunities that apply technology-enhanced instructional strategies to support the diverse needs of learners.

  B. apply current research on teaching and learning with technology when planning learning environments and experiences.

  D. plan for the management of technology resources within the context of learning activities.

  E. plan strategies to manage student learning in a technology-enhanced environment.

III. TEACHING, LEARNING, AND THE CURRICULUM—*Teachers implement curriculum plans that include methods and strategies for applying technology to maximize student learning. Teachers:*

  A. facilitate technology-enhanced experiences that address content standards and student technology standards.

  B. use technology to support learner-centered strategies that address the diverse needs of students.

  D. manage student learning activities in a technology-enhanced environment.

SOCIAL STUDIES

IV. INDIVIDUAL DEVELOPMENT AND IDENTITY—*Social studies programs should include experiences that provide for the study of individual development and identity, so that the learner can:*

  F. explore factors that contribute to one's personal identity such as interests, capabilities, and perceptions.

Lesson Description

TEACHER PREP FACULTY	TEACHER CANDIDATES	FACULTY NOTES
PREPARATION Provide teacher candidates with access to the Social Studies Standards Performance Expectations for strand IV: Individual Development and Identity.	Examine the Social Studies Standards Performance Expectations for strand IV (Individual Development and Identity) and the ISTE NETS for Students.	NAEYC's Position on Technology and Young Children states that "Used appropriately, technology can enhance children's cognitive and social abilities" and suggests that at the classroom level, the use of technology can "facilitate cooperative interactions among children."
In previous class session, direct candidates to review information on scoring rubrics, NCSS Standards, and ISTE NETS for Students.	Review information on scoring rubrics as one will be developed at the end of the demonstration activity.	If you haven't discussed the NAEYC position statement yet, this is a good opportunity to do so.
Provide information on scoring rubrics to prepare candidates to develop one to use at the end of the demonstration activity. At the end of this lesson, a rubric shell is provided as a starting point.	Work individually to locate the Keirsey Temperament Test using an Internet browser. (See Tools and Resources.) Take the Keirsey Temperament Test and print a synopsis of your personality type.	
Assign candidates to take the Keirsey Temperament Test as an online activity prior to class. Assign a short descriptive paper explaining their results and why they agree or disagree with the results.	Write a short paper that tells about why you agree or disagree with the inventory results.	

TEACHER PREP FACULTY	TEACHER CANDIDATES	FACULTY NOTES
INTRODUCTION Provide a rationale for creating learning environments in which the young child can develop a strong personal identity, or sense of self, while learning to be a contributing member of a larger human community. Set the stage for each candidate to explore his or her unique identity in small groups. The Keirsey Temperament Sorter will prepare the candidates for the self-exploration activity. A brief introduction to the Meyers-Briggs personality types might add further information. Invite candidates to provide descriptions of how it "felt" to focus upon one's own personality and share important traits with peers. Using a word processor projected to a large screen, record candidate responses such as: • Interesting • Validating • Insightful Use the Keirsey experience to have the candidates discuss the classroom techniques through which young children can share unique attributes of their personalities with their grade level peers. Prompt discussion to look at interdisciplinary approaches to collecting and analyzing the data.	In small groups, share important personality traits that have been identified in your personal synopsis. Discuss how taking the Keirsey test and learning about others supports building self-esteem and group identity. Suggest descriptors of the feelings, thoughts, and ideas associated with learning and sharing information about your personality. Think about activities in the early childhood classroom setting for having young children share characteristics of their own personality. Consider concepts and skills taught in other curricula as vehicles for collecting and analyzing data.	Taking the Keirsey Temperament Test may be an activity that can be done prior to this class. Access to hardware may be an issue whether done during class time or out of class. Some candidates may be reluctant to discuss the results of their analysis. Keep the groups relatively small for the purposes of discussion to enable all candidates to participate actively. The early grades classroom provides opportunities for interdisciplinary instruction. Mathematics data collection techniques, oral language, and attention to issues of diversity are important areas to draw upon to make a classroom application of the experience meaningful. Other surveys to consider are those related to Gardner's multiple intelligences and Gregorc's learning styles.
IMPLEMENTATION Have candidates in small groups create a "Why Am I Special?" database for primary students. To assist candidates in planning for the construction of their databases, use webbing or concept-mapping software, such as Inspiration, to define potential data fields. Adjust the Main Idea icon to a "New Look" that is 24-point size and can be seen by the whole group. Using "Why Am I Special?" as the main idea, and with the software in Rapid Fire mode, enter the data fields suggested by the candidates. Model the process for creation of a database. Divide candidates into groups to create their own database. Encourage them to brainstorm fields that are appropriate or of interest to specific groups of candidates or take into account cultural or regional differences. Set the scene for entering data in the "Why Am I Special?" databases. Demonstrate a rotation strategy that will move the candidates from one workstation to another. For example: One set of management cards is marked with	In small groups, brainstorm topics for data fields in a first/second grade database entitled "Why Am I Special?" Examples: • Favorite color • Favorite movie • Pets • Favorite ice cream • Hair color • Eye color • Height • Birthday • Favorite food As a group, create a "Why Am I Special?" database that includes fields that are relevant to a specific population or area. Define the population in the title of the database. Rotate groups to add new records to three to five "Why Am I Special?" databases created by the first groups.	As this portion of the activity is taking place, be sure to discuss with the candidates the notion of readable size and shape of font for viewing by young students. Be sure to weave issues of second language learning in the classroom and how the descriptions, word usage, and traits of these learners need to be respected and clarified for common understanding. When the activity moves to the creation of unique databases, several computers or handheld devices in the classroom are essential. If not available, consider breaking the activity at this point to have candidates complete the database development prior to the next class—with that session being in a lab setting. It may be necessary to demonstrate procedures for creating and saving a new record in a database.

TEACHER PREP FACULTY	TEACHER CANDIDATES	FACULTY NOTES
IMPLEMENTATION numbers. One set of management cards is marked with letters. Half of the group will have number cards. Half of the group will have letter cards. "Letters" will exchange places with "numbers" until all candidates have had an opportunity to add a single record to three to five databases. Lead candidates in creating queries within the "Why Am I Special?" databases. The instructor will model: • Creating a sort • Creating a filter Model using the results of a database query as "live data" for the construction of a spreadsheet and data chart. Example database queries: • "Girls who like pizza" • "Boys who like pizza" • "Children who like pizza" Have candidates develop a graph of the class data on "Pizza" using Tom Snyder's Graph Club.	Design queries to identify sets of "unique individuals" using the sort and filter features of a database. Examples: • Girls who like vanilla ice cream • Children who like "Star Wars" and popcorn • Boys who like soccer Create a chart of the class data on "Pizza" using Tom Snyder's Graph Club.	As the lesson proceeds, continually draw the discussion back to how this activity would be carried out in the early childhood classroom. Discuss issues of the use of the technology, managing the students to complete the records, sorting, and so on.
CULMINATION Lead a discussion about the value of using real, meaningful data as the context for teaching young children. The activities modeled will build personal esteem and group identity. In the context of developing conceptual understandings of one's personal and group identity, the young child is simultaneously developing math concepts within the context of meaningful numbers. Have candidates collect the class data in a book using Tom Snyder's Graph Club. Assign candidates the task of taking their experience into the development of a lesson for the classroom. Brainstorm a rubric for assessing the lesson. Major categories of the rubric might include • development of the concept of exploring factors of personality, interests, and perceptions of young children, • technology use and management, and • student management. Have candidates post lesson plans on class Web site for later sharing. If candidates are in a field placement, have them teach the lesson with that group of students.	Create a big book of the class data collected in the "Why Am I Special?" database. Spreadsheets, charts, and graphs will be printed for use in a big book using Tom Snyder's Graph Club. Using information gained from writing rubrics (refer to preparation activity) participate in the development of a rubric appropriate for assessing lesson plans to be developed and taught. In small groups, write a lesson plan for organizing the same lesson for a specific level of students using the database developed in class. Teach the lesson in a classroom of young children with an evaluation by the classroom teacher and/or supervisor using the rubric developed in class.	Access to a bookbinding machine will be necessary for construction of the big books. The development of the lesson plan can be done in small groups or as individuals, in or outside of class, in person or online. An alternative may be to have candidates develop a lesson plan outline during class time for polishing outside of class.

Assessment
Rubric: "Why Am I Special?"

PERFORMANCE INDICATOR	LEVELS OF PERFORMANCE		
	1	2	3
Keirsey Temperament Test and Response Paper			
"Why Am I Special?" Database			
Big Book including Spreadsheets, Charts, and Graphs			
Lesson Plan			

Tools and Resources

SOFTWARE

Tom Snyder's Graph Club, database software, Inspiration or Kidspiration

HARDWARE

Individual stations for completion of Keirsey Temperament Survey

Small group stations for development of database

Demonstration station in classroom for model lesson

Bookbinder for culminating product

WEB SITES

Temperament Types
   Keirsey Temperament Types: www.keirsey.com

Multiple Intelligences
   Multiple Intelligence Online Inventory:
      http://snow.utoronto.ca/Learn2/mod3/miinventory.html
   School Using MI: www.ips.k12.in.us/mskey/

Problem-Based Learning
   Problem-Based Learning:
      www.mcli.dist.maricopa.edu/pbl/
   University of Guelph Teaching Support Services on Problem-Based Learning:
      www.tss.uoguelph.ca/onlineres/pbl.htm
   What Is Problem-Based Learning?:
      http://edweb.sdsu.edu/clrit/learningtree/Ltree.html

Rubrics
   Bibliography for Using Rubrics for Assessment:
      http://stone.web.brevard.k12.fl.us/html/comprubric.html
   Creating Your Own Rubrics:
      www.2learn.ca/projects/together/START/rubricc.html
   Eighmey's Think Tank:
      http://kancrn.kckps.k12.ks.us/Harmon/breighm/rubrics.html
   Kathy Schrock's Guide for Educators (Wholistic and Analytic Rubrics):
      http://school.discovery.com/schrockguide/assess.html
   Rubric Construction Set: www.landmark-project.com/classweb/rubrics/

Standards
   National Council for the Social Studies:
      www.ncss.org/standards/toc.html
   ISTE NETS: http://cnets.iste.org/index2.html

Credits

Beth Holmes, Columbus State University, Columbus, Georgia, Holmes_Elizabeth@colstate.edu

Pam Burish, Metropolitan Nashville Public Schools, Nashville, Tennessee, pjburish@usa.net

Comments/Stories

Depending on the expertise of the candidates, this activity can take one or two sessions. Candidates seem to enjoy taking the Keirsey Temperament Test and often like to discuss the results in some detail. The feedback they receive from their classmates causes many to think about how they perceive themselves. It is this feedback that reinforces the importance of allowing young children to tell each other just how they are special and perceived as such by their peers. Candidates often share that doing the activity in the classroom has fostered newfound understanding by young children of how to be tolerant and get along better with one another.

Technology in Elementary Education Programs

- **Introduction**

- **English Language Arts**
    Electronic Book Discussions
    WebQuest: Content Area Reading Strategies

- **Mathematics**
    What's My Pattern?
    What's Up?

- **Science**
    Data from Our Environment
    Survey of Systems

- **Social Studies**
    Diverse Perspectives on History
    Oral History

TECHNOLOGY IN
Elementary Education Programs

Introduction

Teacher education programs focused on preparing elementary school teachers often have the largest enrollment of all the licensure programs in the college of education. According to most state licensure descriptions, elementary teachers must be prepared to teach the widest span of ages of children—from kindergarten to either sixth or eighth grade. Because of this large program with a wide span of student developmental levels to address, the technology use in elementary teacher professional preparation must focus on preparing the elementary teacher in all curriculum areas instead of just one or two. The program must emphasize student-centered approaches to working in a flexible environment, coping with a host of ways to access equipment and software in the context of addressing the needs of second language learners.

Making the transition from the university methods classroom to the reality of the elementary school tests the bounds of the theory-to-practice dilemma. It is incumbent in colleges of education to provide a variety of experiences for the candidates as learners as well as opportunities to practice using technology in their teaching. The array of experiences should include activities designed for:

▶ *One computer or several computers in the classroom as well as lab settings in the school*

▶ *Independent and cooperative learning classroom organization*

▶ *Open-ended, creative products as well as tightly prescriptive outcomes*

▶ *Performance-based assessment on a given concept as the purpose of the project or product*

▶ *Candidate input on the development of a performance-based rubric as part of the activity*

ACTIVITIES

The activities in this section are designed to provide the university faculty member with choices of how to use technology in the classroom as a replacement for similar activities already part of the methods courses. The variety of assessment rubrics purposefully varies from one activity to the next. While it would have been easy but artificial to create the same type of rubric for each activity, the writing team concluded that having candidates experience many types of performance assessment rubrics would provide additional opportunities for expanding the debate on assessment of student work. To meet the complex needs of the elementary curriculum, the activities include:

Electronic Book Discussions (English Language Arts)

The introduction and implementation stages of this activity take place online as teacher candidates participate in a threaded discussion. The debriefing centers on how learners are able to reread each other's comments and the faculty member is able to monitor participation as well as understanding.

WebQuest: Content Area Reading Strategies (English Language Arts)

Using the model in Section 1, "Using Model Strategies for Integrating Technology into Teaching," teaching candidates participate in an analysis of the WebQuest model centered on developing activities that promote content area reading strategies. This activity takes place as a four-lesson developmental sequence.

What's My Pattern? (Mathematics)

Using electronic and manipulative three-dimensional geometric solids, teacher candidates discover Euler's formula for determining the number of angles, vertices, and faces of an object.

What's Up? (Mathematics)

Candidates create an electronic teaching tool to develop student conceptual understanding of probability and statistics.

Data from Our Environment (Science)

In groups, teacher candidates collect and analyze data in their environment. The data is shared as a class and compared with data from others using the Web.

Survey of Systems (Science)

Candidates explore and learn about the basic elements of systems and how they work to become a system. Presentations are made in a multimedia format.

Diverse Perspectives on History (Social Studies)

Using folk tales that are told from different points of view, teacher candidates explore ways to introduce a unit of study by highlighting the alternative point of view as a way to stimulate discussion. The Internet is used to research the alternative points of view.

Oral History (Social Studies)

Teacher candidates simulate a lesson designed for students in which they learn about either their own family or local history by interviewing elderly individuals and archiving their stories.

Electronic Book Discussions

Program/Grade Range: Elementary

Subject: English Language Arts

Topic: Response Print

Profile: Professional Preparation

Abstract: Discussions in an online environment can significantly enhance the level of participation and the quality of the reflection in reading and comprehension assignments. This activity has three major components: reading, electronic response, and electronic interaction. During the reading, teacher candidates are asked to read an assigned chapter, article, or literature selection by a specific date. Following the reading, the candidates are instructed to post their responses to the assigned reading no later than 48 hours after the specified date. At this point, the candidates do not have access to any of the responses made by their classmates. After all responses have been posted, the site is opened for interaction to allow candidates to respond to each other and the posed questions. The purpose of this activity is to promote the candidates' understanding of the required reading using a model of a technology-mediated instructional strategy to encourage equity in their own classroom practice. (**Note:** The Introduction and Implementation stages of this activity take place online.)

STANDARDS

NETS FOR TEACHERS

I. **TECHNOLOGY OPERATIONS AND CONCEPTS—** *Teachers demonstrate a sound understanding of technology operations and concepts. Teachers:*

    A. demonstrate introductory knowledge, skills, and understanding of concepts related to technology (as described in the ISTE NETS for Students).

V. **PRODUCTIVITY AND PROFESSIONAL PRACTICE—** *Teachers use technology to enhance their productivity and professional practice. Teachers:*

    D. use technology to communicate and collaborate with peers, parents, and the larger community in order to nurture student learning.

ENGLISH LANGUAGE ARTS

1. Students read a wide range of print and nonprint texts to build an understanding of texts, of themselves, and of the cultures of the United States and the world; to acquire new information; to respond to the needs and demands of society and the workplace; and for personal fulfillment. Among the texts are fiction and nonfiction, classic and contemporary works.

4. Students adjust their use of spoken, written, and visual language (e.g., conventions, style, and vocabulary) to communicate effectively with a variety of audiences and for different purposes.

11. Students participate as knowledgeable, reflective, creative, and critical members of a variety of literacy communities.

12. Students use spoken, written, and visual language to accomplish their own purposes (e.g., for learning, enjoyment, persuasion, and the exchange of information).

Lesson Description

	TEACHER PREP FACULTY	TEACHER CANDIDATES	FACULTY NOTES
PREPARATION	Choose a selection to be read by the teacher candidates. It can be a book chapter, article, or literature selection or different titles based on the same author or theme. Develop appropriate probing questions for the candidates to respond to. Set up an electronic bulletin board or forum for candidate responses. Set it so that candidates cannot initially read each other's postings.		Some universities use commercial online course environments that contain areas of electronic discussion. Check with the system administrator to see whether there is an option for keeping initial postings not viewable by the candidates until a predetermined date. The text for this activity can be one that is used in discussion of a literary genre or as background for an upcoming topic. Regardless of the selection, the text rather than the use of the technology should be the focus of the exercise. The online environment should be discussed as a medium for motivating participation in thoughtful discussion.

	TEACHER PREP FACULTY	TEACHER CANDIDATES	FACULTY NOTES
INTRODUCTION	**Note:** The introduction to the activity is briefly given to the class prior to implementation. Give the reading assignment to the candidates and make clear that there is a 48-hour window of posting time on the discussion forum. Answer any questions on posting to the forum. Be sure the candidates understand that they will not have access to the other responses until all the responses have been posted. Share assessment rubrics for various aspects of the activity. Discuss expectations with candidates. Modify the rubric to reflect the discussion and to increase clarity.	Make sure it is clear how to post reactions to the discussion forum before leaving class. Complete the assigned readings and post answers to guiding questions to the discussion forum within the time frame specified. Participate in the discussion of the scoring rubric for the activity. Reflect on how to improve the rubric to optimally assess the outcomes of the activity.	Check equity of access issues with the candidates. Discuss ways to resolve the fact that some candidates may not have access to the technology for completion of the activity. This is a discussion that can be reframed in terms of the access for K–12 students to the technology for posting of comments. You may find it necessary to demonstrate how to access the site or discussion forum as well as enter responses. Keeping the initial posting invisible to the rest of the class is an important part of this activity. This ensures that the first responses are genuine contributions showing initial interpretation and not reactive or restatements of others' work.
IMPLEMENTATION	Acknowledge candidate posting with an e-mail message. Keep track of the postings to determine when all candidates have responded. After all candidates have entered a response on the site, open the access to the site to initiate electronic conversation. Ensure that candidates are aware that a minimum number of postings per candidate are necessary to keep the conversation active.	When the site is opened for general comments, respond to classmates' postings. Consider responses carefully. Note that threads of ideas will begin to emerge. These become apparent only if all the ideas have been read before a response is made. To keep yourself organized, set a plan on the calendar for responding to the postings on a regular basis. Be sure to respond the minimum number of times as stated.	Be sure to ask candidates to report any problems they are having accessing the computer site. Responding to the candidates individually may require a large amount of time. Simple responses are often enough to acknowledge receipt and keep candidates involved. As the responses come in, you may want to suggest some points of debate between candidates to initiate a dialogue.
CULMINATION	Highlight common threads found in the responses. Make explicit any ideas you want all candidates to take away from the reading. Debrief the experience of utilizing the electronic discussion. Assign a journal reflection about the experience and its relationship to teaching elementary students who might be in remote settings.	Examine the responses to find common threads. Participate in a discussion about the experience of the online discussion. In a journal entry, relate the experience of the online discussion to methods that might be used in an elementary classroom with remote learners.	If the reading assignment is a literature selection, having the candidates read and respond to the other candidates may be all that is appropriate. If the reading selection is expository text, it may be necessary to give the class some guidance in identifying the important points. **Extension** If the assigned reading is a selection of children's literature, the candidates may take the activity to a classroom setting for comparing results of responses to questions between elementary students and themselves.

Assessment

The first table shows how the activity is aligned with the specific standards identified at the beginning of the lesson. The tables and rubrics that follow dissect the elements of the lesson for assessment.

Table: Connecting Standards and Electronic Book Discussions Lesson for Assessment

STANDARDS	PERFORMANCE INDICATORS	ASSESSMENT (Processes and Products)
NETS for Teachers I. Technology Operations and Concepts—Teachers demonstrate a sound understanding of technology operations and concepts.	Teachers: A. demonstrate introductory knowledge, skills, and understanding of concepts related to technology (as described in the ISTE NETS for Students).	These skills will be demonstrated by successfully completing the following activities: • Logging on to bulletin board • Accessing information from bulletin board • Responding to instructor's questions on assigned reading on bulletin board • Responding to peers' entries on bulletin board
NETS for Teachers V. Productivity and Professional Practice—Teachers use technology to enhance their productivity and professional practice.	Teachers: D. use technology to communicate and collaborate with peers, parents, and the larger community in order to nurture student learning.	The participation in the electronic dialogue demonstrates the ability to communicate and collaborate on the analysis of the text. Should the activity be extended to students, candidates then demonstrate how it can nurture student learning.
English Language Arts 1. Students read a wide range of print and nonprint texts to build an understanding of texts.... 4. Students adjust their use of spoken, written, and visual language.... 11. Students participate as knowledgeable, reflective, creative, and critical members of a variety of literacy communities. 12. Students use spoken, written, and visual language to accomplish their own purposes....		Candidates create a digital artifact in the form of a word-processed electronic journal entry. Included in this reflection could be: • Different types of print media that could be used by the preservice teacher to engage students • Types of questions or prompts that could be used to encourage reflection with elementary students Candidates participate in an electronic discussion, during which they: • Respond to instructor's questions on bulletin board on assigned reading • Respond to peers' entries on bulletin board

The following rubrics can be used to assess the components of the activity:

Checklist for Basic Operations (NETS•T 1)

	Log on to bulletin board
	Access information from bulletin board
	Respond to instructor's questions on bulletin board
	Respond to peers' entries on bulletin board

Rubric: Participation in Electronic Discussion

	FREQUENCY OF RESPONSES			
	NEVER/FEW	SOMETIMES	OFTEN	REGULARLY
Quality of Responses	Responds to teacher-directed questions	Responds to teacher and candidates' entries	Responds to teacher and candidates entries and contributes independent ideas	Initiates and sustains discussion threads with multiple participants

Rubric: Electronic Journal Entry

| | FREQUENCY OF RESPONSES | | | |
	NEVER/FEW	SOMETIMES	OFTEN	REGULARLY
Quality of Responses	Reflections focused on personal feelings	Responses focused on personal feelings and interpretation of the reading	Responses focused on personal feelings and the skills that are needed for planning and teaching	Responses focused on personal feelings, skills needed for planning and teaching, and how the experience can be used with remotely located students or other situations

Note: Decide on the number of responses appropriate for the given situation. Record those in brackets under the Never/Few, Sometimes, Often, and Regularly categories. Example: 0–5, 6–10.

Tools and Resources

SOFTWARE

Bulletin board, online classroom software, or appropriate browser software

HARDWARE

System with network or bulletin board access

Credits

Ward Cockrum, Northern Arizona University, Sedona, Arizona, **Ward.cockrum@nau.edu**

Kim Kimbell-Lopez, Louisiana Tech University, Ruston, Louisiana, **Kklopez@latech.edu**

Mary Bird, University of Central Florida, Orlando, Florida, **Bird@pegasus.cc.ucf.edu**

Comments/Stories

Having candidates respond to print as a group discussion is a common activity in methods classes. Holding a discussion by means of an electronic bulletin board can significantly increase the quality of the candidates' reflections about the reading. The electronic discussion encourages full participation of the class in an atmosphere of knowing that the responses will be read by others. In an electronic setting, the more vocal or aggressive candidates are not able to dominate an electronic conversation as they might in an in-class setting. Likewise, candidates who are often quiet have an opportunity to be "heard." Because the initial experience is designed not to have other candidates able to see responses until all are posted, individuals do not fear that their idea has already been expressed.

WebQuest: Content Area Reading Strategies

Program/Grade Range: Elementary

Subject: English Language Arts

Topic: Development of Content Area Reading Strategies

Profile: Professional Preparation

Abstract: This activity comprises four distinct lessons that provide an introduction to the elements of a WebQuest project in the context of studying content area reading strategies. The four sequential lessons outlined are designed to be spread over a course as other areas of the English language arts are being developed. The lessons include (1) comparing WebQuest and traditional lesson elements, (2) analyzing WebQuests for critical-thinking skills, (3) modifying WebQuests to include content area reading strategies, and (4) creating WebQuests for developing and using content area reading strategies.

STANDARDS

NETS FOR TEACHERS

II. PLANNING AND DESIGNING LEARNING ENVIRONMENTS AND EXPERIENCES—*Teachers plan and design effective learning environments and experiences supported by technology. Teachers:*

A. design developmentally appropriate learning opportunities that apply technology-enhanced instructional strategies to support the diverse needs of learners.

B. apply current research on teaching and learning with technology when planning learning environments and experiences.

C. identify and locate technology resources and evaluate them for accuracy and suitability.

III. TEACHING, LEARNING, AND THE CURRICULUM—*Teachers implement curriculum plans that include methods and strategies for applying technology to maximize student learning. Teachers:*

A. facilitate technology-enhanced experiences that address content standards and student technology standards.

C. apply technology to develop students' higher-order skills and creativity.

ENGLISH LANGUAGE ARTS

7. Students conduct research on issues and interests by generating ideas and questions, and by posing problems. They gather, evaluate, and synthesize data from a variety of sources (e.g., print and nonprint texts, artifacts, and people) to communicate their discoveries in ways that suit their purpose and audience.

8. Students use a variety of technological and information resources (e.g., library, databases, computer networks, and video) to gather and synthesize information and to create and communicate knowledge.

Lesson Description

For a complete discussion of WebQuests, see the Section 1 chapter "Using Model Strategies for Integrating Technology into Teaching."

	TEACHER PREP FACULTY	TEACHER CANDIDATES	FACULTY NOTES
PREPARATION	Have teacher candidates become familiar with WebQuests by reviewing WebQuest sites listed in Tools and Resources. Make a decision about the lesson plan format to be used for comparison on Lesson 1.	Before class, become familiar with the elements of a WebQuest by previewing the suggested Web sites.	This project can be introduced at the beginning of the term and continued for the duration of the class. Introducing Lesson 1 early in the course, with Lesson 2 soon thereafter, gives candidates time to explore the model WebQuest lessons. Note that although several Web sites are listed that contain WebQuests, a search will yield many additional sites. WebQuests are continually being developed by teachers and shared in many ways.

	TEACHER PREP FACULTY	TEACHER CANDIDATES	FACULTY NOTES

INTRODUCTION	**Lesson 1—Comparison**
	Review the basic components of the WebQuest project (introduction, task, process, evaluation, and conclusion).
	
	Instruct candidates to work in pairs to compare the basic elements of a WebQuest with those of a traditional lesson plan. Conduct a whole class discussion on how the two models compare.
	
	In concluding the discussion, focus on the role of the teacher as a guide and the potentially independent nature of the learner WebQuest. Extend the discussion to include the cautions a teacher would have to keep in mind when developing a WebQuest for elementary students.
		In pairs, compare and contrast basic components of the WebQuest project with those elements typically included in a lesson plan:
		
		• Goal
		
		• Objective
		
		• Materials
		
		• Procedures
		   Introduction
		   Procedures/Development
		   Conclusion/Wrap-up
		
		• Evaluation
		
		How are they the same? How are they different?
		
		Participate in a group discussion about how the two models compare.
			This introductory lesson provides an opportunity to review the basic elements of a lesson plan. Because some teacher preparation programs do not have a common lesson plan format used throughout the program, this review enables candidates to refresh their memory about at least one format to provide a common foundation for discussion. Further, to be able to use technology-based resources, such as WebQuests, appropriately, it is important for candidates to make a connection with the elements of lesson design and how these elements are reflected within a good WebQuest project.

IMPLEMENTATION	**Lesson 2—Analyzing a WebQuest** Review the development of critical-thinking skills. Discuss how this concept can be applied to the WebQuest project. Ask candidates to participate in a WebQuest about WebQuests. (For URL see Tools and Resources.) Following this task, discuss the critical-thinking processes embedded in the task and process sections of the WebQuest design. Assign candidates in pairs or small groups to critique an existing WebQuest for how the task was posed and the type of questions asked as a function of developing critical thinking. Ask candidate groups to suggest modifications for strengthening this component of the WebQuest. (See sites in Tool and Resources or have candidates search for others.)	Participate in a WebQuest about WebQuests to identify what makes one WebQuest project more effective than another. Particular attention can be focused on those projects that promote higher-level thinking skills versus those that call for only basic recall of information. In groups, critique an existing WebQuest in terms of the higher-level thinking skills involved. Suggest changes to strengthen the focus on critical thinking.	This lesson can be done when the course is covering the concept of developing critical-thinking skills. Development of critical-thinking skills is integral to developing good content area reading skills. Therefore, analyzing both the WebQuest model and existing WebQuests for how questions are asked to develop critical-thinking skills is an important prerequisite to the work on content area reading skills. You may want to preselect a WebQuest based on the strength or weakness of the critical-thinking questions asked.
	Lesson 3—Modify a WebQuest Introduce content area reading (CAR) strategies, for example: • Anticipation guide • KWL • Compare/contrast • Concept map • SQ3R • Semantic feature analysis chart Organize candidates in cooperative groups. Have the groups each select a WebQuest designed for elementary school social studies or science. Instruct candidates to answer the questions posed as a part of their analysis.	In small groups, select a WebQuest for analysis of content area reading strategies used to enhance student comprehension of the material. Answer the following questions: • What content area standard is the WebQuest attempting to address? • Does the WebQuest use content area reading strategies? If so, which ones? • Is the CAR strategy appropriate for the context of this lesson? If not, discuss why as well as any modifications that could have been made to improve the use of the particular strategy. • If no CAR strategy is used as part of the lesson, could one have been used that	The exercise of modifying an existing WebQuest is an important skill to increase candidates' confidence in critically analyzing previously developed activities. Too often teachers take material without modifying it to better address the needs of their students. When posing the question about addressing content area standards, you may want to focus on state standards as well as national standards. Find out which sets of standards are used by schools in the region. When making the modifications on the existing WebQuest, consider extending candidates' technology skills by asking them to download the original text, make

	TEACHER PREP FACULTY	TEACHER CANDIDATES	FACULTY NOTES
IMPLEMENTATION	Have groups rewrite the portions of the WebQuest necessary to improve the use of content area reading strategies as a way to increase students' comprehension of the materials needed to meet the content area standards. Have groups share their work and justify the changes made in the WebQuest.	would have helped the elementary students to be more effective in their organization of information? • What other strategies would be appropriate? Rewrite the WebQuest to include appropriate strategies. Share your results and rationale with the class.	the modifications in color, and create a color printout or electronically saved version for easy examination and critique.
CULMINATION	**Lesson 4—Creating a WebQuest** As a whole class, brainstorm a list of possible content area topics appropriate for elementary students that could be developed into quality WebQuest projects. As groups (or individuals) select topics, require them to specify the content area standard being met by the topic. Discuss the importance of using quality Internet resources within the WebQuest project. As a large group, brainstorm a list of qualities that could be found within an appropriate Web site. Review elements of the WebQuest project that should be included (introduction, task, process, evaluation, and conclusion). Have candidates search the Internet for quality sites. Establish a mechanism for sharing WebQuests. Have candidates discuss their WebQuests with peers.	After the brainstorm session, select a topic for the WebQuest that meets content area standards. Once the topic is identified, define the scope of the WebQuest, the desired outcomes, and relevant resources. Search the Internet for quality sites that support the tasks and processes of the WebQuest. Upload the WebQuest onto the class Web site or share the WebQuest with the class in the manner designated. Provide feedback to peers on their WebQuests.	Before making this assignment, decide on how the completed projects are to be shared. Options include uploading to a class Web site, entering the project on one of the many WebQuest database sites, saving it in a single place for pressing to a CD-ROM, and printing it out in paper form. Discuss legal and ethical issues involved in using Internet resources, such as citations, copyright laws, and fair use. As they are developing their projects, it is a good idea to take class time for "status checks." The status check is a good way to • establish a time frame for drafting each of the basic components and • provide for small group sharing and discussion in which peers can offer constructive feedback on each project.

Assessment

The following table is appropriate for tracking how candidates are able to address the standards within the context of a course. Note that in this table, the specific performance indicators provided for the professional preparation profile are not addressed individually. Rather, the elements of the activity are used to justify meeting the standard, in general, with the applicable performance indicators listed as a group as they apply to the development of the WebQuest.

Table: Tracking Standards Met within the Context of a Course

STANDARDS	PERFORMANCE INDICATORS	ASSESSMENT (Processes and Products)
NETS for Teachers II. Planning and Designing Learning Environments and Experiences—Teachers plan and design effective learning environments and experiences supported by technology.	Teachers: A. design developmentally appropriate learning opportunities that apply technology-enhanced instructional strategies to support the diverse needs of learners. B. apply current research on teaching and learning with technology when planning learning environments and experiences. C. identify and locate technology resources and evaluate them for accuracy and suitability.	The WebQuest developed by the candidates should • demonstrate developmentally appropriate reading level and topic, • contain a variety of resources that appeal to the diverse learning styles of students, and • contain all the elements of a WebQuest that reflect effective instructional design and learning with technology. (**Note:** Rubric can be created beginning with these criteria.)
NETS for Teachers III. Teaching, Learning, and the Curriculum—Teachers implement curriculum plans that include methods and strategies for applying technology to maximize student learning.	Teachers: A. facilitate technology-enhanced experiences that address content standards and student technology standards. C. apply technology to develop students' higher-order skills and creativity.	With the analysis and modification of existing WebQuests, candidates will have experience in seeing how the English language arts standards are being met through the lesson taught using the WebQuest. With the development of a WebQuest focused on content area reading strategies, candidates develop a technology-based lesson that meets content area standards as well as English language arts standards.
English Language Arts 7. Students conduct research on issues and interests by generating ideas and questions, and by posing problems. They gather, evaluate, and synthesize data from a variety of sources (e.g., print and nonprint texts, artifacts, and people) to communicate their discoveries in ways that suit their purpose and audience.		Candidates, like their students, are able to select topics for content area reading to provide a way to develop strategies for reading material more effectively. In the process of developing the WebQuest for student use, they are able to evaluate appropriate Web sites and other information for use by students. The design of the WebQuests provides both candidates and their students the opportunity for further exploration and creativity in sharing their results.
English Language Arts 8. Students use a variety of technological and information resources (e.g., library, databases, computer networks, and video) to gather and synthesize information and to create and communicate knowledge.		Because the WebQuest uses digitally stored information, candidates will be using a variety of information resources. Whether the information is stored in a database, occurs as reprints of original print information, or is obtained as a synthesis of other data, the type of information can vary widely.

Tools and Resources

SOFTWARE

Internet browser

HARDWARE

Computer with Internet connection

WEB SITES

Building Blocks of a WebQuest:
http://edweb.sdsu.edu/people/bdodge/webquest/buildingblocks.html (This site identifies the basic components of a WebQuest including introduction, task, process, evaluation, and conclusion.)

Matrix of WebQuest Examples:
http://edweb.sdsu.edu/webquest/matrix.html (A matrix of WebQuest projects categorized by K–3, 4–5, middle school, high school, and adult/college)

The WebQuest Page, Developed by Bernie Dodge:
http://edweb.sdsu.edu/webquest/webquest.html

WebQuest Site Overview:
http://edweb.sdsu.edu/webquest/overview.htm (A resource for teachers using the WebQuest concept to teach with the Web)

WebQuest Training Materials: http://edweb.sdsu.edu/webquest/materials.htm (Links to reading and training materials for WebQuest projects)

A WebQuest about WebQuests: http://edweb.sdsu.edu/webquest/webquestwebquest-es.html

Credits

Kim Kimbell-Lopez, Louisiana Tech University, Ruston, Louisiana, Kklopez@latech.edu

Mary Bird, University of Central Florida, Orlando, Florida, Bird@pegasus.cc.ucf.edu

Ward Cockrum, Northern Arizona University, Sedona, Arizona, Ward.cockrum@nau.edu

Comments/Stories

The methods students often are enrolled in professional education and general classes during the same term. Some candidates who fit this description choose to develop their WebQuest project in connection with one of the general education classes. For example, one candidate developed a project on plate tectonics while enrolled in a basic science class required as part of her plan of study.

I have found that candidates are often unsure as to what theme or topic they should develop. When I build in time for them to explore, investigate, and critique existing projects, they then have a better concept of how to begin. As a support system for the preservice teachers, provide time for share sessions concerning the topic they have selected, identification of appropriate Internet resources, development of their process section, and the means of evaluation. These share sessions help candidates to keep on track with their individual project as well as receive feedback from the instructor or their peers on overall cohesiveness among all elements of the WebQuest.

What's My Pattern?

Program/Grade Range: Elementary

Subject: Mathematics

Topic: Geometry, Algebra

Profile: General Preparation, Professional Preparation

Abstract: The activity begins with a model lesson on exploring three-dimensional geometric shapes to discover the pattern that exists among the number of faces, edges, and vertices. Technology tools are used in the process of the learning to brainstorm and record findings. Following the model lesson, a debriefing discussion takes place covering elements of a discovery-oriented lesson, conceptual understanding of vocabulary for second language learners, developmentally appropriate pedagogy, classroom management issues, and uses of technology. Teacher candidates develop a technology-based tool to teach the patterns discovered in the relationships among the faces, edges, and vertices of the solids. The tools are shared and posted on the class Web site.

STANDARDS

NETS FOR TEACHERS

II. PLANNING AND DESIGNING LEARNING ENVIRONMENTS AND EXPERIENCES—*Teachers plan and design effective learning environments and experiences supported by technology. Teachers:*

  A. design developmentally appropriate learning opportunities that apply technology-enhanced instructional strategies to support the diverse needs of learners.

III. TEACHING, LEARNING, AND THE CURRICULUM—*Teachers implement curriculum plans that include methods and strategies for applying technology to maximize student learning. Teachers:*

  B. use technology to support learner-centered strategies that address the diverse needs of students.

MATHEMATICS

Standard 2: Algebra

Instructional programs from PK–12 should enable all students to—

- understand patterns, relations, and functions.

Standard 3: Geometry

Instructional programs from PK–12 should enable all students to—

- analyze characteristics and properties of two- and three-dimensional geometric shapes and develop mathematical arguments about geometric relationships.

Standard 5: Data Analysis and Probability

Instructional programs from PK–12 should enable all students to—

- develop and evaluate inferences and predictions that are based on data.

Standard 6: Problem Solving

Instructional programs from PK–12 should enable all students to—

- build new mathematical knowledge through problem solving.
- apply and adapt a variety of appropriate strategies to solve problems.

Lesson Description

	TEACHER PREP FACULTY	TEACHER CANDIDATES	FACULTY NOTES
PREPARATION	Obtain enough sets of three-dimensional geometric models for each group of teacher candidates.	Complete readings assigned for background in geometry and instructional strategies.	Because most of the software needed for this lesson is commonly available, it is possible to have candidates bring in one laptop per group, if university computers are not available. The concept-mapping software can be downloaded from the vendor's Web site for a trial period. Consult the Tools and Resources section for vendor options.
	Assign readings on geometry and instructional strategies.		
	Arrange for one computer for each group of candidates. Software provided could include concept-mapping software (such as Inspiration), electronic spreadsheets, as well as presentation software programs (such as PowerPoint or HyperStudio).		
INTRODUCTION	Provide a set of three-dimensional physical models to each group of candidates.	Examine, explore, and describe similarities and differences between the models.	Consider assigning groups different ways of reporting the information, for example, diagrams, charts, pictures, and so on. By doing this, an additional discussion can take place about the various ways of making the concept comprehensible to different types of learners in a classroom.
	Discuss terminology such as faces, edges, and vertices as well as any other vocabulary considered weak in the context of examining the blocks. As the vocabulary is introduced, scaffold the conceptual development as you would for second language learners. Record the vocabulary visually, either electronically or on a whiteboard, review pronunciation, provide examples, and relate concepts to the immediate environment.	Count and record the number of faces, edges, and vertices for a set of six three-dimensional physical models.	
		Describe similarities and differences using Venn diagrams and other graphic organizers. Use concept-mapping software to record brainstorming. Look for mathematical connections as the recording takes place.	
	Focus the discussion around the similarities and differences between the blocks. Have candidates use Venn diagrams or other graphic organizers to describe similarities and differences. Use concept-mapping software to record.	Experiment with creating a table or chart to depict your understanding. Spreadsheet software can be used to create a table recording the number of faces, edges, and vertices for each model.	
	Have candidate create a table or chart of their findings.		
IMPLEMENTATION	Have candidates explore relationships and patterns among faces, edges, and vertices. Have them describe their findings.	Look for any relationships and patterns that exist among the number of faces, edges, and vertices.	The definition of the relationships may lead some groups to develop Euler's formula.
	Question: If you know only pieces of information (i.e., edges, vertices), can you determine the number of the third (i.e., faces)? Encourage candidates to share their charts or diagrams as the discussion takes place.	Provide a description of your discoveries.	The description of discoveries can take place outside of class with posting on a discussion board or other electronic format.
		Develop an electronically communicated "tool" to convey to peers and students that helps to define the attributes of any three-dimensional solid. This tool can be in graphical form, a table, or any other means that clarifies the relationships among the edges, faces, and vertices.	Presentation of the tool can be done with PowerPoint, HyperStudio, or other software. Relationships and patterns must be clearly explained (in online discussions) and must work for all three-dimensional shapes.
	Questions: How do you know this to be true? Will it work for any three-dimensional model?		
	Task: Develop a tool that will help someone "describe" a three-dimensional model if only two of the attributes for the model are known.		
	Have groups share their "tool."		

	TEACHER PREP FACULTY	TEACHER CANDIDATES	FACULTY NOTES
CULMINATION	Debrief the lesson focusing on the instructional methods used. Discuss the amount of time the "teacher" was directing and the amount of time the "students" were engaged in discovering the concept. Discussion should include questions about how the concept and associated vocabulary was developed; what is developmentally appropriate; and how to plan and manage activities to allow children to construct their own knowledge. Further discussion should include how the technology was used in the model lesson. The discussion should progress to debating what technology could be used when, where, and for what purpose. Assign candidates the task of developing a lesson that utilizes the tool they created. Assess the lesson on the criteria specified in the rubric below. Provide a mechanism for candidates to post lessons online for sharing with peers as well as a way to post reflections after teaching the lesson in a field experience. Conduct a class discussion about how implementation of the lesson worked with students.	Reflect on the lesson just experienced. What were the roles of the "teacher" and the roles of the "students"? Develop a geometry lesson that incorporates the tool developed in class. Share the lesson online. Test the lesson during field experience. Follow up with a reflection about the strengths and weaknesses of their lesson. In addition to the effectiveness of teaching the concept, reflect on the use of the technology to convey the concept. Post the lesson reflection, assessment of technology used, and suggested modifications for the lesson plan for sharing with peers. Bring your reflection, assessment of technology used, and suggested modifications to class for a general discussion.	The culminating activity moves from the development of the tool to how it would be used in the classroom to teach children. This portion of the activity can be done in an extended period of time and connected with student teaching or field experience. The reflection, modification, and assessment of the use of technology should not be overlooked. These elements should be brought back into the methods classroom at a specified date to draw out a rich discussion on results. Having a discussion after teaching the lesson allows candidates to reflect on what transpired in the classroom and learn from the results.

Extension of Lesson

Additional physical models can be created using toothpicks and clay based upon the relationships found among edges, vertices, and faces.

What are the results of dipping the three-dimensional model (made of toothpicks and clay) into soapy water with glycerin? Is there a pattern to the soapy "geopanes" formed based upon the faces, edges, and vertices of the three-dimensional model?

Candidates can explore Web sites and software that allow for three-dimensional modeling of physical models. Evaluate and describe appropriate instructional applications of these resources.

Assessment

The following rubric assesses specific elements of the lesson plan but not the elements of an appropriately developed lesson plan. Consult the lesson plan format specified by the college or school district for elements to add to the rubric.

Rubric: "What's My Pattern?"

| CRITERIA | LEVELS OF PERFORMANCE | | | |
	DEVELOPING 1	PROMISING 2	ACCEPTABLE 3	ACCOMPLISHED 4
Type of Activities	Candidate uses only one type of activity that is questionable in its appropriateness for the developmental level of the students.	Candidate uses some developmentally appropriate activities that are a mixture of hands on and technology based.	Most of the activities in the lesson are developmentally appropriate and are a mixture of hands on and technology based.	Candidate uses developmentally appropriate activities that are both hands on and technology based.
Identification of Standards	Candidate lists only one set of standards.	Candidate lists both sets of standards but is incomplete.	Candidate lists both sets of standards with only minor omissions or overstatements.	Candidate lists appropriate standards from NCTM and NETS for Students in developing knowledge and skills.
Uses of Technology	Candidate uses technology but does not enrich conceptual understanding of student.	Candidate uses technology to communicate knowledge of mathematical concepts "discovered" in the lesson activities. Method of use is not necessarily engaging for students.	Candidate uses generally appropriate technology that enhances concept development. Candidate effectively utilizes tool developed.	Candidate uses developmentally appropriate technology that enhances concept development. Candidate effectively utilizes tool developed as an integral part of the lesson.
Reflection	Reflection does not include all elements: strengths, weaknesses, modifications, and evaluation of technologies employed.	Reflection includes a surface-level analysis of the strengths and weaknesses of the lesson taught, explanations of what should be done differently and why, and an assessment of the technologies used.	Reflection includes a reasonable analysis of the strengths and weaknesses of the lesson, explanations of what should be done differently and why, and an assessment of the technologies used.	Reflection includes a thoughtful analysis of the strengths and weaknesses of the lesson, clear explanations of what should be done differently and why, and a critical assessment of the technologies used.

Tools and Resources

SOFTWARE

Concept-mapping software such as Inspiration

Spreadsheet software (Microsoft Works, AppleWorks, Excel, etc.)

PowerPoint and/or HyperStudio

HARDWARE

PC and/or Macintosh computer islands that provide for cooperative group work

WEB SITES

Concept Mapping Software:
   www.inspiration.com/freetrial/index.cfm

Euler's Formula:
   http://www1.lcs.uci.edu/~eppstein/junkyard/euler
   or:
   http://www.math.ohio-state.edu/~fiedorow/ math655/euler.html

Lesson Activity:
   http://forum.swarthmore.edu/alejandre/escot/ cube.prism.html (This site provides a classroom activity.)

Studying Polyhedra:
   http://forum.swarthmore.edu/alejandre/applet. polyhedra.html (This is an excellent digital demonstration that allows users to vary sides and angles.)

Three Dimensional Objects:
   http://jwilson.coe.uga.edu/interMath/MainInterMat/ Strands/WorkshopHTMLs/solids/solid.html (This site provides a classroom activity.)

OTHER

Three-dimensional physical models (these can be obtained through a mathematics education supplier such as Creative Publications, Delta, and Dale Seymour)

Toothpicks and clay (for extensions)

Credits

Sharnell Jackson, Chicago Public Schools, Barrington, Illinois, **sharnellj@aol.com**

Valeria Amburgey, Northern Kentucky University, Highland Heights, Kentucky, **amburgey@nku.edu**

James Wiebe, California State University, Los Angeles, **jwiebe@calstatela.edu**

Comments/Stories

Modeling the lesson, as you would teach it in an elementary school setting, makes the experience more valuable than if it is just described. Teacher candidates seem to find more classroom management issues to discuss when they are in the position of the student in an elementary classroom. The success of the use of technology in the discovery process has increased over time in using this lesson as the candidates have come into the course more comfortable with the concept-mapping software and presentation software. Initially, the candidates were concerned about how the software would work in a math lesson. More often now, they are intrigued with how to create an instructional tool than worried about the mechanics of the software. Since the quality of the tools developed has increased, the class Web site has become a resource for creative tools that are shared with others.

What's Up?

Program/Grade Range: Elementary

Subject: Mathematics

Topic: Experimental Probability

Profile: General Preparation, Professional Preparation

Abstract: Teacher candidates explore and apply concepts of probability and statistics by participating as learners in the first part of the activity. Questions encourage comparisons of expected outcomes (theoretical probability) with simulation outcomes (experimental probability) in both hands-on and electronic simulations of coin tosses. Candidates create an electronic tool for enhancing instruction of probability and the outline of a lesson using the electronic tool. Candidates also participate in developing a scoring rubric for a performance task and completing the assessment rubric for the development of the electronic tool and lesson outline.

STANDARDS

NETS FOR TEACHERS

II. PLANNING AND DESIGNING LEARNING ENVIRONMENTS AND EXPERIENCES—*Teachers plan and design effective learning environments and experiences supported by technology. Teachers:*

  A. design developmentally appropriate learning opportunities that apply technology-enhanced instructional strategies to support the diverse needs of learners.

  B. apply current research on teaching and learning with technology when planning learning environments and experiences.

  D. plan for the management of technology resources within the context of learning activities.

  E. plan strategies to manage student learning in a technology-enhanced environment.

III. TEACHING, LEARNING, AND THE CURRICULUM—*Teachers implement curriculum plans that include methods and strategies for applying technology to maximize student learning. Teachers:*

  A. facilitate technology-enhanced experiences that address content standards and student technology standards.

  B. use technology to support learner-centered strategies that address the diverse needs of students.

  C. apply technology to develop students' higher-order skills and creativity.

V. PRODUCTIVITY AND PROFESSIONAL PRACTICE—*Teachers use technology to enhance their productivity and professional practice. Teachers:*

  B. continually evaluate and reflect on professional practice to make informed decisions regarding the use of technology in support of student learning.

VI. SOCIAL, ETHICAL, LEGAL, AND HUMAN ISSUES—*Teachers understand the social, ethical, legal, and human issues surrounding the use of technology in PK–12 schools and apply that understanding in practice. Teachers:*

  B. apply technology resources to enable and empower learners with diverse backgrounds, characteristics, and abilities.

MATHEMATICS

Standard 5: Data Analysis and Probability

Instructional programs from PK–12 should enable all students to—

  • develop and evaluate inferences and predictions that are based on data.

  • understand and apply basic concepts of probability.

	TEACHER PREP FACULTY	TEACHER CANDIDATES	FACULTY NOTES
PREPARATION	Assign viewing of the Interactive Coin Flipping Web site prior to class. (For the URL see Tools and Resources.) Provide guiding questions and have teacher candidates complete 10, 20, and 30 tosses. Consider posting candidate preparation activities on Web site. Provide enough coins or two-colored counters for groups of candidates to have at least 20 per group. Obtain graphing calculators or computers with a spreadsheet program for each group.	Preview electronic coin toss Web site before coming to class. Make predictions about outcomes, and then complete 10, 20, and 30 tosses. Compare predictions with actual tosses. Be prepared to discuss the similarities and differences between electronically examining coin toss outcomes and physically completing the task.	When looking at the type of technology to use with this activity examine the common spreadsheet programs and calculators used in field placements. If nothing is apparent, look at programs such as Graph Club or TableTop as examples of child-friendly spreadsheet/graphing tools. Depending on how long it is between class sessions, an online discussion can take place debriefing the exercise prior to class.
INTRODUCTION	Pose questions: • If I flip a coin, what is the likelihood of getting a "heads up"? • Will the likelihood remain the same if I flip again? And, again? • Why or why not? Conduct a brief discussion on the multiple ways of symbolically noting the probability of an outcome taking place.	Make predictions about the outcomes of flipping a coin (or two-colored counter). Depict the probability symbolically in the way that makes most sense.	Accept the responses of the candidates at the beginning of the discussion. When the ideas are recorded, use multiple ways of showing the projected outcomes of the coin tosses. It is important to dispense with the issues of the symbolic notation early in the activity as some candidates may become hung up because of prior experience on the issue of notation rather than focusing on the development of the concept.
IMPLEMENTATION	Distribute counters. In pairs, have candidates conduct tossing experiments for 5, 10, and 20 consecutive tosses. Data should be recorded on a chart or spreadsheet. Ask candidates questions about their data and direct them to make comparisons between the numbers they derived in their experiment with the numbers from the samples presented by different groups. Facilitate class discussion about the similarities and differences among individual, small group, and whole class data sets. Pool the small group data on an electronically projected spreadsheet. Question: What would the data sets from 100 or even 500 groups produce? Debrief the outcomes of the electronic coin toss experiment. Discuss the distinguishing characteristics between experimental and theoretical probability. Pause class to direct candidates to record findings and reflections in mathematics journal.	In pairs, conduct an experiment of tossing a coin (or two-colored counter) 5 times (review results), 10 times (review results), and 20 times (review results). Represent the experiment results in a spreadsheet or on a graphing calculator. Pool the data for the group into one graph or table. In groups, share results by discussing the total number of possible outcomes. Enter the theoretical probability next to the experimental probability on the same chart or graph. Compare the results. To what can the difference be attributed? Compare the hands-on experience with the electronic coin toss experiences completed in preparation for the class. Pause to record findings and reflections in mathematics journal.	A lively discussion should ensue about the differing experiences of the hands-on and electronic coin tosses. Move the discussion to topics of developmental appropriateness, the necessity for meeting the many learning styles in the classroom, and special needs students. For clarifying the discussion, consider bringing up the NCTM Web site section that provides information and examples on what the various elements in the standards mean. Look at **http://illuminations.nctm.org.html** Have candidates guide the search to the standard on probability, the box model.

	TEACHER PREP FACULTY	TEACHER CANDIDATES	FACULTY NOTES
CULMINATION	Introduce the use of HyperLogo in HyperStudio as a way to produce an animated character that moves, creating a path. Movements of the animated character will be determined by the results of a coin toss. If the character begins in the center of the screen, for example, it may move to the right for heads and to the left for tails. The location of the character by the end of the series of experiments shows the difference between the number of heads and tails rolled.	To create a teaching tool, use HyperLogo in HyperStudio to create an animated character that moves to create a path. Movements of the animated character will be determined by the results of a coin toss.	The scoring rubric below is partially completed. Rather than providing a completed rubric, consider having candidates complete the elements of the rubric in the context of explaining the expectations for the assignment.
	Have candidates outline a performance task or lesson using the tool to build conceptual understanding of probability.	Outline a performance task or lesson in which the tool can be used to build conceptual understanding of probability with a predetermined classroom of students.	**Note:** As an option, develop the animated character as a whole group in-class activity. The task for the lesson then becomes one of using the developed tool in the context of a lesson for the field. Post the class-created animated character on the Web site for downloading and modification.
	Outline the specifications and complete an assessment rubric for candidates for designing a probability activity that will engage elementary students in simulations of random events using the technology tool that was created. Suggested elements for assessment include:	Develop a rubric for assessment of the performance task in which the tool will be used.	Post class probability tools and tasks on the class Web site.
	1. Developmental appropriateness	Participate in completing the assessment rubric for the assignment.	
	2. Alignment with standards		
	3. Student centered		
	4. Active engagement		
	5. Effective utilization of the tool		
	6. Questioning strategies employed		
	7. Development of an appropriate student performance assessment rubric		

Extension of Lesson

This lesson could involve the use of a robotic device, such as a Valiant Roamer, programmable bricks, and so on as a preactivity or follow-up activity.

Terrapin Logo has a Random Walk exercise as part of its Logo Probability activity, which utilizes coin tossing as a decision maker in the movement of the turtle on the screen.

Assessment

The following table is appropriate for tracking how candidates are able to address the standards within the context of a course. Note that in this table, the specific performance indicators provided for the Professional Preparation profile are not addressed individually. Rather, the elements of the activity are used to justify meeting the standard, in general, with the applicable performance indicators listed as a group as they apply to the development of the electronic tool and lesson plan.

Table: Tracking Standards Met within the Context of a Course

STANDARDS	PERFORMANCE INDICATORS	ASSESSMENT (Processes and Products)
NETS for Teachers II. Planning and Designing Learning Environments and Experiences—Teachers plan and design effective learning environments and experiences supported by technology.	Teachers: A. design developmentally appropriate learning opportunities that apply technology-enhanced instructional strategies to support the diverse needs of learners. B. apply current research on teaching and learning with technology when planning learning environments and experiences. D. plan for the management of technology resources within the context of learning activities. E. plan strategies to manage student learning in a technology-enhanced environment.	Quality of lesson outline Quality of questioning Quality of performance task rubric
NETS for Teachers III. Teaching, Learning, and the Curriculum—Teachers implement curriculum plans that include methods and strategies for applying technology to maximize student learning.	Teachers: A. facilitate technology-enhanced experiences that address content standards and student technology standards.	Design and use of technology tool in lesson outline
	B. use technology to support learner-centered strategies that address the diverse needs of students.	Use of technology tool in lesson outline
	C. apply technology to develop students' higher-order skills and creativity.	Questions developed as part of lesson
NETS for Teachers V. Productivity and Professional Practice—Teachers use technology to enhance their productivity and professional practice.	Teachers: B. continually evaluate and reflect on professional practice to make informed decisions regarding the use of technology in support of student learning.	Discussion of electronic coin toss vs. hands-on experience
NETS for Teachers VI. Social, Ethical, Legal, and Human Issues—Teachers understand the social, ethical, legal, and human issues surrounding the use of technology in PK–12 schools and apply that understanding in practice.	Teachers: B. apply technology resources to enable and empower learners with diverse backgrounds, characteristics, and abilities.	Lesson outline in meeting needs of students defined in classroom
Mathematics Standard 5: Data Analysis and Probability	Instructional programs from PK–12 should enable all students to— • develop and evaluate inferences and predictions that are based on data • understand and apply basic concepts of probability	Discussion, reflection, quality of questions provided in lesson outline; performance rubric created

Completion of the following assignment rubric is part of the class discussion on assignment elements.

Rubric: "What's Up?" Lesson Assignments

CRITERIA	LEVELS OF PERFORMANCE			
	1	2	3	4
Developmental Appropriateness	No grade level or class description provided.	Grade level and class description are provided, but lesson is not developmentally appropriate.		Lesson is developmentally appropriate for grade level and students.
Alignment with Standards	Standard is not defined.		Lesson has elements that are in alignment with the target standard.	
Student Centered				
Active Engagement				
Effective Utilization of the Tool	Technology tool is not utilized.	Technology tool is not utilized appropriately to meet objective of lesson.		
Questioning Strategies Employed				Questioning elicits higher-order thinking while providing assessment information.
Development of an Appropriate Student Performance Assessment Rubric	Assessment rubric is inappropriate for task defined.			Rubric has appropriate levels, well-defined criteria, and _____ (to be completed by candidates).

Tools and Resources

SOFTWARE

Spreadsheet software such as child-oriented tools Graph Club (Tom Snyder) or TableTop (The Learning Company)

HyperLogo/HyperStudio or a Logo programming language such as Terrapin Logo (Terrapin), MicroWorlds, and the Terrapin Logo Probability curriculum

HARDWARE

Computer, graphing calculators

WEB SITES

Box Models Data and Probability:
http://illuminations.nctm.org/illuminations.html?ima th/6–8/BoxModel/index.html~mainFrame

Electronic Kee Books: www.keeboo.com

Interactive Coin Flipping:
http://shazam.econ.ubc.ca/flip/index.html

Kids Can Program: www.kidscanprogram.com/

Credits

Sharnell Jackson, Chicago Public Schools, Barrington, Illinois, sharnellj@aol.com

Valeria Amburgey, Northern Kentucky University, Highland Heights, Kentucky, amburgey@nku.edu

James Wiebe, California State University, Los Angeles, jwiebe@calstatela.edu

Comments/Stories

This is an activity that takes some advanced planning in the use of the technology in conjunction with the content. Because candidates must access the electronic coin toss in advance, they must be aware of the expectations prior to coming to class. This activity has been conducted both having candidates develop the HyperStudio teaching tool as well as having it collaboratively completed in class. Having candidates develop the tool provided much richer outcomes than having it developed collaboratively in class. However, it took students considerably longer to do. When a short time was given to develop the tool, candidates came to class with the tool partially developed, then assisted each other with completion. Because the tool is controlled by the coin flips, the candidates experimented with probability many more times than had they not developed the tool. In examining their reflective journals, candidates commented on the amount of time it took but later recognized the value in "learning by doing" in their own learning.

Data from Our Environment

Program/Grade Range: Elementary, Middle School

Subject: Science

Topic: Collecting and Analyzing Data about the Local Environment

Profile: Professional Education

Abstract: Teacher candidates learn how to create an electronic collaborative project by collecting and analyzing data in their local environment. They share their data with other teams to compare and contrast variables within different environments. Technology is used in collection, analysis, and presentation of data. Candidates collaborate with other teams on the Internet to gain additional insights. This activity is designed to simulate how teachers create a similar project for their own elementary school students while exploring the curriculum and management issues necessary to consider when planning for instruction.

STANDARDS

NETS FOR TEACHERS

III. TEACHING, LEARNING, AND THE CURRICULUM—*Teachers implement curriculum plans that include methods and strategies for applying technology to maximize student learning. Teachers:*

    C. apply technology to develop students' higher-order skills and creativity.

IV. ASSESSMENT AND EVALUATION—*Teachers apply technology to facilitate a variety of effective assessment and evaluation strategies. Teachers:*

    A. apply technology in assessing student learning of subject matter using a variety of assessment techniques.

    B. use technology resources to collect and analyze data, interpret results, and communicate findings to improve instructional practice and maximize student learning.

SCIENCE

Content Standard A: Science as Inquiry

    Grades K–8

    A1. Abilities necessary to do scientific inquiry

    A2. Understanding about scientific inquiry

Content Standard C: Life Science

    Grades K–4

    C1. The characteristics of organisms

    C2. Life cycles of organisms

    C3. Organisms and environments

    Grades 5–8

    C1. Structure and function in living systems

    C2. Reproduction and heredity

    C3. Regulation and behavior

    C5. Diversity and adaptations of organisms

Content Standard D: Earth and Space Science

    Grades K–4

    D1. Properties of earth materials

    D2. Objects in the sky

    D3. Changes in earth and sky

    Grades 5–8

    D1. Structure of the earth system

    D2. Earth's history

    D3. Earth in the solar system

Lesson Description

	TEACHER PREP FACULTY	TEACHER CANDIDATES	FACULTY NOTES
PREPARATION	Assign teacher candidates appropriate background reading on the topic from texts or supplementary materials. Gather materials: • Water testing kits to determine pH, temperature, water composition, etc. • Probeware as available • Soil analysis kits to determine pH, temperature, soil composition, and so on • Weather kits to determine temperature, barometric pressure, humidity, and so on • PDAs or wireless laptops to record data • Digital cameras to take pictures of the environment Identify locations within the community for candidates to investigate that have contrasting environments. Establish collaboration with teams using the Internet. Check accessibility of multimedia equipment for culminating presentations.	Complete background reading as assigned in class.	This activity is designed for each investigating group to have a complete set of materials as outlined. If the project is stretched out over a period of time, the kits can be shared or rotated. Check with the university about loaning equipment to students to collect data. Often there are policies to follow. This activity prompts candidates to develop a multimedia presentation. Consider which technology focus is appropriate for the candidates, either individually or as a whole: a multimedia presentation either using or not using a class Web site. Be prepared to discuss the difference and rationale with the candidates.
INTRODUCTION	Read a story or children's book about the environment to set the stage. Model how to use literature to spark interest in science and its connection to stories both fiction and nonfiction. Suggestions for books are listed in Tools and Resources. Discuss a variety of environments, focusing on those within the local community and the communities candidates will be working in. Divide the class into teams with four to six in each group. Assign the task of investigating one environment of the group's choice. Provide time and guidance as the class and individual teams discuss the task and begin to formulate questions. Have candidates create a plan for collecting data.	Identify elements of the environment in the children's literature read by the faculty member. How many of these are in the local community? Participate in the discussion of local environments. Identify characteristics of the environments that make each unique. In groups choose one specific environment to investigate. As a whole class, formulate three to five questions about each site selected to be answered from an analysis of the data from all groups (e.g., Is the air temperature warmer at the beach or on the mountain top and why? How does the barometric pressure on the mountain top compare with the barometric pressure at the lake and why?). Draft a plan on how to collect data.	Guide the discussion to identify environments where it is possible to collect information about air, water, soil, geology, vegetation, and animal life. Sites should be as environmentally different as possible (e.g., flatland, mountain, beach, riverbed, wetland, forest, lake margin, or desert.) When discussing the elements of the lesson, include information about school district management policies if a class of elementary students were to engage in the same activity. These include • permission forms for field trips, • travel reservations, and • school district guidelines for field trips and chaperones.
IMPLEMENTATION	Demonstrate the use of tools and technology to collect data. Discuss the collaborative group nature of the data collection. Encourage candidates to compare their formulation of a data collection plan with that of elementary students. What concerns and controls might they need to be aware of and plan for?	Make sure that each member of your group knows how to use the scientific and technology-based tools. If not, peer tutor or find alternative ways to help your team members learn what is needed. Within the group, make decisions about who will collect information about the air, soil, water, geology, vegetation, and animal life in each location and from books and Web sites.	To add a different experience for candidates, have them practice using the tools and technology by collecting data from around the campus at as many different environments as possible. The use of PDAs would allow candidates to use spreadsheets and databases and beam each other their responses or upload them onto the server.

TEACHER PREP FACULTY	TEACHER CANDIDATES	FACULTY NOTES
IMPLEMENTATION Discuss and demonstrate how to record the collected data in a way that facilitates sharing among teams. Consider creating a template of required information and posting on a class Web site or through an online discussion forum to facilitate easy sharing of data. Assist candidates in developing a plan to accomplish the task. Direct candidates to develop a multimedia presentation on the results of their investigation in light of the questions posed. Before groups disperse, discuss the assessment rubric below. Make modifications where appropriate. Obtain a schedule of when the groups are visiting the various environments. Consider monitoring or accompanying several of the groups on their investigative trip. Have candidates post data, pictures, and observations on the Web site, and have them compare their information with that of other groups.	Develop a plan to accomplish the task and apply a time line to the plan. Expand plan to include collecting information about the physical and biological interactions and relationships (e.g., How are the number and species of animals related to the physical characteristics of the environment? How is the amount of sunlight related to the type of plants?). Include in plan how to collect appropriate data for multimedia presentation. Participate in discussion of assessment rubric. Adjust the plan to fit assessment needs. Travel to the site and conduct an investigation, collecting required data. Use the laptop, PDA, and/or digital camera to record anecdotal information about taking the data as well as recording the data itself. Post data, pictures, and observations on Web site. Examine the data from groups in other locations and compare and contrast your data with theirs.	The use of wireless laptops can make the examination of Internet-based resources on-site a much richer experience. Multimedia presentations can take many forms. Encourage candidates to use familiar equipment (video cameras, still pictures, etc.) in unfamiliar ways such as documenting characteristics and elements found on their field trip. Preparation to collect visual images and samples should be considered in the work plan. As the lesson is being demonstrated, periodically step outside the role of faculty teacher of the candidates to debrief the rationale and options for working with elementary students. Focus on both management (equipment and student behavior) as well as developing conceptual understanding with young children.
CULMINATION Schedule presentations. Assess presentations using rubric provided. Facilitate a discussion of the use of the activity in an elementary school setting. Consider completing a quick-write posing the question of the applicability of the assignment to the elementary school setting.	Prepare and present a multimedia presentation demonstrating the team's findings and conclusions. Use the rubric to assess the presentations of the other groups. Conclude presentation with adaptation for a school environment.	If a Web-based multimedia presentation is assigned rather than a stand-alone, such as PowerPoint or HyperStudio, adjust the assessment rubric accordingly. The development of a content-based Web site can be a valuable tool for the candidates as they go out to do their student teaching/internship. Candidates can create lessons that access the findings on the class Web site.

Assessment

Rubric: Data from Our Environment

CRITERIA	LEVELS OF PERFORMANCE			
	BELOW EXPECTATIONS 1	APPROACHES EXPECTATIONS 2	MEETS EXPECTATIONS 3	EXCEEDS EXPECTATIONS 4
Quality of the Multimedia Project	Multimedia project is incomplete and scores at the Beginner Level on the "Multimedia Presentation" rubric in Appendix C.	Multimedia project is adequate and scores at the Novice Level on the "Multimedia Presentation" rubric in Appendix C.	Multimedia project is very well done and scores at the Intermediate Level on the "Multimedia Presentation" rubric in Appendix C.	Multimedia project is excellent and scores at the Expert Level on the "Multimedia Presentation" rubric in Appendix C.
Environmental Description	Description of the physical and biological environment is lacking any useful information.	Description of the physical and biological environment is informative, but some facts are not accurate.	Description of the physical and biological environment is factual and informative.	Description of the physical and biological environment is factual, very informative, and rich with data.
Rationale for Ecological Interactions	Explanation of the rationale for various ecological interactions within the environments reflects no research and very little thinking.	Explanation of the rationale for various ecological interactions within the environments reflects some research and thinking.	Explanation of the rationale for various ecological interactions within the environments reflects research and good thinking.	Explanation of the rationale for various ecological interactions within the environments reflects considerable research and higher-order thinking.
Data Collection	Data collection tools were not used effectively and very little data were collected, contributing to an unsuccessful project.	Data collection tools were used to collect less than half the required data, contributing to the partial success of the project.	Data collection tools were used effectively to collect more than half the required data, contributing to the partial success of the project.	Data collection tools were used very effectively to produce a rich data set, contributing to the overall success of the project.

Note: Use only the portions of the "Multimedia Presentation" rubric in Appendix C that are relevant to this project.

Tools and Resources

SOFTWARE

Database software (Filemaker Pro, Access, etc.), presentation software (Web-editing software, PowerPoint, HyperStudio, etc.)

HARDWARE

PDAs or laptop computers with scientific probeware to collect environmental data, digital cameras, and computers with Internet connections

WEB SITES

The Educator's Palm: http://educatorspalm.org/

Using Mobile Computing to Enhance Field Study: www.oise.utoronto.ca/cscl/papers/rieger.pdf

Wade through the Wetlands: www.apple.com/education/k12/success/ (This is only one success story in which students use technology to explore their environments.)

REFERENCE TEXTS

General

Field guides for plant, animal, and geologic identification

Children's Literature
(Use to introduce the lesson.)

Aardema, V. (1981). *Bringing the rain to Kapiti Plain: A Nandi tale.* New York: Dial.

Arnosky, J. (1988). *I was born in a tree and raised by bees.* New York: Simon & Schuster.

Arnosky, J. (1989). *In the forest: A portfolio of paintings.* New York: Lathrop, Lee and Shepard.

Bash, B. (1989). *Desert giant: The world of the saguaro cactus (tree tales).* Boston: Little, Brown, and Co.

Carson, R. (1991). *The sea around us.* Oxford, England: Oxford University Press.

Cole, S. (1985). *When the tide is low.* New York: William Morrow & Co.

Eastman, P. D. (1960). *Are you my mother?* New York: Random House.

Larrick, N. (1983). *When dark comes dancing: A bedtime poetry book.* New York: Putnam.

Lester, A. (1990). *Imagine.* New York: Houghton Mifflin.

Siebert, D. (1988). *Mojave*. New York: HarperCollins.

Whipple, L. (Ed.). (1989). *Eric Carle's animals, animals*. New York: Puffin.

KITS FOR COOPERATIVE GROUP INVESTIGATIONS

Water testing kits to determine pH, temperature, water composition, and so on

Probeware as available

Soil analysis kits to determine pH, temperature, soil composition, and so on

Weather kits to determine temperature, barometric pressure, humidity, and so on

PDAs or laptops to record data

Digital cameras to take pictures of the environment

Credits

Kathy Norman, California State University, San Marcos, California, **knorman@csusm.edu**

Rosie O'Brien Vojtek, Bristol School District and NSDC, Bristol, Connecticut, **rvojtek@home.com**

Louisiana Review Team:

Juanita Guerin, University of Louisiana, Lafayette, Louisiana, **jguerin@louisiana.edu**

Dolores Champagne, THE Quest Project, Lafayette, Louisiana, **djchampagne@louisiana.edu**

Sue Jackson, THE Quest Project, Lafayette, Louisiana, **sujax@louisiana.edu**

Gloria Hendrickson, THE Quest Project, Lafayette, Louisiana, **gloria@louisiana.edu**

Comments/Stories

At the initial assignment, the candidates were overwhelmed with the complexity of the task. However, when they realized that they would have a hands-on experience collecting real data, the adventure of the group-arranged field trip raised the excitement of the exercise. Many candidates brought their own children or siblings along on the trip to provide additional insight. Groups seemed continually amazed at how the use of the technology in the data collection process makes the presentation of the results as well as the on-site analysis far more efficient.

Survey of Systems

Program/Grade Range: Elementary

Subject: Science

Topic: Systems and Interactions

Profile: Professional Preparation

Abstract: This activity combines the learning of a standards-specified science theme and the application of technology with the pedagogy of a cooperative learning model. In preparation for creating a teaching tool on systems for elementary students, teacher candidates investigate systems and interactions in their own environment and community while experiencing Kagan's model of cooperative learning. Technology is used to obtain evidence to support and describe their system as well as to display and present their findings.

Note: Although the Kagan model is used in this lesson, it can be easily modified to fit other models of cooperative learning.

STANDARDS

NETS FOR TEACHERS

I. **TECHNOLOGY OPERATIONS AND CONCEPTS**—*Teachers demonstrate a sound understanding of technology operations and concepts. Teachers:*

A. demonstrate introductory knowledge, skills, and understanding of concepts related to technology (as described in the ISTE NETS for Students).

II. **PLANNING AND DESIGNING LEARNING ENVIRONMENTS AND EXPERIENCES**—*Teachers plan and design effective learning environments and experiences supported by technology. Teachers:*

A. design developmentally appropriate learning opportunities that apply technology-enhanced instructional strategies to support the diverse needs of learners.

B. apply current research on teaching and learning with technology when planning learning environments and experiences.

C. identify and locate technology resources and evaluate them for accuracy and suitability.

V. **PRODUCTIVITY AND PROFESSIONAL PRACTICE**—*Teachers use technology to enhance their productivity and professional practice. Teachers:*

B. continually evaluate and reflect on professional practice to make informed decisions regarding the use of technology in support of student learning.

C. apply technology to increase productivity.

VI. **SOCIAL, ETHICAL, LEGAL, AND HUMAN ISSUES**—*Teachers understand the social, ethical, legal, and human issues surrounding the use of technology in PK–12 schools and apply that understanding in practice. Teachers:*

A. model and teach legal and ethical practice related to technology use.

B. apply technology resources to enable and empower learners with diverse backgrounds, characteristics, and abilities.

C. identify and use technology resources that affirm diversity.

SCIENCE

Content Standards: K–12, Unifying Concepts and Processes

Standard: As a result of activities in Grades K–12, all students should develop understanding and abilities aligned with the following concepts and processes:

- Systems, order, and organization
- Evidence, models, and explanation

Lesson Description

	TEACHER PREP FACULTY	TEACHER CANDIDATES	FACULTY NOTES
PREPARATION	Check equipment access for teacher candidate use for the duration of the activity. Have candidates review Kagan's cooperative learning model.	From previous work in models of student interaction and teaching, review Kagan's cooperative learning model.	This project culminates in the dissemination of the developed projects to class members either through a class Web site or a distributed CD. Make a decision in advance about the means of sharing projects and the appropriate arrangements.

TEACHER PREP FACULTY	TEACHER CANDIDATES	FACULTY NOTES
INTRODUCTION		
Introduce the notion of systems in science as well as in other curriculum areas.	Participate in the discussion about systems in science.	As the activity begins, record in a prominent place the elements of the Kagan model as the sequence proceeds (e.g., Identify the Topic). The recording of the elements will facilitate the debriefing of the model at the end of the discussion.
Facilitate a discussion about the definition of a system and the critical attributes.	Divide into groups of three or four.	
Place candidates into groups of three or four.	**Identify the Topic**—As a group identify the system to be studied. Select a system that is of interest to children at the elementary school age level. If the system is not one discussed in class, be sure to discuss the selection with the professor.	
Have teams brainstorm systems in their environment. Explain and share systems listed as a class discussion. Discuss the interaction and interdependence of the components of each system identified. Brainstorm additional systems that are familiar to children.	Identify three characteristics of the system that make it a system composed of interdependent parts. Focus the investigation on the three interdependent components.	
From the list of systems created during the discussion, have each team select a system to be studied. Teams determine how to approach their investigation, assign roles and tasks, set goals, and establish a time line.		
Describe the culminating project: the development of a Web page designed for elementary students that explains at least three interdependent components of the system.		
IMPLEMENTATION		
Coach teams to collect supporting evidence for each of the three interdependent components. Information resources including Web sites are in Tools and Resources.	**Plan the Investigation**—In teams, locate information about the system.	Encourage teams to select a topic relevant to the grade level they are teaching. They should look at their project from a child's point of view. Have candidates discuss the topics that would make the Web page relevant to the age level targeted.
Ensure teams are clear about the assignment. Assign teams to develop an assessment rubric for the Web page they are creating. (See below as a starting point.) Ask that each team obtain your approval for the scoring rubric before beginning the project.	• Identify the components of the system.	Teams may need to limit the scope of their project based on time constraints. Consider what is reasonable.
Teams should organize their evidence, findings, analysis, and summary to create an effective Web page for posting or linking to from the class Web site.	• Describe the functions of each interdependent component.	The specifications for the rubric should include features of the Web page that push the candidates' technical skill. Be specific about the features required as the minimum.
Have teams	• Explain how the components interact to carry out the shared purpose of the system.	
• locate information about their system,	Select three interdependent components to study in detail.	
• identify at least three interdependent components of the system,	**Carry Out the Investigation**—Collect supporting evidence for each of the three components above. Locate information on the Web, in addition to other sources. Include images.	
• describe the functions of each component, and	Begin to develop a Web page about the system studied for elementary students to use. The Web page must be well organized and include evidence, analysis, and a summary of findings.	
• explain how the components interact to carry out the shared purpose of the system.	As a group, develop an assessment rubric to be used by your team, other teams, and the instructor for assessing Web pages. Include at least two criteria—science content and Web page design.	

TEACHER PREP FACULTY	TEACHER CANDIDATES	FACULTY NOTES

CULMINATION

TEACHER PREP FACULTY

Relate the experience to a discussion of systems in the areas of science including biology, chemistry, and physical science.

Using Inspiration software, record the connections made during a discussion of how the notion of systems can be applied in many ways.

Have candidates share the Web pages in class. Encourage the discussion to center on the use of the Web page for students of the age level targeted. Have peers evaluate the Web page using each team's rubric. Debrief the activity in terms of how the tool can be used in the content of an interdisciplinary unit.

At the conclusion of the presentations, have candidates write a one- to two-page paper to compare and contrast their system with the other teams' systems. Included is the identification of the interdependent components of the other systems. Encourage candidates to make generalizations about systems.

Debrief the experience in terms of participating in an activity designed around the Kagan model for cooperative learning. Elicit the parts of the model from the lesson just completed.

TEACHER CANDIDATES

Participate in a discussion of systems in other areas of science as well as other disciplines. Note the use of Inspiration software to make the connections in a visual form.

Share the Project—Share projects with the class as an oral presentation. The posting of the Web pages will provide additional means of sharing work.

At the beginning of each presentation, share the rubric created including a rationale about how it was designed and the scoring mechanism.

Evaluate and Assess—Complete the evaluation of your own project as well as provide constructive feedback for others. Complete a one- to two-page paper comparing the team's system with that of other teams. Identify each system and its interdependent components. What generalizations can be made from what was presented?

Transfer Learning—Participate in the discussion of how the notion of systems is connected to the areas of science of biology, chemistry, and physical science. Make additional connections to other disciplines.

Participate in the debriefing of the experience in terms of having gone through the steps in the Kagan cooperative learning model.

FACULTY NOTES

Providing constructive feedback to peers can sometimes result in mixed reviews. Encourage candidates to provide feedback that will make their peers' projects more responsive to student needs as well as accurate.

Having candidates use a self-created rubric can be an eye-opening experience. Because there are many ways to write indicators that mean relatively the same thing as well as many ways to interpret criteria, candidates will have additional questions on the writing of rubrics that they may not have had prior to this experience.

Note: Consider having an all-class discussion at the conclusion of this lesson on the lesson itself. Opening up a lesson to candidate debriefing can provide them with an opportunity to reflect on their own experience as well as experience effective modeling by the instructor. Include in the debriefing your own reflection on how the lesson went and why changes were made while the lesson was in progress. Share your own thoughts on how you might modify this lesson in the future to obtain better candidate outcomes.

Assessment

The assessment on this lesson can vary widely as candidates participate in the development of a rubric to suit their own project. This means of assessment is quite different from others presented. This rubric shell is designed for the faculty member to provide skeletal criteria, with the candidates filling in the specifications to meet their perception of an exemplary project. The rubric must be completed prior to the beginning of the project and approved by the faculty member. In this way, candidates set their own target of performance while the faculty member makes the judgment of the equity of the rating of outstanding from one rubric to the next. The rubric created by each team is then used by others to assess the team's end-product. Using another group's rubric can be very enlightening in examining clarity of language and discovering ambiguity in the rubric presented.

Rubric: Web Site Design and Content

CRITERIA	LEVELS OF PERFORMANCE			
	NEEDS IMPROVEMENT 1	EMERGING UNDERSTANDING 2	ACCEPTABLE 3	OUTSTANDING 4
Web Site Design (Specify Minimal Attributes)				
Web Site Content				

Tools and Resources

SOFTWARE

Access to software that helps students complete the project (e.g., image software, Internet, graphic organizers such as Inspiration or Kidspiration)

HARDWARE

Access to hardware and peripherals that help students complete the project (e.g., digital cameras, scanners, CD-ROM burners)

WEB SITES

Cooperative Learning Resources

The Collaborative Classroom:
www.ncrel.org/sdrs/areas/rpl_esys/collab.htm

Cooperative Learning: **www.clcrc.com/pages/cl.html**

Cooperative Learning—The Building Tool Room:
www.newhorizons.org/trm_atriskinstr.html

Cooperative Learning—Elementary Activities:
http://sps.k12.mo.us/coop/ecoopmain.html

The Cooperative Learning Center at the University of Minnesota: **www.clcrc.com/**

Kagan Model

The Essential Elements of Cooperative Learning in the Classroom:
www.ed.gov/databases/ERIC_Digests/ed370881.html

We Can Talk: Cooperative Learning in the Elementary ESL Classroom:
www.cal.org/ericcll/digest/kagan001.html

Science-Related Systems

Anatomy and Physiology of the Cardiovascular System:
www.merck.com/disease/heart/coronary_health/anatomy/home.html

The Circulatory System: **http://gened.emc.maricopa.edu/bio/bio181/BIOBK/BioBookcircSYS.html**

Solar System Live: **www.fourmilab.ch/solar/solar.html**

Solar System Simulator: **http://space.jpl.nasa.gov/**

Credits

Rosie Vojtek, Ivy Drive Elementary School, Bristol, Connecticut, **rvojtek@home.com**

Kathy Norman, California State University, San Marcos, California, **knorman@csusm.edu**

Comments/Stories

The initial discussion of systems, interaction, and interdependence provides the framework for the entire lesson. Some candidates struggle to come up with child-relevant examples. If the candidates are even slightly fuzzy about their understanding of the concept, they struggle with developing child-relevant examples and developing the Web page. However, the struggle is worth the time as the learning is much more deep and results in better application to other curriculum areas. Take the warning about limiting the project very seriously. Some candidates have developed very sophisticated Web pages because they enjoy the process and see the relevance for their own teaching. The total collection of candidate Web pages provides a nice compilation for the class.

Diverse Perspectives on History

Program/Grade Range: Elementary

Subject: Social Studies

Topic: Diverse Perspectives on History

Profile: Professional Preparation

Abstract: The purpose of this activity is to have teacher candidates look at history from a nonmainstream perspective. Nonmainstream includes perspectives from underrepresented populations and those not usually articulated in textbooks. Based on their research, candidates create a multimedia presentation for peers that includes computer, video, audio, and other media of their choosing. Presentations are archived on the class Web site for use by the entire class.

STANDARDS

NETS FOR TEACHERS

II. **PLANNING AND DESIGNING LEARNING ENVIRONMENTS AND EXPERIENCES**—*Teachers plan and design effective learning environments and experiences supported by technology. Teachers:*

   A. design developmentally appropriate learning opportunities that apply technology-enhanced instructional strategies to support the diverse needs of learners.

   B. apply current research on teaching and learning with technology when planning learning environments and experiences.

   C. identify and locate technology resources and evaluate them for accuracy and suitability.

   D. plan for the management of technology resources within the context of learning activities.

   E. plan strategies to manage student learning in a technology-enhanced environment.

VI. **SOCIAL, ETHICAL, LEGAL, AND HUMAN ISSUES**—*Teachers understand the social, ethical, legal, and human issues surrounding the use of technology in PK–12 schools and apply that understanding in practice. Teachers:*

   C. identify and use technology resources that affirm diversity.

SOCIAL STUDIES

I. **CULTURE**—*Social studies programs should include experiences that provide for the study of culture and cultural diversity, so that the learner can:*

   B. give examples of how experiences may be interpreted differently by people from diverse cultural perspectives and frames of reference.

Lesson Description

	TEACHER PREP FACULTY	TEACHER CANDIDATES	FACULTY NOTES
PREPARATION	Refer teacher candidates to prior study of national, state, and district documents or compile a resource list of the areas of history mandated by the state or districts at each of the elementary grade levels. Prepare a model lesson using an area of history you prefer. When you present the lesson, highlight how you obtained some of the information electronically, explain how you evaluated the validity of the information, and provide an overview of the lesson developed using electronic media. Select a presentation medium that candidates have access to. (Check candidate project criteria in the assessment rubric to be sure your example is consistent.)	Review the national standards, state frameworks, and district and regional guidelines for the topics taught in history at the elementary grade level.	Place this lesson within the study of how to teach historical facts (and fiction). Because the selection of topics is based on mandated curriculum materials, candidates should have had experience with the national, state, district, and regional guidelines before this activity is introduced.

TEACHER PREP FACULTY	TEACHER CANDIDATES	FACULTY NOTES
INTRODUCTION Using an Upside Down Tale, such as *Jack and the Beanstalk* and *The Beanstalk Incident*, discuss the notion that historical events can be conveyed from multiple perspectives. In the story, who is at fault in each version of the story? Which version is accurate? Have candidates justify their answer.	Listen to the two versions of the folk tale Jack and the Beanstalk. In small groups discuss your responses to the following questions: What did you learn? Which version is accurate? Why do you think that?	Be prepared to be asked "Why do we need to know this?" This is a pedagogical question. Regarding content, candidates have become accustomed to accepting historical information as presented. Candidate questions tend to center on who, what, when, and where. They seldom ask the why and how with regard to historical content.
IMPLEMENTATION Relate the multiple perspectives to a historical event. For example, discuss limitations of Eurocentric perspectives as presented in the majority of texts. Give specific examples of valid interpretations of history from underrepresented groups. Example: the Lakota perspective on the Battle of the Little Big Horn (Greasy Grass) as opposed to the U.S. Cavalry view (Custer's Last Stand). Using think-pair-share, ask candidates to think of similar or parallel examples from other cultural groups or other perspectives of history. Discuss what those examples mean to candidates. How do candidates interpret the significance of the diversity of perspectives? What value do they place on viewing multiple perspectives of historical events or processes and what does that mean in terms of understanding history in context or as a process? Have candidates share personal experiences in which their awareness of an underrepresented group's perspective changed their thinking. Divide candidates into pairs or small groups. Have each group select a historical event that will effectively introduce a unit. Ensure that the grade levels are distributed, no events are duplicated, and the events selected are in alignment with the state and district guidelines. Instruct candidates that they are to produce a lesson plan that introduces the historical event from a nonmainstream perspective. The manner in which the point of view is presented should cause elementary students to think critically about what is deemed historical fact and engender a desire to research multiple points of view to an incident. The lesson will be presented to the class with the lesson plan and supporting information posted on the class Web site. The manner of presenting the lesson is open-ended but has a time limitation and a required use of technology to enhance audience understanding. (See rubric for specifications of assessment.)	Debrief the historical example provided. Which is the "correct" version? What does this tell you about textbooks? Use think-pair-share to discuss what other events in the elementary curriculum have multiple perspectives that might be particularly interesting to students. In pairs, share personal experiences in which an event from an underrepresented group's perspective influenced your thinking on the event. How does the introduction of diverse perspectives on historical events affect teaching social studies in the elementary school? **Project** In small project groups, select one of the events shared in class or another that is in alignment with the elementary social studies curriculum. Create a lesson plan that uses diverse perspectives on the event to introduce a unit of study. The lesson plan must • be in the approved format following the tenets of a well-designed lesson including age appropriateness and attention to second language learners and special needs students; • use some form of technology appropriately; • use information obtained from a variety of sources including electronic resources; • incorporate high-level questioning techniques that cause students to think about viewing events from diverse perspectives; and • include a synopsis of the unit of study for which the lesson is an appropriate introduction. Be prepared to present the lesson to the class as an oral presentation as well as post the end product on the class Web site.	Professors traditionally steer away from assessing the affective domain of learning (dispositions). However, to meet the objectives of this lesson, affective outcomes (candidates' dispositions) must be measured. For example, is there evidence of motivation to view history from multiple perspectives? Is the candidate committed to acquiring that knowledge? The combination of the discussion, lesson, presentation, and reflection should provide evidence that can be assessed using the rubric provided in the assessment section. As an alternative project, consider having candidates create a WebQuest for elementary students to explore alternative perspectives on the event. For examples, examine the WebQuests on Black History (see Tools and Resources). Look at the chapter on model strategies for additional information on WebQuests. As candidate groups are selecting events to use for their project, ensure that all grade levels are covered as well as underrepresented groups. Strive for balance in the perspectives presented. Before candidates begin work on the project, consider having a brief discussion about the scoring rubric. Allowing candidates to modify the rubric to fit what they consider to be important focuses the conversation on the quality of the outcome. Follow up the discussion by emphasizing that candidate knowledge of and input to the assessment criteria enhance candidates' focus on what the teacher and the candidates agree to be high-quality performance.

CULMINATION	TEACHER PREP FACULTY	TEACHER CANDIDATES	FACULTY NOTES
	Facilitate candidates' presentation of the lesson with accompanying discussion. At the conclusion of all the presentations, conduct a discussion. Ask candidates to share their thinking about common themes they noticed, what they learned that they didn't know before. Did they see patterns in the use of resources, and how do they think they could use this at the grade level they want to teach? Have candidates write a reflection about their individual contribution in the context of group work, what they learned from the lesson, and how they felt about what they learned. Focus on revelations and concerns about approaching events from diverse perspectives with elementary students.	As a group, present the lesson in class and respond to questions from peers. Listen carefully to other presentations. Pose clarifying questions. Participate in a whole class discussion that includes the following questions: • What were the common themes in each situation? • What did you notice about the resources used by each group? • How can these lessons be modified for various ages and maturities of students? Write a reflection about your experience. The reflection must include answers to the following questions: • What was your individual contribution to the lesson development as a member of the group? • What did you learn from the lesson? • How do you feel about what you learned?	Examine the topics in advance of the presentation day. Look at the sequence to see if there is an order that will enhance candidate understanding of how important it is to present diverse perspectives on an event. Consider a chronological presentation based on the date of the event being highlighted or order them by grade level.

Assessment

Lesson Presentation

The following assessment rubric is one in which a generic scoring scale is applied to the specific criteria for the lesson. In this model of assessment, candidates are familiar with the scoring statements as they are applied to multiple assignments and settings. The criteria for the specific project are developed to guide candidates in the development of their project and specify the important elements of the project.

Rubric: Generic Scoring Scale Applied to Lesson Criteria

CRITERIA	PERFORMANCE INDICATORS
Lesson Plan	The lesson plan is in the approved format following the tenets of a well-designed lesson. The lesson is presented in a manner appropriate to the age level of the students, contains vocabulary development techniques to enhance the comprehension by second language learners, and attends to the unique requirements of special needs students.
Technology	The lesson uses appropriate electronic media to enhance the understanding of the diverse perspectives presented. The technology is embedded in the lesson as a natural part of the instruction.
Resources	Multiple resources were accessed and are appropriately cited. Resources include information obtained from the Internet. Primary source information is included.
Questioning	The lesson incorporates high-level questioning strategies that cause students to think about the diverse perspectives on the event presented. Questions challenge students to confront their perceptions of people different from themselves and genuinely consider alternative points of view.
Unit Context	The lesson is preceded by a synopsis of the unit for which it is the introduction. The brief synopsis describes a unit of instruction that is in alignment with the curriculum for the target grade level. The lesson is an appropriate introduction to the unit described.
Oral Presentation	The oral presentation is well organized, interesting, informative, and stays within the time frame requirements. All members of the group participate in the oral presentation. The group interacts with the class and is able to respond knowledgeably to questions.
Web Posting	The lesson plan and supporting material including resource citations are posted on the class Web site in a timely manner and in a format that is accessible to classmates. Any suggested modifications have been made prior to posting. The posting is free of grammatical errors and is of high quality to be shared with anyone who accesses the Web site.
Reflection	Reflection follows general guidelines on reflections. All three questions have been answered in an insightful and thoughtful way. Reflection includes personal reactions that show growth in understanding the need to expose elementary students to diverse perspectives on historical events. The reflection shows a positive disposition toward including teaching that attends to diverse perspectives.

Scoring Scale

5 — The work exceeds expectations and shows an exceptionally high level of creativity and sophisticated application of knowledge and skills. It contains elements that were not considered or discussed in class, thus setting it in a category all of its own. (Rarely given score.)

4 — The work exceeds the standard and shows very strong applications of the knowledge and skills.

3 — The work meets the standard and demonstrates the appropriate application of knowledge and skills. It contains minor errors that do not diminish the quality.

2 — The work does not quite meet the standard. It shows inconsistent application of knowledge and skills. The minor errors are significant enough to detract from the overall quality. Additional work is required.

1 — The work does not meet the standard and shows limited understanding of the knowledge and skills. The work lacks depth and/or is incomplete with significant errors and/or omissions.

0 — No work is presented.

Note: NCATE asks for assessment of candidate knowledge, skills, and dispositions. Disposition is a very difficult area to assess as it is value-laden and subjective. Because this activity attempts to get at issues of disposition toward diverse cultures and points of view, the following scale can be used to assess the reflection. The combination of the disposition assessment in the oral presentation and the reflection should provide assessment data to the faculty member on candidate attitudes at this point in their education.

Through discussion, lesson presentation, and reflection, the candidate:

3 Shows a strong, positive disposition for presenting historical events from diverse points of view, exhibits evidence of continuing to pose higher-level questions causing students to think about multiple perspectives, and is committed to personally acquiring that knowledge.

2 Demonstrates an inconsistent disposition toward presenting historical events from diverse points of view.

1 Is ethnocentric, resistant to multiple perspectives of a historical event, and perceives there is one way to present information to students and one correct interpretation of what occurred.

Tools and Resources

SOFTWARE
Presentation software, concept-mapping software, word processor

HARDWARE
One computer with Internet access for presentations; easy access to computers for students as they prepare assignments; access to video and audio recorders and playback tools (VCR and TV) for preparation of presentation

WEB SITES
American Indian Study Center at UCLA:
www.sscnet.ucla.edu/indian/lib/aiscLibrary.htm (This library's mission is to collect and provide access to accurate and timely information about American Indian cultures in both historical and contemporary perspectives. The site provides a link to the California Digital Library.)

Black History: Exploring African-American Issues on the Web: **www.kn.pacbell.com/wired/BHM/AfroAm.html** (This site contains WebQuests, treasure hunts, and other jewels of information.)

Journal of Negro Education Online:
http://ine.law.howard.edu (This site contains a variety of resources for investigating alternative perspectives to issues of racism. The reading level is above that of elementary education students but the information can be used as a resource.)

National Association for Multicultural Education: **www.nameorg.org** (This site provides information about conferences and speakers who often address topics of interest.)

NativeNET: **http://cs.fdl.cc.mn.us/natnet** (This site provides audio archives as well as links to many specialized Web sites on Native American issues and perspectives.)

Smithsonian: **www.si.edu** (Smithsonian has unprecedented resources. Check search section for topics to be covered.)

Credits
David Whitehorse, California State University, San Marcos, California, **dwhitehorse@csusm.edu**

Joyce Friske, Jenks Public Schools, Jenks, Oklahoma, **friskej@jenksusa.k12.ok.us**

Leslie Conery, ISTE, Eugene, Oregon, **lconery@iste.org**

Comments/Stories
We have found many candidates are initially resistant to looking for resources about groups that are not typically covered well in the textbooks. The research provides them with the realization that not all textbooks cover material completely or with what is considered to be a fair treatment. The increasing number of Web sites emerging on perspectives that are different from the textbooks provides ample resources for teacher candidates. However, the credibility of the some of the Web sites is questionable. A discussion on the source and credibility of information is a very valuable augmentation to this lesson.

Oral History

Program/Grade Range: Elementary

Subject: Social Studies

Topic: Oral History

Profile: General Preparation, Professional Preparation

Abstract: Oral history is the recollections or reminiscences of living people about their past. Unlike role-playing, oral history is historical inquiry by obtaining information or stories from everyday people. The purpose of this activity is to model a lesson in which history comes alive as teacher candidates (and students) are surrounded by and are a part of the making of history. Candidates participate in the creation of an oral history as they interview individuals on a predetermined topic. The oral histories are captured on video, edited, categorized in a database, and archived for later use. Candidates prepare a written account of their experience and post it to the class Web site as a further archive of the experience. The videos and written accounts can later be accessed for use in the classroom as a starting point for further study or as examples of how the project might be done.

STANDARDS

NETS FOR TEACHERS

II. **PLANNING AND DESIGNING LEARNING ENVIRONMENTS AND EXPERIENCES**—*Teachers plan and design effective learning environments and experiences supported by technology. Teachers:*

    A. design developmentally appropriate learning opportunities that apply technology-enhanced instructional strategies to support the diverse needs of learners.

    D. plan for the management of technology resources within the context of learning activities.

    E. plan strategies to manage student learning in a technology-enhanced environment.

III. **TEACHING, LEARNING, AND THE CURRICULUM**—*Teachers implement curriculum plans that include methods and strategies for applying technology to maximize student learning. Teachers:*

    A. facilitate technology-enhanced experiences that address content standards and student technology standards.

    B. use technology to support learner-centered strategies that address the diverse needs of students.

    C. apply technology to develop students' higher-order skills and creativity.

V. **PRODUCTIVITY AND PROFESSIONAL PRACTICE**—*Teachers use technology to enhance their productivity and professional practice. Teachers:*

    B. continually evaluate and reflect on professional practice to make informed decisions regarding the use of technology in support of student learning.

VI. **SOCIAL, ETHICAL, LEGAL, AND HUMAN ISSUES**—*Teachers understand the social, ethical, legal, and human issues surrounding the use of technology in PK–12 schools and apply that understanding in practice. Teachers:*

    B. apply technology resources to enable and empower learners with diverse backgrounds, characteristics, and abilities.

SOCIAL STUDIES

I. **CULTURE**—*Social studies programs should include experiences that provide for the study of culture and cultural diversity, so that the learner can:*

    B. give examples of how experiences may be interpreted differently by people from diverse cultural perspectives and frames of reference.

II. **TIME, CONTINUITY, AND CHANGE**—*Social studies programs should include experiences that provide for the study of the ways human beings view themselves in and over time, so that the learner can:*

    C. compare and contrast different stories or accounts about past events, people, places, or situations, identifying how they contribute to our understanding of the past.

IV. **INDIVIDUAL DEVELOPMENT AND IDENTITY**—*Social studies programs should include experiences that provide for the study of individual development and identity, so that the learner can:*

    G. analyze a particular event to identify reasons individuals might respond to it in different ways.

Lesson Description

	TEACHER PREP FACULTY	TEACHER CANDIDATES	FACULTY NOTES
PREPARATION	Assess the availability of video cameras for use by groups of teacher candidates. Many candidates have access to video cameras while others will need to check one out from university media services. One camera is necessary for each group of candidates. The number of candidates in a group is flexible. Candidates will be editing the video made of the oral history interview. Ensure that candidates have access to video-editing software. Alert university computer lab technicians that the project is being launched and that access to the software will be in high demand. Obtain enough copies of the campus video release form for each group. Have candidates complete background reading on the purpose of oral history and its place in the state and national social studies standards.	Investigate obtaining a video camera for group use later in the project. It is ideal to use a digital video camera, but analog will work when there is a method for digitizing the video. Complete readings on the purpose of oral history. Examine the state and national standards for how oral history fits into a balanced social studies program.	The ability of the candidates to both video the interview and edit the interview for posting on the Web is a function of their skill level with the use of video and Web posting of video. It may be necessary to offer an out-of-class workshop or point to on-campus or online learning opportunities if some members of the class feel weak in the area of using video. Transferring the video from analog to digital (if digital cameras are not used) is very straightforward. See campus services for specific procedures to be used on campus equipment. Assess issues of cultural taboos of videotaping individuals—be sensitive to opposition candidates may encounter. Be prepared with alternatives such as audiotape.
INTRODUCTION	(The introduction to this lesson is done in a modeling or simulation style.) Explain to the class that you are a fountain of information on the topic of _____. (You select the topic. This could be campus information, something you have experienced over time, a hobby, or something fictitious.) Divide the class into groups of three to four candidates. Have each group develop three to four questions to ask you. Have them record the answers. Answer the questions only as asked. Do not embellish the answer with any information. As a class, discussion the information gained through the questioning process. Through class discussion, analyze and evaluate the questions. Make sure that the candidates understand the importance of asking questions that cannot be answered merely by a yes or no.	In small groups, develop three or four questions to pose to the faculty member. Your objective is to be able to get the interviewee to tell his or her own story. You will want to know how he or she gained expertise in the field mentioned, as well as any other objectives that you and your group determine ahead of time are most important. Record the answers given. Based on what is heard and what the objectives were, discuss how the questions could be revised to obtain better answers. Participate in a discussion of the attributes of good questions to ask interviewees.	Oral histories are particularly suited to nonnative English learners and young children as they place emphasis on interviewing subjects rather than on letters, documents, and other written records. Point out that oral history develops higher-order thinking skills in candidates and students as they develop and refine questions; discuss interviewing strategies; make judgments about the point of view of the person being interviewed; and then analyze, synthesize, and evaluate the information they receive.
IMPLEMENTATION	Inform candidates that the oral history project involves creating both a video archive and a written report documenting an oral history on a given theme or subject. Both products will be posted on the Web after an oral presentation. Create project groups. These may be self-selected or preassigned. Have candidates generate questions for the interview.	In groups, participate in the decision of the selection of a topic. Discuss the alignment of the topic with the national and state social studies standards. Explicitly define the desired outcome of the interview. Collaboratively formulate the questions to ask.	Using grade level topics below may provide candidates with the needed experiences in exploring a topic to be used with students before taking the lesson into the classroom.

TEACHER PREP FACULTY	TEACHER CANDIDATES	FACULTY NOTES
IMPLEMENTATION Collaboratively make decisions on the assignment of topics. Brainstorm the resources and procedures necessary for a productive interview. Include in the discussion: • Video release forms for the subjects and ethical use of video and copyright issues • Appropriate equipment including, possibly, a tripod • Methods of transferring the video if not digital • Expectations for the final product both video and written. (Both will be posted electronically.) See rubrics below for suggestions. • A time line Conduct a class discussion to complete rubrics below in the context of discussing the assignment. Review the standards being addressed by the project. Caution candidates on selecting subjects for interviewing. Have candidates complete the project outside of class.	Make a plan for completing the interview, editing the video, preparing the written report, and posting both products on the Web. The plan should include how the tasks in the project are going to be equitably completed, the time line, and so on. Discuss issues of copyright, video release for use on the Internet, and appropriate use of video. Participate in the discussion to complete the rubrics for assessment of the project. Discuss the purpose of the project in alignment with the standards, both national and state. In selecting the subject for the interview, be sensitive to cultural issues and the willingness of the individual to be videotaped. Complete the project outside of class.	An alternative to determining topics is to look at a current issue that has deep historical roots. The entire class may choose to pose the same questions to a series of people to obtain different perspectives on the topic. The campus may require its own video release form be signed in order for the video to be posted on the campus Web site. Have candidates discuss the essential elements of a release form to address liability. Consider collecting examples of video and other release forms from local school districts for comparison. As the discussion of the need for a written record takes place, be explicit about the electronic format of the report. If the reports are to be universally accessible by candidates as they enter into teacher education, consider having them posted in the same format such as Web pages or PDF files.
CULMINATION Groups share videos providing oral presentations of information in the written report. Ensure that the reports are posted on class Web site with video available in QuickTime or RealPlayer format. Facilitate a discussion debriefing the experience. Focus on the history learned. Relate the experience as closely as possible to classroom use.	Work with your group to present the video with an oral presentation on what was learned from the project. Post project on class Web site. Participate in a class discussion debriefing the experience in the context of using the lesson in the elementary school. Focus on: • What was learned about history? • How can different technologies be used? • What classroom management issues would need to be addressed when creating a lesson or project such as this? • How can the archived oral histories be used in the classroom?	The presentation of the videos can be done either from the Web or loaded as cassettes into a VCR. Candidates should have videos queued up for ease of access. Web access does allow the video to be replayed and accessed from various points to illustrate the theme or punctuate the discussion.

Grade Level Topics

Grade 3 **Local History**—What is the oldest house in the community? Who built it? Who has lived there? How has the community changed since it was built? (Example: Interview people who have lived in the community for a long time about their experiences and stories.)

Grade 4 **State History**—When did your family come to (state)? Where did they come from? What are the origins of the names of the places close to where you live? (Example: Interview members of the local Native American community to find out about reservation life now and life in the past.)

Grade 5 United States History—What does being an American mean to you? What experiences have you had that make you proud to be an American? Has anyone is your family been to war? What do they say about it? Has anyone in your family immigrated to the United States? What was his or her experience like? (Example: Interview someone who has recently immigrated or who remembers immigrating to the United States.)

Grade 6 World History—Ancient Civilizations—Beginnings of civilization can focus on ethics and the establishment of rules: When your parents were children, what were the rules in school? How have the rules changed? What qualities of individuals from the past are similar to those of the present? (Example: Interview a member of the Chinese Historical Society to find out how ancient traditions are remembered and influential in the present.)

Assessment

Completion of the rubric is part of the class discussion on assignment elements.

Rubric: Video Project

CRITERIA	LEVELS OF PERFORMANCE				
	1	2	3	4	5
Editing					The editing is respectful of the subject, includes smooth transitions, only the essential footage.
Alignment with Theme					Holistically the information on the video is in alignment with the selected theme.
Quality					The video includes a title screen and credits, has good camera angles, and is of high enough resolution to be posted on the Web site and viewed through a browser.
Archived					Video is posted on the class Web site, within the time line, and is fully functional through the browser.

TO BE COMPLETED BY CLASS

Rubric: Written Report

CRITERIA	LEVELS OF PERFORMANCE				
	1	2	3	4	5
General Information					Report includes objective of the study, grade level, title, description of classroom, and special circumstances.
Rationale					Designated theme meets the national and state standards, citations, and alignment with current adopted materials.
Key Questions					The key questions were in alignment with the objective of the study.
Procedures					Procedures are described in a way that can be replicated, demonstrate equitable distribution of the workload in the group, and respect the interviewee.
Summary of Results					The summary of results describes common themes and an analysis of the outcomes in light of the objective.
Connections to Curriculum					The results are connected to the curriculum as defined by the standards.
Student Assessment					If this project were completed by elementary students, an appropriate assessment mechanism is present.
Reflection (included for each member of the team)					The reflection is personal and applied to individual learning.

Tools and Resources

SOFTWARE

Acrobat for creating PDF files or Web page development software; video-editing software

HARDWARE

Video cameras for each group (digital video is preferred to analog)

Computer access for editing video, development of report for posting on class Web site

WEB SITES

Class Web site for posting projects

Association for Oral History Educators:
www.geocities.com/aohelanman

Oral History Homepage: **www.dickinson.edu/oha/**

Oral History Online:
www.lib.berkeley.edu/BANC/ROHO/ohonline/ (This site attempts to increase online access to firsthand accounts and personal perspectives on historical events.)

Oral History Project:
www.ohs.org/collections/oralhistory/oralhistory.html (Here Oregon history is preserved in sound, with tapes, discs, and transcripts spanning 5,500 hours of recorded sound.)

Other Links: **www.dickinson.edu/organizations/oha/ Othersites.html** (This site includes oral history organizations, publications, centers, and collections.)

University of Connecticut Center for Oral History:
www.ucc.uconn.edu/~cohadm01 (This site contains a catalog of interviews.)

University of Hawaii Center for Oral History:
www2.soc.hawaii.edu/css/oral_hist/ (This site preserves recollections of Hawaii people through oral interviews and disseminates oral history transcripts to researchers, students, and the general community.)

Credit

Laura Wendling, California State University, San Marcos, California, **wendling@csusm.edu**

Comments/Stories

The oral history project has been a rich and valuable project in social studies methods classes. It opens candidates to the notion that history is consistently being made, but it is not necessarily being recorded. The introduction of the technology into the project provides an archive of oral histories that can be used both for the purposes of reference and as an introduction for candidates. The first few times the project included video, the learning curve for the university technical staff seemed very high. However, once they became used to the high volume of video editing taking place during a specific time during the semester, they were able to facilitate candidate needs much more easily. An interesting spillover for the video use has been the candidates' willingness to take video in the classroom and edit it both for their own study and as an archive of student performance.

Technology in Middle School Education Programs

TECHNOLOGY IN
Middle School Programs

Introduction

Middle school education has undergone a tremendous transformation in the last 15 years. From being viewed as "junior" to the high school experience to becoming sensitive to the unique needs of adolescents, the middle school has developed a unique school organization involving teacher collaboration, and often, problem-based and interdisciplinary instruction.

The success of interdisciplinary instruction and alternative assessment strategies piloted in the middle school setting forces middle level teacher education programs to transform themselves as part of the change process. Increasingly, programs preparing middle school teachers are organizing themselves into interdisciplinary teams, organizing candidates into cohort groups, and organizing teams within cohorts to collaboratively complete complex learning projects.

Technology plays an integral part in the changes in middle school education. From connecting teachers to others in the professional middle school network to connecting teacher candidates outside the school walls, technology has enabled communities of middle level educators to share stories, lessons, and ideas.

This sharing of ideas and collaboration among students, teacher candidates, teachers, and others has spawned a demand for interdisciplinary activities that can be repurposed in many ways. Although the activities in this section are organized in the same way as the other sections, by discipline, each lesson has interdisciplinary ideas woven into it that can easily be extracted or expanded as teams of faculty work together. Faculty who piloted the lessons noted that they found many ways to assess an end product that resulted in better writing, computing, and conceptual understanding, thereby discovering the interrelatedness of the curriculum.

ACTIVITIES

The activities in this section are designed to provide the university faculty member with choices of how to use technology in the classroom.

Contained in each activity is a suggested rubric for assessment or a grid aligning the activity with the standards as a way to look at program assessment. The activities vary in length, background knowledge needed, and type of assessment rubric used. All the variability is intentional as it is anticipated that faculty members will customize the lessons to fit their own setting and academic preferences. The activities include:

Responding to Literature (English Language Arts)

Teacher candidates learn to use a newsletter as an alternative way to respond to literature. The newsletter has prescribed elements as well as criteria for the graphics, layout, and design.

Weaving a Multimedia Approach to Literature (English Language Arts)

Using technology to annotate a piece of literature, poem, song, and so on becomes a method for teacher candidates to help students develop understanding of written language. The annotation is electronically completed as pop-up windows and shared as a multimedia presentation.

Design-a-Lesson—Packaging a Product (Mathematics)

Determining the optimum size of packaging for a product is the purpose of the lesson. Teacher candidates work with the variables of volume, surface area, maximum and minimum values, and graphing to determine the best package.

Phone Phunctions (Mathematics)

Teacher candidates participate in a simulated lesson to discover which is the best cellular phone plan.

Bounce Back—The Long and Short of It (Science)

A motion detector, probeware, and graphing software are used to develop concepts of motion and elasticity using sports balls.

Frankenfoods? (Science)

The topic of genetic engineering is introduced as a way to get middle school students to explore the social and ethical issues around bioengineering.

Wearing Your Geography (Social Studies)

Many students wear T-shirts with the names of places or sports teams prominently displayed on the front or back. Teacher candidates use the locations on their own shirts to explore the five themes of geography using the Internet as a primary source of information.

What Will They Buy? (Social Studies)

Invention has always been a hallmark of the American economic system. Teacher candidates will examine economic concepts by exploring how to manufacture, market, and sell a new product.

Responding to Literature

Program/Grade Range: Middle Level

Subject: English Language Arts

Topic: Literary Criticism

Profile: Professional Preparation, Student Teaching/Internship, First-Year Teaching

Abstract: People respond to literature in many ways, but teacher candidates may be comfortable in designing and assessing only activities that are familiar to them (book reports, essays, or tests). This activity provides candidates with an experience that combines graphics and graphic design, creative writing, and interdisciplinary writing as a response to literature. Candidates reflect upon planning and assessment issues involved in the creation of such a product. In this activity, candidates will use simple desktop publishing software to create a four-page newsletter to accompany the reading of a period-based piece of literature (examples: *To Kill a Mockingbird, Beloved, The Things They Carried*). The newsletter contains articles based on the novel's characters and events, as well as events from the period.

STANDARDS

NETS FOR TEACHERS

II. **PLANNING AND DESIGNING LEARNING ENVIRONMENTS AND EXPERIENCES—***Teachers plan and design effective learning environments and experiences supported by technology. Teachers:*

   B. apply current research on teaching and learning with technology when planning learning environments and experiences.

   C. identify and locate technology resources and evaluate them for accuracy and suitability.

   D. plan for the management of technology resources within the context of learning activities.

   E. plan strategies to manage student learning in a technology-enhanced environment.

V. **PRODUCTIVITY AND PROFESSIONAL PRACTICE—***Teachers use technology to enhance their productivity and professional practice. Teachers:*

   C. apply technology to increase productivity.

VI. **SOCIAL, ETHICAL, LEGAL, AND HUMAN ISSUES—***Teachers understand the social, ethical, legal, and human issues surrounding the use of technology in PK–12 schools and apply that understanding in practice. Teachers:*

   A. model and teach legal and ethical practice related to technology use.

   B. apply technology resources to enable and empower learners with diverse backgrounds, characteristics, and abilities.

   C. identify and use technology resources that affirm diversity.

ENGLISH LANGUAGE ARTS

6. Students apply knowledge of language structure, language conventions (e.g., spelling and punctuation), media techniques, figurative language, and genre to create, critique, and discuss print and nonprint texts.

Lesson Description

	TEACHER PREP FACULTY	TEACHER CANDIDATES	FACULTY NOTES
PREPARATION	Prepare a model newsletter by following the steps in this activity in advance. Make a final copy, but keep the parts separate on disk so creating the model can be demonstrated by flowing the original text into the formatted newsletter. Acquire some good and poor models of newsletters. These may be about novels or an unrelated topic. Direct teacher candidates to consider literature they would like to use for a literary response activity.	Be thinking about a novel or piece of literature, or core literature that is used in the schools that you are familiar with. This will be the subject of a literary response activity.	Before doing this exercise, the candidates should be comfortable with scanning images, downloading images from the Internet, or creating images using graphics software. To acquire model newsletters, do a search on the Internet on literature newsletters. To use nonliterature newsletters, consider acquiring those that are used on campus for distribution of information. Many campus or district entities publish printed newsletters.

TEACHER PREP FACULTY	TEACHER CANDIDATES	FACULTY NOTES
INTRODUCTION		
Ask candidates how they have been required to respond to literature in their own past courses in high school and college (essay, book report, test, etc.).	Participate in a large group discussion about required responses to literature and their purposes.	Candidates should be ready to discuss past experiences in their own English language arts classes.
Discuss the purpose of these various responses to literature. What is each meant to assess?	Brainstorm ways a newsletter might assess student knowledge about a book.	Candidates should have discussed or worked with assessment issues previously.
Introduce the concept of a newsletter response to a novel. In a large group discussion, brainstorm what such a newsletter about a book might contain. Use a currently familiar work such as *Harry Potter* as an example.	Work in a small group to generate eight article headlines that might be contained in a newsletter about *Harry Potter* or other example book used in class.	Consider having the candidates select a piece of core literature from their grade level of preference or an award-winning book of their choice. See Tools and Resources for the URLs for the following sources:
In small groups, have candidates brainstorm a list of eight article headlines that might be contained in a newsletter about the novel. (As candidates work, go to groups to see what they have included and suggest other things to consider. For example, in *Harry Potter,* consider history, characters, upcoming events, political issues, social and cultural issues, special needs of characters, ways to cope with home and school stress, and so forth.)	As a group, decide on a piece of literature to use for creating a literary response newsletter. Collaboratively assign each member of the group a character from the novel. Write a short essay about one of the characters. Share these with others in the group. Make a list of the information that was presented.	John Newberry Medal Books Coretta Scott King Award Books Caldecott Medal Books Children's Book Awards As an alternative, select a piece of literature that is part of a children's literature course or a specific genre of literature being studied, or a fictional story about teaching or teachers and students that is customarily used in another course.
Have each group decide on a piece of literature to use for creating a literary response newsletter. Ask each member of the group to write a short essay about one of the characters.		
IMPLEMENTATION		
Using the elements of the model newsletter created during the preparation time, model desktop publishing skills to be used by candidates (either in the computer lab or at an instructional station). Include the creation of a headline, placement of text in columns, importing images, and importing clip art. Display and/or distribute the model newsletter.	As you watch the presentation, make a list of those parts of a newsletter that should be used and the processes needed.	Candidates should have access to a scanner and the Internet to obtain images. Both instructor and candidates should be proficient in obtaining, creating, and accessing digital images.
Discuss elements that may be assessed in a given newsletter (e.g., mechanics, graphic design, adherence to the novel or time period).	Examine a newsletter. Brainstorm the elements that might be assessed (the ones that might form the first column of a rubric).	Discuss the issues of fair use.
As part of the class discussion, construct a rubric for evaluating a newsletter.	Use the empty rubric shell provided with this lesson to evaluate some models of newsletters. Use only the columns provided at this time. Do not fill in the shaded area now.	Candidates can examine the sample newsletters and decide what elements they want to grade. Two categories are provided (content and newsletter format). Candidates may come up with others.
Provide some good models and some poor models to allow candidates practice in assessing newsletter elements.	What made some newsletters fit one level and others another?	In completing the assessment rubric, candidates may need some help with an exact statement of expectation. Provide them with an example to start with if necessary.
Have candidate groups create one page of their newsletter, using the character "essay" they have already written. (This may become more than one article.)	Fill in the cells of your rubric with exact statements of expectations.	If issues of copyright and appropriate citation have not been covered at this point, be sure to emphasize the need for adhering to copyright guidelines as in print media. The appropriate citation format can be found in the university library or through the APA Web site: www.apa.org. See Section 1, "Using Model Strategies for Integrating Technology into Teaching," for more Web sites on this topic.
When the pages are complete, do a pair peer evaluation, assessing design, mechanics, and adherence to text (that is, do the articles stay true to character and plot?).	Design one page of a newsletter, using the content of the character essay completed as homework. In pairs, assess each other on content (adherence to text) and newsletter design. Individually or in small groups, revise the first page and complete the remaining three pages of the newsletter. The pages should be saved and printed.	

TEACHER PREP FACULTY	TEACHER CANDIDATES	FACULTY NOTES
Have candidates complete the rest of the newsletter. The newsletter must contain at least: • Two articles per page • One scanned or downloaded graphic per page • One piece of clip art or original art • Two articles about historic events taking place during the novel's time period The completed newsletter is to be 11 x 17" and folded.	Compile the newsletter, copying pages one and four to one side of an 11 x 17" sheet, and pages two and three to the other side. Turn in the completed product with a copy of the completed rubric as self-assessment.	
In a whole group, reflect on the assignment—the task, the pitfalls, the possibilities for use in their future classrooms, modifications for this assignment, and modifications for students of various levels. In small groups, ask candidates to expand on their candidate-generated rubric and determine weights for the pieces of the product. (This may be a whole group guided exercise if candidates have not yet done any work with assessment.) Have candidates write a reflection that is focused on how the newsletter as a response to literature could be used in the classroom. It should include the following elements: a needs assessment (hardware, software, prior knowledge, technology skills), scheduling needs, possible problems, means of assessment, and consideration of whether and how they might use this activity with a future class.	Discuss the task, pitfalls, possibilities, and how this might be used in your own classroom in the future. Work to refine the earlier generated rubric. Discuss the weighting of each component. Fill in the shaded area with the weights. Write a reflection that focuses on how the newsletter can be used in the classroom. The reflection should include a needs assessment (hardware, software, prior knowledge, technology skills), scheduling needs, possible problems, means of assessment, and consideration of whether and how you might use this activity with a future class.	Candidates should have an understanding of needs assessment and task analysis. Candidates should look for ways that the newsletters (articles, graphics, layout) could be improved. Candidates should also consider how they wish to weigh the various elements of the newsletter. For example, candidates may wish to give the most weight to the articles about the novel, then to articles about events during the time period. The newsletter format may receive more or less weight, depending on the focus of the class (English language arts or technology). Candidates might discuss how individual articles could be assessed. A sample is provided using the Six Trait Analytical Writing Assessment. At the end of this activity, candidates should have composed a scheme for assessing all elements of the newsletter, including those elements having to do solely with technology (use of computer graphics, for example).

CULMINATION

Assessment

Rubric: Empty Shell for Teacher Candidate Use

	LEVELS OF PERFORMANCE		
	UNACCEPTABLE	ACCEPTABLE	TARGET
Article (Content and Writing)			
Newsletter Format (Elements of Graphic Design)			
Other Category			

Rubric: Partially Completed Shell for Teacher Candidate Use

	LEVELS OF PERFORMANCE		
	UNACCEPTABLE	ACCEPTABLE	TARGET
Article (Six Trait Analytical Writing Assessment Model)			
Ideas and Content: Adherence to the Novel and Time Period			
Organization			
Voice			
Word Choice			
Sentence Fluency			
Conventions			
Newsletter Format—Elements of Graphic Design			
Balance			
Flow			
Use of White Space			
Use of Fonts and Formatting			
Creativity			

Note: For additional assessment, modify the "Written Reflection" rubric in Appendix C.

Tools and Resources

SOFTWARE

Simple desktop publishing software (ClarisWorks, AppleWorks, MS Publisher)

HARDWARE

Computer with Internet access, scanner, printer, copy machine

WEB SITES

Caldecott Medal Books:
www.ala.org/alsc/caldecott.html

Children's Book Awards:
www.acs.ucalgary.ca/~dkbrown/awards.html

Coretta Scott King Award Books:
www.ala.org/srrt/csking/index.html

International Reading Association: www.reading.org/

John Newberry Medal Books:
www.ala.org/alsc/newbery.html

National Council of Teachers of English:
www.ncte.org/standards/

Six Trait Writing Assessment:
www.nwrel.org/eval/toolkit98/traits/

Credits

Bryan Miyagishima, St. Cloud State University, St. Cloud, Minnesota, **bmiyagishima@stcloudstate.edu**

Nancy Patterson, Portland Middle School, Portland, Michigan, **patter@voyager.net**

Comments/Stories

In this activity, the instructor may ask candidates to apply many different levels of understanding to a piece of literature. Newsletter articles may demonstrate understanding of character and plot. Editorials may demonstrate understanding of theme. Articles about historic events may demonstrate understanding of context. The instructor may also use this activity to focus on writing style (journalistic) and audience. When candidates are given the opportunity to produce this newsletter in small groups, candidates of varying abilities all play a valuable role.

Weaving a Multimedia Approach to Literature

Program/Grade Range: Middle Level

Subject: English Language Arts

Topic: Literary Criticism

Profile: Professional Preparation

Abstract: Technology allows language arts teachers to move beyond printed text to convey ideas and meaning. Teacher candidates select a short piece of literature (poem, song, short story) and identify key elements of the piece they wish to annotate, clarify, enhance, or explicate (such as rhyme, rhythm, alliteration, allegory, figures of speech, word meaning, etc.). Using the library and the Internet, candidates research and locate various media that can be used to illustrate the key elements. Web page creation and editing software allow students to link other text, graphics, audio, and video to enhance meaning or demonstrate new understandings to the printed text. Presentation software allows them to combine various media (e.g., text, graphics, audio, and video) to turn text into a multimedia format. This models a lesson that preservice candidates may choose to use in their own middle school classrooms. It may also be adapted for younger or older students.

STANDARDS

NETS FOR TEACHERS

II. PLANNING AND DESIGNING LEARNING ENVIRONMENTS AND EXPERIENCES—*Teachers plan and design effective learning environments and experiences supported by technology. Teachers:*

    A. design developmentally appropriate learning opportunities that apply technology-enhanced instructional strategies to support the diverse needs of learners.

    B. apply current research on teaching and learning with technology when planning learning environments and experiences.

    C. identify and locate technology resources and evaluate them for accuracy and suitability.

III. TEACHING, LEARNING, AND THE CURRICULUM—*Teachers implement curriculum plans that include methods and strategies for applying technology to maximize student learning. Teachers:*

    A. facilitate technology—enhanced experiences that address content standards and student technology standards.

    B. use technology to support learner—centered strategies that address the diverse needs of students.

VI. SOCIAL, ETHICAL, LEGAL, AND HUMAN ISSUES—*Teachers understand the social, ethical, legal, and human issues surrounding the use of technology in PK–12 schools and apply that understanding in practice. Teachers:*

    A. model and teach legal and ethical practice related to technology use.

    B. apply technology resources to enable and empower learners with diverse backgrounds, characteristics, and abilities.

ENGLISH LANGUAGE ARTS

3. Students apply a wide range of strategies to comprehend, interpret, evaluate, and appreciate texts. They draw on their prior experience, their interactions with other readers and writers, their knowledge of word meaning and of other texts, their word identification strategies, and their understanding of textual features (e.g., sound-letter correspondence, sentence structure, context, and graphics).

5. Students employ a wide range of strategies as they write and use different writing process elements appropriately to communicate with different audiences for a variety of purposes.

7. Students conduct research on issues and interests by generating ideas and questions, and by posing problems. They gather, evaluate, and synthesize data from a variety of sources (e.g., print and nonprint texts, artifacts, and people) to communicate their discoveries in ways that suit their purpose and audience.

8. Students use a variety of technological and information resources (e.g., libraries, databases, computer networks, and video) to gather and synthesize information and to create and communicate knowledge.

12. Students use spoken, written, and visual language to accomplish their own purposes (e.g., for learning, enjoyment, persuasion, and the exchange of information).

Lesson Description

TEACHER PREP FACULTY	TEACHER CANDIDATES	FACULTY NOTES
PREPARATION		
Have teacher candidates select a short piece of literature or poetry to annotate or explicate.	Select a short piece of literature or poetry to annotate or explicate.	The low-end user might copy and paste the text from the Internet and use only a linked Word document. The high-end user could use audio and video clips, presentation or Web page software, or possibly create his or her own clay animation. Consider basing one of the assessment criteria on growth of candidates' technology skills. An alternative is to require candidates to meet a specified level of technology skill in use of multimedia as demonstrated through the end product.
Arrange for the computer lab at least once or twice during the development of the project. This time should be targeted at checking on the status of the developing projects, sharing ideas, and resolving dilemmas.		
Assess candidate technology skill level to determine the level of assistance that may be necessary. This base level information can also be used to assess candidates' growth in technology skills at the end of the activity.		Posting end products to a Web site requires candidates having access to posting whereas presentation software is readily available. It is also mandatory to have written permission for any pieces that are not original or public domain. Posting to a Web site allows for the end product to be easily shared with local and remote audiences.
Decide whether the multimedia end product will be a Web page or electronic presentation, or whether candidates can choose between the two.		
Establish an electronic mail list for candidate communication or a threaded discussion on the class Web site.		In addition to the use of poetry or literature, suggest the use of a video or film that could be digitized and then develop a means of annotating in keeping with the project. Other candidates may select song lyrics, a poem, or an excerpt from a larger work. Candidates could be expected to bring their piece of literature to the next class meeting.
INTRODUCTION		
Ask candidates how they believe the Web and presentation software can be used to enhance one's thinking about literature, including alternative forms of literature like songs, video, and film.	Think about how the Web and presentation software might be used to demonstrate a person's understanding of literature.	Establish guidelines for electronic mail list conversations and perhaps a minimum participation requirement of one meaningful or substantive posting per week either initiating conversation or responding to others.
Introduce the concept of how a Web or presentation software project might help a writer think critically about a piece of literature and exhibit that thinking in a visual and print manner.	Examine a sample of digitally annotated literature. Think of other key elements that might be annotated. What other ways can you think of to annotate key elements?	Consider introducing the candidates to some examples at this point or later in the lesson. (See annotation example Web sites in Tools and Resources.)
Guide candidates through a short poetry annotation activity, using a poem such as Tennyson's *Eagle*. Encourage candidates to find key images, words, and phrases they would like to investigate or research further. These elements could also be literary allusions or figures of speech. Point out that each explanation can be turned into a slide or a Web screen.	Participate in the online discussion on the class electronic mail list. Follow the lead questions posed by the instructor. The first portion of the discussion will focus on instructional and literary criticism theory that supports the project and the learning that is taking place.	
Refer back to the candidates' responses to the question about the use of presentation software as the explanations are being presented.		

	TEACHER PREP FACULTY	TEACHER CANDIDATES	FACULTY NOTES
INTRODUCTION	Explain that participation on the class electronic mail list is expected in order to continue discussion regarding instructional and literary criticism theory that supports the learning taking place in this project. Pose specific questions to ensure that conversations continue to be active. The first questions should focus on instructional and literary criticism theory supporting annotations of text.		
IMPLEMENTATION	Display examples of Web pages and hypermedia or multimedia presentations that annotate, explicate, or enhance works of literature. Conduct a discussion of the attributes of each in terms of how each helps students construct meaning from text. (See Faculty Notes from Introduction above.) Have candidates work in small groups to share the piece of literature they have selected and to brainstorm ways the piece can be annotated, explicated, or enhanced. Ask candidates to reflect on how they might create their project. This reflection can be shared in class or on the class electronic mail list, or brought to the next class or session for sharing in a small group. The reflection should include the ways such projects can enhance student literacy. In the context of discussing how information, images, sound or music, and video might be found and inserted, discuss with candidates fair use guidelines for using digital and print materials and the legitimacy of sources. Present the assessment rubrics below as a point of discussion. Modify the rubrics based on the class discussion.	Participate in a whole class discussion focusing on the attributes of the annotated examples. Take notes on the points made for future sharing or online discussions. Work with a small group to examine each other's piece of literature. Brainstorm ways each piece can be annotated, explicated, or enhanced. Focus on how the particular addition will enhance student understanding of the literature. In a written reflection, include ways your piece of literature might guide your selection of a presentation strategy and ways such projects can enhance student literacy. Review fair use guidelines for using materials from other sources to annotate, explicate, or expand your piece of literature. Contribute to the class discussion on the assessment rubric.	It may be necessary to discuss technology concerns regarding access or skill level. Suggest ways candidates can find tutorials or campus facilities that will help them with their technology concerns. To facilitate the discussion of appropriate use of Web materials, review Teaching Kids to Be Web Literate (available online at the URL in Tools and Resources). It may be helpful to introduce candidates to the Curry School's Multicultural Model for Evaluating Educational Web Sites to determine whether the materials are appropriate to use with the selected piece of literature when candidates take their completed project for use with students. See Tools and Resources for the URL. Provide time and direction once the project has begun so that candidates can share their perceptions, in class or online, regarding the difficulty of the project and can provide input regarding their perceptions of what a good project should look like. This discussion can also be woven into one about how middle grade students should be assessed on projects of this nature, and what literacy issues are involved in these composing processes. This might be a good opportunity to reinforce the concept that composing processes vary from individual to individual and from task to task. Candidates need to understand that the composing process, whether it involves computer technology or not, is a fluid, recursive process rather than one that is lock step.
CULMINATION	Ask candidates to present their annotations to the class for discussion. Presentations can take place online if finished projects are posted to a course Web site or digitally (computer, disk/CD, projector) if they are not. Direct candidates to provide feedback to peers based on the rubric.	Present annotated selection to peers. Provide a rationale for the presentation format (Web, presentation software, etc.). Include an explanation of how the annotation contributes to student understanding of the selection. Provide feedback on peer presentations based on the rubric collaboratively developed.	Much of the work on this project can be done out of class, but time should be set aside for candidates to display their projects, using a projector for presentations and possibly disk-stored Web pages. Web pages can also be uploaded to the Internet and viewed. Project exhibitions may show excerpts if time is short or candidates may present within small groups if multiple resources are available.

CULMINATION

TEACHER PREP FACULTY	TEACHER CANDIDATES	FACULTY NOTES
Following the presentations, conduct a discussion of 1. how the process of constructing such a project can provide a meaningful literacy event in a classroom, 2. how the attributes of each can help students construct meaning from text, and 3. the effect of the two delivery systems on student outcomes. Following the presentations, have candidates think-pair-share other ways annotation might be used in teaching. Ask candidates to write a closing reflection regarding the processes they used to create their project, their rationale for the portions annotated, and how annotated literature can contribute to student understanding. Candidates are also expected to support the points they make in their reflection with readings done as part of their coursework.	Think-pair-share on ways the process of annotating selections can be used in other contexts in teaching. Complete the guided reflection discussing the process used, the rationale for the portions of the selection that have been annotated, references to prior learning, and general contributions to improving your professional practice.	Consider having Web site presentations viewed electronically as homework while software-based presentations are given in class. One powerful discussion that candidates might want to engage in is how this particular project can be done in a less technologically advanced environment. Some candidates may find themselves in a first-year teaching situation that does not have adequate access to technology for this project to be duplicated. Have candidates brainstorm ways this project can be modified in an environment that does not have computers. Connections to student teaching, teaching, and personal lives might include annotated letters of introduction, newsletters, and greeting cards.

Assessment

The following example rubric can be adapted in a teacher and candidate discussion. For reflections and assessment of Web pages, consider using the rubrics in Appendixes C and D.

Rubric: Sample for Annotation Project Assessment

CRITERIA	LEVELS OF PERFORMANCE			
	1	2	3	4
Selection of Items	Items are selected arbitrarily.	Items are selected with some sensitivity to audience.	Items are selected on the basis of their effectiveness in increasing the understanding of the text in the intended audience.	Items are selected to foster deep understanding not only of the text but also of the cultural and literary context of the text.
Richness of the Annotations	Annotations are not clear.	Annotations are reasonably clear and help explicate the text.	Annotations are clear and they enrich the text by providing insight into the document.	Annotations are clear, concise, and creative; they enrich the reader's understanding of the text with insights about the document and its context of meaning.
Multimedia Enhancements	No multimedia enhancements are included.	Some multimedia items are included.	Multimedia enhancements significantly enhance the effect of the annotations.	Multimedia items are appropriate to the items and are creative enhancements to the meaning of the text in several dimensions.

Tools and Resources

SOFTWARE

Web-editing software such as Netscape Composer or Dreamweaver, and presentation software such as PowerPoint or HyperStudio

HARDWARE

Computers with Internet access, preferably in a lab situation. Students would also be expected to have access to a computer and the Internet in their out-of-class time.

WEB SITES

Annotation Examples

"The Hands of Mary Jo," by Mary Tall Mountain: **www.npatterson.net/sara/index.html** (This is a poetry annotation by Sara, a middle school student.)

The Victorian Web: **http://landow.stg.brown.edu/victorian/victov.html** (This annotation about Victorianism is a good example of a hypermedia annotation.)

Other Web Resources

A Multicultural Model for Evaluating Educational Web Sites: **http://curry.edschool.virginia.edu/curry/ centers/multicultural/net/comps/model.html** (This site helps determine the appropriateness of Web sites for use with various groups.)

Teaching Kids to Be Web Literate: **www.techlearning.com/db_area/archives/TL/200103/ webliterate.html** (This site provides ways to check the links to a Web site.)

University of Toronto English Library: **www.library.utoronto.ca/utel/rp/poems/tennyson12. html** (This site includes original source poetry.)

Credits

Nancy G. Patterson, Portland Middle School, Portland, Michigan, **patter@voyager.net**

Bryan Miyagishima, St. Cloud University, St. Cloud, Minnesota, **bmiyagishima@stcloudstate.edu**

Comments/Stories

This annotation project was used with eighth graders as a vehicle for teaching students about Web technology as well as introducing them to the idea of annotation and literary criticism. Students selected a poem, designed a rubric, and created and presented an annotation. They used online sources as well as traditional print sources to find more information about the historical context of the poem, background information about the author, and information that further explained what they as middle school students found important in the poem. Students reflected regularly in a response journal about the processes they used to create their Web site, their frustrations or triumphs with the technology, and what they were learning about the literature they were annotating. Students published their Web pages on the Internet or on the local area network.

Design-a-Lesson—Packaging a Product

Program/Grade Range: Middle Level

Subject: Mathematics

Topic: Maximum and Minimum

Profile: Professional Preparation, Student Teaching/Internship, First-Year Teaching

Abstract: This problem-based activity addresses consumer-related issues that involve volume, surface area, minimum and maximum values, and graphing. The problem is to determine optimal packaging size for a given volume of a product. The activity addresses a teacher candidate's ability to design modifications of this lesson and to make a judgment about whether to use technology and, if so, what technology.

STANDARDS

NETS FOR TEACHERS

II. PLANNING AND DESIGNING LEARNING ENVIRONMENTS AND EXPERIENCES—*Teachers plan and design effective learning environments and experiences supported by technology. Teachers:*

A. design developmentally appropriate learning opportunities that apply technology-enhanced instructional strategies to support the diverse needs of learners.

B. apply current research on teaching and learning with technology when planning learning environments and experiences.

D. plan for the management of technology resources within the context of learning activities.

E. plan strategies to manage student learning in a technology-enhanced environment.

IV. ASSESSMENT AND EVALUATION—*Teachers apply technology to facilitate a variety of effective assessment and evaluation strategies. Teachers:*

C. apply multiple methods of evaluation to determine students' appropriate use of technology resources for learning, communication, and productivity.

V. PRODUCTIVITY AND PROFESSIONAL PRACTICE—*Teachers use technology to enhance their productivity and professional practice. Teachers:*

B. continually evaluate and reflect on professional practice to make informed decisions regarding the use of technology in support of student learning.

C. apply technology to increase productivity.

D. use technology to communicate and collaborate with peers, parents, and the larger community in order to nurture student learning.

VI. SOCIAL, ETHICAL, LEGAL, AND HUMAN ISSUES—*Teachers understand the social, ethical, legal, and human issues surrounding the use of technology in PK–12 schools and apply that understanding in practice. Teachers:*

B. apply technology resources to enable and empower learners with diverse backgrounds, characteristics, and abilities.

MATHEMATICS

Standard 2: Algebra

Instructional programs from PK–12 should enable all students to—

- understand patterns, relations, and functions.
- use mathematical models to represent and understand quantitative relationships.
- analyze change in various contexts.

Standard 3: Geometry

Instructional programs from PK–12 should enable all students to—

- use visualization, spatial reasoning, and geometric modeling to solve problems.

Standard 4: Measurement

Instructional programs from PK–12 should enable all students to—

- understand measurable attributes of objects and the units, systems, and processes of measurement.
- apply appropriate techniques, tools, and formulas to determine measurements.

> **Standard 6: Problem Solving**
> Instructional programs from PK–12 should enable all students to—
> - build new mathematical knowledge through problem solving.
> - solve problems that arise in mathematics and in other contexts.
> - apply and adapt a variety of appropriate strategies to solve problems.
> - monitor and reflect on the process of mathematical problem solving.

Lesson Description

	TEACHER PREP FACULTY	TEACHER CANDIDATES	FACULTY NOTES
PREPARATION	Review math concepts and cooperative learning strategies as needed in the class prior to introducing the activity. Check to be sure that spreadsheet software is available on the teaching station in the classroom. Be sure to increase the font size to make it viewable from the back of the room.	Review the mathematical concept of the ratio of surface area to volume.	There are several suggestions embedded in the Faculty Notes portion of this activity that change the setup of the lesson. Review this section carefully, making special equipment arrangements, if necessary.
INTRODUCTION	Discuss involvement of middle school students in real-life problem-based activities or the problem-based learning model. Introduce the problem: "You will be marketing a new brand of dog food. One unit of this item will be packaged in a metal cylindrical can. Each unit will contain 750 cc of dog food. You have several competitors in the market. You want to charge a competitive price for your product, so you want to keep production costs as low as possible. One way to help cut costs is to use the least amount of material possible in making the can. Knowing that the volume of dog food contained in each can is 750 cc, what should be the radius and height of the can so that the least amount of material is used in making the can? Use the metric system for all measurements." In pairs, have teacher candidates restate the problem in comprehensible language appropriate for a multilingual student. Pose the question "How can we use a spreadsheet to get at the notion of maximum volume with minimum packaging?" Using a think-pair-share technique, have candidates share how they would organize the spreadsheet to arrive at an answer. Using a blank spreadsheet displayed on a large screen, discuss the ways the spreadsheet can be developed, the formulas needed to illustrate the concept, appropriate labeling, and so on.	Participate in the discussion of real-life problems as a vehicle for teaching concepts to middle school students. Listen to the problem presented. In pairs, state the problem in comprehensible language appropriate for a multilingual student. Provide input on how a spreadsheet can be used to solve the problem. Think about the formulas that may be needed. Contribute to the discussion on how to organize the spreadsheet and how your suggestion contributes to the conceptual understanding of the middle school students. Think about how you might introduce a problem such as this. What "hook" would get middle school students interested in a maximum and minimum problem? What characteristics should the problem presentation and context have to sustain their interest?	Instead of presenting the example as a whole class activity, consider using a lab setting for pairs or small groups such as one computer for each group of four to six candidates. Consider using Geometer's Sketchpad in addition to a spreadsheet. Have candidates compare the pros and cons of both. If the class has not experienced many hands-on activities, you may want to use an alternative problem to emphasize visualization using a model. An alternative problem is: From a piece of poster board of a given size, make a box (by cutting out the corners) that could carry the maximum volume of a certain material. Consider using graphic organizing software such as Inspiration to capture the candidates' brainstorming on ways to introduce lessons. The visual representation can be saved and posted on the class Web site for later reference. At the end of the discussion, close the spreadsheet and reopen it in the customary font (usually 10 point). Point out that 10-point font when used in a whole setting is too small for students to see. As a teacher, the size of the characters must be large enough to be viewed from the back of the room.

	TEACHER PREP FACULTY	TEACHER CANDIDATES	FACULTY NOTES
INTRODUCTION	Step out of the teacher role and into a role of debriefing with the candidates about the presentation of the problem. Discuss with candidates the many ways of introducing a problem based on situations that occur in business for which there are economic consequences for the business. Brainstorm ways in which this problem, or a modification of the problem, could be introduced to middle school students to pique their interest.		
IMPLEMENTATION	Assign candidates into teams. Assign the task of developing a lesson appropriate for middle school students based on a problem that teaches the concept of maximum and minimum. Discuss the expectations for the problem, lesson plans, the presentation of the solution, participation in the online discussion, and reflections. In the context of the discussion, introduce the scoring rubric below. Discuss the elements of the rubric, soliciting modification. Direct candidates to create a work plan and assign roles to group members. As the teams begin to work on their own, post questions on the class discussion list such as: • On your next trip to the grocery store, look at the packaging that catches your eye. What is it about the packaging that is interesting? • When you look at the generic brands section of the store, is there one type of packaging that is more often found than another? Why do you think that is so? • What preproblem hands-on activities are you considering? • What "reasonable" openers have you discarded in your discussion? Why did you discard them? • What problems are you having in creating your lesson? Encourage teams to present their lessons in the most comprehensible way possible. Suggest that the presentation role is not just one of sharing a lesson, but one of teaching their peers in a professional development setting. Presentation software or some other easily viewable medium should be used.	Listen carefully to the task at hand. In teams define the problem, limitations, standards to be addressed, assessment techniques, and technology to be used. Make a work plan for completing the task. Determine the role for each member of the group. Specifically appoint a team member to monitor the work plan through e-mail communication with the members of the group. As the group is designing the lesson, keep in mind that you must design and develop the following for the lesson: • Outcomes • Assessment scoring tool • Opening activities for students prior to introduction of the problem-based activity • Teaching strategies and grouping to be used • Activities that will develop conceptual understanding • Student products, how they will be presented, and the presentation format • Potential technologies to be used in finding solutions to the problem • Closing or culminating activity • Suggestions for extension activities and adaptations Plan the group presentation in such a way as to highlight the mathematics, the use of technology to enhance student conceptual understanding, and a way of making a professional presentation.	If groups have been used in the past, make a concerted effort to mix up the group members. Ensure that at least one person in the group is adept at using a spreadsheet while another is familiar with a graphic organizer. If a specific scheme is used to organize the groups, be sure to debrief the ideas with candidates at the end of the lesson. When introducing the need for participation in the online discussion, set minimum standards for participation. Check the software to be sure that the number of candidate responses can be tallied, if necessary. Candidates should be aware of the need to contribute positively to the discussion with thoughtful responses. Some examples of extensions for this activity include: • Vary volume, vary shape of packaging • Design labels • Develop a marketing plan • Design advertising materials • Determine cheapest method of packaging for distribution

	TEACHER PREP FACULTY	TEACHER CANDIDATES	FACULTY NOTES
CULMINATION	Provide an opportunity for teams to present their lesson. Keep the discussion lively by posing questions to the class on how the lesson presented could be improved, extended, and adjusted to meet the needs of multilingual students and special needs students. Be sure to include potential classroom management issues that may arise. Have teams post lesson plans on the class Web site. Discuss the process of designing a problem-based activity lesson. Assign candidates to write a reflection on • how the technology worked to build conceptual understanding for students, • what they learned from the lesson development process, and • what they would do differently when the lesson is implemented in their classroom.	Present lesson to peers. At the conclusion of the presentation, discuss the process of designing the lesson. What were the major concerns, issues, and so on? Having heard all the presentations and the discussion, individually reflect on the lesson design experience. Provide your thinking on how the technology worked with building conceptual development of the concept of maximum and minimum, what you learned in the process, and what you will do differently when you implement the lesson in your classroom. Consider packaging the lesson plan and reflection as an entry into your professional portfolio.	Using the rubric below, assess teamwork. This may provide an opportunity for peer assessment. Consider using the rubric for each team to evaluate the work of others. If peer assessment is to be used, be sure to inform the candidates in advance and decide whether the peer assessment is considered part of the graded assessment of this activity. Use the "Written Reflection" rubric in Appendix C.

Assessment

The following scoring rubric combines a checklist and a holistic scoring rubric. The final work receives a score based on the fit of the final product to the description. The holistic rubric is used when the body of work is interdependent on the component parts, especially if the technology is designed to be an integral part of the lesson. However, if a detailed, categorical rubric is desired, the elements can be separated into a table and scored individually.

Rubric: Checklist and Holistic Scoring

CHECKLIST FOR LESSON CONTENTS	LEVELS OF PERFORMANCE			
	RETURN—NEEDS ADDITIONAL WORK 1	MARGINAL 2	GOOD 3	EXCELLENT 4
___Outcomes ___Assessment scoring tool ___Opening activities for students prior to introduction of the problem-based activity ___Teaching strategies and grouping to be used ___Activities that will develop conceptual understanding ___Student products, how they will be presented, and the presentation format ___Potential technologies to be used in finding solutions to the problem ___Closing or culminating activity ___Suggestions for extension activities and adaptations		• Lesson contains all the required elements.	• Lesson contains all the required elements. • The use of technology enhances the conceptual development. • Lesson reflects attention to needs of second language learners.	• Lesson contains all the required elements. • The use of technology greatly enhances the conceptual understanding of the maximum and minimum problem presented. • Lesson effectively integrates techniques to support second language learners in a natural way.

Note: To assess the reflection, use the "Written Reflection" rubric provided in Appendix C.

Tools and Resources

SOFTWARE

Spreadsheet software available on the teaching station; graphic organizing software (see Faculty Notes section); Geometer's Sketchpad, Key Curriculum Press (see Faculty Notes section)

HARDWARE

Teaching station in the classroom

WEB SITES

As candidates are pondering the subject of their lesson, encourage them to visit commercial Web sites that provide amounts of purchasable items. Web sites include online grocery shopping services, gift producers, candy manufacturers such as Hershey and Mars, and so on.

OTHER

Manipulative materials for candidates to experiment with as they create their lessons, including centi-cubes, base-10 blocks (ones blocks are metrically measured), centimeter grid paper with glue, and rulers for creating models

Credits

Marcia Cushall, Frostburg State University, Frostburg, Maryland, **mcushall@frostburg.edu**

James Wiebe, California State University, Los Angeles, **jwiebe@calstatela.edu**

Comments/Stories

This activity has come toward the end of the semester when many of the core concepts in teaching mathematics have been covered. Candidates have had a lot of experience in working in groups and developing lessons. Sometimes the content, maximum and minimum, is difficult to teach to middle school students. Therefore, making this lesson one that utilizes many of the techniques taught with simpler concepts enables candidates to bring it all together to create a lesson that focuses on conceptual understanding. When given the freedom and encouragement, the teams became very creative in the storyline to draw the middle school students into the problem. The creativity continues through the extensions as a way to expand the lesson. The candidates found many ways to link this lesson into interdisciplinary work by drawing in economics, reading, and art. Many created ways to utilize technology tools to further extend the lesson into those areas as well as increase students' technology skills through the use of graphics and desktop publishing.

Phone Phunctions

Program/Grade Range: Middle Level

Subject: Mathematics

Topic: Functions

Profile: Professional Preparation

Abstract: Experiencing the activity as middle school students, teacher candidates reflect on a cooperative learning activity during which they apply the concept of functions to answer the question "What is the best cellular phone plan for our client (a middle school student)?" Candidates use Web-based research to collect information about cellular phone plans and the phone habits of middle school students, spreadsheets to organize their findings, and technology to present their findings to the class. Candidates must justify their answer using the concept of function from the graphical, numerical, and algebraic perspectives. As a class, candidates reflect on the lesson, giving particular attention to the importance of the mathematics taught, the part technology played in conceptual development, and the appropriateness of the methodology.

STANDARDS

NETS FOR TEACHERS

II. PLANNING AND DESIGNING LEARNING ENVIRONMENTS AND EXPERIENCES—*Teachers plan and design effective learning environments and experiences supported by technology. Teachers:*

  A. design developmentally appropriate learning opportunities that apply technology-enhanced instructional strategies to support the diverse needs of learners.

  C. identify and locate technology resources and evaluate them for accuracy and suitability.

  D. plan for the management of technology resources within the context of learning activities.

  E. plan strategies to manage student learning in a technology-enhanced environment.

III. TEACHING, LEARNING, AND THE CURRICULUM—*Teachers implement curriculum plans that include methods and strategies for applying technology to maximize student learning. Teachers:*

  A. facilitate technology-enhanced experiences that address content standards and student technology standards.

  B. use technology to support learner-centered strategies that address the diverse needs of students.

  C. apply technology to develop students' higher-order skills and creativity.

MATHEMATICS

Standard 1: Number and Operations

Instructional programs from PK–12 should enable all students to—

  • compute fluently and make reasonable estimates.

Standard 2: Algebra

Instructional programs from PK–12 should enable all students to—

  • understand patterns, relations, and functions.

  • represent and analyze mathematical situations and structures using algebraic symbols.

  • use mathematical models to represent and understand quantitative relationships.

Standard 5: Data Analysis and Probability

Instructional programs from PK–12 should enable all students to—

  • formulate questions that can be addressed with data and collect, organize, and display relevant data to answer them.

  • select and use appropriate statistical methods to analyze data.

Standard 6: Problem Solving

Instructional programs from PK–12 should enable all students to—

  • build new mathematical knowledge through problem solving.

  • solve problems that arise in mathematics and in other contexts.

  • apply and adapt a variety of appropriate strategies to solve, problems.

  • monitor and reflect on the process of mathematical problem solving.

Lesson Description

	TEACHER PREP FACULTY	TEACHER CANDIDATES	FACULTY NOTES
PREPARATION	Have teacher candidates review NCTM principles for math, NCTM standards for Grades 6–8, and NETS for Students for Grades 6–8. In preparation for the activity, divide the class into groups to locate specific information and have them be prepared to share their findings as well as the source of the data. One group should locate each of the following: • Rates of local cellular phone plans with options (assign one plan per group) • Demographic data on adolescent cell phone users • Use data on adolescent cell phone users including how many minutes they typically use in a month, what price they are willing to pay for the service, and when they typically use their cell phones—days, nights, or weekends • Cell phone companies who have special plans for individuals with handicapping conditions—define the services and the prices	Review the NCTM principles for school mathematics, the NCTM standards for Grades 6–8, and the NETS for Students profile for Grades 6–8. Locate the Web-based information for the work topic assigned to your group. Be prepared to bring the source of the information as well as to answer questions from classmates.	Candidates may hold one or more of the following attitudes that are barriers to using this lesson: • Activity-based learning takes too much time. • This lesson will not prepare students for the state exam. • My cooperating teacher said this lesson would not work. • This technology is not in my school. Finding the demographic and research data may be time-consuming. Examine the resources available in your area before making the assignment. If cell phone usage data are not available, make this assignment during the study of data collection, probability, and statistics prior to this lesson.
INTRODUCTION	Have groups share their data. Limit the discussion of the data to quickly observable conclusions. Have candidates relay what they learned about cell phone plans for people with handicapping conditions. Review the mathematics behind the notion of a function, variables, and so on. Introduce the activity by stating "Today you will experience a problem-based lesson designed for middle school students. I will be modeling strategies that illustrate the standards. Your job is to complete the activity by role-playing a middle school student. After the activity you will be asked to reflect on the lesson as you are, a teacher candidate, and to create a lesson that shows your mastery of the objectives." Inform the candidates that they are to find the best cellular phone plan as if they were a group of middle school students. (Distribute the presentation scoring rubric for a brief discussion before proceeding.) Assign collaborative groups of three to five candidates. These groups may be different than those used for the introductory research. Have them assign roles and create a time line.	Participate in having your group share the data brought to class. Listen for any commonalties and unusual information. What did you learn about cellular phone plans for persons with handicapping conditions? Review functions and variables. Become part of a collaborative work group. Assign roles and responsibilities for completion of the task. Make a time line for completing the tasks.	The activity may take too long for your time period. Consider where to break or alter the activity. Candidates may become enamored with the technology and neglect the mathematics of the activity. Keeping them focused can be quite a task. If this is the case, be prepared to debrief the activity heavily on classroom management techniques needed to control the use of technology in the classroom. Take time to look over the proposed scoring rubric below. Alter the rubric to fit your needs. When distributing the rubric to candidates, be open to the addition of other criteria and modification of performance indicators.

	TEACHER PREP FACULTY	TEACHER CANDIDATES	FACULTY NOTES
IMPLEMENTATION	Have candidates conduct their research. Have them assign roles and create a time line. The group's presentation must compare at least three cellular plans, determine costs for one year of all the plans, consider fixed and variable costs, address what happens if the client goes over the allotted number of minutes allowed by the plan, and so on. Groups should • research the topic using Web-based resources; • use the concept of function to solve a problem; • justify a solution from the graphical, numerical, and algebraic perspectives; • organize and analyze data using a spreadsheet; and • use technology such as presentation software to report to the class. Have candidates present their findings. Assign candidates to write a reflection on what they learned from the lesson, how different a problem-based lesson is than others they have experienced, and any concerns they have.	Conduct research about cell phone plans and organize findings in a spreadsheet. To complete your project: • Create a detailed description of your client (a middle school student). • Plan how you are going to use technology to describe the client in the presentation. • Identify the independent and dependent variables, create symbolic expressions for cost functions, create a spreadsheet of numerical data, and graph the functions using an appropriate viewing rectangle. Present your findings to the class. Complete an individual reflection on your experience in the lesson. Include in your reflective writing what you learned, how the problem-based lesson was a different learning experience for you than others you have experienced, and any concerns or other thoughts about this model of teaching.	Use observation to determine the following: • Did candidates identify reliable and appropriate Web sites? • Did candidates use the concept of function to solve the problem? • Are justifications correct, complete, and clearly stated? • Does the spreadsheet show that data have been organized and analyzed logically? • Do the electronic product and the presentation show sufficient expertise with the software? Getting candidates to focus on the mathematics may be difficult at first. Keep prodding with questions about the variables, depicting what they find in graphical form, and so on.
CULMINATION	Facilitate a discussion of candidate reflections, emphasizing important ideas that they might have missed. Assign collaborative groups to develop the skeleton or outline of a lesson that uses problem-based learning. The outline must include: • The standard being addressed with meaningful mathematics using the appropriate conceptual development • A topic of interest to middle school students • A problem requiring Web-based research and technology to complete and/or display Have the class peer-assess the outlines on the Web. Use the lessons as a topic for threaded discussion by the class.	Participate in the discussion of the lesson. Include information written in your reflection. In working groups, outline a problem-based lesson you would use with middle school students. This outlined lesson must require students to use Web-based resources for current information. The mathematical topic is of the group's choosing. Submit the lesson to the class Web site. As other lessons are submitted, participate in an evaluation of the lesson based on the posed questions.	The lesson outline assignment is designed to extend the experience into one that causes the candidates to think about their own practice and how they would use the techniques in their own classroom. The outline is used instead of a fully written lesson plan to save time. From a lesson outline, the readers should be able to answer the peer evaluation questions. Issues of classroom procedures, management, and other considerations used in creating a full lesson plan are left unaddressed in this exercise. However, if time allows, a full lesson plan is always preferable. The use of the outlines as a topic in threaded discussions can extend the learning of the candidates. Additionally, the posting of the outlines on the class Web site forces the groups to write for a larger audience. Knowing that their work will be responded to increases the level of concern for quality performance.

Assessment

The assessment rubric below is one in which a generic scoring scale is applied to the specific criteria for the lesson. In this model of assessment, candidates are familiar with the scoring statements as they are applied to multiple assignments and settings. The criteria for the specific project are developed to guide candidates in the development of their project and specify the important elements of the project.

Rubric: Phone Plan

CRITERIA	PERFORMANCE INDICATORS
Presentation	The presentation is well-organized, engaging, uses technology, and presents the information in a comprehensible format.
Phone Plan	A rationale is provided for the plan presented that identifies the independent and dependent variables, creates symbolic expressions for cost functions, displays a spreadsheet of numerical data, and graphs the functions using an appropriate viewing rectangle.
Research	Credible Web-based resources are used in the decision making and the presentation.

Scoring Scale

5 The work exceeds all expectations. It shows an exceptionally high level of creativity and sophisticated application of knowledge and skills. It contains elements that were not considered or discussed in class, thus setting it in a category all of its own. (Very rarely given score.)

4 The work exceeds the standard and shows very strong applications of the knowledge and skills.

3 The work meets the standard and demonstrates the appropriate application of knowledge and skills. It contains minor errors that do not diminish the quality.

2 The work does not quite meet the standard. It shows inconsistent application of knowledge and skills. The minor errors are significant enough to detract from the overall quality. Additional work is required.

1 The work does not meet the standard and shows limited understanding of the knowledge and skills. The work lacks depth or is incomplete with significant errors and/or omissions.

0 No work is presented.

Peer Evaluation of Lesson Outlines

- Was the lesson based on the interests of middle school students?
- What concepts and processes were addressed?
- Will students learn meaningful mathematics?
- Is Web-based research essential?
- What part did technology play? Was it essential? Did it detract from the mathematics?
- How can the lesson be improved?
- Would you use this lesson in your classroom? Why or why not?

Tools and Resources

SOFTWARE

Presentation, spreadsheet, class Web site, and threaded discussion forum

WEB SITES

Phone plan comparisons:
www.letstalk.com
ComSearch: **www.comsearch.net/**

Credits

Lucy Carpenter Snead, Columbia College, Columbia, South Carolina, **lsnead@gandalf.colacoll.edu**

James Wiebe, California State University, Los Angeles, jwiebe@calstatela.edu

Comments/Stories

Teacher candidates could not believe the variety of information available on cellular phone plans. Because many of the candidates carry cellular phones, the research itself was a valuable exercise. Candidates were surprised how many middle school students were using cellular phones to keep in touch with parents. However, the research was expanded to look at cellular phone use over time. The older the students, the higher the cellular phone use. Again, the data spawned mathematically rich conversations about the function that resulted from the information.

Bounce Back—The Long and Short of It

Program/Grade Range: Middle Level

Subject: Science

Topic: Motion and Elasticity

Profile: Professional Preparation

Abstract: Teacher candidates use motion detector probeware and graphing software to build concepts of motion and elasticity. Following a demonstration using basketballs, candidates test other sports balls to determine the optimal conditions and type for the sport. Using an interdisciplinary approach to teaching, candidates graph data and use it to create an advertisement for the sports ball. Reflecting on their experience, candidates develop a lesson plan for middle grade students on teaching motion using probeware.

STANDARDS

NETS FOR TEACHERS

I. **TECHNOLOGY OPERATIONS AND CONCEPTS**—*Teachers demonstrate a sound understanding of technology operations and concepts. Teachers:*

B. demonstrate continual growth in technology knowledge and skills to stay abreast of current and emerging technologies.

II. **PLANNING AND DESIGNING LEARNING ENVIRONMENTS AND EXPERIENCES**—*Teachers plan and design effective learning environments and experiences supported by technology. Teachers:*

A. design developmentally appropriate learning opportunities that apply technology-enhanced instructional strategies to support the diverse needs of learners.

B. apply current research on teaching and learning with technology when planning learning environments and experiences.

C. identify and locate technology resources and evaluate them for accuracy and suitability.

D. plan for the management of technology resources within the context of learning activities.

E. plan strategies to manage student learning in a technology-enhanced environment.

III. **TEACHING, LEARNING, AND THE CURRICULUM**—*Teachers implement curriculum plans that include methods and strategies for applying technology to maximize student learning. Teachers:*

A. facilitate technology-enhanced experiences that address content standards and student technology standards.

B. use technology to support learner-centered strategies that address the diverse needs of students.

C. apply technology to develop students' higher-order skills and creativity.

D. manage student learning activities in a technology-enhanced environment.

V. **PRODUCTIVITY AND PROFESSIONAL PRACTICE**—*Teachers use technology to enhance their productivity and professional practice. Teachers:*

D. use technology to communicate and collaborate with peers, parents, and the larger community in order to nurture student learning.

SCIENCE

Content Standard A: Science as Inquiry

A1. Abilities necessary to do scientific inquiry

A2. Understanding about scientific inquiry

Content Standard B: Physical Sciences

B1. Properties and changes of properties in matter

Content Standard E: Science and Technology

E1. Abilities of technological design

Lesson Description

TEACHER PREP FACULTY	TEACHER CANDIDATES	FACULTY NOTES
PREPARATION Assign background reading on motion, force, and elasticity. Gather materials needed for the activity: a meter stick, several brands of basketballs or other sport ball, probeware for motion detection, and graphing software. (Compatible probeware can be found for both the computer and the graphing calculator.) Collect advertising examples of how elasticity is used to sway the buyer in purchasing the type or brand of ball.	Complete assigned background reading on motion, force, and elasticity.	It is ideal to have multiple stations equipped with probeware. Should this not be possible, consider another form of classroom organization such as combining the lesson with other nontechnology related activities to keep teacher candidates engaged when rotating through the stations. Other electronic tools such as handheld devices are increasingly compatible with various probeware.
INTRODUCTION Check that the probeware device is hooked to a computer interface or graphing calculator to record the data electronically. Demonstrate use of the probeware. Be sure to include how to connect and care for probes with a computer or graphing calculator. Address issues of student safety. Introduce terminology: elasticity, kinetic energy, gravitational potential energy, thermal energy, and composite materials. Have candidates consider how to present terminology for special needs students and second-language learners. Introduce possible research questions. • Does the composition of a ball determine the elasticity (bounce) of the ball and is there a reason that some sports use balls that bounce more? • How can we find out the answer to the above question? • Why would the athlete care about the elasticity of the ball? • How can this lesson be used with middle grade students to engage them in inquiry in concepts of motion and elasticity? Have candidates brainstorm any additional research questions they consider pertinent. Record hypotheses on a chart for later use.	Observe the demonstration of the equipment. Make notes on how to teach middle grade students to appropriately use the equipment. Think about classroom organization to ensure the success of the activity. Record issues of care of equipment and safety concerns for inclusion in your own lesson. Check yourself on knowledge of the vocabulary presented. If any concepts are unfamiliar, make a plan to understand the concepts before the project begins. Think of ways of adding meaning to specialized vocabulary for special needs students and second language learners. Brainstorm additional research questions to augment those posed.	Consider using a KWHL (Know, Want to know, How to learn, and what was Learned) chart to complete the activity. The activity should then include prompts for completing the chart. Prompts should include: • K and W in the Introduction • H in the Implementation • L in the Culmination If constructing KWHL charts is unfamiliar, see the Graphic Organizers Web site listed in Tools and Resources.
IMPLEMENTATION Demonstrate the first data collection activity by testing the bounce of several basketballs. Try different brand names or one slightly flat and one slightly overinflated. Use the meter stick to ensure that the ball is dropped from the same height. After the ball is dropped, record the height of the return bounce using a motion detector device.	Observe the demonstration of the basketballs. Make notes of any conceptual or procedural issues that come to mind in how this can be used to foster student understanding in a classroom setting. Participate in debriefing of the data collection activity.	Consider expanding the activity by conducting three tests of each bounce of each type of basketball. Discuss issues of consistency of procedure and reliability of the experimental data.

	TEACHER PREP FACULTY	TEACHER CANDIDATES	FACULTY NOTES
IMPLEMENTATION	Debrief with candidates any issues or concerns about how the measurements are taken, how the data are recorded, and the unit of measurement recorded by the probeware's software. During the debriefing, refer back to the hypotheses recorded during the Introduction.	Form teams of two to three. Create a work plan that includes assigning cooperative group roles and equitable distribution of tasks.	Some software programs allow you to superimpose the graphs for each kind of ball on top of each other. The super-imposed graphs allow candidates to more accurately compare their results. Note that issues of scale, altitude, and amplitude may arise when examining the graphs.
	Model effective classroom organization by placing candidates into groups of two or three. Have candidates determine which ball they will use for their experiment and have them bring one to the next class session.	Select a sports ball. Review the original research questions. Modify the questions to fit the ball being tested. Questions might include: • Do flat soccer balls get kicked farther? • What is the optimal inflation of a soccer ball? • What is the optimal bounce for a basketball?	As candidates look into sports balls, elasticity, advertisements, lesson plans, and so on, on the Internet, you may find they need coaching on effective search techniques. In addition to Web-based search tutorials, a quick peer advice session on tricks they have learned in conducting Internet searches can be very beneficial. If necessary, check with the library media center staff for a brief review of searching.
	Review procedures for conducting experiments. Have groups review their research questions prior to beginning their testing. Have candidates conduct their experiment.	• Do varying brands significantly differ in their bounce? Design and perform the experiment. Collect and graphically represent the data.	
	As the data come in from each group, ask candidates to graph and compare their results and draw some conclusions. Have candidates debrief the process by referring to the research questions and analyzing the results in reference to the questions.	Analyze the data and draw conclusions. Participate in a debriefing comparing research questions with the result.	
CULMINATION	Show examples of real-world advertising that uses elasticity data. Assign the development of a brochure advertising one of the balls used. The brochure should be written in persuasive language, use graphics, and have data presented in table or graph form.	Design an advertising flyer based on the data collected from the experiments. The advertisement must be written in persuasive language, use graphics, and have data presented in table or graph form.	Candidates might want to work with other content area instructors: language arts, graphic arts, and so on. As the learner-based activities are being developed, consider extending the activity by developing a rubric to score candidates' work.
	Facilitate the sharing of the brochures. Sharing can occur electronically if brochures are posted on the class Web site as Web pages or PDF files. Have candidates debrief the activity in small groups.	Present the flyer to the class. The flyer can be presented as a draft hard copy, but the finished flyer will be converted to a Web page or posted as a PDF file. Debrief the activity in small groups.	The lesson plan to be completed outside of class can be finished either collaboratively or individually. If used as an artifact for assessment, an individually completed lesson plan may yield more interesting information about each candidate. The lesson plans can be posted on the class Web site for class sharing.
	Have groups collaboratively develop a lesson plan for middle grade students based on the debriefing of their experience. This lesson plan can be quickly sketched in class and more fully developed outside of class.	Collaboratively develop a classroom activity for use with middle grade students based on the experience. Complete the lesson plan outside of class.	Ensure that a digital artifact is collected on the experiments that took place in class (digital pictures or video), the advertisements created (PDF files), and the lesson plans developed (Word files).

Assessment

The following rubric lists the general areas of assessment for this activity. The specific items within each category can be expanded to become separate criteria nested under each element. Likewise, unique rubrics can be developed for each product or process. This chart is partially completed to give flexibility to the teacher preparation faculty member as well as to provide practice for candidates in developing assessment rubrics.

Rubric: "Bounce Back"

CRITERIA	LEVELS OF PERFORMANCE			
	NOVICE	APPRENTICE	PROFICIENT	DISTINGUISHED
Advertising brochure: • is effectively designed. • conveys desired concept using data appropriately. • demonstrates effective use of technology tools.	CANDIDATES TO COMPLETE AS PART OF CLASS DISCUSSION			**Brochure:** • creatively meets all design criteria in visual appearance. • conveys the desired argument with convincing accurately portrayed data including graphs, charts, and narrative. • is an example of effectively using technology tools in creative and interesting ways.
Collaborative work: • meets goal. • demonstrates equitably distributed tasks. • equitably uses technology. • is effectively communicated.	**The group:** • had most of the work done by one or two people and was not complete by the end of the time period.			**The group:** • completed conducting the experiment and collecting the data. • identified and equitably distributed the tasks among all members of the group. • equitably distributed the responsibility of using the technology among its members to reinforce each member's skills and experience. • easily and frequently communicated with one another both in face-to-face work as well as in electronic communications.
Lesson plan includes: • elements of inquiry. • elements of appropriate lesson plan design. • accurate scientific generalizations and language. • attention to special needs students. • scaffolding for language development. • appropriate use of technology. • classroom management. • safety issues and use of probeware.				**The lesson plan:** (meets the criteria and specifications set by the college of education.)

Tools and Resources

SOFTWARE

Graphing and/or data collecting software appropriate for the probes being used; HTML editing software; desktop publishing and word processing software

HARDWARE

Motion detector, graphing calculator and/or computer attached to motion detector probe, digital camera (optional)

WEB SITES

Bouncing Balls: **www.exploratorium.edu/baseball/bouncing_balls. html** (Site provides an Exploratorium Baseball Activity.)

Graphic Organizers: **http://graphic.org/kwhl.html** (This site provides information on how to create KWHL charts.)

How Things Work: **http://rabi.phs.virginia.edu/HTW/bouncing_balls.html**

Measurement in Sports: **www.science.org.au/nova/033/033key.htm** (Site is sponsored by the Australian Academy of Science.)

Racquets and Balls: **www.science.org.au/nova/033/033box04.htm** (Site is sponsored by the Australian Academy of Science.)

REFERENCE TEXTS

Antinone, L., Gough, S., & Gough, J. (1997). *Modeling motion: High school math activities with the CBR.* Dallas, TX: Texas Instruments, Inc.

Brueningsen, C., Brueningsen, E., & Bower, B. (1997). *Math and science in motion: Activities for the middle school.* Dallas, TX: Texas Instruments, Inc.

Carlson, R. J., & Winter, M. J., (1998). *Transforming functions to fit data: Mathematical explorations, using probes, electronic data-collection devices, and graphing calculators.* Emeryville, CA: Key Curriculum Press.

Credits

Virginia Reid, Thurgood Marshall Middle School, Olympia, Washington, **vreid@osd.wednet.edu**

John Spagnolo, Appalachian State University, Boone, North Carolina, **spagnolojt@appstate.edu**

Bonnie Mathies, Wright State University, Centerville, Ohio, **bonnie.mathies@wright.edu**

Comments/Stories

Middle school students are often involved in sports of some kind, making this activity appealing to most students. Even the most nonathletic student rolls a ball or fiddles with a spherical rubber toy at some time. This includes candidates! Because this activity is very active, it provides a golden opportunity for the faculty member to discuss with the candidates issues of classroom management and materials control. The use of a bouncing ball in the middle school requires the confident skill of a teacher to keep the activity to one of a learning nature rather than a competitive athletic event. Often candidates behave as their worst student might. Using the candidates' way of behaving in the classroom as a starting point makes for a lively discussion of how to effectively manage active, hands-on science. This discussion, in addition to the potentially complex environment of probeware and the focus on the conceptual understanding of motion and elasticity, makes the activity extremely rich.

Frankenfoods?

Program/Grade Range: Middle Level

Subject: Science

Topic: Genetic Engineering

Profile: Professional Preparation

Abstract: Teacher candidates explore the potentially volatile topic of genetic engineering to engage middle grade students in examining the social and ethical issues surrounding biogenetics. An inquiry-based lesson is modeled for candidates with the expectation that they will then develop a lesson appropriate for middle level students. Two to three candidates work together in collaborative research design teams. The teams select a bioengineering dilemma with the task of creating a lesson that includes appropriate use of technology to increase student conceptual understanding of the topic.

STANDARDS

NETS FOR TEACHERS

II. PLANNING AND DESIGNING LEARNING ENVIRONMENTS AND EXPERIENCES—*Teachers plan and design effective learning environments and experiences supported by technology. Teachers:*

A. design developmentally appropriate learning opportunities that apply technology-enhanced instructional strategies to support the diverse needs of learners.

C. identify and locate technology resources and evaluate them for accuracy and suitability.

VI. SOCIAL, ETHICAL, LEGAL, AND HUMAN ISSUES—*Teachers understand the social, ethical, legal, and human issues surrounding the use of technology in PK–12 schools and apply that understanding in practice. Teachers:*

A. model and teach legal and ethical practice related to technology use.

SCIENCE

Content Standards A: Science as Inquiry

A1. Abilities necessary to do scientific inquiry

A2. Understanding about scientific inquiry

Content Standard C: Life Science

C2. Reproduction and heredity

Content Standard E: Science and Technology

E2. Understanding about science and technology

Content Standard F: Science in Personal and Social Perspectives

F5. Science and technology in society

Content Standard G: History and Nature of Science

G2. Nature of science

G3. History of science

Lesson Description

	TEACHER PREP FACULTY	TEACHER CANDIDATES	FACULTY NOTES
PREPARATION	In preparation for the lesson, have teacher candidates access the following Web sites (URLs are listed in Tools and Resources): • Hot Topic—Genetic Engineering/Genetically Modified Plants and Animals, Strategian • More Food, Cleaner Food—Gene Technology and Plants, Australian Academy of Science	Look at the assigned Web sites prior to coming to class. Compare both the information on the Web sites and the manner in which the information is presented. Evaluate the Web sites for use in the school classroom. If you find your background is weak in genetics, consult some of the references cited on the Web sites for additional independent learning.	The unique feature of the Strategian Web site is that it is constantly updated with new citations and summaries on the topic. As you reuse this activity, be sure to access the Strategian Web site before introducing the lesson as new articles will be posted that may slant your lesson. The Australian Academy of Sciences Web site has hot-buttoned links to definitions

	TEACHER PREP FACULTY	TEACHER CANDIDATES	FACULTY NOTES
PREPARATION	• Designer Genes: Punnett Squares, ThinkQuest entry		and examples embedded in the text to assist in understanding the concepts. The ThinkQuest Web site was created by students. Be sure to comment on the Web site development as you debrief or introduce this assignment.
INTRODUCTION	Using the Rapid Fire feature in Inspiration, conduct a discussion on the current debate on bioengineering. Consider starting the discussion with the statement "The U.S. House of Representatives passed a bill on July 31, 2001, forbidding human cloning. What are the scientific and ethical implications of the legislation?" Lead the discussion into the pros and cons of scientists' work in genetic engineering.	Participate in the discussion on genetic engineering. Carefully consider the pros and cons of current research. What ethical issues emerge? What is the dilemma in the scientific community? What boundaries would you draw for genetic engineering?	Many current materials are available to generate discussion: newspaper articles, news stories, films, and the Internet. Depending on the time constraints in class, make use of a Web search on the topic. Discuss the source of the information, how current it is, and so on. Be sure to point out the use of "Page Info" data from the browser to be able to verify how current the information is.
IMPLEMENTATION	Use an example of a genetically engineered product to discuss the science of genetics as well as the ethical issues involved. For example, although an urban legend, the KFC advertisement of featherless chickens may spawn a rich conversation. Drawing on the discussion and the concept map created above, have the class identify the main issues as areas for further study that would assist middle school students in understanding the topic of genetics and heredity. The objective of the assignment is to explore bioengineering or genetics in a way that will help each member of the class teach the topic with a rich background of resources and a full understanding of the complexity of the topic. Divide the class into groups of two to three candidates. Have each group: • Select an ethical or social issue related to biogenetics • Develop a research lesson appropriate for middle grade students that includes interdisciplinary activities, cooperative learning, and an appropriate use of technology • Align the lesson with state and national standards Have candidates develop a work plan with a time line. Work should be divided equitably among the candidates. Model rubric development by leading a discussion of how to develop an appropriate set of rubrics for middle grade students when they complete the projects	Participate in the discussion of the genetically engineered product (such as wingless chickens). Think about the implications for teaching middle school students. How would they tie into this urban legend? How will you elicit topics from students that are of interest to them? As part of a group of two or three, examine the topics generated in the introductory portion of the activity. Make a decision about which topic or subject your group wants to explore. Approach the topic from the standpoint of creating a lesson that middle school students will be able to understand that is of high interest to them. Your lesson must include: • The objective • The standards being addressed • Interdisciplinary linkages • The appropriate use of technology by middle school students • A clear set of directions for other teachers to follow • Clear scientific evidence for student use • An assessment instrument or rubric • A list of resources consulted In groups, create a work plan with a calendar to ensure that each member of the group is able to participate as equally as possible. Participate in the construction of a rubric for assessment of middle grade students' work.	An alternative to exploring the various issues related to biogenetics is to have candidates create a bioengineered food that meets a specific need. The activity is altered to include a discussion of the characteristics of the combined or altered food that improves the food. Research is conducted on the food to find dominant and recessive characteristics of the desired food. After completion of the discussion portion, step aside to discuss the value of debriefing and questioning strategies as an introduction to exploring a topic. Use Inspiration or a different concept-mapping software in each brainstorming session. Encourage candidates to use the same software in working out the elements of their plan and as a tool to use in their lesson. Show candidates how to change the map into an outline form to address the various learning styles of students. For topics, consider some of the following: • Feeding the people of the world • Genetic engineering or selective breeding • Hemophilia • Scientists on the cutting edge—ethical or not? • Should Congress legislate science? • What product do you wish was significantly different? What is necessary to do that? • Religious and cultural barriers to genetic engineering Consider having candidates create a Web page for their project rather than a paper

	TEACHER PREP FACULTY	TEACHER CANDIDATES	FACULTY NOTES
IMPLEMENTATION	being developed. Be sure to include both content and technology standards assessments. Before the groups begin work, develop or present a completed project scoring rubric as a whole class activity. Refer to the rubrics below as a starting point.		version. As the instructor, create a navigational or title Web page to make all the projects accessible to all in the class.
CULMINATION	Set aside class time for presenting projects. (If a Web page was created, show pages as the catalyst for the presentation.) Hold a feedback discussion for each project. If projects require editing, post the projects on the class Web site after the edits are made. Have candidates write a reflection on this activity. Suggest to candidates that this project is an appropriate addition to their electronic portfolio.	Present your project to the class. Participate in the discussion about others' projects. Frame the discussion around the use of the lessons with middle school students. Write a reflection about what you learned from this activity as well as what you think will be of most value in what you observed from your colleagues in creating a unit on heredity.	Consider having candidates evaluate each other's project using the assessment rubric developed. Provide the presentation team time to read the class assessments. Consider debriefing the activity in terms of the range of opinions in the class. The range may be representative of the range of ideas in a classroom. Discuss how to deal with the range of ideas, acknowledging that diverse points of view are important for a challenging discussion.

Assessment

Rubric: "Frankenfoods?"

CRITERIA	LEVELS OF PERFORMANCE			
	UNACCEPTABLE 1	MARGINAL 2	ACCEPTABLE 3	EXCEPTIONAL 4
Objective	Objectives are poorly stated, not measurable, and not in alignment with standards.	Objectives are in general alignment with standards but are difficult to measure and have confusing aspects.	Objectives are in alignment with the standards, are measurable, but have minor edits necessary to be clear.	Objectives are clearly stated, measurable, age appropriate, and in alignment with standards.
Standards	There is a mismatch between standards and activities or the section is incomplete.	Standards are included but are either overstated or missing a few relevant portions.	Standards are stated with a few minor edits required.	Standards are appropriate, complete, and accurate. Standards include both science and technology.
Interdisciplinary Characteristics	Lesson includes superficial and/or inauthentic inclusion of interdisciplinary linkages.	Some thought was given to interdisciplinary linkages. Some are well done while others are poor or superficial.	All disciplines are included showing thought and authenticity.	Lesson provides creative, valuable, embedded, and authentic use of language arts, mathematics, and social science concepts.
Technology	No technology is included or there is an inappropriate use of technology.	Technology is embedded but there is a weak use of technology for either student or teacher.	Appropriate use of technology is included for both the teacher and the students.	Lesson provides rich opportunities for teacher modeling and student use of technology that significantly enhance student conceptual understanding.

Rubric: "Frankenfoods?"
(Continued)

CRITERIA	LEVELS OF PERFORMANCE			
	UNACCEPTABLE 1	MARGINAL 2	ACCEPTABLE 3	EXCEPTIONAL 4
Directions	Directions show poor alignment with objectives and standards. Directions are muddled, out of sequence, and/or sketchy. Assessment link is marginal.	The alignment with objectives and standards is generally accurate but muddled. Directions are in sequence but barely provide enough information to replicate. Assessment link is marginal.	Directions are clear and sequential. Alignment with objectives and standards is mostly clear. Assessment is obvious and appropriate.	Directions are clear, sequential, complete, and include student management strategies. Directions are in alignment with objectives and standards. There is a logical flow into assessment from the sequence of activity.
Scientific Evidence	No scientific evidence or link is provided. Students do not engage in any exploration or inquiry of the scientific evidence.	Scientific evidence is marginal or weak. Students do engage in exploration or inquiry of the scientific evidence but the manner in which it takes place is superficial and seems marginally related to the topic.	Scientific evidence is present and embedded in the lesson. Students engage in an exploration or inquiry of the scientific evidence in a meaningful way.	Scientific evidence is strong and embedded in the lesson. There is an exploration of scientific evidence or inquiry into multiple points of view, or students are provided with the opportunity to validate their findings.
Assessment	The assessment is not in alignment with objectives or standards, and/or activities are unclear. Not all objectives are assessed. The assessment is not measurable.	The assessment is somewhat in alignment with the objectives and standards but introduces other unrelated elements. The assessment is single dimensional and does not provide for multiple measures of student achievement. The assessment includes both science and technology.	The assessment is mostly in alignment with the objectives and standards. The assessment is reasonably clear and provides for multiple measures of student performance. The assessment includes measures of both science and technology.	The assessment is in alignment with the objectives and standards. The assessment is clear, authentic, and provides for multiple measures of student performance. The assessment includes measuring understanding of the science content and the use of technology.
Resources	Resources are inadequate in quality and quantity. Resources are inadequately cited.	(None) THIS CRITERIA HAS NO MARGINAL OR ACCEPTABLE OPTIONS	(None)	Resources are appropriately cited. The resource portion provides a section for students. The resource portion provides a background section for peers.

Tools and Resources

SOFTWARE

Presentation software or Web page design software; Inspiration or a different concept-mapping software

HARDWARE

Multimedia presentation station

WEB SITES

Biotechnology Information Series, Genetically Engineered Fruits and Vegetables: **www.biotech.iastate.edu/biotech_info_series/bio8.html**

Create Your Own Chocolate Milk Cow: **www.sun-sentinel.com/graphics/science/clone.htm** (Site is sponsored by Sun-Sentinel.)

Designer Genes: Punnett Squares: **http://library.thinkquest.org/18258/noframes/punnettsquares.htm** (Site is sponsored by ThinkQuest Entry.)

Flying Pigs and Featherless Chickens: **www.oneworld.org/ni/issue293/pigs.htm**

"Frankenfoods" or Part of Solution: **www.news-journalonline.com/2000/Jun/1/ORTS.htm** (Site is sponsored by News Journal Online.)

Genetically Engineered Seeds Grew Well Aboard Space Shuttle: **http://seattletimes.nwsource.com/news/health-science/html98/grow_010299.html** (Site is sponsored by the Seattle Times.)

Hot Topic—Genetic Engineering/Genetically Modified Plants and Organisms: **www.strategian.com/genetic.html** (Site is sponsored by Strategian.)

Integrated Pest Management—The Good, The Bad, and the Genetically Modified: **www.science.org.au/nova/041/041key.htm** (Site is sponsored by the Australian Academy of Science.)

More Food, Cleaner Food—Gene Technology and Plants: **www.science.org.au/nova/009/009key.htm** (Site is sponsored by the Australian Academy of Science.)

Pharming, a Biopharmaceutical Company: **www.pharming.com/**

Public Perceptions of Agricultural Biotechnology: A Survey of New Jersey Residents: **www.nal.usda.gov/bic/Pubpercep/** (Site is sponsored by Rutgers.)

Credits

Virginia Reid, Thurgood Marshall Middle School, Olympia, Washinghton, **vreid@osd.wednet.edu**

John Spagnolo, Appalachian State University, Boone, North Carolina, **spagnolojt@appstate.edu**

Bonnie Mathies, Wright State University, Centerville, Ohio, **bonnie.mathies@wright.edu**

Comments/Stories

The activity has been done using both biogenetics as a general topic and food as a specific topic. When completed with candidates using the general set of topics, a rich Web site was created that candidates felt was a great resource for their teaching. When food was used as a specific topic, the candidates had a wonderful time being creative with the invention of bioengineered products that meet personal needs. The usability of the end products of the bioengineered food became good models for using the lesson in the classroom.

Wearing Your Geography

Program/Grade Range: Middle Level

Subject: Social Studies

Topic: Five Fundamental Themes of Geography

Profile: Professional Preparation, Student Teaching/Internship, First-Year Teaching

Abstract: Teacher candidates will demonstrate their understanding of the five themes of geography by participating in a simulated lesson appropriate for middle school students. Based on a geographic location depicted on a commonly worn T-shirt, the lesson will include an exploration of a specific location to illustrate the principles of the five themes. Candidates will conduct research using the Internet, e-mail, and electronic resources (CD-ROMs) to research the location shown on their T-shirt. They will report their research by selecting from the following technology tools: presentation, publication, or Web development. The overall result of the project will provide structure and organization to a student's way of thinking about the world.

STANDARDS

NETS FOR TEACHERS

I. **TECHNOLOGY OPERATIONS AND CONCEPTS—***Teachers demonstrate a sound understanding of technology operations and concepts. Teachers:*

   A. demonstrate introductory knowledge, skills, and understanding of concepts related to technology (as described in the ISTE NETS for Students).

   B. demonstrate continual growth in technology knowledge and skills to stay abreast of current and emerging technologies.

II. **PLANNING AND DESIGNING LEARNING ENVIRONMENTS AND EXPERIENCES—***Teachers plan and design effective learning environments and experiences supported by technology. Teachers:*

   A. design developmentally appropriate learning opportunities that apply technology-enhanced instructional strategies to support the diverse needs of learners.

   B. apply current research on teaching and learning with technology when planning learning environments and experiences.

   C. identify and locate technology resources and evaluate them for accuracy and suitability.

III. **TEACHING, LEARNING, AND THE CURRICULUM—***Teachers implement curriculum plans that include methods and strategies for applying technology to maximize student learning. Teachers:*

   A. facilitate technology-enhanced experiences that address content standards and student technology standards.

SOCIAL STUDIES

III: **PEOPLE, PLACES, AND ENVIRONMENTS—***Social studies programs should include experiences that provide for the study of people, places, and environments so that the learner can:*

   A. create elaborate mental maps of locales, regions, and the world that demonstrate understanding of relative location, direction, size, and shape.

   C. use appropriate resources, data sources, and geographic tools such as aerial photographs, satellite images, geographic information systems (GIS), map projections, and cartography to generate, manipulate, and interpret information such as atlases, databases, grid systems, charts, graphs, and maps.

   D. estimate distance, calculate scale, distinguish other geographic relationships such as population density and spatial distribution patterns.

   F. describe physical system changes such as seasons, climate and weather, and the water cycle and identify geographic patterns associated with them.

   H. examine, interpret, and analyze physical and cultural patterns and their interactions, such as land use, settlement patterns, cultural transmission of customs and ideas, and ecosystem changes.

   J. observe and speculate about social and economic effects of environmental changes and crises resulting from phenomena such as floods, storms, and drought.

Lesson Description

TEACHER PREP FACULTY	TEACHER CANDIDATES	FACULTY NOTES
PREPARATION Prior to the beginning of the lesson, introduce the five themes of geography. Instruct teacher candidates to bring a T-shirt to class with a location printed on it. For example, a common T-shirt acquired during traveling is "My mom went to ___ and all she brought back was this dumb shirt." Wear or bring your own T-shirt or other location-oriented clothing to class. Research your location according to the five themes of geography in preparation for the demonstration. Have candidates observe popular middle school T-shirts. What locations are depicted? Have a map of the U.S. and the world available to have Post-its placed in locations represented by the T-shirts.	Review the five themes of geography: • Location • Place • Human/environment interaction • Movement • Regions Wear a T-shirt to class that depicts the name of a location outside your city. The location can be a city, state, country, or team or company representing a location. Because this is a simulated lesson, observe the T-shirts middle school students are wearing. What locations are on the shirts worn in your area?	This lesson could also be adapted by having the candidates research a geographic location and then use paint or draw software to create their own T-shirt design. For those without appropriate T-shirts for this activity, you may want to have locations on paper for a random drawing of places to research. If you do not have a map of the world, you may want to restrict your candidates to locations in the U.S.
INTRODUCTION Using the T-shirt you wore, begin the questioning by explaining where you obtained the shirt. Place a Post-it on the map on the location depicted on your shirt. Discuss the location in terms of the five themes of geography. Have candidates place a Post-it on the map on the locations of their shirts. Discuss the geographic distribution.	Consider the five themes of geography as you discuss the location depicted on the professor's shirt. Place a Post-it on the map for the location of your shirt. Discuss the geographic distribution of the shirts worn by the class as shown by the Post-its on the map. Is there a region more highly chosen than another? Why?	If candidates bring in shirts that duplicate a location, have strips of paper with alternative locations on them for selection. An additional way to handle duplication is to have candidates examine where their shirt was made. Often this results in international locations being added to the discussion of the five themes.
IMPLEMENTATION Discuss the content criteria for the presentation of the five themes of geography. See Web sites listed in Tools and Resources for additional help. Additional guiding questions on the five themes are provided in the Faculty Notes section. Use these questions as a model in preparing your discussion of your location. Instruct candidates that their assignment is to prepare a 5 to 10 minute presentation on their location following the guidelines in the Teacher Candidates column. Divide candidates into discussion groups to consider how to approach preparing for their presentation. Provide brainstorming and feedback time in class. Following the discussion of the assignment, conduct a discussion examining the scoring rubric below. Be prepared to modify the rubric based on candidate feedback.	Discuss with your group how you are going to represent the five themes of geography using the location depicted on your T-shirt. As you create your presentation, keep in mind the following guidelines: A. The T-shirt you use for this presentation must be nonoffensive, in good taste. B. The presentation must: • demonstrate an understanding of at least three of the five themes of geography with a rationale for why the remaining two were not used; • be completed using a technology-based tool such as PowerPoint, HyperStudio, and so on; • cite sources of information for learning more about the location; and • be appropriate for use in the middle school social studies classroom, intriguing to students, and provide an introduction to a larger unit of study.	In discussing the five themes, the following questions may be used: **Location**—Include a map that shows the location of the campus in relation to the location of the T-shirt place. Information must include absolute location, time zone and relative time compared with campus location, directions from campus, and distance from campus. Use map Web sites listed in Tools and Resources. **Place**—What's it like where you are talking about? Is your place flat or mountainous, wet or dry? Compare the current campus temperature with that of the location. What's the average temperature compared to the campus location? What types of physical features are visible? What resources? Elevation? **Human/Environmental Interaction**—How do people respond and modify their environment? What is going on there? How is the land used? What are the products of your place? What are the people like in your place? What are the occupations of your place?

	TEACHER PREP FACULTY	TEACHER CANDIDATES	FACULTY NOTES
IMPLEMENTATION		Examine the scoring rubric below. You will be evaluating others as well as yourself based on the rubric. Participate in a class discussion to modify and extend the rubric.	**Movement**—A study of movement includes learning about major modes of transportation, an area's major exports and imports, and ways people communicate. Consider population patterns as they exist today, then ask how people got there. **Region**—Geographers categorize regions in two basic ways: physical and cultural. Physical regions are defined by landform (continents and mountain ranges), climate, soil, and natural vegetation. Cultural regions are defined by political, religious, linguistic, and other human characteristics.
CULMINATION	Organize the class into groups for presentation of the projects. Using three to five computer stations, multiple presentations can be taking place at the same time. Have candidates critique each others' presentations using the rubric below. Following the presentations, instruct candidates to complete a reflective journal entry focusing on what they learned from constructing their own presentation and observing others. Have candidates post their electronic presentation on the class Web site.	Divide into audience groups for the presentation. These groups can be organized by geographical region as well as randomly. Using electronic media, present your T-shirt and information on your location. Conduct a discussion about your location, eliciting feedback on your presentation. Your peers should evaluate your presentation based on the rubric below. In your journal, self-evaluate your experience in developing the presentation, the results, and what you learned from others.	As an alternative to having individuals present each T-shirt, this lesson culminates in a presentation to groups. The smaller audience allows the candidate to obtain specific feedback in a less public forum. Additionally, a class period of one presentation after another fatigues the audience and diminishes the quality of feedback. This activity relies on peers for evaluation of the product. If you want to evaluate individual projects, posting them on the Web allows you to do that outside of class.

Assessment

Rubric: "Wearing Your Geography"

CRITERIA	PERFORMANCE INDICATOR
Knowledge of five themes of geography	The presentation of the T-shirt location is organized by the five themes of geography. The content provided leaves no doubt in the audience's mind that the presenter understands and is able to apply the five themes of geography. At least three of the five themes are presented thoroughly.
Accuracy of information presented	The information presented about the location shows thoughtful consideration of much research information found centered on the five themes. Appropriate citations are mentioned or visually documented for sources used.
Developmental appropriateness of lesson	The presentation is developmentally appropriate for middle school students. The presentation is rich in content and contains interesting features that would retain the interest of middle school students and cause them to think and develop accurate generalizations about the location.
Appropriate and creative use of technology	The use of technology in the presentation is appropriate, makes use of the capabilities of the technology, and significantly contributes to student understanding of the content.
Other	(Space for additional criteria.)

Scoring Scale

⑤ The work exceeds expectations. It shows an exceptionally high level of creativity and sophisticated application of knowledge and skills. It contains elements that were not considered or discussed in class, thus setting it in a category all of its own. (Very rarely given score.)

④ The work exceeds the standard and shows very strong applications of the knowledge and skills.

③ The work meets the standard and demonstrates the appropriate application of knowledge and skills. It contains minor errors that do not diminish the quality.

② The work doesn't meet the standard. It shows inconsistent application of knowledge and skills. The minor errors are significant enough to detract from the overall quality. Additional work is required.

① The work does not meet the standard and shows limited understanding of the knowledge and skills. The work lacks depth or is incomplete with significant errors and/or omissions.

⓪ No work is presented.

Tools and Resources

WEB SITES

General

T-Shirt Day:
www.mwsc.edu/~hist465/99shirtemes.html

T-Shirt Day Worksheet:
www.mwsc.edu/~hist465/shirtwksheet.html

Five Themes of Geography

www.siskiyous.edu/class/geog10/fivethemes.html
www.siskiyous.cdu/class/geog10/shastathemes.htm
www.ed.gov/pubs/parents/Geography/
www2.una.edu/geography/statedepted/themes.html
http://yn.la.ca.us/cec/cecsst/cecsst.168.txt
http://district.moundsview.k12.mn.us/schools/dsc/socialstudies/themes97.html

Location, Place, and Region

Calculating Distance: www.indo.com/distance/
Earthwatch:
www.earthwatch.com/SKYWATCH/RDUS2D.html
Intellicast: www.intellicast.com/localweather
Map Collections: www.lib.utexas.edu/maps/map_sites/states_sites.html#M
Weather Underground: http://wunderground.com

Human Interaction

Fact Books: http://odci.gov/cia/publications/factbook/
Stately Knowledge: www.ipl.org/youth/stateknow
States On Line: www.unitedstates-on-line.com

Country Information

e-Conflict World Encyclopedia: www.emulateme.com

Credits

Jerry Aschermann, Missouri Western State College, St. Joseph, Missouri, ascher@mwsc.edu

Al Smith, Utah State University, Logan, Utah, asmith@cc.usu.edu

Carol Shields, Intel Teach to the Future, Fort Worth, Texas, carols@tenet.edu

Comments/Stories

This is a fun project that never ceases to amaze candidates and their students with the diverse locations found on T-shirts. Often middle school students think nothing of wearing T-shirts of sports teams and exotic places visited by family. Doing research on the locations provides insights into why, for example, the Green Bay Packers always seem to be playing football in the snow. Using the organizational pattern of the five themes of geography provides candidates with an activity that they can use to teach the breadth of concepts in geography. Additionally, with modification, this lesson could be used in geography lessons in foreign language classes.

What Will They Buy?

Program/Grade Range: Middle Level

Subject: Social Studies

Topic: Economic Concepts of Production, Distribution, and Consumption

Profile: Professional Preparation

Abstract: The purpose of this activity is to demonstrate to prospective teachers strategies they can use to translate abstract economic concepts into real-world experiences. Preservice teachers conduct market research to develop a new product idea (a new food or clothing item, according to age-appropriate interests). Cooperative groups use technology to brainstorm product ideas, create a data survey, and report data findings. Groups complete a final class presentation (using presentation software) to highlight their findings.

STANDARDS

NETS FOR TEACHERS

II. **PLANNING AND DESIGNING LEARNING ENVIRONMENTS AND EXPERIENCES**—*Teachers plan and design effective learning environments and experiences supported by technology. Teachers:*

   A. design developmentally appropriate learning opportunities that apply technology-enhanced instructional strategies to support the diverse needs of learners.

   B. apply current research on teaching and learning with technology when planning learning environments and experiences.

   C. identify and locate technology resources and evaluate them for accuracy and suitability.

   D. plan for the management of technology resources within the context of learning activities.

   E. plan strategies to manage student learning in a technology-enhanced environment.

III. **TEACHING, LEARNING, AND THE CURRICULUM**—*Teachers implement curriculum plans that include methods and strategies for applying technology to maximize student learning. Teachers:*

   B. use technology to support learner-centered strategies that address the diverse needs of students.

   C. apply technology to develop students' higher-order skills and creativity.

V. **PRODUCTIVITY AND PROFESSIONAL PRACTICE**—*Teachers use technology to enhance their productivity and professional practice. Teachers:*

   C. apply technology to increase productivity.

VI. **SOCIAL, ETHICAL, LEGAL, AND HUMAN ISSUES**—*Teachers understand the social, ethical, legal, and human issues surrounding the use of technology in PK–12 schools and apply that understanding in practice. Teachers:*

   A. model and teach legal and ethical practice related to technology use.

   B. apply technology resources to enable and empower learners with diverse backgrounds, characteristics, and abilities.

   D. promote safe and healthy use of technology resources.

   E. facilitate equitable access to technology resources for all students.

SOCIAL STUDIES

VII. **PRODUCTION, DISTRIBUTION, AND CONSUMPTION**—*Social studies programs should include experiences that provide for the study of how people organize for the production, distribution, and consumption of goods and services, so that the learner can:*

   A. give and explain examples of ways that economic systems structure choices about how goods and services are to be produced and distributed.

   B. describe the role that supply and demand, prices, incentives, and profits play in determining what is produced and distributed in a competitive market system.

   E. describe the role of specialization and exchange in the economic process.

   F. explain and illustrate how values and beliefs influence different economic decisions.

   I. use economic concepts to help explain historical and current developments and issues in local, national, or global contexts.

Lesson Description

TEACHER PREP FACULTY	TEACHER CANDIDATES	FACULTY NOTES
PREPARATION Assign teacher candidates to review the Web site for the National Council of Economic Education (NCEE) to look at the concepts of production, distribution, and consumption. For the URL see Tools and Resources.	Review the assigned Web site. Pay particular attention to the standards, concepts covered by the standards, and teacher resource material.	The NCEE Web site offers "one-stop shopping" for information on using economics in the classroom. Many other sources are linked on the site to make access easy for the teacher. Familiarity with the site will provide candidates with another resource to use.
INTRODUCTION Discuss the information discovered on the Web site. Using think-pair-share, introduce this activity by asking candidates to identify consumer products that have experienced success or failure in the marketplace (for example, failure: New Coca Cola/Classic Coca Cola; success: Pepsi One). Have candidates think alone about why they believe the products failed. Have individuals pair up to share their ideas, coming to a consensus on several of the best. Using the Rapid Fire feature in Inspiration, list the products and brainstorm the reasons for success or failure of a product. Have candidates speculate on how the failures could have been avoided. Insist that candidates relate their initial proposals to what they learned about the characteristics of adolescents. Introduce the lesson project by proposing the following scenario: "You are a product developer for Adolescent-Perfect Engineering (APE). The corporate managers have asked you to design a new product that will appeal to today's adolescent. How would you do this? Investigate the steps that the developer takes from product inception to the market research data reporting." Have candidates further consider the steps in production, cost range of the product, and means of marketing and distribution.	Participate in a discussion about the NCEE Web site. Divide into pairs to participate in the think-pair-share to identify products that have been successes and failures in the marketplace. Participate in the use of the Inspiration Rapid Fire technique to discover the connection of success and failure to concepts in adolescent development that have been covered in previous coursework. Add another dimension to the discussion by suggesting ways that the failures could have been avoided. Reframe the discussion by brainstorming the steps necessary to solve the problem posed in the development of a new product. Address the issues brought up in the discussion of what became successes as well as failures.	Discussion of product success or failure may be limited depending on candidates' preexisting experiences and misconceptions about marketing. **Note:** Check out the science lesson called "Frankenfoods?" for possible interdisciplinary connections. The economics elements of this lesson can be combined with the creative, bioengineering aspects of the science lesson.
IMPLEMENTATION Provide project guidelines that include: • Identifying project tasks with assignment of tasks to group members • Market research on proposed product including justification/rationale • Developing a project production time line • Creating an enticing product marketing plan • Developing a rubric to determine product originality and creativity (for use	Project guidelines: • Divide into groups of three to four. • Brainstorm to identify product ideas. • Select product; create a rationale for your selection. • Develop survey instrument to determine target audience and need for product. • Conduct an electronic survey of adolescents to obtain information. • Analyze survey results.	The product identification can be the most interesting part of the project. Encourage candidates to complete a needs assessment survey as well as a cost analysis. Conducting a market survey of adolescents will provide candidates with insight into the buying habits and desires of students they will encounter in their student teaching and first years of teaching. Aside from the multimedia presentation, each element of the product can specifically target the use of a technology tool. For example:

	TEACHER PREP FACULTY	TEACHER CANDIDATES	FACULTY NOTES
IMPLEMENTATION	with own students as well as part of assessment of the group work) Conduct a discussion on the assessment rubric for the project. Include elements of technology assessment as well as a reflection of economics concepts covered. Have groups prepare a multimedia presentation on their product, steps of production, and results of their survey.	• Alter the product plan based on the feedback. • Create a production plan. • Create a marketing plan. Participate in development of a rubric for the project. Prepare a multimedia presentation on the steps in development of the product as well as a description and rationale for the product.	**Project Task**—Inspiration can be used to create a map of task assignments as well as a flow chart of the tasks. **Market Research**—In addition to electronically conducting the research, candidates can display the research on a spreadsheet with associated charts and graphs. **Project Production Time Line**—Timeliner can be used as well as a word processing program for creating a variety of time lines. **Marketing Plan**—A PowerPoint presentation can be used stemming from one of the business templates that comes with the program. If a CAD program is available, the product can be drawn in a three-dimensional form such as one used to create a prototype.
CULMINATION	Have candidates present their findings and provide feedback. After group presentations, discuss ways to extend this activity to the middle school level. The Invention Convention, a common activity sponsored by many local economic councils, can be highlighted. Assign candidates an individual assignment to develop a lesson plan sequence for middle school students to engage in a similar experience. Be sure to revisit student standards in economics. Be specific about technology requirements, as well as accommodations for the needs of special populations of learners.	Present your group's multimedia presentation. Provide feedback to other groups on their product and marketing plan. Develop a lesson plan based on your experience. Customize the plan to meet the needs of the students you have in field experience or you are anticipating teaching in student teaching. Carefully plan for the use of technology, management of resources, and organization of the classroom activities. Follow the lesson plan format designated in class.	Be sure to allow enough time for group presentations. Between presentations, provide the class with the scoring rubric to check their ability to observe the elements decided on in the development of the rubric. As an addendum to the multimedia presentations, invite a focus group of middle school students to observe the presentations. Have the students provide feedback on the products designed. An alternative way to complete the focus group activity is to post the presentations online, and contact a few middle schools to provide feedback and/or rate the products. Consider having candidates include a reflection on how their experience influenced the development of their own lesson plan sequence.

Assessment

The following table is appropriate for tracking how candidates are able to address the standards within the context of a course. Note that in this table, the specific performance indicators provided for the professional preparation profile are not addressed individually. Rather, the elements of the activity are used to justify meeting the standard, in general, with the applicable performance indicators listed as a group as they apply to the development of the multimedia presentation on the product developed and the follow-up lesson plan.

Note: Generic multimedia presentation rubrics are available in Appendix C. Draw from group-developed rubrics on creativity in product development if additional forms of assessment are desired.

Table: Tracking Standards Met within the Context of a Course

STANDARDS	PERFORMANCE INDICATORS	ASSESSMENT (Processes and Products)
NETS for Teachers II. Planning and Designing Learning Environments and Experiences—Teachers plan and design effective learning environments and experiences supported by technology.	Teachers: A. design developmentally appropriate learning opportunities that apply technology-enhanced instructional strategies to support the diverse needs of learners. B. apply current research on teaching and learning with technology when planning learning environments and experiences. C. identify and locate technology resources and evaluate them for accuracy and suitability. D. plan for the management of technology resources within the context of learning activities. E. plan strategies to manage student learning in a technology-enhanced environment.	As candidates prepare middle school lessons based on their experience, the lessons can be assessed based on the extent to which the design of the lesson meets the indicators.
NETS for Teachers III. Teaching, Learning, and the Curriculum—Teachers implement curriculum plans that include methods and strategies for applying technology to maximize student learning.	Teachers: B. use technology to support learner-centered strategies that address the diverse needs of students. C. apply technology to develop students' higher-order skills and creativity.	The lesson plan developed should reflect learner-centered needs. Additionally, the reflection on their experience as learners should bring out a recognition of the learner-centered nature of the activity. Survey information is accurately analyzed through correct use of data analysis technology. Develop the rubric with candidates to determine criteria for product originality.
NETS for Teachers V. Productivity and Professional Practice—Teachers use technology to enhance their productivity and professional practice.	Teachers: C. apply technology to increase productivity.	This standard is demonstrated by the use of the various technology tools within each portion of the product development.
NETS for Teachers VI. Social, Ethical, Legal, and Human Issues—Teachers understand the social, ethical, legal, and human issues surrounding the use of technology in PK–12 schools and apply that understanding in practice.	Teachers: A. model and teach legal and ethical practice related to technology use. B. apply technology resources to enable and empower learners with diverse backgrounds, characteristics, and abilities. D. promote safe and healthy use of technology resources. E. facilitate equitable access to technology resources for all students.	The standards are demonstrated by the candidates' analysis and use of NCEE Web resources in preparation for the activity and as part of the student lesson. If video or other data gathering technologies are used, safe access and legal considerations must be demonstrated.
Social Studies VII. Production, Distribution, and Consumption—Social studies programs should include experiences that provide for the study of how people organize for the production, distribution, and consumption of goods and services, so that the learner can:	F. explain and illustrate how values and beliefs influence different economic decisions. H. compare basic economic systems according to who determines what is produced, distributed, and consumed.	Display and explain survey results. Candidates are able to construct survey questions, target a potential survey audience, and appropriately analyze survey results.

Tools and Resources

SOFTWARE

Inspiration Software (for brainstorming and discussion activities); Microsoft Excel or other spreadsheet software (for analyzing data); Microsoft PowerPoint or other presentation software (for reporting data). If specific tools are used for each element of the project, additional software packages needed are spreadsheet, CAD, and Tom Snyder's Timeliner.

HARDWARE

Computer, printer, copier, projection device

WEB SITES

National Council for Economic Education:
www.nationalcouncil.org

Nebraska Economic Education Web Resource:
http://ecedweb.unomaha.edu/teach.htm

University of Kansas Center for Economic Education:
www.cee.soe.ukans.edu/

Credits

Jerry Aschermann, Missouri Western State College, St. Joseph, Missouri, **ascher@mwsc.edu**

Al Smith, Utah State University, Logan, Utah, **asmith@cc.usu.edu**

Carol Shields, Intel Teach to the Future, Forth Worth, Texas, **carols@tenet.edu**

Comments/Stories

This project has proven to be wildly successful in that the candidates thoroughly enjoy the interaction with the middle school students. The process of doing the market research provided insights into what the students liked and didn't like. Every semester, there are several product groups who initially feel they have a solid sense of what middle school students like. They are invariably surprised by the reaction of the students. Further, some groups took the initiative to digitize video of some of their research. The middle school students' reactions embedded in their product presentation added credibility to their work.

Additionally, foreign language classes could adapt this lesson. Preservice teachers could identify international products not available in the United States and conduct market research on these products to determine their potential success.

Technology in Secondary Education Programs

- Introduction

- English Language Arts
    - Assessing Research Materials
    - Literature Is More than Just a Book

- Mathematics
    - Trigonometric Tables: Tangent
    - WebQuest: Meeting of Mathematical Minds

- Science
    - Cool Liquids
    - Gravity

- Social Studies
    - Who's in Control Here?
    - Why Are Things Where They Are?

TECHNOLOGY IN
Secondary Education Programs

Introduction

Because responsibility for teaching methods in secondary education varies from being that of the academic departments to the college of education, finding a consistent way to develop technology experiences can be problematic. Regardless of who has responsibility for teaching the courses, the content of the secondary curriculum provides almost limitless opportunities for the effective use of technology. The close link between the high school course content and prerequisite coursework for successful academic experiences in college makes collaboration between the academic departments and the college of education imperative.

After surveying secondary education programs that had self-identified as having successfully integrated technology into coursework, the following recommendations were found to be most common:

1. Have enough portable and lab equipment for the number of groups using probeware. Permitting candidates to check out equipment for use at school sites significantly increased the number of candidates who implemented technology-rich sessions in their student teaching.

2. Examine the technology use in both the lower division and major level courses while developing the plan for technology implementation in the secondary methods courses. Ensure that skills and expectations for use in the major field are methodically developed before making the connection to teaching at the secondary level.

3. Use the secondary education advisory committee to recommend secondary teachers who are well recognized as using technology effectively in the major field. Create a liaison with the teacher group to: (a) advise on current trends in technology in the major field in regional schools; (b) communicate the expectations of new teachers; and (c) provide feedback on graduates and their strengths and weaknesses in utilizing technology with students. This advisory group is the best source for cooperating teachers and identifying other potential cooperating teachers.

4. Make use of well-equipped regional secondary schools as professional development schools or small cohort sites as a way to consistently connect to secondary students as well as to assist in providing consistent access to hardware for candidates.

5. Provide candidates with a checklist of skills and experiences or performances that must be demonstrated throughout the program. The checklist provides the listing of performance indicators by standard with electronic space to list all artifacts containing elements that meet the standard. Have candidates use the checklist as an artifact for the digital portfolio.

6. Designate targeted technology-based activities in the methods courses and the content area courses that are consistently carried out and used for performance assessment. Over time, faculty will often embellish the activities and link the skills with other coursework.

ACTIVITIES

The following activities were designed to connect common secondary education methods course content with examples of effective uses of technology. As stated earlier, the activities are not meant to be at the forefront of utilizing emerging technologies. Rather, they are designed to utilize currently available technologies in ways that are accessible to most faculty members.

Assessing Research Materials (English Language Arts)

Exploring the validity of research materials available on the Web and creating an assessment rubric to examine sources is an activity that candidates can easily modify for use in the classroom.

Literature Is More than Just a Book (English Language Arts)

Electronically annotating a key piece of literature provides teacher candidates with an opportunity to create a customized learning tool for second language learners and other students who require alternatives to increase comprehension.

Trigonometric Tables: Tangent (Mathematics)

Learning the relationship between the often formulaic trigonometric function table and how it is used in a realistic situation is the goal of this activity.

WebQuest: Meeting of Mathematical Minds (Mathematics)

Using the model outlined in the Section 1 chapter "Using Model Strategies for Integrating Technology into Teaching," candidates participate in a WebQuest to create a debate among famous mathematicians on a current issue.

Cool Liquids (Science)

Using a temperature time graph, candidates explore the phase changes of a liquid as it evaporates.

Gravity (Science)

"The falling rate of objects" is the subject of this activity, which uses a variety of technologies including probeware.

Who's in Control Here? (Social Studies)

Using the Internet and presentation tools, candidates explore the multifaceted nature of sovereignty.

Why Are Things Where They Are? (Social Studies)

Using Web-based information, satellite technology, and other geographic software, teacher candidates explore the concept of urban place location.

Assessing Research Materials

Program/Grade Range: Secondary

Subject: English Language Arts

Topic: Evaluation of Research Sources

Profile: Professional Preparation

Abstract: The task of teaching the research process often falls to the English language arts teacher. An important part of this process is guiding teacher candidates through the creation of a useable rubric for assessing the value of resources in terms of validity and usefulness to the assignment at hand. In this activity, candidates (1) select a topic, problem, or dilemma to research; (2) formulate a plan of action to access and evaluate a variety of resources (electronic, print, audio, and human resources); (3) collect and organize the information; (4) create a resource evaluation rubric; and (5) communicate their findings to the class. This is an activity that can be replicated in the secondary classroom.

STANDARDS

NETS FOR TEACHERS

II. **PLANNING AND DESIGNING LEARNING ENVIRONMENTS AND EXPERIENCES**—*Teachers plan and design effective learning environments and experiences supported by technology. Teachers:*

C. identify and locate technology resources and evaluate them for accuracy and suitability.

III. **TEACHING, LEARNING, AND THE CURRICULUM**—*Teachers implement curriculum plans that include methods and strategies for applying technology to maximize student learning. Teachers:*

A. facilitate technology-enhanced experiences that address content standards and student technology standards.

C. apply technology to develop students' higher-order skills and creativity.

VI. **SOCIAL, ETHICAL, LEGAL, AND HUMAN ISSUES**—*Teachers understand the social, ethical, legal, and human issues surrounding the use of technology in PK–12 schools and apply that understanding in practice. Teachers:*

E. facilitate equitable access to technology resources for all students.

ENGLISH LANGUAGE ARTS

7. Students conduct research on issues and interests by generating ideas and questions, and by posing problems. They gather, evaluate, and synthesize data from a variety of sources (e.g., print and nonprint texts, artifacts, and people) to communicate their discoveries in ways that suit their purpose and audience.

8. Students use a variety of technological and information resources (e.g., libraries, databases, computer networks, and video) to gather and synthesize information and to create and communicate knowledge.

Lesson Description

	TEACHER PREP FACULTY	TEACHER CANDIDATES	FACULTY NOTES
PREPARATION	Before scheduling this activity, decide whether the topics to be researched are limited to topics that expand this course or are selected in collaboration with requirements from other courses. Instruct teacher candidates to have the topic selected and a few resources to support the topic brought to class. When giving the preliminary assignment, include the format for reporting the resources (APA, MLA, etc.). In preparation for modeling the assessment of resources, select several resources, at least two of which are electronic. The demonstration can be more	Select a research topic, within the guidelines provided by your professor, that will allow you to use both print and nonprint resources. Search for print and nonprint resources that will be evaluated later. Develop a plan for cataloging and saving the resources you find. Consider a Word file or database for cataloging the resources, or a Web address book. Format each entry in a format provided by the faculty member or as assigned (MLA, APA, other).	This activity can be done in collaboration with other methods or discipline courses as a content-based assignment is made. Collaboration with another course adds further meaning to the resources being evaluated as well as models multidisciplinary assignments. It is important, also, to note that the culmination of the activity does *not* result in the production of a research paper on this topic, but in the evaluation of resources that will support the writing of the paper. The presentation of the final resource list may be done in a number of ways depending upon available technology. Some possibilities include

	TEACHER PREP FACULTY	TEACHER CANDIDATES	FACULTY NOTES
PREPARATION	engaging when revealing your own system for filing and retrieving resources that you have located and want to keep for future use. Make sure that those you select include one that is credible and one that is suspect.		development of or posting on a class Web site, individual PowerPoint presentations, and so on. Encourage creativity. Familiarize yourself with the literature on assessing electronic resources. Some sites are noted in the Tools and Resources section (Evaluating Electronic Resources).
INTRODUCTION	Have candidates work in small groups to list reasons for evaluating print and nonprint resources. Provide in-class time for candidates to share their lists. Encourage candidates to think in terms of secondary students' use of resources, what they might find, and what they might accept as fact. Have groups write a brief summary paragraph about the need to evaluate print and nonprint resources to use as a rationale for the criteria they develop. Ask candidates to reword their reasons into criteria statements for evaluating the credibility of resources. Raise their awareness of ethics concerns regarding plagiarism, copyright, crediting, and credibility of sources.	In small groups, brainstorm reasons why resources need to be evaluated. Share your thoughts with other groups in the class. Add reasons others suggest to your list if you don't have them. With your group, write a brief summary paragraph (a rationale) about the need to evaluate print and nonprint resources. Follow this paragraph with an opening, "The following criteria should be used to determine the credibility and validity of resources:...." Reword the reasons on your list into statements of criteria for credible and valid sources of information. Add these to the brief summary paragraph.	Candidates will find value in generating these lists. Much discussion will take place over whether certain items should be considered reliable sources of information. If candidates have already had this experience, the activity could be modified to have them locate several online forms for assessing the value of Web sites to compare and contrast. Regardless of prior experience, candidates should be able to articulate an understanding of the need for evaluating print and electronic resources. The first part of this activity, in the Introduction section, could take more than an hour or one class session. The actual generation of a rubric for assessing resources could be given as group homework or saved for another day's class. Collaborative work on the specific rubrics is necessary regardless of the individual topic and resource list.
IMPLEMENTATION	Assist candidates in creating a rubric that can be used to evaluate print and electronic resources for general validity and topic-specific usefulness in a research setting. (Some Web resources are provided in the Tools and Resources section.) Separate from the rubric development, work with the candidates to determine the criteria on which this rubric will be assessed. (How will the candidates know they have developed an effective rubric?) Set the stage for using the rubric by introducing the resources you collected and explaining why you collected them. Show the candidates how you file your resources for later use. Provide time in class for candidates to work on evaluating two resources you provided (one reliable, one not) using the rubric developed. Once the scoring on the rubrics has been completed in evaluating your resources, have the candidates work in groups to compare and contrast their results and reach consensus on each item.	Use the criteria generated in the first part of this activity to design a rubric of at least five criteria and three levels of accomplishment. Be sure to include general validity and usefulness to the topic as two of the criteria. Work cooperatively with the faculty member to develop a rubric to assess the rubric you generate (Rubric on Rubrics). Use the rubric created to assess the two demonstration resources. Reach consensus in your group on each criteria. Make notes on where you think the rubric is not clear or adequate. As groups, share results of the assessment of the two resources. Come to consensus on the evaluation of the resources. Participate in the group discussion on modifying the resource assessment rubric. As a group, modify the Rubric on Rubrics as needed. As homework, individually, critically analyze at least three print and five nonprint resources gathered on your topic.	Candidates may become very involved in the creation process of the general rubric, but it is essential that this process be a collaborative effort. It is tempting to pull ready-made rubrics from the Internet to assess Web sites and other electronic media. Some of those resources are listed in Tools and Resources. After the candidates have had the experience of developing useful rubrics themselves, the introduction of ready-made rubrics will cause them to be more critical of what they see. Throughout the teacher preparation program there should be opportunities to create rubrics. This activity focuses specifically on rubric development while intertwining ideas of validity of resources. Keeping that objective in mind, avoid concentrating on writing the research paper itself at this point. Subsequent activities can concentrate on the writing process. For candidates who need further guidance in how to report their information, offer

	TEACHER PREP FACULTY	TEACHER CANDIDATES	FACULTY NOTES
IMPLEMENTATION	Before they proceed to evaluating their own collection of resources, assist candidates in modifying the resource assessment rubric based on their experience. Modify the in-class generated Rubric on Rubrics to reflect their experience. Assign candidates to critically analyze at least three print and five nonprint resources using the class-generated rubric. Add a rationale for the results. Have candidates modify a presentation rubric to accommodate the assignment.	Add a rationale for accepting or rejecting a resource. Participate in modifying a presentation rubric to fit the needs of the assignment.	some alternatives: an oral report, a written report, an annotated table, a chart, a PowerPoint presentation, a set of Web pages, an editorial essay, and so on.
CULMINATION	Provide the time and the environment for the presentations of candidate resource evaluation results. Include in the discussion references to perceived differences between print and nonprint resources. Ask candidates to write a closing reflection (what they did, what problems they encountered, what they would do differently next time). Conclude the reflection with thoughts on how this lesson would be used with students.	Present your findings to your classmates. Complete a written reflection on this lesson to include what you did, what problems you encountered, and what you would do differently next time. Conclude the reflection with ways to use this lesson with high school students.	The presentation of the findings offers rich opportunities for evaluating candidate understanding of the development and use of rubrics as well as the assessment of resources. Time constraints may not allow for presenting and discussing the assessment of the resources. Consider other means of sharing and debriefing results that do not take class time, such as an electronic threaded discussion, reflective journals, electronic study groups, and so on.

Assessment

The lesson contains three items that might be assessed: (1) a rubric, (2) a presentation, and (3) a written reflection. (See Appendix C for a "Multimedia Presentation" rubric and a "Written Reflection" rubric.) Consider using these criteria in the development of an assessment rubric for this lesson.

Rubric: "Assessing Research Materials"

CRITERIA	LEVELS OF PERFORMANCE		
	EMERGING 1	ACCEPTABLE 2	DISTINGUISHED 3
Assessing Resources			
Variety of reference materials	Candidate evaluated three print and five nonprint resources from the same or similar sources (such as articles from the same journal).	Candidate evaluated three print and five nonprint resources, each from unique sources.	Candidate evaluated more than three print and five nonprint resources from varied sources with a rationale for the selection of the resource.
Evaluating Credibility of Resources			
Evaluating each resource for topic-specific usefulness in a research setting	Many of the resources are not specifically related to the topic. Further research on appropriate resources is necessary.	All of the resources are directly related to the topic.	All of the resources directly relate to the topic. Some of the resources provide unique points of view that will enrich the discussion of the topic in unanticipated ways.
Use of rubric	Use of the rubric does not indicate understanding of the criteria or the resource.	Use of the rubric indicates some understanding of the criteria or the resource.	Use of the rubric indicates understanding of the criteria and appropriate evaluation of the resource.
Presenting conclusions from research	Conclusions are presented based on the evaluation of the resources. The conclusions cannot be generalized and do not extend experience into teaching.	Generalizations are made from the experience of evaluating the resources that inform further searches on the topic.	Generalizations are made based on the experience that inform further searches on this topic and other topics. Guideline statements are suggested for evaluating resources with students.
Oral presentation*			
Effectiveness of presentation	Presentation did not engage class, lacked continuity, was disorganized.	Presentation caught the attention of the class; content was conveyed.	Presentation sustained the attention of the class in an informative and entertaining way, leaving the audience with a strong understanding of the generalizations and conclusions of the research.

*Note: See also the "Multimedia Presentation" rubric in Appendix C.

Tools and Resources

SOFTWARE

Internet access, CD-ROM databases, presentation software, word processing programs, rubric construction software (not required)

HARDWARE

Computer with Internet connectivity, presentation devices

WEB SITES

Content

American's Freedom Documents:
www.education-world.com/a_lesson/lesson190.shtml

BBC Online History: www.bbc.co.uk/history

Biographies: www.biography.com

EdSitement: www.edsitement.neh.gov (This provides subject-based access to top humanities sites.)

Great Sites for Teaching about American History and Culture: www.education-world.com/a_sites/sites028.shtml

Search Yahoo for "oral history."

Evaluating Electronic Resources

Assessing Electronic Sources:
http://cwolf.uaa.alaska.edu/~afdtk/assess.htm (This site contains categories to evaluate and several links to other evaluation sites.)

Evaluating the Quality of Internet Information Sources:
http://itech.1.coe.uga.edu/faculty/gwilkinson/Webeval.html

How to Critically Analyze Information Sources:
www.library.cornell.edu/okuref/research/skill26.htm

Scholarly Research and Electronic Resources:
www.wwp.brown.edu/project/newsletter/vol04num02/scholarly042.html

Tips for Evaluating a World Wide Web Search:
www.uflib.ufl.edu/hss/ref/tips.html

Rubrics

Creating Rubrics: www.rubristar.4teachers.com

Kathy Schrock's Rubrics and Assessment:
http://school.discovery.com/schrockguide/

Oral Presentation:
http://memorial.sdcs.k12.ca.us/LESSONS/WWII/WWIIunit/oralpresentation.html

Presentations: www.ncsu.edu/midlink/rub.pres.html

Rubric Construction Set: www.landmark-project.com/classweb/rubrics/

Ruminating on Rubrics:
www.accessexcellence.org/21st/SER/JA/rubrics.html

Using Rubrics in Middle School:
www.middleweb.com/rubricsHG.html#anchor352906

Credits

Marylee Boarman, Bishop Dunne Catholic School, Dallas, Texas, **mboarman@bdhs.org**

Dale Allender, National Council of Teachers of English, Urbana, Illinois, **dallender@ncte.org**

Comments/Stories

Many of the teacher credentialing programs require all candidates to take the language arts course as language arts is a subject that is reinforced across the curriculum. Because the candidates may have done their major coursework in other departments, their experience with evaluating resources may vary widely. This activity is particularly helpful when done at the beginning of the semester as it levels the experience in the class in evaluation of resources. It also provides a good reinforcement for the creation of rubrics.

Literature Is More than Just a Book

Program/Grade Range: Secondary

Subject: English Language Arts

Topic: Multicultural Literary Study and Web Site Production

Profile: Professional Preparation

Abstract: The study of any piece of literature will ideally involve more than just a reading and analysis of the assigned text. Using collaborative learning groups, teacher candidates explore the richness of a multicultural literary work, searching for cultural and primary source information to support contextual knowledge and construct Web sites that connect both. The process includes analyzing the text for content and structure, searching for primary source and other appropriate contextual information, analyzing the structure of an existing Web site, constructing a Web site by locating and adding information, initiating conversations on electronic mailing lists, scanning visual images, embedding video, linking sites, and so on.

STANDARDS

NETS FOR TEACHERS

II. **PLANNING AND DESIGNING LEARNING ENVIRONMENTS AND EXPERIENCES**—*Teachers plan and design effective learning environments and experiences supported by technology. Teachers:*

   A. design developmentally appropriate learning opportunities that apply technology-enhanced instructional strategies to support the diverse needs of learners.

   C. identify and locate technology resources and evaluate them for accuracy and suitability.

III. **TEACHING, LEARNING, AND THE CURRICULUM**—*Teachers implement curriculum plans that include methods and strategies for applying technology to maximize student learning. Teachers:*

   A. facilitate technology-enhanced experiences that address content standards and student technology standards.

   C. apply technology to develop students' higher-order skills and creativity.

ENGLISH LANGUAGE ARTS

1. Students read a wide range of print and nonprint texts to build an understanding of texts, of themselves, and of the cultures of the United States and the world; to acquire new information; to respond to the needs and demands of society and the workplace; and for personal fulfillment. Among these texts are fiction and nonfiction, classic and contemporary works.

2. Students read a wide range of literature from many periods in many genres to build an understanding of the many dimensions (e.g., philosophical, ethical, and aesthetic) of human experience.

Lesson Description

	TEACHER PREP FACULTY	TEACHER CANDIDATES	FACULTY NOTES
PREPARATION	Select novels or text with multicultural themes for reading by teacher candidate literature circles. Using a common search engine such as Yahoo! for "author sites," provides a myriad of sites from which to choose. (Or see sample resources at the end of this lesson.) Use these as samples for discussion. Review the Web site evaluation instrument from Appendix D. Select this one or one that best fits your needs from those listed in Tool and Resources. Set up an electronic mailing list to enable candidates to work together online. Investigate campus resources for Web site construction software such as FrontPage or	Read and discuss the novels or text in literature circles. Search the Internet for possible related sites and information.	This lesson can be altered to focus on a single piece of literature. The development of the Web site can be distributed among the candidates with each element assigned to a group. Elements may include politics of the time, historical context, geography, cultural foundations, religion, and so on. Spot-check and conduct mini-lessons on "surfing" tips, as needed, using the collections of search engines suggested in Tools and Resources. If technology to build Web sites is unavailable, adapt the lesson for PowerPoint, HyperCard, or other presentation media. When implementing this exercise in a high school classroom, it is recommended that

	TEACHER PREP FACULTY	TEACHER CANDIDATES	FACULTY NOTES
PREPARATION	Pagemill as well as training for candidates who may need additional help.		student teachers and first-year teachers communicate with building administration regarding the use of potentially controversial Web sites and issues in light of existing district and building policies on acceptable use, CHIP, and COPPA. Use NCTE's Rationales for Challenged Books as a resource for this discussion.
INTRODUCTION	Place the candidates in their literature circles to discuss the contextual knowledge necessary to understand the selected piece of literature. What historical, geographic, visual, biographical, spiritual, or religious information, for example, will support a broader understanding of the assigned reading? Help candidates to articulate and identify categories that might not be recognized. Show several model Web sites in class. Conduct a whole-class exploration of the Web sites, analyzing for visual appeal, ease of navigation, and access to and depth of information. Use or design a rubric to evaluate this Web site. (See Tools and Resources.) Assign groups the development of a Web site focused on the contextual background of each piece of literature. This site should address gaps in their knowledge based on the literature piece selected. Discuss issues of fair use, plagiarism, and ethical conventions for presenting information such as copyrights and credits. Discuss assessing the credibility of sources.	In small groups, discuss the contextual knowledge necessary to understand the assigned piece of literature. As the discussion takes place, outline knowledge gaps and list areas of content that will support a broader understanding of the text. Examine a Web site for visual appeal, ease of navigation, and access to and depth of information. Suggest other features that might be of value. Use or design a rubric to assess Web sites to serve as a guide in developing your own. In small groups, begin the development of a contextual Web site. Keep issues of fair use, plagiarism, copyright, and crediting sources in mind as well as determining the credibility of sources.	Monitor literature circles, ask probing questions, and do an ongoing analysis of candidate responses to ensure that discussions are appropriate in depth. It is important to establish a climate in which candidates can articulate the gaps in their own knowledge as a springboard for exploring topics otherwise left alone. Consider using a Web site evaluation tool to analyze the Web sites you have located for candidates. One is in Appendix D and several are provided in the Tools and Resources section. An alternative organization of this lesson is to assign each group a unique aspect of the context of the literature, such as contemporary historical events, lives of people, cultural mores, and so on.
IMPLEMENTATION	Monitor and facilitate the research process and Web site construction. Initiate a mailing list conversation to engage feedback on the site as it is being built.	Gather information, images, documents, video clips, sound bites, and so on to build a Web template. Use Web links listed as resources at the end of this lesson as a beginning (contextual information). Participate in a mailing list conversation as you work with your group to construct your Web site.	It may be necessary to prod or suggest the location of appropriately thorough and authentic Web sites that address knowledge gaps, including political and cultural organizations appropriate to the literary text. Several Internet resources are provided at the end of this lesson.
CULMINATION	Facilitate the group presentations of Web sites. Have candidates evaluate their own sites using the class-generated rubric. Encourage candidates to save their sites for an electronic portfolio entry.	Launch the Web site. Present a tour of your Web site to your classmates or allow for independent exploration. Do a self-assessment of your site using the class-generated rubric. Consider saving your site as an electronic portfolio entry.	Suggest that candidates modify this lesson to use during student teaching and their first year to meet ISTE NETS for Students standards and indicators.

Assessment

Rubric: Shell for In-Class Completion

CRITERIA	LEVELS OF PERFORMANCE		
	UNACCEPTABLE	ACCEPTABLE	TARGET
Contextual Knowledge			
Historical			
Geographic			
Visual		CLASS TO DEVELOP DESCRIPTIVE PERFORMANCE STATEMENTS	
Biographical			
Spiritual or Religious Information (Modify options to fit assignment)			
Web Site			
(Insert desired design features)			

Note: See Appendix D for the rubric "Evaluating Web Resources for Reliability and Credibility."

Tools and Resources

SOFTWARE
Web development software, Internet access, search engines

HARDWARE
Computer with Internet connectivity, scanner, computer projection device

WEB SITES
Contextual Information
American Memory: http://lcWeb2.loc.gov/ (This is an online digital library with historical photographs.)

BBC Online History: www.bbc.co.uk/hsitory (Search for a topic in history and get the British perspective.)

Curry School of Education Multicultural Pavilion: http://curry.edschool.virginia.edu/curry/centers/multicultural/sites1.html

EdSitement: The Best of Humanities on the Web: www.edsitement.neh.gov/

Multicultural Education and Ethnic Groups: Selected Resources: wwwlibrary.csustan.edu/lboyer/tmp/multicu.htm

National Council of Teachers of English-American Collection: www.ncteamericancollection.org

Scribbling Women: Online Resources for Teaching American Women's Literature: www.scribblingwomen.org

This Day in History: www.historychannel.com/thisday (This site provides links to happenings on any day in history.)

Author and Literature
Edgar Allan Poe National Historic Site: www.nps.gov/edal/

Goosebumps: http://place.scholastic.com/goosebumps/index.htm

The HoBBit Site: www.mi.uib.no/~respl/tolkien/

The Official Jean Craighead George Web Site: www.jeancraigheadgeorge.com/

Robert Louis Stephenson Web Site: www.unibg.it/rls/rls.htm

Evaluating
The ABCs of Web Site Evaluation: http://kathyschrock.net/abceval/

The ABCs of Web Site Evaluation: Teaching Media Literacy in the Age of the Internet: www.connectedteacher.com/newsletter/abcs.asp

Blue Web'n Site Evaluation Rubric: www.kn.pacbell.com/wired/bluewebn/rubric.html

Critical Evaluation Information: http://school.discovery.com/schrockguide/eval.html

Evaluating Web Sites for Curriculum Use: www.germantownacademy.org/Academics/US/Library/Internet/Evaluation/teacher.htm

Internet Searches

Kid Friendly Search Engines: **www.rcls.org/ksearch.htm** (This is a collection of search engines located on one page.)

Search the Net: Your Top Ten Resources: **www.windweaver.com/searchtools.htm**

Cultural

4directions: **http://4directions.org/**

African American Web Connection: **www.aawc.com/aaa.html**

Chinese Cultural Center: **www.c-c-c.org/**

Heard Museum: Native Cultures and Art: **www.heard.org/**

Institute for Korean American Culture: **www.KAMuseum.org/**

Japanese American Experience: **www.balchinstitute.org/japanese/japanese.html**

Japanese American National Museum: **www.janm.org/**

Korean American Museum: **www.KAMuseum.org/**

Pacific Islander Cultural Association: **www.pica-org.org/**

REFERENCE TEXT

NCTE/IRA. (1998). *Rationales for challenged books* [CD-ROM]. NCTE/IRA [Producer and Distributor]. (See description at www.ncte.org/chronicle/CC98119rationales.html.) CD-ROM holds more than 200 rationales (references to reviews, plot summaries, redeeming qualities, teaching objectives, methods, and assignments) and covers 170 books and films.

Credits

Dale Allender, National Council of Teachers of English, Urbana, Illinois, **dallender@ncte.org**

Marylee Boarman, Bishop Dunne Catholic School, Dallas, Texas, **mboarman@bdhs.org**

Comments/Stories

This activity has been done both ways—one book and many books. The advantage of doing one book is that the resulting Web site is very rich for each contextual element. Candidates have commented how useful the site is as they go into their student teaching. The advantage of using multiple pieces of literature is that the candidates are exposed to more literature and have access to more Web sites that have been created. However, generally, the Web sites created under those conditions are not as well developed and lack the depth that the efforts of a whole class can provide. An additional note: The Web site development skills of the candidates seem to improve each semester. Advancements in Web development software are making this process easier and easier.

Trigonometric Tables: Tangent

Program/Grade Range: Secondary

Subject: Mathematics

Topic: Understanding Trigonometric Tables

Profile: Professional Preparation

Abstract: This model lesson focuses on developing the concept of the trigonometric table of tangents using Geometer's Sketchpad. The lesson uses the initial problem of how to measure the heights of rockets launched in a science class. Upon completion of the activity, teacher candidates will have developed a trigonometric function determined as a procedure for finding the height of a succession of rockets launched, developed a table of tangents for angles, created a scenario for use in a classroom that uses tangents as a solution, and explored possible student misconceptions in developing understanding of the tangent table. This activity can be an introductory exercise to Geometer's Sketchpad.

STANDARDS

NETS FOR TEACHERS

I. **TECHNOLOGY OPERATIONS AND CONCEPTS—**_Teachers demonstrate a sound understanding of technology operations and concepts. Teachers:_

   A. demonstrate introductory knowledge, skills, and understanding of concepts related to technology (as described in the ISTE NETS for Students).

   B. demonstrate continual growth in technology knowledge and skills to stay abreast of current and emerging technologies.

MATHEMATICS

Standard 3: Geometry

Instructional programs from PK–12 should enable all students to—

  * analyze characteristics and properties of two- and three-dimensional geometric shapes and develop mathematical arguments about geometric relationships.
  * specify locations and describe spatial relationships using coordinate geometry and other representational systems.
  * apply transformations and use symmetry to analyze mathematical situations.
  * use visualization, spatial reasoning, and geometric modeling to solve problems.

Standard 4: Measurement

Instructional programs from PK–12 should enable all students to—

  * understand measurable attributes of objects and the units, systems, and processes of measurement.
  * apply appropriate techniques, tools, and formulas to determine measurements.

Standard 6: Problem Solving

Instructional programs from PK–12 should enable all students to—

  * build new mathematical knowledge through problem solving.
  * solve problems that arise in mathematics and in other contexts.
  * apply and adapt a variety of appropriate strategies to solve problems.
  * monitor and reflect on the process of mathematical problem solving.

Lesson Description

	TEACHER PREP FACULTY	TEACHER CANDIDATES	FACULTY NOTES
PREPARATION	Prior to this lesson, the teacher candidates should have completed readings and a discussion about how students develop conceptual understanding of mathematical ideas. Select an on-campus setting such as a flagpole, building, or some other vertical object to use as a real, comparative object for the lesson. This should be a location that the candidates pass by each day or have visual reference to from the classroom window. Take a digital picture of the setting. Upload the digital picture into Geometer's Sketchpad for a projection to use in comparison with a diagram of a triangle. Bring to class small weights such as washers and string for making clinometers.	Complete all reading on ideas of developing conceptual understanding of mathematical ideas.	Localizing the object of comparison to something that is easily seen is an important feature of this lesson. Discourse should focus on how to make the development of the concept of the trigonometric function of tangent have a realistic basis for high school students.
INTRODUCTION	Set the context for the experiences with the following scenario: "A science class is building rockets that they will launch later in the week. When the rockets are launched, they want to be able to determine which rocket went the highest. Their teacher suggests they use a clinometer, sometimes called an anglometer." Demonstrate to candidates how to make the clinometer. Explain that for practice before the rocket launch, they will be going outside in pairs to measure the height of an object (one that you preselected). Outside, instruct pairs to measure the angle using the clinometer while standing 10 meters from the object. Each member of the pair should take readings. Have candidates discuss what they think the readings mean as they draw a diagram of a triangle showing the height of the object, the 10 meter baseline, and where the angle reading from the clinometer belongs in the drawing. Continue the modeling of the scenario by explaining that measuring the object is like measuring the height of the rocket being launched. The question posed is: Is there any easier way to do this? What if rockets were launched quickly in succession. How would you be able to calculate the heights quickly? In transitioning to the next portion of the activity, discuss what misconceptions high school students could have in creating the clinometer, doing the readings, and drawing the diagram.	Watch the demonstration of how to attach the string to the protractor to make the clinometer: Using a protractor, hang a piece of string with a weight attached from the zero point on the protractor. Sight the top of the object by turning the protractor upside down with the straight edge up. Measure 10 meters from the base of the object and mark that spot. Look along the straight edge of the protractor to the top of the object while standing 10 meters from the base. Record the angle crossed by the hanging string. What does that angle of measure mean? Determine the angle of elevation. Draw a diagram of the triangle created by the base line (10 meters from the base), the height of the object, the hypotenuse of the triangle connecting the base and height, and all angles you know. Based on your experience and the discussion, create a list of possible responses high school students would have to solving the problem posed about the rocket measurements at this point in their knowledge and conceptual understanding. Additionally, brainstorm misconceptions high school students could have while doing this portion of the lesson.	It is important for candidates to struggle with the reading of the clinometer in relation to the problem at hand. Merely showing the clinometer and telling them how to determine the angle of elevation from the clinometer reading reinforces a stand-and-deliver style of teaching. To save time, a demonstration of how to attach the string to the protractor and sight the top of an object can be done during the prior class meeting. As homework, candidates can measure the 10 meters from the object and take the readings. For a traditional lesson, the introduction of the trigonometric table listing the tangent ends here with showing how the table works. The introduction of Geometer's Sketchpad as a tool to solve the problem and develop understanding of the ratio created provides an important foundation. Avoid allowing preservice students to solve directly from their prior knowledge of using trig tables or a graphing calculator.

IMPLEMENTATION

TEACHER PREP FACULTY	TEACHER CANDIDATES	FACULTY NOTES

Introduce Geometer's Sketchpad by drawing a right triangle ABC where B is the vertex of the right angle. Drag the vertex of the vertical side up and down to show the dynamic nature of the software as the angle measures change on the screen.

Ask the candidates to use a think-pair-share strategy to answer the following question: What type of triangle is this? Review how students can predict the measure of the angles of the right triangle when only one acute angle is known.

Have the candidates work in small groups to explore the following questions and explorations:

- Can the "rightness" of this triangle be altered? Explore by changing the length of the sides and the measure of the angles.

- Experiment by making the measure of angle CAB and then ABC equal to the measure of the angle you took with the clinometer. Which triangle looks like the one you drew?

- Make a generalization for determining the angle of elevation.

- Calculate the height of the object. (Do not use Geometer's Sketchpad for this step.)

Using Geometer's Sketchpad, show a digital picture of the object to be measured. Compare and discuss the digitized picture of the object and the diagram previously used.

- How much bigger is the real situation than the diagram created on Sketchpad? What is the "stretch factor" of the diagram to the real situation?

Allow candidates the time to arrive at the ratio between the sets of sides. Discuss the need for high school students to use the skill of determining ratios before using the electronic means. Discuss again what misconceptions could occur at this point.

Return again to the original situation of having to determine the height of many rockets that are launched. Note that the rockets will be launched in reasonably quick succession. Therefore, there must be a faster way to determine each height. It would be easier if there was a table of every possible "stretch factor" for the range of heights likely to be found during the contest.

Introduce the definition of a tangent in relation to a unit circle. Have candidate groups draw the tangent using Geometer's Sketchpad.

Observe the drawing of a right angle using Geometer's Sketchpad.

In pairs, think-pair-share about how to know the measure of the angles of a right triangle.

In pairs or small groups, explore the right triangle by answering the questions posed and doing the suggested explorations. Compare the drawing made outside with an electronic drawing using the same angle measure as the angle of elevation.

Observe the comparison of the digital picture of the object measured outside and the diagram created on the computer. Determine the "stretch factor."

Stop the discussion of the activity to clarify what misconceptions could occur at this point when working with high school students. What other factors must a teacher consider when doing this lesson to this point?

Consider again the rocket-launching problem. To look at the "stretch factor," or ratio, create a tangent to a unit circle. To draw a tangent in Geometer's Sketchpad, do the following:

- Draw a unit circle.

- Draw a radius AB (radius measures 1 unit).

- Highlight line AB and point B.

- Using the construction menu, draw perpendicular BC.

- Draw line segment AC and BC.

- Measure angle BAC and segment BC.

What is the relationship between the triangle created and the one used to determine the height of the object?

Drag the vertex of C up and down. What happens? How can you use the dynamic nature of the software to alter the vertex of C to explore tangents?

Using Geometer's Sketchpad, find the "stretch factors," or tangents for the angles assigned to your group. Record the results on a spreadsheet. Transfer your results onto a single spreadsheet for the class that includes all the angles from 1 to 90.

Discuss the following questions:

- What happens when angle BAC gets closer to 90 degrees?

- What happens when it gets closer to 0 degrees?

- Using the table of "stretch factors," or tangents, how would you determine the height of the rockets?

Think-pair-share is a technique for promoting participatory discussion in the classroom. Provide for individual time to think about the question posed, prompt pairs to share their thinking with one another, then call on several to share their conclusions.

Pay close attention to candidates' willingness to walk through the activity using the software. All too often, candidates rely on their prior conceptual knowledge to answer the questions and not "walk in the shoes" of a high school student. Using the software, ensure that they thoroughly explore what a right triangle is, manipulating the sides and angles to formulate generalizations, and comparing the diagram created with the digital picture. The power of the technology comes in the candidates' ability to motivate their students to explore the possibilities, answer their own questions, and thus increase their understanding of the concepts.

Be sure to take a few moments to discuss management issues in terms of the many configurations of hardware in classrooms. What if there is only one computer available? How can this lesson be done? What if it is in a lab setting? What about the use of PDAs with Geometer's Sketchpad installed? How would the lesson change?

	TEACHER PREP FACULTY	TEACHER CANDIDATES	FACULTY NOTES
IMPLEMENTATION	Divide the numbers from 1 to 90 between the groups. Using Geometer's Sketchpad, have each find the "stretch factor" or tangents for each. Collapse all the values into one table. Have candidates make generalizations based on their findings. Debrief the experience again in terms of possible misconceptions high school students might have.	• What procedure can you create to make measuring the height of the rocket launch as quick as possible? Stepping out of the activity again, discuss the misconceptions high school students could have at this point in the lesson.	
CULMINATION	Assign candidates to develop a scenario through which they could use the teaching sequence to engage students in the study of tangents. As part of the preparation for writing a full lesson plan, have candidates identify four major misconceptions students may have and address how the lesson design would ameliorate the potential misconceptions. Have candidates share their scenarios and a few possible misconceptions in class. Following the class discussion, have the scenarios posted on the class Web site for sharing. Have candidates write a reflection discussing their experiences.	Develop a scenario to engage students in the study of tangents. Identify four misconceptions your students may have and how you would use the scenario and lesson design to avoid the potential misconceptions. Share your scenario and key points in your lesson with your peers. Post your scenario on the class Web site for others to use. Before posting, however, consider the feedback given in class and make appropriate adjustments to the scenario and lesson. Complete your reflection on your experience with the lesson in class. Include an assessment of your own beliefs and actions, and consider the salient issues in classroom practice.	In debriefing the lesson, consider having a discussion about the pacing of the elements of the lesson. Where are good breaking points? How can the lesson be divided into portions done independently and those requiring whole class work?

Assessment

Rubric: "Trigonometric Tables: Tangent"

CRITERIA	LEVELS OF PERFORMANCE			
	NEEDS REVISION 1	MARGINAL 2	ADEQUATE 3	WELL DONE 4
Scenario and Lesson Outline				
Scenario context	The scenario is not engaging to high school students and not adequately developed.	The scenario is of some interest to high school students but is contrived.	The scenario is moderately motivating to students.	The scenerio is well written and highly motivating to students.
Appropriateness to trig function solution	The situation posed is inappropriate for use of the tangent. It does not make sense.	The situation posed is appropriate for use of the function although contrived.	The situation posed is a good example of the use of the trig function.	The situation posed is a rich, realistic example of the appropriate use of the trig function.
Addresses possible student conceptual misconceptions	The candidate identifies some misconceptions with weak means of addressing.	The candidate identifies three misconceptions with inconsistent means of addressing.	The candidate identifies four misconceptions with mostly strong means of addressing.	The candidate identifies four major misconceptions with valid means of addressing those within the lesson.
Scenario posted on class Web site	(None)	(None)	(None)	Scenario is posted.
		This is a completed/not completed criteria		
Reflection*				

*Note: See "Written Reflection" rubric in Appendix C.

Tools and Resources

SOFTWARE

Geometer's Sketchpad (Key Curriculum Press), spreadsheet, digital camera editing software (optional)

HARDWARE

Demonstration station, stations for each collaborative group, digital camera

WEB SITES

Manipulating Math with Java: **www.ies.co.jp/math/java/**

Nathaniel Bowditch: **www-groups.dcs.st-andrews. ac.uk/~history/Mathematicians/Bowditch.html**

SOS Mathematics: Trigonometry: **www.sosmath.com/trig/trig.html**

Trigonometry and Astronomy, Measuring the Distance to the Stars: **www.geocities.com/Hollywood/Academy/8245/**

REFERENCE TEXTS

Charischak, I. (1996). Measuring heights, or what trigonometry tables are all about. *Learning & Leading with Technology, 23*(5), 13–16.

Latham, J. L. (1955). *Carry on, Mr. Bowditch.* Boston: Houghton Mifflin Company.

Credits

Peggy Kelly, California State University, San Marcos, California, **pkelly@csusm.edu**

James Wiebe, California State University, Los Angeles, **jwiebe@calstate.edu**

Comments/Stories

I have struggled with how to develop conceptual understanding of trigonometric functions outside the procedural understanding using the ratio of sides. The use of the technology permits candidates to really see what is happening with the sides as the angles are altered. This is an excellent activity as an introduction to the use of Geometer's Sketchpad. The dynamic nature of the software enables candidates to move the triangle in a variety of ways that cannot be done with static triangular shapes. The window that allows the ratio to be instantaneously displayed as the angles of the triangle are altered leads the candidates to see that pattern much more quickly than when it is derived from a table. There is an excellent story format in the issue of *Learning and Leading with Technology* cited above. The article is written from the perspective of a teacher completing a similar exercise.

WebQuest: Meeting of Mathematical Minds

Program/Grade Range: Secondary

Subject: Mathematics

Topic: History of Mathematics

Profile: Professional Preparation

Abstract: Teacher candidates are introduced to the WebQuest model of higher-level thinking in the context of learning about the history of mathematics. After researching information on the Web, they select a role as one of four mathematicians from different time periods, genders, and backgrounds. Candidates produce a video, play, reader's theatre, screenplay, multimedia presentation, or other creative performance showing the interaction among the mathematicians. The four mathematicians discuss a 21st century problem using their mathematical talent and perspective. The candidates demonstrate their knowledge of the contribution of each mathematician by applying the individual's contribution to mathematics to a 21st century problem.

STANDARDS

NETS FOR TEACHERS

III. TEACHING, LEARNING, AND THE CURRICULUM—*Teachers implement curriculum plans that include methods and strategies for applying technology to maximize student learning. Teachers:*

B. use technology to support learner-centered strategies that address the diverse needs of students.

C. apply technology to develop students' higher-order skills and creativity.

D. manage student learning activities in a technology-enhanced environment.

VI. SOCIAL, ETHICAL, LEGAL, AND HUMAN ISSUES—*Teachers understand the social, ethical, legal, and human issues surrounding the use of technology in PK–12 schools and apply that understanding in practice. Teachers:*

B. apply technology resources to enable and empower learners with diverse backgrounds, characteristics, and abilities.

C. identify and use technology resources that affirm diversity

MATHEMATICS

An underlying theme of the NCTM 2000 standards is the notion of connections. Connections means both to concepts within mathematics and to application of concepts to the real world. This activity focuses on both the historical development of mathematics and the connections with current problems. Every standard can be addressed depending on the historical figures selected for use.

Lesson Description

The WebQuest model is discussed in Section 1, "Using Model Strategies for Integrating Technology into Teaching," with additional references and resources cited.

	TEACHER PREP FACULTY	TEACHER CANDIDATES	FACULTY NOTES
PREPARATION	Preview the database of mathematical biographies at the MacTutor History of Mathematics Archive site (see URL in Tools and Resources). Develop a five-item scavenger hunt using the information on the MacTutor database. An example question is: What English mathematician spent her academic career at Bryn Mawr? Select a set of 21st century problems that are relevant to the teacher candidates. See Section 1, "Using Model Strategies for Integrating Technology into Teaching," for an overview of WebQuests.	View the scavenger hunt developed from the MacTutor database of biographies.	There are other Web sites that have the biographies of mathematicians. This Web site is only a suggestion. Although the WebQuest is provided in print in this lesson, consider having candidates access the digitally stored WebQuest to ensure that the activity simulates what high school students would be doing.
INTRODUCTION	Introduce the WebQuest model of inquiry-based learning. Facilitate a paired discussion of candidates' experiences doing the scavenger hunt. What was learned? What is the relationship of the activity to the development of mathematical understanding? Brainstorm some key 21st century problems facing the U.S. for which mathematicians could contribute to the solution. Open this discussion to include the notion that mathematics can be considered an integral part to most real-world problems. Divide the class into teams of four or five. Have teams select one of the 21st century problems identified in the discussion as the focus of their work. Review the criteria in the scoring rubric, completing missing elements before beginning the WebQuest. Assign teams to begin the WebQuest.	In pairs, share your strategy for finding the information in the MacTutor database site. What other sites did you use? What was found to be helpful? Relate the experience to working with students. Share your perception of key problems facing the U.S. in the 21st century. Be as broad as you can in your thinking. Participate in the discussion of identifying the mathematical concepts that would contribute to the solution of the problems identified. Divide into WebQuest teams. Select one of the problems identified as the focus of the group's project. Contribute to the discussion of the elements of the assessment rubric for the assignment. Begin the WebQuest as outlined.	If the class is not adept at finding information on the Web for use in research, the scavenger hunt provides an overview and reacquaints them with the process. If they are very competent Web searchers, consider deleting the scavenger hunt. The identification of the 21st century problem has the potential of expanding candidates' perceptions of how mathematics can be practically applied to real-world situations. Take the time to explore how mathematical concepts contribute to potential solutions.

IMPLEMENTATION

Note: This section is the WebQuest and is designed for use by the candidate groups.

WEBQUEST: MEETING OF MATHEMATICAL MINDS

Introduction

Picture this: You and a team of learners are presented with the task of solving a contemporary problem of the 21st century. Instead of looking in an encyclopedia or checking with experts, you are each assuming a new role as a famous mathematician. Each member of the group will use the Internet to find out more about what your background is as a famous mathematician. Based on what each of you learn, you will discuss a 21st century problem from the perspective of your role and assist in creating a script of the discussion among the mathematicians selected. Present the group's findings in the form of a video, play, reader's theatre, screenplay, multimedia presentation, or other creative performance.

The Quest

You must use a minimum of four mathematicians: (1) one Western male mathematician, (2) one female mathematician, (3) one non-Western mathematician, and (4) a nonspecific mathematician who also acts as a moderator. For example, you might phrase your question as:

How would Benjamin Banneker, Maria Agnesi, Pythagoras, and John Tukey plan for year 2100 in terms of population growth and energy consumption?

The Process and Resources

In this WebQuest you will be working together with a group of candidates in class. Each group in the class should select a different contemporary question and different cast of four characters (famous mathematicians) based on the four roles. For example, you will explore Web pages about people all over the world who care about population and energy consumption. Because these are real Web pages we're tapping into, not those made for classrooms or students, the reading level and vocabulary might be challenging. Feel free to use the online Webster dictionary or one in your classroom. (Note: As you modify this activity for classroom use, you may also need to scaffold or shelter this activity based on the background of your candidates.)

Begin with everyone in your group getting some background with MacTutor with a scavenger hunt developed by your professor and then by some dyads in your class at the university before dividing into roles for role-playing in which team members reveal some expertise on one part of the topic.

Phase 1—Background: Something for Everyone

Use the Internet information to answer the basic questions of who, what, where, when, why, and how. Be creative in exploring the information so that you answer these questions as fully and insightfully as you can. Remember that you will all be writing a script for your play. (See URLs in the Tools and Resources section for additional information.)

Phase 2—Looking Deeper from Different Perspectives

Instructions:

1. Individuals or pairs from your larger WebQuest team will explore one of the roles below.

2. Read through the files linked to your group. If you print out the files, underline the passages that you feel are most important. If you look at the files on the computer, copy sections you feel are important by dragging the mouse across the passage, copying it, and pasting it into a word processor or other writing software. **Note:** Remember to write down or copy and paste the URL of the file you take the passage from so you can quickly go back to it if you need to prove your point. You will also need to record the URL in your bibliography.

3. Be prepared to focus what you've learned into one main opinion that answers the Big Quest(ion) or completes a task based on what you have learned from your role.

   Role 1: Western Male Mathematician—Use the Internet information to answer the question specifically related to role 1, Western male mathematician. Keep in mind the historical perspective of males at the time as well as the Western viewpoint.

   Role 2: Female Mathematician—Use the information at the Famous Women Mathematicians Database hosted at Agnes Scott College in Scotland (see Tools and Resources) to answer the question specifically related to role 2, female mathematician. Keep in mind the role of females at the time the mathematician lived as well as the individual's cultural background.

   Role 3: Non-Western Mathematician—Use the Internet information to answer the question. Identify the perspective of the non-Western mathematician both historically and culturally as you examine the individual's contribution to mathematics.

   Role 4: Additional Member—This member serves as moderator as well as another mathematician. Use the Internet information to answer the questions specifically related to role 4.

Phase 3—Debating, Discussing, and Reaching Consensus

You have all learned about your 21st century problem, for example, population growth and energy consumption. Following completion of the research, members come back to the larger WebQuest team with expertise gained by searching from one perspective. You must all now answer the quest or complete the task as a group. Each of you brings a certain viewpoint to the answer; some of you will agree and others disagree. That conversation becomes the play—live or on video. Use information, pictures, movies, facts, opinions, and so on from the Web pages you explored to persuade your teammates that your viewpoint is important and should be part of your team's answer, such as to the population growth and energy consumption dilemma. Your WebQuest team should write a script for a video, play, reader's theatre, screenplay, multimedia presentation, or other creative performance that reflects the viewpoint of the character you are playing, the character's mathematical philosophy, and the time period in which the character lived.

Phase 4—Real-World Feedback

You and your teammates have learned a lot by dividing up into different roles. Now's the time to put your learning to use by producing that video, play, reader's theatre, screenplay, multimedia presentation, or other creative performance for real-world feedback by your peers. Be sure to document the process and retain a copy of the product as you may wish to include it as a digital artifact in your electronic portfolio.

	TEACHER PREP FACULTY	TEACHER CANDIDATES	FACULTY NOTES
CULMINATION	Have groups present their performance to the class. Provide a question and answer period for the audience to query the historical figures on their perspective to the solution of the problem. Have candidates complete peer evaluations. Relate the experience to classroom use. Discuss the techniques of scaffolding the learning when using the combination of electronic tools with the historical nature of the assignment. Further debrief the activity by discussing the WebQuest model as a Web-based activity. Discuss the strengths and weaknesses of using a Web-based activity in the classroom. Have candidates post their presentations on the class Web site.	Make the presentation in class. As you are listening to other groups, formulate clarifying questions to pose at the conclusion of the presentation. Complete the peer evaluation of the presentation to provide constructive feedback to the group. Participate in a discussion about using the WebQuest in the classroom. Following the presentations, post your group's presentation on the class Web site for sharing and dissemination.	Provide information and guidelines on how to post the final product to the class Web site. In discussing the activity, localize the issues to situations that the candidates might experience in the classroom. Issues of equity and access may be apparent as well as issues for second language learners. **Extension** Have candidates write a modified WebQuest to meet the needs of their field experience class.

Assessment

Rubric: "WebQuest: Meeting of Mathematical Minds"

CRITERIA	LEVELS OF PERFORMANCE		
	BEGINNING	**EMERGING**	**TARGET**
Plays the role of the famous mathematician	Candidate parrots some of the words that might be said by the famous mathematician.	Portrayal demonstrates a partial understanding of the background and time the mathematician lived.	Portrayal demonstrates an accurate and complete understanding of the background and time of the mathematician.
Demonstrates understanding of the mathematician's contribution to the field of mathematics	In the presentation, the explanation of the contribution demonstrates surface or rote level understanding.	In the presentation, the candidate explains the contribution in a way that shows conceptual understanding.	In the presentation, the candidate's explanation of the contribution shows conceptual understanding and the ability to relate the contribution to the field of mathematics.
Connects mathematician's contribution to a 21st century problem	Presentation makes an attempt to connect the mathematician's contribution to the solution of a 21st century problem but is lacking depth.	Presentation makes an accurate connection between the contribution of the mathematician and the solution of a 21st century problem.	Presentation makes an accurate and complete connection between the contribution of the mathematician and the solution of a 21st century problem in concert with other mathematicians being studied by the group.
Includes reflection on activity	Reflection contains superficial comments.	Reflection includes self-assessment, connection of teaching, and goals, but is incomplete.	Reflection contains appropriate self-assessment, connection of experience to teaching, and setting of goals for improvement for next similar assignment.
Peer-assesses group work	Peer assessment is superficial and does not provide evidence for assessment.	Peer assessment includes comments that are inconsistently backed by evidence.	Peer assessment provides critical analysis of strengths and weaknesses with all comments backed by evidence.

Tools and Resources

SOFTWARE

Word processing program for the script. Additional software is necessary depending on the creative production determined by the teams.

HARDWARE

Minimum—Internet access for each team of candidates

WEB SITES

Female Mathematicians:
www.agnesscott.edu/lriddle/women/women.html

MacTutor History of Mathematics Archive:
www-history.mcs.st-and.ac.uk/history/ (This site has an extensive database on mathematicians.)

The Math Forum Internet Mathematics Library:
http://mathforum.org/library/ (This site provides background information on mathematicians.)

Meeting of Minds WebQuest:
www.kn.pacbell.com/wired/fil/pages/ webmeetingja.html

The WebQuest Page at San Diego State University:
http://edweb.sdsu.edu/webquest/webquest.html (This site provides resources on creating and using WebQuests.)

REFERENCE TEXT

Allen, S. (1990). *Meeting of minds: The complete scripts, with illustrations, of the amazingly successful PBS-TV series.* Buffalo, NY: Prometheus.

Credit

Janet Miller, Huntington Park High School, Santa Monica, California, **jamille7@earthlink.net**

Comments/Stories

The WebQuest is designed to be modified into an interdisciplinary unit. The language arts class can concentrate on the writing of the script, dialogue, citations, appropriate sources, and so on. The history or social science class can examine the time in history, the location of the historical figure, and the cultural context in which the individual lived. Each of these investigations colors the perspective of the students as they investigate the mathematician in terms of the 21st century problem being investigated. In creating an interdisciplinary unit, many teachers have found that the use of the mathematical concepts developed by the mathematician are given new meaning as they are applied to a current situation. Rather than mathematics being viewed as an isolated discipline, the use of mathematics in current problems adds motivation for learning the concepts and considering research in ways that contribute to contemporary issues.

Cool Liquids

Program/Grade Range: Secondary

Subject: Science: Physical Science/Chemistry

Topic: Evaporation of Liquids

Profile: Professional Preparation

Abstract: This is a model lesson in which teacher candidates experience the use of technology as their high school students would. The temperature probe is used to dramatically illustrate the process and effects of evaporation. A variety of technologies, such as graphing calculators, temperature probes, a data collection system, Internet sites, and computer software, are all used to teach phase-change concepts, which are often difficult for high school students to conceptualize. The activity presents the candidates with opportunities to use probes, compile data, and develop mathematical models to define relationships, design micromodels using digital flipbooks, present their results electronically, and cooperatively develop a lesson plan to teach the concept of evaporation using the developed flipbooks.

STANDARDS

NETS FOR TEACHERS

I. TECHNOLOGY OPERATIONS AND CONCEPTS—*Teachers demonstrate a sound understanding of technology operations and concepts. Teachers:*

   A. demonstrate introductory knowledge, skills, and understanding of concepts related to technology (as described in the ISTE NETS for Students).

II. PLANNING AND DESIGNING LEARNING ENVIRONMENTS AND EXPERIENCES—*Teachers plan and design effective learning environments and experiences supported by technology. Teachers:*

   A. design developmentally appropriate learning opportunities that apply technology-enhanced instructional strategies to support the diverse needs of learners.

   D. plan for the management of technology resources within the context of learning activities.

   E. plan strategies to manage student learning in a technology-enhanced environment.

V. PRODUCTIVITY AND PROFESSIONAL PRACTICE—*Teachers use technology to enhance their productivity and professional practice. Teachers:*

   C. apply technology to increase productivity.

   D. use technology to communicate and collaborate with peers, parents, and the larger community in order to nurture student learning.

SCIENCE

Content Standard A: Science as Inquiry

   A1. Abilities necessary to do scientific inquiry

   A2. Understanding about scientific inquiry

   • Scientists rely on technology to enhance the gathering and manipulation of data.

   • Scientific explanations must adhere to criteria such as: a proposed explanation must be logically consistent; it must abide by the rules of evidence; it must be open to questions and possible modification; and it must be based on historical and current scientific knowledge.

Content Standard B: Physical Science

   B2. Structure and properties of matter

Lesson Description

	TEACHER PREP FACULTY	TEACHER CANDIDATES	FACULTY NOTES
PREPARATION	Set up the graphing calculators or data collection system and temperature probes at laboratory workstations. For each workstation, prepare small quantities (about 50 ml) of various liquids such as water, isopropyl alcohol (rubbing alcohol), acetone (fingernail polish remover), pentane, or methanol in small containers. Use families of liquids such as alcohols, alkanes, and ketones. Before class, have teacher candidates prepare a lab journal on the computer.	Prior to class, prepare a laboratory journal on the computer that includes a data table or spreadsheet for three families of liquids—alcohols, alkanes, and ketones.	Ensure that candidates are familiar with the use of the graphing calculator as well as the setup and operation of probeware prior to the introduction of this activity. The activity needs to be preset in a laboratory because of chemical safety issues. If it is not possible, discuss safety issues as the candidates are setting up for the experiment. Consider rotating candidates in to assist in setting up laboratory activities.
INTRODUCTION	Lead a class discussion on the process of evaporation and factors that could affect the evaporation of liquids. Some guiding questions are: 1. Why do you feel cooler when you step out of a swimming pool? 2. What are some possible laboratory techniques that can be used in the high school lab to explore the process of evaporation? 3. What physical properties of the liquids would cause evaporation more quickly? 4. Which liquid will produce a greater cooling effect to its surroundings? 5. How can you describe the flow of energy involved in the process of evaporation? 6. Is it possible to establish a relationship between the rate of cooling and the type of liquid? How can you do that? In class, examine the rubric in the Assessment Section on conducting the experiment. With the candidates, create a rubric to use at the end of the lab period as a group self-assessment device.	Actively engage in the discussion focused on how evaporation occurs. Brainstorm possible answers to the discussion questions. Make notations of discussion items, key points, your own ideas, and any additional questions. Participate in the development of the self-assessment rubric.	Periodically step out of the teaching mode and into the debriefing mode to relate the steps in this lesson to teaching it in the classroom. Issues of classroom management with the equipment and chemicals, student behavior and motivation, and lesson sequencing can easily be periodically discussed. Additionally, elements of the lesson plan, such as preparation, introduction, concept development, inquiry, and so on, can be debriefed as each element takes place or as a separate discussion at the end of the lesson. Consider developing a parallel lesson plan as the activity is progressing to demonstrate how a lesson plan is written to reflect an inquiry-based lesson. Focus on the preparation necessary and the sequential nature of how the lesson progresses by recording every step. The assessment rubric for the lab period is a self-assessment. Have candidates consider restructuring the rubric to a yes and no format or checklist. Discuss the pros and cons of a modified rubric as part of assessing the group process.
IMPLEMENTATION	Provide an overview of the investigation including a reminder of the goal of the lesson, the methods being used, and the assessment criteria. Divide the class into enough groups to use the lab stations, usually two to six candidates per group. Have them develop a cooperative work plan. Guide the setup of a temperature time graph to collect data for a 4-minute period. As an example, the setup will be 5 seconds between samples of each of 5 liquids, collecting 48 samples for a total time of 240 seconds or 4 minutes.	Divide into working teams. Consider the tasks involved. Create a cooperative work plan to ensure that all members of the groups have equal responsibility for the outcome. Create the first time graph by labeling the axis and setting up the probe attached to the computer. Take a small piece of filter paper, wrap it around the temperature probe, and secure it with a small rubber band. Place the temperature probe into one of the liquids. Start the data collection and	Consider using a candidate performance laboratory checklist to assess laboratory techniques, safety, and teamwork. If not enough data are collected for different liquids, candidates may not observe a direct relationship between change in temperature and molecular mass. Also, they may not be able to determine the exceptions to this model such as water. The digital flipbook is designed to use micromodels that demonstrate the process of evaporation by showing what happens to a few molecules at a time.

TEACHER PREP FACULTY	TEACHER CANDIDATES	FACULTY NOTES

IMPLEMENTATION

When all teams finish collecting data for several different liquids, gather and compile class data for each of the different liquids.

Ask the candidates to rank the liquids according to the change in temperature. Guide a discussion of the properties of the individual liquids in relation to their rank. Follow this discussion with the question "Can we determine a relationship between the change in temperature and the molecular mass of the liquids?"

Organize groups to share data and compile a list of temperature changes and molecular mass in order to prepare a graph.

Facilitate a discussion about the results of the graph. Inquire about ways the data displayed on the graph can be represented in a mathematical equation. Ask: "Can you tell what would happen at 5 minutes, 6 minutes, and so on?"

Assign candidates to develop a digital micromodel of the process of evaporation. (See Faculty Notes.) Candidates should use the presentation software of their choice to design a presentation that includes their experimental findings and micromodels to present to the class.

Collaboratively adjust the rubric to assess the micromodels.

take the probe out of the liquid.

Secure the probe with a piece of tape to the edge of the lab table so that the liquid soaked filter paper is over the edge of the table.

Type the readings from the probe into the computer spreadsheet.

When data collection is completed, store the data in a graphing program or copy and paste it into your spreadsheet. Reset the probe software, change the filter, and begin testing the next liquid.

Organize and rank the change in temperature for the liquids.

Record and graph the change in temperature and the molecular mass for each liquid using the graphing calculator or computer graphing software.

Participate in a discussion about your results.

Design a mathematical model or equation that will depict what you see happening with the data.

Participate in collaboratively adjusting the flipbook assessment rubric.

Use presentation software to develop a digital flipbook that shows the phase-changes as evaporation takes place.

The micromodels should demonstrate the movement and behavior of particles during the process of evaporation. Each slide is created slightly differently than the previous slide either by using the automatically advanced slide feature or built-in animation to show movement of the molecules to demonstrate how the concept works.

Use a rubric to assess the digital flipbook micromodels of the evaporation process.

If multiple types of presentation software are not available, such as PowerPoint, HyperStudio, AppleWorks, and so on, use what is available and adjust the rubric.

CULMINATION

Facilitate the presentation of the digital flipbook micromodels to demonstrate the process of evaporation.

Lead a discussion to address the following questions:

A. What were some unexpected outcomes that you observed while:

- doing the experiment with probes?
- compiling and analyzing the data?
- answering the experimental questions?
- designing the micro-model flipbook?
- organizing your presentation?

B. What are the advantages and disadvantages of using the different types of technology during this activity?

Complete a journal entry focusing on the experimental process and outcomes.

Based on the classroom lab experience, have groups develop a lesson plan appropriate for high school students to learn the concept of evaporation. The lesson plan should include accommodations for special needs and second language learners.

Present flipbook micromodel.

Participate in the discussion while taking notes for a journal entry on the important points leading to implementing the lesson in a secondary classroom.

Work in groups to develop a lesson plan for teaching the concept to a specific set of students. Use the flipbook that was created as a part of the lesson plan. Post the lesson plan on the class Web site for sharing and discussing.

This activity provides an opportunity to make candidates aware of safe management and storage of chemicals.

Encourage candidates to push the limits of the presentation software to be able to depict the process of evaporation accurately and in an engaging manner.

Preservice candidates often overlook the difficulties that students with special needs may have in working with equipment and in group settings. Encourage candidates to make accommodations for students with special needs including language acquisition needs. Scaffolding the development of the concept as well as focusing on understanding the vocabulary is an effective way of making the content accessible to all students.

Assessment

Use the "Written Reflection" rubric in Appendix C.

Use a program-specific or generic rubric for assessing the lesson plan.

Rubric: Group Assessment of Laboratory Experience

CRITERIA	LEVELS OF PERFORMANCE		
	NEEDS IMPROVEMENT 1	ADEQUATE 2	EXEMPLARY 3
Stayed on task			
Assigned tasks equitably			
Followed safety procedures			
Followed experiment procedures		HAVE THE CLASS COMPLETE THE CELLS OF THE RUBRIC AS PART OF THE CLASS DISCUSSION.	
Completed task			
Collaborated in helping all members of the group understand the concept			
Cleaned up materials and equipment appropriately			

Rubric: Micromodels Flipbook Assessment

CRITERIA	LEVELS OF PERFORMANCE			
	INADEQUATE 1	MINIMAL 2	ACCEPTABLE 3	EXEMPLARY 4
Concept Accuracy	The depiction of evaporation has enough errors as to confuse learners and question developers' understanding of the concept.	The depiction of evaporation has minor errors.	Evaporation is depicted accurately.	Evaporation is depicted accurately with considerable detail to enhance student understanding.
Organization of Presentation	Presentation seems jumbled or incomplete.	Presentation is organized but lacks engaging layout, introduction, or conclusion.	Presentation contains introductory slides, animation or automated sequencing, and concluding slides.	Presentation is well organized and interestingly presented with introductory slides, animation or automated sequencing that is engaging, and a concluding or closure slide.
Use of Technology	An inappropriate presentation tool was selected. The presenters demonstrate a lack of knowledge of the tool.	An appropriate tool was selected, but the presenters do not seem to be well versed in its use.	An appropriate presentation tool was selected; the presenters seemed moderately comfortable with its use.	The presenters have selected the appropriate presentation tool and demonstrate comfort and ease in using it.

Tools and Resources

SOFTWARE

Graphing software, presentation software, spreadsheet software, Internet access

HARDWARE

Computers and/or graphing calculators, temperature probe, data collection system

WEB SITES

Chemistry Web Resources

Interactive Guide to Chemistry:
http://library.thinkquest.org/3659/

Mr. Guch's Cavalcade o' Chemistry:
www.chemfiesta.com/

Phase Change Resource:
http://eee.uci.edu/97w/40090/phases.html

Welcome to Rader's CHEM4KiDS!:
www.kapili.com/chem4kids/index.html

REFERENCE TEXT

Holmquist, D., & Volz, D. (2000). *Chemistry with calculators*. Beaverton, OR: Vernier Software.

OTHER

Containers for liquids for each group

Isopropyl alcohol

Water

Acetone

Pentane or methanol

Another liquid that evaporates easily

Credit

Arlene V. Cain, Sam Houston High School, Lake Charles, Louisiana, **acvid53@aol.com**

Comments/Stories

The development of the micromodel flipbook forces candidates (and secondary students) to think about how the process of evaporation takes place. Candidates seem to spend a lot of time figuring out how to make the various software tools move the molecules around. The discussion that takes place about how to depict the phase changes reveals how much they really know about how molecules move. Candidates have found that the development of a flipbook provides a good model to use once they get into the classroom. The model can be applied to other concepts that show development of movement.

Gravity

Program/Grade Range: Secondary and Middle School

Subject: Science

Topic: Properties of Gravity

Profile: Professional Preparation

Abstract: In response to the question "Do objects fall at the same rate?", teacher candidates discuss a model experiment for secondary students to discover the answer, including recording and analyzing data. One of the proposed experiments is conducted in class and thoroughly debriefed. In response to "What is the rate of acceleration of gravity?", candidates design an experiment using available technology (rulers, stopwatches, computers, photo gates, probes, etc.) to obtain the most accurate answer. Experiments are discussed and results compared to known values of gravity. As a result of their experience, candidates develop lessons with experiments to address different grade levels with accommodations for second language and special needs learners.

STANDARDS

NETS FOR TEACHERS

I. TECHNOLOGY OPERATIONS AND CONCEPTS—*Teachers demonstrate a sound understanding of technology operations and concepts. Teachers:*

   A. demonstrate introductory knowledge, skills and understanding of concepts related to technology (as described in the ISTE NETS for Students).

II. PLANNING AND DESIGNING LEARNING ENVIRONMENTS AND EXPERIENCES—*Teachers plan and design effective learning environments and experiences supported by technology. Teachers:*

   A. design developmentally appropriate learning opportunities that apply technology-enhanced instructional strategies to support the diverse needs of learners.

   D. plan for the management of technology resources within the context of learning activities.

III. TEACHING, LEARNING, AND THE CURRICULUM—*Teachers implement curriculum plans that include methods and strategies for applying technology to maximize student learning. Teachers:*

   A. facilitate technology-enhanced experiences that address content standards and student technology standards.

   B. use technology to support learner-centered strategies that address the diverse needs of students.

   D. manage student learning activities in a technology-enhanced environment.

SCIENCE

Content Standard A: Science as Inquiry

   Grades 5–8

   A1. Abilities necessary to do scientific inquiry

   A2. Understanding about scientific inquiry

Content Standard B: Physical Science

   Grades 5–8

   B2. Motion and forces

Content Standard A: Science as Inquiry

   Grades 9–12

   A1. Abilities necessary to do scientific inquiry

   A2. Understanding about scientific inquiry

   • Scientists rely on technology to enhance the gathering and manipulation of data.

Content Standard B: Physical Science

   Grades 9–12

   B4. Motions and forces

Lesson Description

	TEACHER PREP FACULTY	TEACHER CANDIDATES	FACULTY NOTES
PREPARATION	Set up five stations, each with • a ruler and stopwatch with instructions, • a calculator or computer-based lab with instructions, • a photo gate and CBL with instructions, • a ramp and stopwatch with instructions, and • a station for unique ideas given by the teacher candidates or professor. Assign candidates background reading. If necessary, make arrangements for candidate lesson plans to be disseminated in one of the ways listed in the Culmination—Faculty Notes section.	Complete content background reading as assigned.	You may choose to have candidates involved in the setup of the classroom in preparation for the lesson. As this is happening, discuss with the candidates the issues related to room arrangement and classroom management. This discussion can also take place at the end of the lesson as part of the debriefing.
INTRODUCTION	Organize candidates in collaborative groups. Explain to the candidates that they must take the role of learners even if they know the final answer. The purpose for assuming this role is to look at the activity through the eyes of both the teacher and students they will have. Display guiding question, "Do objects fall at the same rate?" To set the stage for the lesson, pose the following questions focused on the force of gravity: • Why do some people float easily? • What would happen if the force of gravity was cut in half? • Why do astronauts bounce while on the moon? • What would happen if gravity ceased to exist? Encourage candidates to participate in the discussion and record their ideas.	Participate in the discussion by recording ideas and conjectures in your science journal or notebook. Share your ideas with the group. Record your own reactions to the discussion. Record your hypotheses for comparison with the results of your investigation. This will enable you to track your own learning.	As candidates share their answers, have them record possible answers students might give that show potential misconceptions of the concept. Relate answers to prior knowledge and ideas. Discuss issues of comprehensible vocabulary in expressing these ideas—especially in relation to second language learners. If the activity is conducted in a room with adequate computers, consider having the journal portion of the class time completed electronically. As an alternative way to organize the time, consider e-mailing or posting the guiding question in advance of class. Have candidates electronically record or post their hypothesis and rationale.
IMPLEMENTATION	Return to the focus question, "Do objects fall at the same rate?" **Model**—Have each group design a model for answering the question. This should include a hypothesis, an experiment using the materials at their table, data collection, and a method for analysis. In large group discussion, perform an experiment suggested by the candidates from their discussions and guide them to analyze their hypothesis.	**Model**—In the small groups, design a model for answering this question by developing a hypothesis, creating an experiment, collecting data, analyzing the results, and drawing conclusions. Answer the question as posed without having done any experimentation. If an answer is known, how exact is the answer? Observe the experiment as part of the whole group discussion. Participate in the modification of the question and the discussion following the experiment.	As the lesson is taking place, be sure to model vocabulary development and methods of accommodating special needs students. The notion of understanding what a scientific question is asking is an important issue with middle level and secondary students. Candidates should understand how the question should be asked in order to make more sense. If the question were changed, how would the experiment have to change?

	TEACHER PREP FACULTY	TEACHER CANDIDATES	FACULTY NOTES
IMPLEMENTATION	• Is the hypothesis an answer to the question? • How should we modify the question so that it will make more sense to students? • How should we modify the experiments to answer the new question? The modification of the question might be "Do all objects fall at the same rate in a vacuum?" Debrief the modeling by discussing the appropriateness of using the technology to answer the question, posing good questions to lead students into the scientific process, the notion of measurable variables, and so on. **Implement**—Ask or write the question "What is the acceleration value of gravity?" Ask for hypotheses that might be given by middle or secondary students. Require the collaborative groups to use some form of technology in conducting their experiment. Have candidates discuss the question in their groups, then share main points in the large group setting. Have groups collaboratively design an experiment to answer the question. Have the candidates implement their experiments, obtaining empirical data, and record their plans and procedures. In large-group discussion, compare and contrast different approaches to the problem.	**Implement**—Discuss the question again focusing on the scientific process needed to answer the question. What is acceleration? What is gravity? How do we measure acceleration? What would be the accuracy we really need? Design an experimental inquiry to answer the question. Use technology in some portion of your experiment. Collect empirical data from the experiments, no matter how strange or "wrong." Be sure to record your plan to answering the question as well as your procedure of what took place and why. Discuss the accuracy of the data depending on the mode of experimentation. How did the required use of technology enhance or detract from the experimental process? What are the benefits and detriments of the use of technology in this context?	Other topics for discussion include how to ensure that students document the inquiry process, experimental procedure, laboratory procedure, results, and conclusions as well as ensuring class participation as the debriefing in the classroom takes place.
CULMINATION	After the results are shared, there are four major points to address. 1. When did the answer "all objects fall at the same rate" become conceptually easy to understand during the activity? What difficulties would students at your grade level have? When exploring this question, would technology-based experiments be beneficial? 2. Would the experiments answer "How does the acceleration value of gravity help or hurt your conceptual knowledge of gravity?" When exploring using inquiry and experimentation, was using technology beneficial? 3. How can we enhance a current teacher-centered lesson using the techniques we explored? 4. On reflection, which experimental procedure do you feel provided the best overall results? What modifications of this lesson would you make and why?	Record in your journal a quick-write that includes what you learned and how you would apply what you learned to a classroom situation. Create a lesson with an experiment to discover the concept of gravity for a specified grade level of students that includes: • Identifying an objective focused on the appropriate level of the concept • Adapting the experiment for linguistically diverse learners and special needs students • Appropriately integrating the use of technology • Assessing student outcomes • Aligning the lesson with local, state, and national standards • Considering essential conditions to effectively implement the lesson plan and where you can find them if needed	Although the scoring rubric is provided, consider using the assignment sheet as the basis for developing a scoring rubric determined by the candidates. As the candidates create their lesson plan, think about the many ways that they could share their lesson plan. Using electronic dissemination methods, choices include posting to a Web site, uploading to peers as an attachment, creating a PowerPoint presentation, sharing with a small group that is required to attach a critique of the lesson, and so on.

	TEACHER PREP FACULTY	TEACHER CANDIDATES	FACULTY NOTES
CULMINATION	Direct candidates to complete a quick-write in their journals about what they learned and how they would apply this to a classroom situation. Direct candidates to complete a lesson plan that includes the elements listed to the right.	• Identifying common traits of an effective inquiry-based lesson	

Assessment

Rubric: Gravity Lesson Plan

CRITERIA	LEVELS OF PERFORMANCE			
	INADEQUATE 1	MINIMAL 2	ACCEPTABLE 3	EXEMPLARY 4
Objective	The objective is inappropriate and/or does not address the concept of gravity.	The objective addresses the concept of gravity but is not completely appropriate to the grade level targeted.	The objective addresses the concept of gravity, focuses on gravity, and is mostly appropriate for the targeted grade level.	The objective is well written and appropriately covers the concept of gravity for the targeted grade level.
Adaptation for second language learners and special needs students	Inappropriate or no adaptations for second language learners and special needs students are included in the lesson.	Minimal attention to the second language learners and special needs students is included.	Attention to the needs of second language learners and special needs students is integrated into the lesson.	Methods of attending to the needs of second language learners are woven throughout the lesson in appropriate and creative ways.
Technology	Technology is superficially included and does not support the learning.	Technology is included with unclear support of the learning.	The technology included clearly supports the learning.	The technology is integrated into the lesson in a creative way that clearly supports the learning.
Assessment of student outcomes	Student assessment is present but is not in alignment with the objectives and/or outcomes.	The student assessment is vaguely in alignment with the objectives and vaguely connected to the student outcomes.	The student assessment is in alignment with the objectives and is connected to the student outcomes.	The assessment is clearly in alignment with the objectives and is exemplary in its connection to the outcomes.
Alignment with standards	The lesson addresses standards that are not listed.	The lesson minimally addresses the standards identified.	The lesson addresses all of the standards identified.	The lesson provides conceptual understanding to clearly address all of the standards identified.
Essential conditions	Few essential conditions are described.	Essential conditions are described in a sketchy manner with incomplete options of where or how to meet them.	Essential conditions are described with ways to meet those needs.	The essential conditions to be successful are thoroughly described with multiple options of where to locate the needed materials and make the necessary conditions described happen.
Common traits of an inquiry-based lesson	Few traits are described.	*There are no variations on this criterion.*		Common traits of an effective inquiry-based lesson are thoughtfully and thoroughly described.

Note: A "Written Reflection" rubric can be found in Appendix C.

Tools and Resources

SOFTWARE

Calculator or computer-based learning software (e.g., Pasco, Vernier, TI-83), data recording and depicting software associated with probes and photo gate

HARDWARE

A demonstration station for whole modeling, multiple stations for groups to work at. (It is ideal to have one station available for every group.) Calculator or computer depending on software, probes, photo gates, and motion sensors that work with above software

WEB SITES

Explorezone.com:
   http://explorezone.com/101/gravity.htm
Exploring Gravity: www.curtin.edu.au/curtin/dept/
   phys-sci/gravity/index2.htm
Fourmilab Interactive Experiments in Gravity:
   www.fourmilab.ch/gravitation/
NASA Reduced Gravity Student Flight Opportunities
   Program: www.tsgc.utexas.edu/floatn/
Society of Exploration Geophysics Virtual Museum:
   www.seg.org/museum/VM/gravity_items_main.html

REFERENCE TEXTS

Green, J. (2000). *The mad scientist handbook: The do-it-yourself guide to making your own rock candy, anti-gravity machine, edible glass, rubber eggs, fake blood.* New York: Perigee Books.

Narlikar, J. (1999). *Motion & gravity.* Pune, India: Shekhar Phatak & Associates.

Provenzo, E. F., & Provenzo, A. B. (1990). *47 easy-to-do classic science experiments.* Mineola, NY: Dover Publications.

Tyler, D. (1971). *A new and simple theory of gravity.* Carlisle, MA: Discovery Books.

Vancleave, J. (1992). *Janice Vancleave's gravity.* New York: John Wiley & Sons.

Wheeler, J. (1999). *Journey into gravity and spacetime.* New York: WH Freeman & Co.

OTHER

Rulers, stopwatches, and items to drop

Credits

Scott Kirst, Oconto Falls High School, Abrams, Wisconsin, sctkirst@aol.com

Louisiana Review Team:

   Dolores Champagne, University of Louisiana at Lafayette, djchampagne@louisiana.edu

   Juanita Guerin, University of Louisiana at Lafayette, jguerin@louisiana.edu

   Gloria Hendrickson, University of Louisiana at Lafayette, gloria@louisiana.edu

   Sue Jackson, University of Louisiana at Lafayette, sujax@louisiana.edu

Comments/Stories

Depending on the length of time available in the methods class, this lesson can take multiple periods. However, the benefit of modeling and implementing the lesson is well worth the time. Candidates seem to ask good questions after they see the technology used in a whole class activity, then break into groups to answer a related question. When they work with the probes, photo gate, and so on, they have a better notion of what might go wrong in the secondary classroom. Classroom management seems to become a rich discussion as they are concerned about how to control the equipment and yet ensure that their students are really involved in an inquiry-based lesson rather than a forced lesson.

Who's in Control Here?

Program/Grade Range: Secondary

Subject: Social Studies

Topic: Sovereignty and Control

Profile: Professional Preparation

Abstract: Sovereignty is a major theme in social studies. Sovereignty is the exercise of, or right to exercise, supreme power, dominion, sway, supremacy, or independence. Sovereignty can have social, political, economic, historic, geographic, psychological, religious, social, and cultural applications. This lesson uses cooperative groups to explore global aspects of sovereignty employing simulation software and Internet resources, including primary source documents, geographic software, and world literature sources. The lesson culminates with a desktop publishing project.

STANDARDS

NETS FOR TEACHERS

III. **TEACHING, LEARNING, AND THE CURRICULUM**—*Teachers implement curriculum plans that include methods and strategies for applying technology to maximize student learning. Teachers:*

A. facilitate technology-enhanced experiences that address content standards and student technology standards.

B. use technology to support learner-centered strategies that address the diverse needs of students.

C. apply technology to develop students' higher-order skills and creativity.

D. manage student learning activities in a technology-enhanced environment.

SOCIAL STUDIES

VI. **POWER, AUTHORITY, AND GOVERNANCE**—*Social Studies programs should include experiences that provide for the study of how people create and change structures of power, authority, and governance, so that the learner can:*

A. examine persistent issues involving the rights, roles, an status of the individual in relation to the general welfare.

B. explain the purpose of government and analyze how its powers are acquired, used, and justified.

F. analyze and evaluate conditions, actions, and motivations that contribute to conflict and cooperation within and among nations.

Lesson Description

	TEACHER PREP FACULTY	TEACHER CANDIDATES	FACULTY NOTES
PREPARATION	Based on resources available, make a decision about the form and options of the final product. Teacher candidate options for the final product could be open-ended or very restrictive depending on the resources available and technology-related objectives targeted. Acquire simulation software appropriate to exploring the concept of sovereignty. Examples include Tom Snyder's Decisions, Decisions series. Have candidates form collaborative groups.	In preparation for working on the teaching of a concept, form a collaborative group whose final product is a technology-based presentation.	Decide the most appropriate way to share the results of the investigation. If oral presentations are to be given, define the type. (This activity is written to provide an array of possibilities for conveying the information. Brochures and newspapers are viable options as well as PowerPoint, etc.) If this is the first group-created multimedia assignment, consider doing a brief skills assessment of the types of media you want to highlight. For example, if the choices you want to use include simulation software, a desktop publishing product, PowerPoint, video, and HyperStudio, survey the candidates using a quick self-assessment of their competency and preference. Experience with particular software may form the basis of the groupings. An alternative is to purposefully compose the groups of some individuals who are well-versed in the technology with those who want to learn more.

	TEACHER PREP FACULTY	TEACHER CANDIDATES	FACULTY NOTES
INTRODUCTION	Begin by telling the story of "Knight of Sovereignty" from the Knights of the Round Table Web site (see Tools and Resources). At the critical juncture of the story, poll the candidates for their response to the critical question. It is important to hold a discussion and hear candidate input concerning possible solutions. As candidates respond, ask for a justification or rationale for the proposed outcome. Question candidates about the relationship of the story to the notion of sovereignty. Review the outcomes suggested. How does each interpret or affect the sovereignty of the characters? Finish reading the story. Debrief the printed conclusion in light of the proposed outcomes in terms of sovereignty.	Listen carefully to the story. Participate in the poll and brainstorm possible outcomes of the story. Provide a rationale for your suggestion. Participate in the discussion of the questions: • What does the story say about the concept of sovereignty? • Review the various outcomes suggested. What does each of the proposed outcomes say about the notion of sovereignty? • After listening to the conclusion of the story, discuss the relationship between the written conclusion and the proposed outcomes. How is sovereignty the same or different?	The old English version is available at the URL listed in Tools and Resources. For candidates, the story illustrates the fact that empowerment in the classroom can come from ceding power to others. The methods classroom needs to be a place of respect, especially acknowledging the power that every teacher has in his or her classroom. It is vital for the methods classroom to model this concept of shared governance and empowerment. This notion of shared governance and empowerment should be a thread of discussion that continues throughout the course as a way to expand understanding into the student teaching classroom and beyond to the K–12 arena (NCSS/NCATE theme 10, Civic Ideals and Practices). If candidates have not had significant experience or stated expectations in appropriately citing and evaluating information from Web sites, a segment of the lesson should be devoted to those issues.
IMPLEMENTATION	Divide the class into groups of three to four candidates. Assign or allow groups to select a different kind of sovereignty: • Political • Economic • Social • Historic • Geographic • Psychological • Religious • Cultural Assign groups to research the meaning of sovereignty in the context of the topic. Use Web-based as well as print resources to teach the class the chosen aspect of sovereignty through a technology-based presentation. The groups may choose the media most appropriate for their topic. Prior to beginning research, facilitate a discussion about the scope and nature of the assignment and the associated scoring rubric.	In groups, select one aspect of the concept of sovereignty. Find two diverse examples that clearly depict the type of sovereignty selected. Use print-based documents, simulation software (provided by the professor such as Tom Snyder's Decisions, Decisions), online folk tales, historic examples, and so on. Develop a presentation to convey the distinctive or dual perspectives of the assigned type of sovereignty. This presentation can take the form of a desktop published newspaper, brochure, multimedia presentation, or candidate-created simulation.	Be open to candidate selections of multiple views of sovereignty that arise for the different social science disciplines. Development of the rubric can include: • Quality of information • Comprehensiveness of presentation • Disparity of examples • Empathy toward alternative perspectives For multimedia presentation guidelines, see the generic rubric in Appendix C or the URL for Multimedia Mania Rubric in the Tools and Resources section. In the development process, consider having each group specifically assigned to another group for the purpose of preliminary in-depth feedback. This enables each class member or group to concentrate on in-depth, appropriate feedback for just one presentation.
CULMINATION	Provide feedback to candidates upon completion of each presentation. Complete this feedback in an electronic form for inclusion in candidates' working portfolio. Distribute a group assessment and self-	Present project in class. Complete the self-assessment and group assessment. Participate in the discussion about working	As the projects are completed, the notion of debriefing the activity based on the content and the pedagogy used is important in assisting candidates in making the link between the activity and

TEACHER PREP FACULTY	TEACHER CANDIDATES	FACULTY NOTES
assessment rubric for each class member to complete. Rubrics should include elements of evaluating the effectiveness of the use of technology in the research and presentation process. Debrief the group process of completing the task. Have the class share issues of organizing and working in groups in terms of using the technique in the classroom. Have candidates write a reflection on the activity.	on a single product in a group setting. Debrief the organization of the groups and why it was used. Contribute ideas to how this technique might work in the high school classroom. Complete a reflection of what you learned about the concept of sovereignty, ideas you have acquired for teaching, as well as concerns.	implementation in the classroom. Because the groups were organized based on the preference or skill in the technology, the outcome may be different than having had groups organized by interest in the topic. Be sure to discuss the considerations in creating groups. If appropriate, consider saving the presentations for posting on the class Web site. Encourage candidates to save their results for inclusion in their portfolio. Prompt candidates to attach their reflection with the entry. Additionally, consider having candidates tag the entry by the standard or criteria identified for the program for later use in completing a culminating assessment portfolio.

(Left vertical label: CULMINATION)

Assessment

The table below offers an assessment for looking at the degree to which programs structure activities that meet specified standards. Use this table as a guideline for analyzing the activity as a potential performance product.

Table: Tracking Standards Met by Activities

STANDARDS	PERFORMANCE INDICATORS	ASSESSMENT (Processes and Products)
NETS for Teachers III. Teaching, Learning, and the Curriculum—Teachers implement curriculum plans that include methods and strategies for applying technology to maximize student learning.	Teachers: A. facilitate technology-enhanced experiences that address content standards and student technology standards. B. use technology to support learner-centered strategies that address the diverse needs of students. C. apply technology to develop students' higher-order skills and creativity. D. manage student learning activities in a technology-enhanced environment.	Candidate presentation rubric guidelines are available at: **www.ncsu.edu/midlink/rub.mm.st.htm** The Instructor can utilize the ISTE HyperSIG's rubric available at: **www.ncsu.edu:80/midlink/rub.mm.2000.htm**
Social Studies Standards VI. Power, Authority, and Governance—Social Studies programs should include experiences that provide for the study of how people create and change structures of power, authority, and governance, so that the learner can:	A. examine persistent issues involving the rights, roles, an status of the individual in relation to the general welfare. B. explain the purpose of government and analyze how its powers are acquired, used, and justified. F. analyze and evaluate conditions, actions, and motivations that contribute to conflict and cooperation within and among nations.	Candidate presentations include: • Quality of information • Comprehensiveness of presentation • Disparity of examples • Empathy toward alternative perspectives

Tools and Resources

SOFTWARE

Presentation software such as PowerPoint or HyperStudio

Desktop publishing software such as MS Word

Tom Snyder's Decisions, Decisions series

HARDWARE

Simulation software installed on open-access stations for candidate use. If simulation software is to be used in the presentation, software must be available on the presentation station that is accessed in the methods classroom.

Access to computer stations outside of class to complete product/presentation

Access to the Internet for acquiring resources

WEB SITES

Knight of Sovereignty Story:
http://patriot.net/~nachtanz/SReed/GawainLL.html
(This site is based on Knights of the Round Table.)

Multimedia Mania Rubric:
www.ncsu.edu/midlink/rub.mm.st.htm

Multimedia Rubric:
www.ncsu.edu:80/midlink/rub.mm.2000.htm

Old English Version of Knight of Sovereignty:
www.bulfinch.org/tales/chiv05.html or
www.lib.rochester.edu/camelot/teams/marriage.htm)

Credits

Candy Stocker, Denver Public Schools, Lakewood, Colorado, candy_stocker@ceo.cudenver.edu

Barbara Slater Stern, James Madison University, Winchester, Virginia, sternbs@jmu.edu

D. Mark Meyers, Rowan University, Glassboro, New Jersey, meyers@rowan.edu

Comments/Stories

The social sciences seem to be generally well understood by candidates when they reach this point in their professional preparation. However, the complex idea of sovereignty is one that they have not had to examine across the areas of the social sciences. In retrospect, candidates have commented that the process of looking at sovereignty through another lens (economics, geography, etc.) provided them with a far deeper understanding of the concept as well as a way to relate it to student-centered experiences when out in the classroom. Of note, one social studies methods class combined all their presentations together into one using a common fictitious character. Members of the class who were completing a dual credential in literature wrote a story that linked all the presentations together using the fictitious character to weave all the elements together. The result was informative, useful, and a bit comedic in a way secondary students would enjoy.

Why Are Things Where They Are?

Program/Grade Range: Secondary

Subject: Social Studies

Topic: Geographic Concepts of Region and Place

Profile: Professional Preparation, Student Teaching/Internship, First-Year Teaching

Abstract: Have you ever wondered why places are located where they are? In this model lesson, geographic, historic, economic, social, and political factors are introduced to help explain how certain places came to be populated and developed into what they are today, and to predict what they might become in the future. Using Internet information, satellite technology, CD-ROM databases, and other geographic software, teacher candidates explore concepts of urban place location. Through active knowledge creation, candidates explore the connections between geography and the other social science disciplines.

STANDARDS

NETS FOR TEACHERS

II. **PLANNING AND DESIGNING LEARNING ENVIRONMENTS AND EXPERIENCES**—*Teachers plan and design effective learning environments and experiences supported by technology. Teachers:*

   A. design developmentally appropriate learning opportunities that apply technology-enhanced instructional strategies to support the diverse needs of learners.

   C. identify and locate technology resources and evaluate them for accuracy and suitability.

V. **PRODUCTIVITY AND PROFESSIONAL PRACTICE**—*Teachers use technology to enhance their productivity and professional practice. Teachers:*

   A. use technology resources to engage in ongoing professional development and lifelong learning.

   B. continually evaluate and reflect on professional practice to make informed decisions regarding the use of technology in support of student learning.

   D. use technology to communicate and collaborate with peers, parents, and the larger community in order to nurture student learning.

SOCIAL STUDIES

III. **PEOPLE, PLACES, AND ENVIRONMENTS**—*Social studies programs should include experiences that provide for the study of people, places, and environments, so that the learner can:*

   A. refine mental maps of locales, regions, and the world that demonstrate understanding of relative location, direction, size, and shape.

   E. describe, differentiate, and explain the relationships among various regional and global patterns of geographic phenomena such as landforms, soils, climate, vegetation, natural resources, and population.

   H. examine, interpret, and analyze physical and cultural patterns and their interactions, such as land use, settlement patterns, cultural transmission of customs and ideas, and ecosystem changes.

VIII. **SCIENCE, TECHNOLOGY, AND SOCIETY**—*Social studies programs should include experiences that provide for the study of relationships among science, technology, and society, so that the learner can:*

   B. make judgments about how science and technology have transformed the physical world and human society and our understanding of time, space, place, and human-environment interactions.

IX. **GLOBAL CONNECTIONS**—*Social studies programs should include experiences that provide for the study of global connections and interdependence, so that the learner can:*

   B. explain conditions and motivations that contribute to conflict, cooperation, and interdependence among groups, societies, and nations.

   E. analyze the relationships and tensions between national sovereignty and global interests, in such matters as territory, economic development, nuclear and other weapons, use of natural resources, and human rights concerns.

Lesson Description

TEACHER PREP FACULTY	TEACHER CANDIDATES	FACULTY NOTES
PREPARATION		
Preview geographic software (electronic atlases) to select the desired software package appropriate for the class.	Read the social studies standards that focus on	It is important to recognize the dynamic nature of the geographic information available on the Internet. Most geography sites are constantly being updated with current information. Before beginning this lesson, check and update the links. (If possible, select software that is currently available at the school sites most used by candidates in their field experiences.)
Create a handout that contains the list of Web sites provided in the Tools and Resources section. Add others, especially local or regional resources, you are familiar with.	• geography; • production and distribution; • science, technology, and society; and • global connections. Be familiar with student expectations.	
Select a presentation program and a slide template for the teacher candidate presentation. Prepare an introductory presentation to define and present the scope of the geographic concept of place. This presentation becomes the introductory slides to a cumulative class slideshow on the concept of place.		The purpose of selecting a presentation program and slide template is to ensure that the candidate's final presentation is consistent and thoroughly illustrates theories of place, rather than offering a series of individual reports.
Have candidates review the appropriate social studies standards and discuss with them student expectations.		
INTRODUCTION		
Show an outline map of an island such as New Zealand. Ask candidates to predict where people might settle. Record reasons for predictions as well as dilemmas that arise.	Divide into collaborative groups to examine the map.	The introductory activity can be completed again using a map of an inland region with no transportation lines defined. Again ask groups to predict based on geographical features. Add information such as an east/west orientation, proximity to a coast, climatic conditions, and so on. Compare the two activities in terms of knowing the coasts versus seeing only a snapshot of an interior region of land.
Divide candidates into groups.	Reach a consensus on where the population might settle. Provide a rationale.	
Distribute topographic maps of the same region. Ask the groups to again predict where the population might settle. Discuss factors that are necessary to consider.	After being given a topographic map of the same region, again predict where the population might settle. Provide a rationale.	Some atlas programs have separate maps for each feature. Candidates can explore these features independently.
Following the activity, facilitate a brief class discussion of the ideas raised during the activity, and move to the guiding question for this activity: Why are things where they are?	Participate in a discussion of the ideas raised by your group. Begin to think about the question: Why are things where they are?	If the course is being offered concurrently with fieldwork, consider grouping candidates by grade level or common course/topic being taught in schools. For example, those teaching U.S. history may focus their examples on geographic areas of the colonization.
IMPLEMENTATION		
Use the prepared presentation to define the scope of the geographic concept of place, highlighting candidates' responses to the introductory activity. Point out the template used in the presentation as the template for the groups to use to create four slides on selected factors of the concept of place.	Form groups to complete the lesson. Each group is to provide four slides for the class presentation on "place," selecting one or more of the factors of place and ensuring that all are covered and none are duplicated. Factors can include, but are not limited to:	As candidates view the introductory presentation, have them begin to consider the template and make possible suggestions for modifications before the work on their final presentation begins.
Divide the class into groups. Have candidates select an attribute or attributes to investigate and supply them with the Web site handout. Be sure that all the factors have been assigned and no attribute is duplicated. Encourage	• River valleys • Transportation breaks • Ports and harbors • Religious or cultural events • Mountain or fall lines	See the Northern Lights folder system as a possible organizational pattern (the reference is in the Web Sites section of this lesson). As the assignment is given, do not forget to remind candidates about copyright issues and appropriate citations of images and information gathered from the Web. Check your university policy on citations.

TEACHER PREP FACULTY	TEACHER CANDIDATES	FACULTY NOTES
IMPLEMENTATION candidates to add to the list of Web sites as they search the Internet to complete this lesson. Create a folder on the university or college server (Yes, you can!) in which candidates may store their slides. Initially, the folder should contain documents including an evaluation rubric and appropriate Web sites on factors of place. (It may be necessary to create a brief handout on how to upload files.) After discussing the assignment, introduce the scoring rubric. Conduct a class discussion to complete the cells of the rubric. When they are completed, candidates place the four slides in a single folder labeled by the attribute they selected. Members of the class should be able to access those slides as a way of examining each other's work.	• Extractable resources • Power sources • Tourism • Historical significance • Military presence • Business centers • Transportation hubs **Slide 1**—A definition of the geographic or economic factor selected. **Slide 2**—Downloaded maps demonstrating places containing the attributes of the factor. **Slide 3**—Other places or illustrative examples of the application of the factor. **Slide 4**—An infrared map or satellite image from the Internet or CD-ROM. Use the image to have the class predict where the chosen factor would be located. After the group has completed its work, post or upload the four slides for others to view and provide feedback. View the work of other groups. Consider modifying the slides based on what is learned from other groups' work.	Often your library services has the policy posted on the library portion of the university Web site or as a handout. An incomplete rubric is presented on the following page to provide candidates with additional practice creating rubrics. The exercise in itself often clarifies the assignment and ensures that candidates are aware of the expectations. You may choose to change the headings to numbers or other scoring mechanisms consistent with college program assessments. On the class Web site, be sure to provide access to a Web site evaluation form as well as live links to the Web sites listed on the handout. An alternative to having candidates upload their slides to the university server is to set the class Web site such that the slide file can be uploaded onto the Web. Because program files such as those created in PowerPoint can be viewed on a Web site, posting on the Web becomes a viable way for groups to examine each other's work. Consider setting a date for the slides to be uploaded in a draft form. Encourage groups to electronically examine each other's work after the posting date. Allow groups additional time to edit and upgrade their slides based on what they learn from one another.
CULMINATION Facilitate the assembly of a class presentation on the concept of place. Schedule time for the presentation. Ask for group representatives to narrate the presentation. Discuss the effectiveness of the final product. Ask candidates to reflect on (1) the process, (2) the product, (3) the functioning of the group, and (4) how they might modify the lesson to meet the needs of middle or high school students. Post the presentation on the class Web site for disseminating or downloading by the class, or for use in their field experience or with their own students.	View the class presentation. Participate in a discussion about the effectiveness of the final product as well as the process. E-mail a reflection to the faculty member addressing these issues: (1) the process, (2) the product, (3) the functioning of the group, and (4) how the lesson might be modified to meet the needs of middle school or high school students. Download a copy of the presentation for your own reference and professional use. Separate your section of the presentation as an artifact for an electronic portfolio.	You can either assemble the presentation yourself prior to class or ask representatives from each group to complete the assembly. Putting this responsibility in the hands of the candidates forces them to make decisions about the order of the factors. For some, this additional responsibility can be extra credit. Consider responding to the reflections written and sent by the candidates, asking further probing questions and providing perhaps another "link" to increase their understanding. **Note:** Candidates who have had experience with Geographic Information Systems (GIS) in a prior class have a significant advantage in being able to access databases of information, satellite images, and remote-sensing data. These candidates can provide an inservice experience for others in the class on these rich resources. This is an example of content area faculty providing experience in the arts and sciences courses that markedly changes the discussion in methods courses.

Assessment

Each group's slide sequence is assessed using the following rubric. The class should complete the descriptors of the other elements of the table.

Rubric: Slide Presentation

CRITERIA	LEVELS OF PERFORMANCE		
	INCOMPLETE	ACCEPTABLE	TARGET
Content			
Accuracy of content			Candidate relates his or her knowledge of topography to patterns of settlement and development. Candidate provides other places or illustrative examples of the application of the factor/attribute.
Slide 1—Definition of the geographic or economic factor selected			Definition is clear and accurate. Candidate uses at least one map example and other reference materials to illustrate the definition of the factor.
Slide 2—Downloaded map demonstrating a place containing the attributes of the factor			Candidate uses multiple technologies to obtain appropriate maps and information.
Slide 3—Examples of other places or illustrative examples of the application of the factor			Candidate provides at least two examples that show the attribute with connections to at least three real locations as examples.
Slide 4—Using an infrared map or satellite image from the Internet or CD-ROM, asks appropriate questions to have the class predict where the chosen factor would be located			Candidate povides a clear infrared or satellite image of an area such that the class can predict where the factor might be placed. Slide also has a completed map of where the factor is actually placed as a way to check the prediction.
Technology			
Graphic design and adherence to template			Sequence of four slides utilizes the template presented according to the guidelines agreed on in class. The design of the slides is pleasing to the eye and readable from an appropriate distance with each slide connecting one to the other in the appropriate order.
Written Reflection (by E-mail)			
Elements to consider: (1) the process, (2) the product, (3) the functioning of the group, and (4) how they might modify the lesson to meet the needs of middle school or high school students			Candidate clearly expresses newly created knowledge of technology, multimedia presentations, cooperative/collaborative learning groups, and the connections to the secondary classroom.
Collaboration			
Roles			Roles were defined and performed effectively.
Collaborative group work			All candidates worked together cooperatively and enthusiastically, sharing responsibility equitably, using necessary listening and leadership skills.

Note: The collaboration component is modified from Cooperative Learning Project Rubric B: Product: www.phschool.com/professional_development/assessment/rub_coop_product.html.

Tools and Resources

SOFTWARE

Electronic atlas (Microsoft Encarta Virtual Globe, 3-D Atlas), presentation software (PowerPoint, HyperStudio, Astound, Flash, etc.)

HARDWARE

Projection device and Internet access, space on the university server to create a class folder to save the common files that all candidates will be accessing

WEB SITES

Maps

Ask USGS—Educational Resources:
http://ask.usgs.gov/education.html (This site is sponsored by the U.S. Geological Survey.)

Expedia Travel: www.expedia.com/daily/home/ (Click on "Maps" to make a selection.)

Geography with Matt Rosenberg:
http://geography.about.com/science/geography/?once=true& (Click on "World Atlas and Maps" or "Cities and Urban Geography.")

Northern Light Search: City and Urban Geography:
www.northernlight.com/nlquery.fcg?cb=0&qr=city+and+urban+geography (This search engine uses a folder system.)

UT Austin Maps:
www.lib.utexas.edu/Libs/PCL/Map_collection/map_sites/map_sites.html

Sample Lessons

Cities of Today, Cities of Tomorrow:
www.un.org/Pubs/CyberSchoolBus/special/habitat/index.html (This site is sponsored by the United Nations.)

Global Poster Education:
www.eloff.com/~poster_ed/NGSstds.html

Ideal City Unit:
www.un.org/Pubs/CyberSchoolBus/special/habitat/ideal/ideal.htm (This site is sponsored by the United Nations.)

Iditarod WebQuest:
http://inkido.indiana.edu/w310work/Iditarod_webquest/

The National Geography Standards:
www.eloff.com/~poster_ed/NGSstds.html (This site offers lesson plans.)

The Three Gorges Dam WebQuest:
http://library.thinkquest.org/27384/dam.html

Understanding Cities: Discovery Channel:
http://school.discovery.com/lessonplans/programs/cities/standards.html

Geography Games

GeoGlobe: Interactive Geography:
http://library.thinkquest.org/10157/

Online Geography Games: www.geography-games.com/index.html

Geography Content

Geographic Learning Site:
http://geography.state.gov/htmls/teacher.html (This site is sponsored by the U.S. State Department.)

Geography World:
http://members.aol.com/bowermanb/101.html (This site offers geography resource listing.)

GeoResources: www.georesources.co.uk/index.htm (This UK site contains links, virtual fieldwork, case studies, outline maps, weather data, etc.)

The Urban Geography of Leeds: An Historical Analysis of Urban Development:
www.brixworth.demon.co.uk/leeds/#Leeds

General Resources

Ask USGS—Educational Resources:
http://ask.usgs.gov/education.html (This site is sponsored by the U.S. Geological Survey.)

Geography Matters: GIS and Mapping Software:
www.esri.com

The Great Globe Gallery:
http://hum.amu.edu.pl/~zbzw/glob/glob1.htm

Radical Urban Theory: The Geography of Urban Sprawl:
www.rut.com/mjalbert/AntelopeValley/index.html

Teaching Geography through the Internet: Internet Resources for Geography Education:
www.oranim.macam98.ac.il/geo/ndx_geo.html

Credits

Candy Stocker, Denver Public Schools, Lakewood, Colorado, candy_stocker@ceo.cudenver.edu

Barbara Slater Stern, James Madison University, Winchester, Virginia, sternbs@jmu.edu

D. Mark Meyers, Rowan University, Glassboro, New Jersey, meyers@rowan.edu

Comments/Stories

This project has been done with both preservice and inservice teachers. The teachers were excited by the content and the expanded electronic availability of information coupled with the ability to empathize with the perspectives of others. When candidates enter the field, they will be exposed to an environment of collaboration, diverse learners, and learning styles. The candidates need to have prior experience working together to create a single product; the project models the work a curriculum development team in the school would do as well as a method for use with students.

Integrating Technology in the Classroom

- Technology in Student Teaching and Internships
- Technology in First-Year Teaching and Professional Development
- Assessing Technology Preparation of Teachers

Technology in Student Teaching and Internships

The student teaching experience is at the heart of the teacher preparation program. Whether it is taken as an internship under the supervision of an on-site teacher and a university faculty member or completed as a fully supervised experience in the classroom of a master teacher, it is the point when theory becomes practice with real students in a real classroom setting. (Note: The master teacher is sometimes called a cooperating or supervising teacher, overseeing the classroom in which the teacher candidate becomes the student teacher. In this chapter, we'll be using the term "master teacher.")

The implementation of the NETS for Teachers during the student teaching or internship experience takes on a different set of characteristics than that discussed in earlier profiles. The first standard, Technology Operations and Concepts, is emphasized in the General Preparation Performance Profile, as an integral part of the general education or major study experience. The Professional Preparation Performance Profile concentrates on the second standard, Planning and Designing Learning Environments and Experiences. The Student Teaching/Internship Performance Profile focuses on using all that has occurred before, thus completing the teaching cycle of **planning** (Standard II), **teaching** (Standard III), and **assessing** (Standard IV).

Although each of the prior profiles covers elements of each standard, the developmental nature of the profiles helps teacher preparation programs emphasize the appropriate standard at each point in the education of teacher candidates. Productivity and Professional Practice (Standard V) and Social, Ethical, Legal, and Human Issues (Standard VI) run as threads through all programs at all stages.

The use of technology for professional productivity for preservice, novice, and experienced teachers grows in sophistication and specialization as their needs change. Likewise, the application of social, ethical, legal, and human issues moves from monitoring personal use to modeling, promoting, and facilitating student understanding and appropriate behavior. The student teaching/internship phase of teacher preparation must ensure that candidates are able to apply productivity tools, develop their own professional plan, and progress from merely having a dialogue about social, ethical, legal, and human issues to demonstrating how those ideas play out in planning, teaching, and assessing in the classroom.

This chapter focuses on addressing the NETS for Teachers by examining the

- essential conditions,
- supervision of student teaching/internships,
- student teaching placements, and
- transfer of university experiences into classroom practice.

Essential Conditions

The student teaching or internship experience is a collaborative endeavor between the partnering schools and the university. Ideally, every aspect of the essential conditions outlined for this profile should be in place at the school site.

Experience tells us that not every situation is an ideal learning environment for teacher candidates. Each school setting carries a unique set of variables that creates both positive and negative experiences; the continuous struggle schools undergo in their effort to meet the essential conditions is a valuable experience in itself for student teachers to witness.

Additionally, cooperating schools are under pressure from many sectors to push the learning outcomes of their students as high as possible. With a focus on student outcomes, schools are placing time and resources toward endeavors they believe will pay off in higher test scores and student performance.

The essential conditions for the Student Teaching/Internship Performance Profile are generally met when

- there is a climate of promoting student conceptual understanding and technology competence to meet the curriculum standards and ISTE NETS for Student, and

- the school community creates a setting focused on learning for all members of the community, including students, student teachers, teachers, administrators, and parents.

The following section elaborates on each of the essential conditions in building an ideal environment to support student teaching and internship experiences.

Shared Vision—*University personnel and teachers and administrators at the cooperating school site share a vision for technology use in the classroom.*

It should be apparent to the teacher candidate that there is consistency in the vision at the school site. From the custodian to the principal and the parents to the outside community, there is a shared commitment for the presence of technology and the manner in which it is utilized at the school. The teacher candidate is able to participate in or witness how the vision is revisited, as well as share in the recommitment to keep the school community moving forward. Clarification and recommitment may happen at faculty meetings, working meetings, back-to-school nights, or other public events.

Access—*Access to current technologies, software, and telecommunications networks is provided for student teachers/interns and their master teachers in the classroom and professional work areas.*

Access to current technologies at the school site is not limited to a few teachers' rooms, the library, or the office. Technology is present in every classroom and the faculty workroom. Teacher candidates can prepare lessons on the school site, observe teachers using technology to prepare lessons, and, especially, engage in teaching students. Access to technology is available to the students in such a way that student teachers and interns can prepare lessons in which their students will be able to use the resources without undo hardship and scheduling dilemmas.

Skilled Educators—*Master teachers and university supervisors model technology use that facilitates students meeting the ISTE NETS for Students.*

As with any desired pedagogy, teacher candidates are able to observe the effective use of technology within the classrooms they are placed. The master teacher models good teaching practice in using technology to create learning opportunities for students and to support professional practice, thereby demonstrating his or her ability to meet the ISTE NETS for Teachers. Additionally, master teachers consciously include opportunities for students to meet ISTE NETS for Students or the state equivalent.

Professional Development—*Master teachers are readily provided with professional development in applications of technology in teaching.*

The professional development opportunities provided by the school or district are shared with student teachers, thus furthering student teachers' awareness that maintaining and improving professional skills are expectations of the profession. Student teachers observe master teachers making these opportunities part of their annual professional development plans.

Technical Assistance—*In field-experience settings, technical assistance is on-site to ensure the reliability of teaching resources.*

Although the reality of having highly trained technical assistance on-site—especially in elementary, small, or rural schools—is economically problematic, the school has enough technical expertise and a plan for ready access to needed expertise that makes use of technology an assumption, not a risk. Student teachers are aware of how to access the assistance and are supported by master teachers in doing so.

Content Standards and Curriculum Resources—*Technology-based curriculum resources appropriate in meeting the content standards in teaching areas and grade ranges are available to teacher candidates at the school site.*

Teachers at the school site have made strategic and informed decisions about their purchases for professional and student use. These resources are not hidden away for the exclusive use of a few. Rather, they are easily accessible and encouraged to be used by student teachers.

Student-Centered Teaching—*Opportunities to implement a variety of technology-enhanced, student-centered learning activities are provided for student teachers/interns.*

Master teachers provide opportunities for student teachers to deal with the ambiguity of diagnosing student needs. Student teachers are coached on how to use this information to plan, teach, and assess technology-rich, student-centered instructional activities while under the tutelage and support of their master teachers.

Assessment—*Master teachers work with student teachers/interns to assess the effectiveness of student learning and technology use in supporting that learning.*

Multiple sources of data and a variety of assessment techniques are modeled by master teachers in evaluating both content standards and technology standards. Master teachers model and share their own reflective practices as a consequence of the teaching process. Learning experiences are then collaboratively modified based on teacher reflection and analysis of student outcomes.

Community Support—*Student teachers/interns teach in partner schools where technology integration is modeled and supported.*

The extended educational community works collaboratively with the university to provide school sites that have the necessary technology, and model appropriate integration of the technology, in teaching and learning. Unlike a deficit model, the educational community willingly provides its best settings and master teachers for the training of novice teachers.

Support Policies—*Student teaching/internship sites are located where administrative policies support and reward the use of technology.*

As student teaching and internship placements are assessed, the existence of administrative support for the effective use of technology and the presence of incentives for teachers and schools to demonstrate good practice are taken into account in making placement decisions.

These essential conditions are targets for schools and programs to strive toward. In an era of teacher shortages, it is easy to assume that the bar must be lowered to provide enough placements for student teachers. However, when colleges of education have an ongoing dialogue with partner schools, a symbiotic relationship can develop in which the quality of student teaching placements and the relevance of the teacher preparation program in meeting the school needs are jointly improved as a consequence of open communication.

Supervision of Student Teaching/Internships

With as much as 50% of the course unit credit assigned to student teaching and field experiences, colleges of education cannot afford to ignore the importance of the university supervisor in ensuring that concepts taught in methods courses are implemented in the field setting. Candidates may be able to meet many of the performance indicators through a university classroom course that uses microteaching and other simulated experiences. But until teacher candidates can demonstrate knowledge and skills in a classroom setting, they are not prepared to take over the full responsibility for a classroom of students.

ADJUNCT FACULTY

Often the breakdown between articulating what happens in the program coursework and validating performance in the student teaching/internship comes with the lack of communication between those teaching the courses and those supervising the field experiences. At many institutions, the largest proportion of supervisors are adjunct faculty who often have no other role with the university than to supervise student teachers and interns. Most often, the supervisors are experienced teachers who are either on loan, on leave, or retired from teaching. They typically have no experience teaching the methods courses and very little ownership of the program.

Although adjunct faculty members usually bring a wealth of teaching experiences to the role of university supervisors, they typically are not well versed in technology and lack depth of experience in its use in teaching and learning. Adjunct faculty members usually have limited access to or communication about professional-development opportunities provided by the university and generally don't attend faculty meetings or have the opportunity to attend conferences at university expense. As a course of habit, colleges of education have disenfranchised adjunct faculty in providing access to university-sponsored opportunities to remain current in their field of expertise.

For the integration of technology to take place in a seamless, well-supported manner, every supervisor must

- be able to recognize the effective use of technology in a lesson,

- be aware of current thinking on the use of technology,

- be familiar with core curriculum software, and

- be able to coach candidates based on models of good practice.

Adjunct faculty members need to be updated on the uses of technology as a condition of continued employment.

SCENARIO 1

Holding Workshops to Improve Supervision

As coordinator of student teaching supervision, Dr. Gray was well aware that more than half of the student teaching/intern supervisors at No Name State University (NNSU) had been working in an adjunct capacity for more than 10 years. Each was a very accomplished teacher selected for depth of experience and ability to coach teacher candidates.

Although the NNSU engaged in periodic professional development for adjunct faculty, it had become painfully apparent that the teacher candidates' level of technology capabilities had far outpaced the supervisors' knowledge. To him, the supervisors seemed unwilling to learn about technology in the context of teaching and learning in K–12 classrooms. This was compounded by the fact that the job description for newly hired supervisors included a provision that they have familiarity with and the ability to critique and coach technology-based lessons in alignment with NETS and district student performance indicators.

Dr. Gray wanted all teacher candidates to be supervised by individuals who could effectively coach candidates on using technology appropriately in the classroom. In an effort to assist existing supervisors to meet the current hiring requirements, a workshop series was designed focusing on model lessons from NETS for Students—Connecting Curriculum and Technology (ISTE, 2000).

In one of the workshops, NNSU faculty members in both educational technology and curriculum and instruction worked with the supervisors to analyze selected lessons as if a teacher candidate or intern had implemented the lessons. Standards were discussed as well as the appropriate use of the technology in supporting student learning. Besides discussing technology use in the classroom, the faculty assisted supervisors in creating their own student teaching seminar presentation that highlighted the use of graphic organizing software, such as Inspiration or Kidspiration.

As a result of this session, supervisors left with a working knowledge of the graphic organizing software, an awareness of several model lessons using the same graphic organizing software, and a list of topics to discuss with each other concerning observing technology-based lessons. The next workshop was slated to view several videos of teacher candidates from the previous semester who were engaged in teaching technology-rich lessons with a focus on observational skills in technology-rich settings.

Although Dr. Gray was initially concerned about how successful the workshop series was going to be, after the first session, which focused on the use of e-mail and attachments, he was pleasantly surprised at how enthusiastic the supervisors were to use specialized educational software as well as productivity tools. In an assessment of supervisor motivation taking the workshops, supervisors reported that in the past, lack of time and targeted professional development to meet their needs were the initial stumbling blocks. After the first three workshops, Dr. Gray received more ideas and requests than he could handle. That, he concluded, was a good problem to work on.

TECHNOLOGY USE IN THE SUPERVISION PROCESS

There are many good examples of how the supervisor can enhance the supervision process by using technology. Simple use of e-mail can make the process far more efficient. For example, requiring candidates to upload lesson plans to the supervisor at least 48 hours in advance of the observation gives the supervisor time to examine the lesson plan, provide written feedback nested in the file as part of the word processor's editing and reviewing function, and have the candidate revise the lesson plan an additional time before the observation takes place. The supervisor is then able to "preconference" with the candidate in a substantive and thoroughly documented way, making the time on-site for the observation much more efficient.

Taking a laptop or personal data assistant (PDA) with a keyboard along to the observation permits instantaneous recording of notes as well as the ability to send the observation notes to the candidate and master teacher following the observation. Furthermore, post-conference discussions can be documented, including pulling up the original lesson plan for oral review and reflection. The process of documenting changes and having recommendations instantaneously available provides the candidate with timely feedback and potential artifacts for a digital portfolio.

SCENARIO 2

Planning, Scheduling, and Organizing with Technology

Melissa finished her weekly planning session with her master teacher on Thursday afternoon. Based on her plan book, she knew she would be preparing a series of lessons for the following week for her first graders on the concept of telling time on an analog clock. Her supervisor would be coming on Tuesday for an observation during her teaching time.

In considering the lessons on developing the concept, she realized that Tuesday's lesson would focus on sequencing time in the context of a series of events by using the book Grouchy Ladybug, *by Eric Carle. Melissa wrote her lesson incorporating Kidspiration software in a whole-class activity both in the introduction of the vocabulary and sequencing the events of the story. By Friday evening, Melissa had sent her lesson plan to her supervisor, Dr. Andre, attached to an e-mail message confirming the observation time for Tuesday.*

Dr. Andre picked up Melissa's e-mail message on Sunday evening as she was preparing for her Monday class. In reading the lesson plan, Dr. Andre had concerns about the type of questions Melissa planned to ask her students about the story. Additionally, since classroom management had been an issue for Melissa in keeping her students actively engaged, Dr. Andre inserted questions in the lesson plan regarding managing students' movements that hadn't been addressed. By 9 p.m., Dr. Andre had attached the queried lesson plan to an e-mail to Melissa, and copied her master teacher on the message.

Monday, Melissa downloaded the lesson plan from Dr. Andre. The issues Dr. Andre raised prompted Melissa to conference with her master teacher. Since the master teacher was aware of the questions raised, she worked with Melissa to revise her lesson plan to look closer at student engagement and the type of questions that foster higher-level thinking in first graders. Melissa sent the revised lesson plan back to Dr. Andre on Monday evening.

Before leaving for the observation, Dr. Andre had received the revised lesson plan, made notes of things to look for, and downloaded it onto her laptop. Before stepping into the classroom to observe Melissa, Dr. Andre was familiar with the lesson being taught, had provided input, and had seen the revised version.

On the day of the observation, Melissa had saved both versions of the lesson plan in a folder on her computer. Because Dr. Andre provided an orientation to student teaching that included the electronic exchange process and expectations for observations, Melissa was aware of the type of write-up Dr. Andre would be providing for her at the conclusion of the observation. Through the documents she received from this observation and others, Melissa was able to track her own growth.

On her computer, Dr. Andre had created a folder for the observation that now contained two versions of the lesson plan. In the end, the folder would contain a document that had the observation notes, reflective comments made by Melissa following the observation, the collaboratively established goals for the next observation, and the completed observation rubric. This document would be sent to Melissa and her master teacher once Dr. Andre returned to campus and had an opportunity to complete a final edit. For each observation Dr. Andre completed, she created a folder for the documents and any substantive e-mail exchanges with her student teachers.

Because Melissa was responsible for maintaining her working portfolio in an electronic form, she had retained all of her lesson sequences that showed how she had grown in her questioning strategies as well as other key points on which Dr. Andre and her master teacher had coached her. Melissa's university required teacher candidates to present their credential portfolio organized by the Model Standards for Beginning Teacher Licensing and Development, available through the Interstate New Teacher Assessment and Support Consortium (INTASC) at **www.coe.ilstu.edu/ncate/intascprinciples.htm.**

Eventually, she would select what she considered to be appropriate lesson sequences as artifacts to demonstrate growth over time in meeting INTASC Principle 4, Multiple Instructional Strategies—Understands and uses a variety of instructional strategies to encourage students' development of critical thinking, problem solving, and performance skills.

TECHNOLOGY AS A TOOL OF SUPERVISION

Various colleges of education have experimented with remote observation of student teachers and interns. Some have placed a camera in the corner of a room and recorded the lesson onto videotape in an unedited form, while others have used live video streaming of student teachers giving lessons in a remote setting, sending the information back to the supervisor at the university. There is always the concern that what the supervisor is seeing through the technology is not all that is happening in the classroom. The feeling and tone of the classroom, interactions with the master teacher, the atmosphere of the school, outside distractions created by the physical setting of the classroom, and so on are all difficult elements to add to the context of the lesson when transmitted electronically. Other detractors from using technology-mediated supervision include the potential high cost of equipment, access to adequate bandwidth, and the need for additional staff to support or control the equipment.

In spite of concerns about technology-mediated supervision, there will always be pressure to meet the needs of rural settings in cost-effective ways. Capturing student teachers and interns on video, whether it is digital or analog, provides an artifact for discussion of the teaching process, live or delayed. This evidence of teaching can be more accurately analyzed and revisited than can a live observation.

SCENARIO 3

Rural Routes—Keeping Connected

Dr. Thomas at Flexible State University (FSU) always had a cadre of students from rural areas in the region who wanted to return to their own communities for their student teaching. In the past, finding adequate supervision for their field experience had been problematic because of the lack of expertise in the region. Or, it had been expensive because of the enormous travel time.

With the installation of an Internet-based videoconferencing system and a variety of videotaping systems, the use of e-mail, and the introduction of threaded discussion, Dr. Thomas was able to work with six student teachers in six different locations. After an on-campus orientation at the conclusion of the semester preceding student teaching, Dr. Thomas found that he needed to visit the sites only once during the semester if all was proceeding well.

One of Dr. Thomas' students, Mark, used the simplest combination of technologies to make the process work. Mark was in a region that lacked access to video streaming or a high bandwidth with which to send video of his teaching. Therefore, his master teacher videotaped his lessons with the rule that once the lesson started, the videotape had to roll continuously until the lesson was over. Mark wore a wireless microphone to ensure that everything he said was recorded.

Mark and his master teacher did a preliminary analysis of the tape the afternoon following the lesson. A copy of the tape was then sent by overnight mail to Dr. Thomas. Dr. Thomas reviewed the lesson and tagged frames that he wanted to discuss with Mark. He then e-mailed Mark the frame numbers and set up a conference call. Together, Mark, his supervisor, and his master teacher discussed the lesson, listened to Mark's assessment of his own performance, and mutually set goals for the next observation.

For weekly seminars, Dr. Thomas scheduled either a videoconference session or Internet-based live chat on a specific issue. At the beginning of the semester, he outlined topics for each seminar with an open time for burning issues. The teacher candidates found that the videoconferencing enabled them to remain connected with the university and each other, thereby bridging that feeling of isolation and the perception of not having someone with whom to share and consult.

Student Teaching Placements

An experienced classroom teacher, who lends expertise as well as her students to the university for teacher training, facilitates the student teaching experience. Without the support, guidance, and coaching from an accomplished master teacher, even the most promising student teacher can become frustrated, disillusioned, and unsuccessful.

Finding appropriate placements for student teachers is an enormous job. The larger the teacher preparation program, the more complex the process becomes. It is ideal but unrealistic to believe that every school and every classroom is appropriate for a student teacher. As stated above in the essential conditions, several attributes of placements and master teachers need to be considered before selecting student teaching situations. These attributes include selecting master teachers who are able to use and model technology effectively. Placing student teachers in settings where technology *is not* used sends the message that implementation of technology standards is not an important characteristic of teaching in the 21st century.

The following scenario addresses the dilemma one university faced in finding well-prepared, technology-savvy master teachers for placements.

SCENARIO 4

Partnering Brings "Freeway" School up to Speed

With a major expansion of the teacher education program, Collaborative University (CU) knew it was going to have a serious problem finding appropriate placements that modeled the effective use of technology. The surrounding school district was building schools at such an alarming rate that filling the teaching positions would necessitate a major effort to recruit from out of state. At the same time, the faculty members in educational technology were being pressured to offer more sections of their courses for professional development to meet the credential needs of the out-of-state teachers.

CU faculty members had a reputation for working with the school district to meet local needs. Many were personal friends with teachers and administrators and often had Friday afternoon discussions about initiatives that were only in the idea stage. In one of those discussions, a newly named principal of a "freeway" school, a temporary school site designed to relieve overcrowding, came up with a solution to solve both the placement issue and provide inservice for the out-of-state teachers.

Because many of the teachers at the new school were experienced but new to the area, CU offered the technology course at the school site. Student teachers and their master teachers enrolled in the course together as teams. The school set up a wireless network to quickly enable all classrooms to have access to the Internet, electronic library resources, and the local area network. With the acquisition of wireless equipped laptops, the inservice/preservice class was up and running in less than a week.

The partnering of the student teachers and master teachers brought a rich, classroom-based context to the course. Each team prepared technology-rich lessons while exploring various tools. The teacher candidates often brought more experience with the technology into the team, thus becoming lead team members. The master teacher brought a depth of experience in teaching and a knowledge of students and curriculum that made the team complete.

Within a year, the entire faculty of the "freeway" school was highly technology-literate and had a shared vision of how technology could be integrated into their teaching. Once the new school was built and the faculty moved into the new building, the wireless technology became an assumed characteristic of each classroom. As new student teachers came into the building, the CU faculty offered different technology courses to meet the needs of the faculty. With each course, incentives were provided for teaching teams and student teacher/master teacher teams to take the course. Involving student teachers in maintaining technology expertise was now part of the school's culture.

Transferring University Experiences into Classroom Practice

As teacher candidates progress through a well-articulated preparation program, the transfer of learning experiences to teaching experiences in the classroom should become a natural step. The activities outlined in the General Preparation phase can have corollary learning experiences in the Professional Preparation phase of university work. Building on this learning, teacher candidates can create standards-aligned, technology-rich experiences for their own students. These lessons can be further honed as the teacher candidates become novice teachers and gain in experience. The lessons selected for this volume are intended to provide an array of technology implementation strategies that can be modified and transferred to many different situations.

The following two scenarios demonstrate how model lessons used at the university can be modified to become developmentally appropriate lessons planned, taught, and assessed by student teachers. Each scenario is a composite of stories from many institutions that have shared their experiences and tested the activities in Section 2. Additional scenarios that extend to the first year of teaching can be found in the next chapter, "Technology in First-Year Teaching and Professional Development."

SCENARIO 5

English Language Arts

General Preparation

Wanting to be a primary grade teacher, Juan took the prerequisite course in children's literature thinking that reading children's books might be boring. He found that he thoroughly loved the course and especially the introduction to Living Books software or interactive books. He had never considered how much imagination and language could come out of taking a wonderful story and examining all the pictures and other events that may not be obvious to the reader. He completed a project on Mercer Mayer's Just Grandma and Me *in the genre of picture books.*

Professional Preparation

During the literacy course, Juan was part of a team that completed the "Creating Literacy-Rich Learning Environments" activity (see Section 2, "Technology in Early Childhood Education Programs," English Language Arts). He insisted that electronic books become part of the presentation. Others in his team had experiences with electronic books, big books, and other forms of presenting literature. As part of their data gathering, the team interviewed several primary grade teachers and toured their classrooms. Juan learned about both independent and whole-class use of electronic forms of literature to enhance student comprehension of the story and their ability to infer from pictures. The team's PowerPoint presentation included a visit to one teacher's Web site that showed what her first-grade students had done with the electronic books, a review of several sites that had books directly online, and other aspects of a literacy-rich learning environment.

Student Teaching/Internship

Juan was placed in a kindergarten for his first student teaching experience. As Grandparents' Day approached, he was asked to do a whole-class lesson while the grandparents were visiting. Juan chose to use Just Grandma and Me. *Juan read the book to the students in English first. Because his class had second-language learners in both Spanish and Japanese, Juan followed up by having the book read electronically in Spanish, then Japanese. The students had never experienced a book that was presented in multiple languages. Additionally, the Japanese grandparents, some of whom did not speak English fluently, were thrilled to be able to understand the story and interact with their grandchild about the content of the story. Juan then showed the children and their grandparents how to control and explore the story themselves at one of the centers. The following day, Juan conducted a reinforcement lesson with a discussion about the story, the words used, and other linguistic elements.*

SCENARIO 6

Science

General Preparation

In an environmental science course, Marta participated in a research study looking at the change in the chemical composition of a stream during two semesters. Every week, the team visited points along the stream above and below a housing development and a light industrial park. For her part in the project, Marta took samples to measure the conductivity or salinity of the water. The samples were taken back to the lab and tested with a conductivity probe connected to a computer. The results were graphed both per sampling period and over time.

Professional Preparation

In her science methods courses, Marta completed the activity "Bounce Back—The Long and Short of It" (Section 2, "Technology in Middle School Education Programs," Science) with a team of teacher candidates. They used the motion-detector probe connected to a computer to graph the bounce of sports balls. The interface used was similar to the one used in the environmental science course. Setting up the graph, reading the data, interpreting results, and modifying variables were all familiar experiences.

Also, Marta participated in completing the "Gravity" activity (Section 2," Technology in Secondary Education Programs," Science), in which she and her colleagues used a photo gate attached to a computer to design experiments testing a variety of objects to decide whether they fall at the same rate. Through that activity, they learned about classroom management, lab materials, and misconceptions students can have based on poor lab instructions. Her familiarity with the interface and the use of probeware allowed her to be more specific in her design of a lesson for students.

Student Teaching/Internship

As with every well-designed lesson in the artificial setting of the university, Marta hoped to use her lessons on gravity and acceleration in her student teaching. She was delighted when her master teacher showed her the probeware and computers in the school. The motion detector and photo gate weren't among the probeware available. However, the school did have the low-g accelerometers for lab groups.

Taking what she had learned from creating student-centered problems, Marta developed a lesson in which the student groups placed the accelerometers on cars on an incline and measured the acceleration down the incline. She expanded the lesson by mounting the accelerometer on the hood of a car in the school parking lot. With the permission of her master teacher, the manual transmission car drove down the side of the parking lot recording the drop in acceleration with each manual shift. The experiment was conducted again on an automatic transmission car and the results compared. The technology provided accurate as well as graphical data for analysis.

Marta's conductivity probeware experience became very valuable because her second student teaching placement was in an environmental biology class. She and her students collaborated with university researchers to collect data on the changing salinity in a local estuary. A year later, she discovered that many of her former students were still monitoring the salinity in the estuary by logging on to the project Web site as others continued the research.

Important Factors

The following are important factors contributing to the ability of the student teacher or intern to implement technology in teaching and learning:

- Teacher preparation program design

- Training of the university supervisors

- Technology training and use by the master teacher

The realities of the classroom and the university make these factors difficult to ensure for every teacher candidate. As schools and universities each struggle with implementing technology in the curriculum, it is likely that one partner may be ahead of the other in implementation. The final two scenarios illustrate that, in spite of difficulties, there can be synergistic gains when public schools and faculties of education are open to learning from each other.

SCENARIO 7

Low-Tech Metropolitan College, High-Tech Rural School

To learn about technology in schools, students at Metro U.S.A. (MU) spent two years in their teacher education program working with faculty who themselves had little preparation to teach their students how to use technology in classrooms. Struggling, the college worked to acquire updated computers for the lab, although most faculty had antiquated hardware in their offices. A grant provided training for faculty, but many were reluctant to participate as they could spare little time to add something new or different to their already-packed classes. Also, they had little vision of the use of technology in classrooms where the teacher candidates would be teaching.

A few stalwart faculty members worked to demonstrate the use of technology in their classrooms and how to "punt" when the equipment wouldn't work. Their smiles showed the teacher candidates that laughing at yourself is sometimes the best you can do. The schools the candidates visited for field placements were those that had computers— mostly in labs and used primarily for programmed instruction during library time. There seemed to be a mismatch between what they were reading should happen in teaching and learning with technology and what was happening in the schools. Because most candidates would teach in local schools, both the faculty and teacher candidates became less interested in trying to use technology in the schools or teaching others to do so.

Two recently married students asked to be allowed to student teach in their small rural home community 200 miles away, in order to live with and assume partial care for their aging grandparents. A supervisor was located at a nearby community college and the capstone teaching seminar was to be facilitated by a faculty member on campus through e-mail. The first seminar assignment asked for the demographics of the community and an exploration of the school policies and procedures that would affect their time in the schools. The town's population was 2,500 and the number of students in the district was 400. The school board had recently provided laptops for all administrators and teachers and for all students in Grades 3–12. Students, teachers, and administrators used technology seemingly in everything they did—planning lessons, communicating with each other and parents, sending and receiving assignments, tracking student progress, and so on.

The seminar assignment on legal issues was returned with references to hurricane plans, chemical spills, fire exits, acceptable use of technology resources, and fair use of technology resources. Neither the teacher candidates nor the faculty member had ever seen the acceptable use or fair use policies. The faculty member became intrigued. After visits with the dean and online communication with the two students, all agreed to save all assignments, reflections, and e-mails to share with other teacher candidates and faculty.

In the meantime, the online e-mail instructor felt compelled to support the two candidates, who were already isolated. He shared their situation with his own students, whose interest was piqued in using technology in new and exciting ways. When he found Web sites that told about the use of wireless computing in classrooms, he forwarded the URLs to the teacher candidates at the rural site along with other ideas that teacher candidates back on campus shared. He encouraged the remote student teachers to keep a journal about the ways they saw technology used and then to think about their own lessons and how technology might fit their lessons. He called the district offices to inquire about professional development experiences for the teacher candidates and received permission for them to participate. He worked with the district Web master and discovered a way to have the teacher candidates post their lessons online so the teacher candidates on campus could follow the implementation. The result? Lots of interest by other teacher candidates and teacher education faculty. With the modeling of the rural school district, the two remotely located candidates brought the effective use of technology to the college in a very real way.

SCENARIO 8

Teacher Candidates Teaching Teachers

Innovative University (IU) has a college of education that is housed in a small structure built in 1975 as a state-of-the-art facility. There are eight classrooms in the building, which serve to house the 300–500 undergraduate students who attend primarily during the day and 500–800 graduate students who attend one to four nights a week and on weekends. With the onset of technology in the early '70s, IU attempted to have cutting-edge technology provided as the building was being built by having overhead projectors and televisions in all classrooms. In addition, video cameras, tripods, VCRs, and tape players were available for checkout; these were used to videotape teacher candidates during student teaching and practicum experiences. With the emergence of computers in the early '80s, one room was dedicated as a computer classroom. It held 20 Apple IIEs, each with a printer.

Rapid changes in technology have required innovative use of the space within the building. To accommodate the lack of space and the need for technology in teaching and learning, the IU college of education has developed and supports two mobile labs of 24 laptops, each with wireless connections to the network and Internet. As faculty integrate technology into their instruction, the mobile labs are rolled into the existing classrooms and students work where classes are held. By doing this, computers can be used in three classrooms at a time, or if faculty are creative and split the 24 computers on the cart with the faculty member next door, multiple classes can be using the computers at the same time.

At IU, technology activities are tied closely to the curriculum. In the foundations courses, students design and take a technology survey to see the hardware, software, and skills they have independently and as a class. (See the activity "Achieving Equitable Access in and out of School" in Section 2, "Educational Foundations.") In addition, they explore various legal and ethical issues in education and spend some time focusing on those clearly associated with the use of technology. (See "Analyzing Legal, Moral, and Ethical Dilemmas" in Section 2, "Educational Foundations.") In their multicultural course they examine the Digital Divide and go into the community to research various cultures. (See "Exploring Cultural Differences" in Section 2, "Educational Foundations.") In all methods coursework students participate in technology-enhanced activities and design them for use in their field placements. Technology is tied to assessment. Students design digital portfolios beginning the first semester of their five-semester program and continue through their first year of teaching. (See "Becoming a Digital Packrat" in Section 2, "Educational Foundations.") Within all of their classes, teacher candidates experience the use of computers in a variety of ways—the use of one computer in a classroom, the use of five computers in a classroom, and the use of a computer lab. (See "Grouping Students for Learning" in Section 2, "Educational Foundations.") All teacher candidates are expected to demonstrate their use of technology in professional practice and in teaching and learning during their student teaching placement.

Four students from IU were assigned to a small rural community for their student teaching experience. Upon arrival they found that there was limited use of technology in the building. In fact, all that was there was one Internet-connected computer on the desk of each of their teachers, and one in the office for the administrator and secretary to share. Basically, the computers were not used because no one in the district really knew how to use them, neither from a technical perspective nor from a curricular perspective. In their first seminar with IU faculty, the students shared their frustration. Technology had become such a necessary part of their lives as students and potential teachers, they really wondered how they could, or if they should, get along without it. Additionally, they wondered how they were going to be able to demonstrate their proficiency using technology in teaching. A brainstorming session resulted in the following suggestions of how that one computer in the classroom might be used.

- *In professional practice students could write and save lesson plans and accompanying worksheets, establish grade sheets, write newsletters to parents, design name tags and certificates of accomplishment, and design a Web page for their teacher.*

- *Borrowing a projector from the university, the students in the classroom could view news and weather sites from the Internet as part of the "homeroom" portion of the day, check up on their place or animal using Web cams, view the photo of the day to use as a writing experience, or view talking books or documentaries.*

- *Teacher candidates could design a set of learning center activities for a thematic unit and use the one computer as the basis for one of the centers. Because there was no firewall, if they were to use the Internet, the screen of the computer would have to be turned to the center of the classroom for teacher view at all times, and teacher candidates would have to design simple WebQuests to control the sites students entered. In this center, four to five students would work cooperatively to do research on the Internet; use online and CD-ROM dictionaries and encyclopedias (checked out from the university library); enter data and make graphs; use discipline-specific software; write reports with accompanying pictures, diagrams, and graphs; and create slideshows.*

Last, but not least, the teacher candidates asked whether they could check out a hub and wireless laptops to use with their own students in the building. Through much discussion about liability, they were granted permission to do so. In fact, faculty members suggested they take a mentor and a member of the tech staff with them.

The IU supervisor visited with the principal and master teachers about expectations in general for the student teachers and asked whether the school personnel would be willing to allow the students to use the one computer in the classroom for instruction in the ways described above. They wholeheartedly agreed. The teacher candidates became teachers not only of students, but also of teachers. Everyone was a winner.

Summary of Recommendations

1. Colleges of education must provide continuous professional development for adjunct supervisors.

2. Maintenance of technology skills and knowledge of models of promising practice are a condition of continued employment for supervisors.

3. University supervisors use e-mail as one technology-enhanced method to enrich the preobservation conference activity.

4. Technology such as a PDA or laptop is used to record observation data. Observation notes are sent to teacher candidates using e-mail.

5. Use technology-mediated observations in settings where on-site observation is restricted by time and geography.

6. The appropriate use of technology must be a factor in identifying appropriate student teaching placements.

References

International Society for Technology in Education. (2000). *NETS for students—Connecting curriculum and technology.* Eugene, OR: ISTE.

M. G. (Peggy) Kelly is a professor of education at California State University, San Marcos, and co-director of the ISTE NETS Project.

Jeri Carroll is a professor of education at Wichita State University, Kansas, and a member of the ISTE NETS Writing Team.

Technology in First-Year Teaching and Professional Development

As novice teachers approach their first days of school many emotions emerge. Feelings fluctuate between excitement and apprehension as their students look to them expecting experience and knowledge in the form of a guide and mentor. Saddled with a stack of district and state expectations, the task can seem overwhelming. The day-to-day realities that consume new teachers' every waking minute of organizing their own time, planning appropriate lessons, meeting professional obligations, and adjusting to a new way of life have the potential to erode a new teacher's self-confidence.

Data on the retention of teachers have emerged from a variety of sources. Included in the data is the rationale for individuals leaving the profession. In the final analysis, retention and satisfaction as a teacher hinges on the level of support provided by the school and the school district. Colleges of education can train the very best candidates for the field using all that research says represents good practice, but if universities and districts are not able to create a seamless path for the novice teacher to transition from a highly supervised setting to the realities of being solely responsible for the learning of a class of children, the retention rate after five years in the profession will continue to hover around 30% (Darling-Hammond, 2001, p. 14).

ISTE's NETS for Teachers were purposefully drafted with a set of profiles to assist colleges of education and school districts in building support mechanisms for new teachers. Additionally, the fourth profile presents performance tasks a new teacher should be engaged in if all the other performances in the preceding profiles have been met. The profiles are an incremental approach to meeting the standards.

Because school districts hire new teachers from all over the country in addition to the regional teacher preparation institution, they cannot be assured that the level of technology preparation of all candidates is equal. Therefore, this chapter focuses on both supporting first-year teachers as they transition from teacher preparation programs into teaching as well as experienced teachers who require professional development to demonstrate that they are able to meet the standards.

Essential Conditions

The ISTE NETS provide essential conditions for the standards with further elaborations for each profile. The First-Year Teaching Performance Profile describes the final iteration of the essential conditions as they relate to all teachers' experiences in schools in their efforts to implement the use of technology in teaching and learning. The following expansion of the essential conditions is designed to enable schools and collaborating universities to assess the conditions that are present. This self-study helps to determine what support structures are in place that contribute to the success of not just novice teachers, but all teachers.

Shared Vision—*Schools, districts, and universities share a vision for supporting new teachers in their use of technology in the classroom.*

A shared vision is exemplified through proactive leadership and administrative support throughout the entire school system. The school's vision for the use of technology is in alignment with the district vision. Ideally, this vision is also in alignment with that of the university, thus providing a seamless transition from university preparation for the novice teacher and consistency for all teachers.

Access—*Access to current technologies, software, and telecommunications networks is provided for new teachers for classroom and professional use, including access beyond the school day.*

All teachers have access to hardware, software, and communications tools in the classroom, workroom, and from home through electronic means. The distribution of school technology assets is equitable regardless of seniority at the school site.

Skilled Educators—*Peers and administrators are skilled users of technology for teaching and school management.*

The schoolwide level of technology knowledge, professional use, and application to teaching may vary, but there is a common base level of expertise such that mentors and models exist at the school to provide the novice teacher and others with consultation and coaching.

Professional Development—*Faculty have continuous access to a variety of professional development opportunities in several delivery modes, with time to take advantage of offerings.*

All teachers in the district have access to consistent ongoing professional development to support continuous improvement in technology skills and curriculum integration. The professional development ranges from individually attended or accessed opportunities to group or grade level situations. Novice teachers are coached in making the best selections for improving their professional practice.

Technical Assistance—*Technical assistance for faculty is timely, on-site, and includes mentoring to enhance skills in managing classroom software and hardware resources.*

All classroom teachers have equitable access to timely, supportive technical assistance. The purpose of the technical assistance is to ensure that teaching and learning continues in an unobstructed manner and that teachers are continuously learning to increase their own repertoire of trouble-shooting skills. As a matter of course, personnel providing technical assistance orient and support novice teachers on classroom hardware, software, and procedures for acquiring additional assistance.

Content Standards and Curriculum Resources—*The school district provides professional development opportunities related to local policies, content standards, and the technology-based resources available to support the new teacher's efforts to address those standards.*

As part of professional development to meet academic standards in an environment of collaboration, all teachers have the opportunity to influence the acquisition of technology-based resources that will support student achievement of content standards. Novice teachers are mentored on currently available resources as well as able to play a role in new acquisitions.

Student-Centered Teaching—*Faculty routinely use student-centered approaches to learning to facilitate student use of technology.*

Faculty members are able to demonstrate that the use of technology in the classroom is balanced between teacher and student technology use. Student-centered approaches to learning guide faculty in creating learning opportunities that require active engagement of students and interaction between students and resources while using technology as a tool for learning.

Assessment—*The district and school site support the classroom teacher in the assessment of learning outcomes for technology-supported activities to inform planning, teaching, and further assessment.*

Technology-rich activities are an integral part of performance-based assessment tasks. All teachers are supported in their efforts to evaluate their students' use of technology as part of ongoing assessment and to use technology to aggregate and disaggregate data for instructional improvement.

Community Support—*Schools provide beginning teachers with connections to the community and models of effective use of local and other resources.*

Teachers support each other and coach novice teachers in making community connections that will benefit both their classroom and the whole school learning community. Community connections are viewed as a whole school effort, rather than competitive or an individual teacher's responsibility.

Support Policies—*School induction-year policies, budget allocations, and mentoring assignments support the first-year teacher's use of technology. Hiring practices include policies regarding technology skills of prospective hires.*

School policies are routinely examined to ensure that structures do not hinder the use of technology for teaching and learning. These policies include the areas of teacher evaluation, time schedules, and building access. They ensure equitable distribution of the budget across faculty and school needs and support for technology-savvy mentors.

Many educators use the absence of one or more of the essential conditions listed above as a reason for not using technology in their instruction. These essential conditions are not identified to create fear of technology but instead to provide goals to work toward for individuals as well as the entire learning community. Effective instruction using technology can occur with few of the essential conditions in place and often does. However, teachers have consistently communicated that the failure to meet the essential conditions contributes to a lack of consistency in the use of technology in the classroom and a disincentive to creativity in its use. The expanded statements above provide issues to consider in developing plans to create new learning environments.

First-Year Teacher Profile

The NETS for Teachers provide a roadmap for first-year and continuing teachers as they plan to integrate technology into their curriculum, instruction, and assessment. Meeting Standard I—Technology Operations and Concepts is now an assumption with the added caveat that competency in new technologies will continue to grow over time.

As with the Student Teaching/Internship Performance Profile, the First-Year Teaching Performance Profile takes the development of the lesson cycle—planning, implementing, and assessing (Standards II, III, and IV)—and pushes the expectations to consistently making instructional decisions that include the effective use of technology. Emphasis is now on the breadth and depth of experiences for students as they work to meet content standards with technology as a vehicle for learning.

It is expected that meeting Standard V—Productivity and Professional Practice becomes a nonissue as the use of technology becomes integral to efficiently and thoughtfully engaging in the profession. Using communication tools, engaging in professional development opportunities, and becoming an exemplar of lifelong learning are elements of expected professional practice.

Standard VI—Social, Ethical, Legal, and Human Issues should now become integral to classroom function and teacher behavior. Additionally, as teaching experience increases, the ability to meet the needs of individual students, taking into account social and human issues, elicits a variety of plausible options in the mind of the teacher. At the same time, teachers conduct themselves as exemplars of professional behavior by making appropriate ethical and legal decisions.

The NETS have been aligned with national content and staff development standards. Schools, school districts, and higher education institutions that work to collaboratively support teacher induction and long-term professional development programs should align individual and group staff development activities with the standards. An increased awareness of the need for educators to include the NETS in their professional development plans is further supported by groups such as INTASC and the National Board for Professional Teaching Standards.

Working with Novice Teachers
THE WELL-TRAINED NOVICE TEACHER

Colleges and universities that have trained their teacher candidates well in the use of technology in teaching and learning send out individuals ready, willing, and able to use technology in all facets of their job. They are typically enthusiastic, full of ideas, idealistic, and yet frightened of the reality of being in total control of student learning for a whole year. Ideally, that novice teacher is placed in a school in which most of the essential conditions are met, where support exists, and where mentors are ready to coach to ensure the novice teacher's easy transition to becoming part of the learning community.

In spite of how well trained a new teacher may be and how supportive the school may be, there are always issues with the introduction of new personnel in a school site. The scenario below captures a multitude of issues faced by even well-trained novice teachers. Note how Jess solves the issues that at first seem overwhelming.

SCENARIO 1

Platform Issues

Jess attended High Tech University (HTU), which supported the integration of technology in all aspects of the university—in liberal arts and sciences, in fine arts, and in teacher education. Jess worked in a high-tech environment on campus, in the dorms, in the classrooms, in the labs, and in the student center. It was no surprise when the student teaching placement was also a high-tech environment where administrative tasks were executed efficiently with an integrated software package, where the nonteaching tasks of teachers were performed effectively on personal computers that were connected to the school and district servers and parents could log on to home computers and check up on their students any time of day, where students were active using both the in-class computer islands and the computer labs, and where both students and teachers used SmartBoards and robotics kits.

Jess and several other teacher candidates attended a job fair set up by the job placement service on campus. The fair had more than 250 personnel directors from both large and small districts from surrounding states. In addition to live interviews, the fair offered a uniform application process for their state uploaded onto several computers. Other districts, physically absent from the fair, participated in synchronous interviews through their district courseware and through videoconferencing.

Jess took along to the interviews a PDA that contained a list of questions about technology to ask during the interview. In each interview, Jess began with an open-ended question about how technology was used. Other questions were asked around issues of tech support, computers for teacher use, Internet access (including policies and filters), software used, and professional development opportunities. Jess finally got the answers he wanted to help make his decision; he decided over the summer on a position in a high-tech unified district at High Tech Middle School (HTMS). Although he was unable to visit the school because of summer renovations, he was comfortable with the responses he received.

Armed with the personal computer his parents bought him for graduation, Jess headed off to his first teaching position. He quickly realized that there was one question he had neglected to ask in the interviews. When he walked into the classroom at HTMS, shiny brightly colored laptops adorned the computer islands, the teacher's desk, the office, and the computer lab. Jess had come from one platform for his personal computer, computer training, and use at HTU and was entering another at HTMS. Although confident until now, many prejudices quickly returned to his mind with anger and anxiety setting in. It was going to be bad enough to struggle with beginning to teach in an unfamiliar environment, but to change computer platforms too? All his resources were on PCs. All work at school was to be done on Macs. No electronic whiteboards were in the rooms—no robotics kits available for math or science. Jess realized he was due for professional development activities in the area in which he felt most prepared. He now faced a new job, a new school, a new grade, a new curricular approach, and now, a new platform.

Jess was assigned a new iBook for personal and professional use, which he took home over the weekend. Frustration grew when it took several minutes and a reading of the resource book just to turn on the computer. And then horror set in when he realized that all his work was on PC floppies and the computer assigned for personal and professional use accepted only CDs requiring external drives that were not included in the box. Utterly frustrated, he turned toward planning for the first couple of days in the new classroom using nontechnology activities. At the first break of the morning, Jess asked a neighboring teacher about tech support and professional development; it was suggested that he use some of the elementary school's "help sheets" developed to train the younger students in how to use the equipment. Shaking his head, Jess logged on to the school's Web site designed for students, teachers, and parents and found the help sheets. Delighted to find answers to the off/on problem encountered the weekend before and also for the floppy/CD problem, Jess vowed to overcome anxiety and head into technology use as an expert student rather than an expert teacher.

His next contact was a to call his student teaching supervisor, who had worked with him on the development of his interview portfolio and job interview strategies. He asked her to make sure that future teacher candidates knew to ask the platform question as part of the interview. Initial conversations with the supervisor revolved around whether platform should really be a question or whether the university ought to spend more time working with teacher candidates to become dual-platform users. The supervisor helped Jess further by making a few quick calls to some Mac-user friends to provide Jess with some initial trouble-shooting. He discovered that most PC disks could be read by the Mac, if the machine had drivers to support the disks (floppy or Zip). Commands were basically the same on both machines for similar software. Jess could upload his disks onto the school servers and copy them to the iBook hard drive.

Armed with a few solutions, Jess headed out—with a smile on his face. He had important work to do, too, such as finding all the technology hardware in the room, school, and lab (and learning to use what he didn't already know how to use); finding, examining, and evaluating the software available; learning how to file work orders on broken equipment; and assessing the skills and needs of the students. He could do this! Technology was a tool. And he had learned to use it in creative and innovative ways. He knew he would need to slip back into the skills-learning mode for a while, but the computer would still do those creative and innovative tasks he was accustomed to. Maybe for a while, the students would be the ones completing the creative and innovative projects while he learned the ropes.

Although platform mismatches may prove troublesome, differences in hardware may be the least of the worries of the first-year teacher. Being able to cling to a lesson sequence that is familiar, is aligned with content standards, and has been successful in student teaching often turns out to be the best beginning. The following scenarios each illustrate how the use of technology throughout the teacher preparation program can make the transfer of experiences more likely to take place for novice teachers.

SCENARIO 2

Mathematics

General Preparation

In an economics course, Jamal learned about conducting cost benefit analyses, graphing supply and demand curves, and determining the optimum price for a product or service. One project in the course asked the students to compare all offerings of a service and provide a rationale for their selection of the service. Jamal chose television cable or satellite service options as he was in the process of considering what it would cost to meet his needs. Jamal used the Internet to obtain most of his data. His professor threw another variable into the project by asking the students to locate Web sites that shared complaint information on the service being researched. As part of the project, Jamal was required to use a spreadsheet to show the comparison of services and options provided, incorporate graphs showing use of the service over time, quantify complaint information, and provide a rationale for his selection based on economic principles. The final product consisted of an oral multimedia presentation and accompanying printed document.

Professional Preparation

As part of the mathematics methods course, Jamal participated in the "Phone Phunctions" activity (See Section 2, "Technology in Middle School Education Programs," Mathematics). Where his economics class focused on the economics of comparing a service, this activity focused on the mathematics. Jamal could easily see that the economics fell into applied mathematics. He was able to use the same searching and information gathering techniques as in the previous experience. However, in the methods course, he worked in a group, discussing the various attributes of cellular phone services and the needs of the buyer. The group not only researched online, but communicated often about their results as they put their presentation together. The culminating activity allowed Jamal to translate his experiences into a lesson plan for students.

Student Teaching/Internship

Jamal's student teaching assignment was to teach middle school mathematics and co-teach one language arts block with another teacher who was part of the interdisciplinary team. He already had a lesson plan outlined for use of the "Phone Phunctions" activity. In the process of having his master teacher critique his lesson plan, Jamal and the master teacher began to develop an interdisciplinary unit on home services including cellular phones. In addition to the requirements for the "Phone Phunctions" activity, Jamal and his master teacher created a simulation that took place over 10 days. In the simulation all services were disrupted at some time, including phone services, rates changed, and students fictitiously moved residences. Students had to examine the "fine print" in service contracts and evaluate the various options the service policy offered on handling the situations presented. Jamal was able to integrate the technology through the use of the Internet to coach students on using search techniques, keeping online journals, communicating with service vendors and public entities, and making presentations on what they had learned. The middle school team collaboratively developed the interdisciplinary unit; Jamal left with a completed unit of instruction and the school team learned from Jamal's contribution.

First-Year Teaching

Jamal took a teaching position out of state to be close to his extended family. He was initially concerned about how his professional experience would transfer to the new setting. Having obtained a position in a middle school, Jamal consulted with his new colleagues about using his unit. Although the teachers were initially skeptical, Jamal was able to persuade them that the interdisciplinary unit would tie together many concepts typically taught by the end of November according to their long-range plan. Jamal had retained all the lesson plans as well as examples of student work. It was the quality and complexity of the student work that impressed his new team. Using the unit developed during the student teaching, the team expanded the notion of finding the best phone (or service) to alternative ways of obtaining the service such as solar, Internet-based long distance, and so forth. The interdisciplinary nature of the unit expanded from mathematics and language arts to include more social studies and a strong component of science.

SCENARIO 3

Social Studies

General Preparation

As part of a women's history course, Elisabeth was a member of a group whose task was to obtain the history of the role of women on a local Native American reservation. The class had been studying the techniques and the purpose for oral histories. The group carefully created a set of open-ended questions, then checked with the tribal elders before proceeding with their project. Through much discussion and becoming sensitized to cultural issues, they obtained permission to use only audio recordings and still pictures. The digital still pictures and audio clips were placed into an electronic presentation. They presented their finding to the tribal council, who asked that it be placed on multiple CDs for all to view. As a result of the experience, the council began working collaboratively with the professor as part of a service learning project to record as many oral histories as possible from the elders of the tribe as a way to preserve their culture.

Professional Preparation

As part of the social studies method course for elementary teachers, Elisabeth's professor introduced the "Oral History" activity (see Section 2, "Technology in Elementary Education Programs," Social Studies). Because Elisabeth had experience with oral history, she shared the cultural constraints she ran into with using electronic media for obtaining the information. Her group's assignment was to learn as much as possible about the history of one of the local schools that was being demolished. Through school district records of administrators and teachers and a visit to a local retirement home, the group created a plan for focusing on the changing lives of the teachers over time. Among the elderly, the teacher candidates identified five retired teachers. The group used audio, video, still photos, and basic note-taking during the five in-depth interviews. As an outcome of the project, their presentation was placed on the university Web site and buttoned from the school's Web site as part of a growing archive of historical information. The reflective journals completed by Elisabeth and her group confirmed that the outcomes of the project provided a window into teaching as a lifelong endeavor.

Student Teaching/Internship

During her student teaching, Elisabeth was required to teach social studies in a fourth grade assignment. The curriculum centered on state history. Her initial thought was that the topic was still being covered in the same way as when she was in fourth grade. Recalling her experience with oral history, Elisabeth decided to give her students a different view. At the local retirement home, she inquired whether there were any people who had been living in the state all their lives. She located nine individuals who had never lived outside the state and each of whom were raised in different parts of the state. Together the class created a set of questions about the interviewees' lives at specific times in the state's history. After considerable discussion and coaching, they took a walking field trip to the retirement home. Equipped with laptops, small groups interviewed each individual under the watchful eye of staff and parent volunteers. Digital pictures were taken of interviewees; residents even lent the students personal pictures to be scanned for their presentation. The project resulted in an oral presentation to a public audience, the residents, and their families, and posting the end product on the school Web site. What Elisabeth perceived as a potentially boring part of the curriculum was enlivened with a local perspective of state history.

First-Year Teaching

Elisabeth obtained her first teaching position in a fifth grade in a highly urban school. There were no local Native American reservations and no retirement home close at hand. Her social studies focused on American history. Obviously there were no Revolutionary War heroes in the neighborhood. In discussing with her colleagues the possible questions she could use with family members or the elderly, Elisabeth discovered that many residents in the area had served in a war—a war for freedom in another country. Through a discussion with her students, Elisabeth was reminded that many of her students' families had immigrated fairly recently and were living with relatives who had firsthand experience with the notion of a revolutionary war. The oral history project Elisabeth created combined what she had learned from her previous experiences. She took the technical expertise she had gained in creating PowerPoint presentations; the ability to use audio, video and laptop technology; the planning skills necessary to gain good information; and the attention to cultural and legal issues and applied it all to this situation. As a result of the project, her students shared how much they learned about the concept of revolution and their family history. Elisabeth shared how much she had learned about the students and their community; she acquired good examples of how they met social studies, language arts, and technology standards.

THE MISMATCH

All the best training and best intentions of a teacher preparation program cannot predict what teacher candidates will find in their first teaching experience. Often there occurs some level of mismatch between the experiences at the university and the reality of the school setting. Aside from hardware differences, novice teachers can find themselves as the most expert person in a building in which the faculty have either been reluctant or lacked the support and other essential conditions to make technology part of teaching practice. The following scenario has been played out innumerable times as schools gear up for the use of technology in teaching and learning. However, at this point in the new teacher's career, it is not his or her role to be technology coordinator for the school or provide staff development for peers.

SCENARIO 4

Pushing the New Teacher too Far

Evan had loved using the technology during his undergraduate experience. The university required students to carry laptops and access resources in a wireless environment in class and in cooperative group settings. This was the norm.

When Evan received his position in an elementary school, he was shocked to see that computers were stored in corners of rooms. The computer lab was used all day, every day for integrated learning system use.

In the opening staff meeting, Evan asked questions about access to technology including available resources. The administrator and staff responded very well to Evan's questions. Very quickly all knew that Evan had brought additional expertise that was not anticipated. In what seemed to be a whirlwind of discussions and decisions, Evan was elected to the technology committee and asked to update the school plan. Teachers came to Evan asking for help with anything related to technology. The lack of on-site technical assistance made Evan the first target for help.

Evan had great plans for the use of technology for himself and the school. But the pressure placed on Evan was enormous in addition to the reality of preparing to meet the needs of his own students. By the end of the year, Evan was burned out, feeling that he hadn't done a good job at anything. His first-year evaluations were marginal and he was considering not returning to the classroom. He also had received some informal queries for positions outside teaching in a local high-tech firm. After a frank discussion with his principal and the district technology coordinator, Evan was able to facilitate obtaining additional help for the school and realized that although his feelings were normal, the situation was unique.

Three years into his teaching career, Evan became one of the district specialists in technology. Upon reflection, Evan advised principals and new teachers not to place a new teacher in the position of leading technical assistance for peers for the first few years. Evan regretted that he did not have all the time he would have liked to concentrate on his teaching.

Likewise, new teachers can find themselves in a situation in which the university technology experience is not as comprehensive as the expectations of the school district. Every region of the country has gone through periods of funding imbalance between K–12 and higher education. Where technology has been funded well at the higher education level and inadequately funded at the K–12 level, the teacher candidates have the opportunity to bring about change in the schools. When technology funding for K–12 has outpaced higher education, the onus for professional development bears heavily on the school district. Not only are novice teachers needing support to survive and grow, but additional support is needed to enable them to teach with technology in a way that is reasonably commensurate with their colleagues. This situation can result in high stress, frustration, and early burnout for new teachers.

BEGINNING TEACHER SUPPORT

To prevent the loss of new teachers early in their careers, many supportive school districts and state programs have emerged. These programs are not specifically designed to address technology needs. Rather, they are designed to support the whole environment of the new teacher. One of the many exemplary programs is California's Beginning Teacher Support and Assessment (BTSA) program.

Founded on the principles of ensuring that new teachers meet the California Standards for the Teaching Profession, the program is built around a highly structured formative assessment and support system. The California standards include engaging and supporting all students in learning; creating and maintaining effective environments for student learning; understanding and organizing subject matter for student learning; planning instruction and designing learning experiences for all students; assessing student learning; and developing as a professional educator.

Using an individual "support provider," new teachers are led through a series of activities that are designed to emphasize the process of teaching. "[The program] is grounded in a developmental view of teaching and recognizes that this complex, demanding profession is learned over the course of several years of study, consultation, and reflective practice beyond professional preparation" (California Commission on Teacher Credentialing and California Department of Education, 1998, p. 3).

Because the organization of the BTSA program focuses on the standards that apply to all teachers and is in alignment with INTASC and NCATE standards, meeting the ISTE NETS for Teachers becomes an extension of the teacher preparation program. The performance-based tasks and rubrics developed by BTSA have been incorporated into many teacher preparation programs as a way to incrementally assess movement on a continuum of expertise. Likewise, the work of the NETS Assessment Team, discussed in the following chapter, makes the process of preparing teachers to use technology in a teacher preparation program part of the larger continuum of professional development in the induction years.

As new teachers complete the BTSA program they have become familiar with the professional development opportunities available to them. An integral part of the BTSA program is the creation of a professional development plan for the short term as well as projected over time. This plan is also part of meeting NETS for Teachers—Standard V, Productivity and Professional Practice.

There are still teachers who are transitioning between programs and standards that may be lost between the cracks. The following scenario illustrates how the flexibility of the BTSA program can meet a need.

SCENARIO 5

The Beginning Teacher and the Experienced Teacher

As part of the BTSA program, beginning teachers were offered an optional integrating technology course after school. Over the years, attendance had slowed down. The first explanation was that the teachers were coming in more prepared because beginning teachers had grown up with computers or were prepared in college and didn't need assistance. In response, the basic course was eliminated. The staff development at the school site began at a much higher level.

A couple of years ago, Alice began teaching as her second career. Alice was 50 years old when she began teaching and had never touched a computer. Alice completed her preliminary certification before the technology standard was required at the preliminary level. Alice had taken a few years off to care for an elderly parent. She was now a new teacher in a school district that was nationally known for its technology. She was faced with six computers in her classroom and confessed that every time she looked at them she would feel panic.

The on-site BTSA support provider mentioned to Alice that an after school course for beginning teachers was taught on-site and it could connect to the requirement for her clear credential. No one thought that she would enroll because of her apprehension...but she did!

At the first class meeting, she sat paralyzed most of the time because all the other teachers in the course had experience with the machines. After the first class meeting, Alice came to the instructor in tears. She doubted everything about teaching. The first month of teaching takes all new teachers by surprise and they become disillusioned. Now this computer class was confirming all her insecurities. After Alice aired her concerns, Alice and her instructor came to the decision that they needed to proceed as a team at her own pace (and not try to follow the structure set for the others).

The instructor used her BTSA coaching time with Alice to set goals that involved personal and instructional use of technology. They designed a plan in which Alice could immediately transfer knowledge she'd learned to the classroom, so that the kids did not have to wait to use the technology in their learning. Alice found that it was a wonderful way for her to learn from her kids. Her BTSA support provider would often come in during technology-based lessons to assist her in managing the program.

It was obviously difficult in the beginning, but Alice turned an obstacle into a huge opportunity. After two years, Alice had a personal digital portfolio, a classroom Web site that featured student work and, most important to her, she had her own computer at home. Alice taught the BTSA support providers that previous background and age are only factors of where to start the learning, not insurmountable obstacles.

Professional Development for All Teachers

As stated in the 1995 report *Technology and Teachers: Making the Connection* (U.S. Congress, Office of Technology Assessment, 1995), the lack of teacher training or professional development is one of the greatest hindrances to integrating technology into a school's curriculum. With an expenditure of less than 15% of the technology budget on staff development, school districts have struggled with the relative importance of professional development as a growing budgetary item with other competing needs.

Although professional development has become a well-recognized need in staying current in the curriculum areas, the need is even more critical in the area of technology. All teachers learned to read and write as a process of their own education; few have grown up in the digital age. Technological competence has been a self-taught or peer-taught set of skills, which are often acquired on a need-to-know basis. The pedagogy of appropriately using technology as a teaching tool has been a part of the teacher preparation curriculum within only the last 10 years and not required until recently. Therefore, the professional development needs for teachers in the field are immense. If colleges of education are to complete the cycle of creating programs that support novice teachers in transferring their university experience into classroom practice, teachers who take the role of mentoring teacher candidates and novice teachers must be users and infusers of technology into their teaching practice.

As universities, intermediate administrative units, professional development consortia, and school districts collaborate to create a myriad of professional development opportunities for new and experienced teachers, the basic principles of high-quality staff development apply. As an example, summarizing the results of many professional development projects, the report on outcomes of the PBS Mathline project given at the RAND Corporation Workshop on Teacher Professional Development stated, "Teachers did not want a model nor an ideal classroom. They wanted situations in which they could learn from both their achievements and mistakes. They wanted sustained staff development; not short term programs. They wanted teacher-controlled programs, not top-down directives. They wanted programs that would advance them intellectually and professionally. And they want flexibility in terms of the time when the programming was offered—so they could complete the program on their own schedule" (Harvey & Purnell, 1995). Although Mathline is a professional development project offered online with supplementary programming, the results of the participant survey provided data that are in concert with other studies and can be generalized outside of the area of mathematics.

Research on professional development in technology has shown that the following considerations are important as professional development programs and plans are developed for both individuals and groups (Brand, 1997):

Time—Participants in the RAND study workshop "repeatedly name time as the most common barrier to change. The education system as currently structured does not pretend to make available to teachers the amount and kind of time needed to develop professionally. Time not spent in front of the class is considered somewhat wasted" (Harvey & Purnell, 1995).

In support of the RAND report, a recent report by the California Department of Education's Professional Development Task Force, chaired by Linda Darling-Hammond of Stanford University, made 10 recommendations to improve professional development. Among the recommendations was to "redesign schools so that they can focus on student and teacher learning. Add and recognize time to enable collaborative teacher planning and inquiry." Time to engage in inquiry regarding their own practice, collaborate with others, and assimilate new learning is not new to learning but is finally being recognized as a necessary element to teacher professional development (Darling-Hammond & Meno, 2001).

Time for learning to use technology can be different from time set aside to learn a new curriculum. As illustrated through the standards, basic skills and operations are foundational to being able to think about how the technology can support teaching and learning. For example, practicing the skills can come in the form of creating materials for the classroom, researching online alternative means of teaching a concept, connecting with other teachers through electronic means, and reviewing software options. These examples may or may not require a peer-to-peer or formal class setting. Increasingly, the time allocated to learning occurs at the discretion of the educator. But how can teachers be compensated for non-workday time? How can time be allocated that takes into account the varying needs of teachers with busy professional and personal lives? These are issues yet to be resolved in the current structure.

Varying Needs—Like teaching students, professional development must be student-centered. In this case, the learners are the teachers. The level of knowledge is as wide in attendees at professional development in technology as it is in any other area. However, the level of apprehension for the emerging user is high. Using identified strengths of the participants, individual mentors can be assigned in a peer-to-peer model. The Profiler (**www.profiler.pt3.org**) is one of the many online tools for examining self-report data about skills or other competencies. This tool can be used to quickly assess the strengths and weaknesses of a group. Acknowledging the expertise in a group is critical to retaining interest and building on strengths. Other tools include NCREL's Learning with Technology profile (**www.ncrtec.org/capacity/profile/profwww.htm**). Like the Profiler, this tool is designed to compare an individual's current instructional practices with a set of indicators for engaged learning and high-performance technology use.

Knowing the variety of needs, single professional development opportunities and entire professional development programs must create a balanced presentation from the simple to the more complex to meet the needs of teachers.

Flexibility—Professional development does not lend itself to a "one-size-fits-all" model. Flexibility in offerings can be provided by having individual and group options, by holding staff development on-site rather than in remote locations, and by presenting opportunities to complete projects at the teacher's pace rather than adhering to a rigid schedule. Additionally, there must be instructional variety to effectively model the manner in which technology can support the varying needs and styles of learners. Time, content, and delivery flexibility all contribute to making a malleable package of opportunities.

On-Site Support—Just as stated by the essential conditions, the presence of on-site support provides another avenue of professional development that is specific to the needs of the individual. Teachers are more willing to invest the time and energy in beginning the process of infusing technology into the curriculum if they know that there is someone to whom they can turn who is knowledgeable about the technology as well as the curriculum.

Recognition—Recognition comes in many forms. The most direct recognition is to have time compensated for by extra pay or release from other duties. Having adequate incentives to make any major change and maintain momentum requires that school districts make long-range professional development plans that include recognition and rewards. The recognition should reward those who continue to upgrade their skills and demonstrate effectiveness of implementation through high-quality student work. Recognition can also come with publicity, access to specialized resources, and publicly acknowledged incentives for those who continue to make progress.

Continued Professional Development—It is a well-recognized notion that one-shot opportunities have very little affect on the overall change process. Using technology is not easy in the first efforts. Learning how to integrate technology in the context of the classroom takes time and support. The support necessary must be sustained over an extended period of time such as a calendar year. Therefore, the structure of professional development focusing on the use of technology in teaching and learning must include sustained, ongoing opportunities to obtain feedback and coaching, examine incremental gains, analyze student outcomes, and continue the process of professional development. And as with ensuring a variety of means of delivery, there should be a variety of means of sustaining the support. Online options work for some teachers while face-to-face is the preferred mode for others. Regardless of the means for sustaining the learning, professional development cannot be concentrated in a single event but requires methodical, prolonged support.

Intellectual Stimulation—The balance between providing enough opportunities for the various levels of experience and ensuring intellectual stimulation for all attendees is a delicate one. Professional development must be worth a teacher's time and energy. To intellectually challenge teachers to rethink their practice, focus on student learning, and increase their own skills requires carefully tying the technology learning to the curricular outcomes required in the current atmosphere of high-stakes testing. This, in itself, is an intellectual challenge for educators. While strictly skill development workshops are necessary, the true worth of the learning is how the teacher applies the newly learned skill to teaching and learning; therein lies the intellectual stimulation.

Administrative Support—In concert with the essential conditions discussed earlier, administrative support is key to effective professional development. The administrator holds the purse strings, controls the atmosphere of the school, doles out the rewards and sanctions, and has the power to alter policies and procedures that can potentially hinder effective staff development. Administrators who are technology users themselves, who meet the requirements specified by the Technology Standards for School Administrators (2001), make a significant difference in the understanding of and support for technology use in their school.

Each of the above elements contributes to creating professional development opportunities for teachers, both novice and experienced. Coupling the ISTE NETS and profiles with the elements of effective professional development defined by research provides the guidelines necessary to develop a plethora of options to meet the needs of teachers.

Professional Development Models

As early as the 1980s, new models of professional development were being tested that broke away from the traditional course-style delivery mode. The Teacher Advisor Project provided early insight into the effects of peers, mentors, or coaches as the primary means of delivering staff development. Operating on the basic premise that teachers learned best when they learn from, and are supported by, other teachers, enables participants to more comfortably apply their learning as they try out new ideas in the classroom (Johnson, 1985).

Many models of professional development have emerged that have been successful and replicable. The following examples are merely a representation of many outstanding professional development projects that focus on technology in teaching and learning. Each model incorporates the principles cited above in different ways with varying degrees of emphasis. Like any uniquely designed program, the best professional development plan is often one that is a combination of promising practices learned from others then configured in a way that meets the needs of the region, district, or specific population.

ILAST (www.csusm.edu/cwis/ilast/)

Emphasizing the power of partnering, ILAST (Improving Learning for All Students through Technology) is a collaborative professional development project that includes a university, a county office of education, a regional technology consortium, a regional professional development consortium, and more than 20 school districts. The ILAST Partnership consists of a year-long commitment of 120 hours of professional development delivered through a combination of face-to-face, online, and videoconferencing meetings. Forty hours are spent at regional institutes while 80 are completed under the guidance of a mentor with multiple means of maintaining contact. The curriculum has evolved into five areas that reflect the expanding nature of the needs:

1. Foundation—for new participants

2. Project-based—for second-year participant

3. Administration—for principals, administrators, and technology leaders

4. Mathematics and technology—a collaboration with a mathematics professional development project

5. BTSA support—for specific support to new teachers

TAPPED IN (www.tappedin.org)

Established as a way to collect research data by SRI International, Tapped In, currently a free resource, "helps professional development projects, education agencies, philanthropic organizations, and for-profit organizations use the Internet to connect with and support teachers via the Web" (Tapped In, www.tappedin.sri.com/info/services.html). The Tapped In online environment provides a campus-style simulated graphical interface that connects the user to buildings, rooms, and services that include a calendar, e-mail groups, a newsletter, and a special area called "Teachers' Corner." Resources in the corner are organized by category with some contributed by organizational partners as well as teachers. The calendar provides regularly scheduled offerings of real-time chats by both topic and recognized individuals in the field. The list of activities is consistently updated and rich with opportunities. Other features include spaces for groups to meet electronically and share resources, a process for linking classrooms to do joint projects, a scheduled array of already created collaborative school-based projects, and forums for discussing issues. The topic of integrating technology in teaching is a consistent thread that runs through most areas of the site.

The strength of Tapped In lies not only in its resources but in the ability of staff developers to use its environment to customize opportunities for individuals and groups. Professional development organizers work with groups in private spaces or collaborate among themselves to create online opportunities to share teaching strategies, generate ideas, debate issues, or meet any other educational communication need.

WINGS ONLINE (http://emissary.ots.utexas.edu/wings)

Judi Harris, University of Texas, Austin, has taken what she has learned from her Electronic Emissary Project to create an online support environment for new teachers. Using technology as a tool for professional development and communication, WINGS Online offers telementoring, public discussion, and information-on-demand resources exclusively to Texas teachers.

Like BTSA, WINGS Online acknowledges that personal relationships and one-to-one mentoring are the major contributing factors to a new teacher's ability to get questions answered and ideas for unfamiliar situations. New teachers can connect immediately with online curriculum specialists to get content area questions answered and participate in online discussions as part of a virtual learning community, as well as other activities. To add to the individual communications, the Web site is building a database of carefully annotated answers to professional information requests. Although in its infancy, the WINGS Online design holds promise as an exemplary learning environment for novice teachers.

Summary of Recommendations

1. Even a technology-experienced new teacher needs to focus on improving teaching skills and gaining experience before assuming a leadership role in the school.

2. Novice teachers who lack the desired level of expertise in using technology require the same level of coaching and mentoring in technology as any novice teacher in remedying deficiencies in expertise.

3. Professional development opportunities in technology should follow the same promising practices in design and support as other professional development activities.

4. Professional development programs in the use of technology will never be static. Teachers and administrators must commit themselves to continuous learning of skills, considering applications to new teaching environments.

5. Teachers must recognize that integrating technology into their teaching practice will result in fundamentally different ways of teaching and learning.

References

Brand, G. A. (1998). What research says: Training teachers for using technology. *Journal of Staff Development, 19*(1), 10–13.

California Commission on Teacher Credentialing and the California Department of Education. (1998). *Beginning teacher guidebook: Beginning teacher support and assessment and California formative assessment and support system for teachers.* Sacramento, CA: California Department of Education.

Darling-Hammond, L. (2001). The challenges of staffing our schools. *Educational Leadership, 58*(8), 12–17.

Darling-Hammond, L., & Meno, L. (2001). *Report of the professional development task force.* Sacramento, CA: California Department of Education.

Harvey, J., & Purnell, S. (1995). *Technology and teacher professional development* [Online]. Available: **http://ed.gov/Technology/Plan/RAND/Teacher.html**.

Johnson, J. N. (1985). *The teacher advisor project: A handbook for implementing a new approach to staff development.* San Francisco: Far West Laboratory.

Tapped In. (n.d.). *Tapped In virtual environment and support services* [Online]. Available: **www.tappedin.sri.com/info/services.html**.

Technology Standards for School Administrators. (2001). *Technology standards for school administrators* [Online]. Available: **http://cnets.iste.org/tssa/**.

U.S. Congress, Office of Technology Assessment. (1995). *Teachers and technology: Making the connection.* (OTA-EHR-616). Washington, DC: U.S. Government Printing Office.

Lynn Nolan is director of Professional Development Services for ISTE and a member of the NETS Leadership Team. She is a former director of Clemson University's PT[3] grant.

M. G. (Peggy) Kelly is a professor of education at California State University, San Marcos, and co-director of the ISTE NETS Project.

Jeri Carroll is a professor of education and the president of the Faculty Senate at Wichita State University, Kansas, and a member of the ISTE NETS Writing Team.

Leslie Conery is acting Chief Executive Officer of ISTE and a member of the NETS Leadership Team.

Assessing Technology Preparation of Teachers

Assessment is an ongoing process aimed at understanding and improving student learning. It involves making our expectations explicit and public; setting appropriate criteria and high standards for learning quality; systematically gathering, analyzing, and interpreting evidence to determine how well performance matches those expectations and standards; and using the resulting information to document, explain, and improve performance. When it is embedded effectively within larger institutional systems, assessment can help us focus our collective attention, examine our assumptions, and create a shared academic culture dedicated to assuring and improving the quality of higher education. (Angelo, 1995, p. 7)

The components of an effective assessment process include determining the purpose or reason for collecting the information, selecting appropriate methods of measurement, evaluating the results, and using the information to inform teaching and learning. To accomplish these purposes, the assessment system should follow a balanced approach. The elements include performance assessment (projects, presentations, student teaching), a portfolio (a purposeful collection of items to demonstrate efforts, progress, and achievement), as well as traditional assessment strategies (multiple choice, true and false, essay, teacher-made, and standardized tests). Within the context of general assessment strategies, this chapter will explore the ISTE NETS assessment model by discussing

- Attainment of ISTE NETS for Teachers,
- General Preparation—the candidate readiness benchmark,
- Professional Preparation and Student Teaching/Internship—the initial certification benchmark, and
- Portfolios.

Assessing Attainment of ISTE NETS for Teachers

The NETS for Teachers Project developed the NETS for Teachers Assessment Model (see Figure 1) to effectively measure progress toward attainment of ISTE educational technology foundation standards and performance indicators in a sustainable, scalable system. This model includes multiple measures for ongoing formative performance measurement and summative assessment to address both individual progress and program effectiveness. Providing guiding principles and feedback for continuous improvement supports NCATE's (2000) Principles for *Performance-Based Assessment Systems in Professional Education Programs* and ISTE's mission of advocating career-long professional development in the use of technology to enhance teaching and improve student learning.

The NETS for Teachers Assessment Model illustrates the relationship between the NETS for Teachers and the phases of professional growth in teacher preparation including levels beyond initial certification, such as the first year of teaching and accomplished teaching.

NETS for Teachers Assessment Model

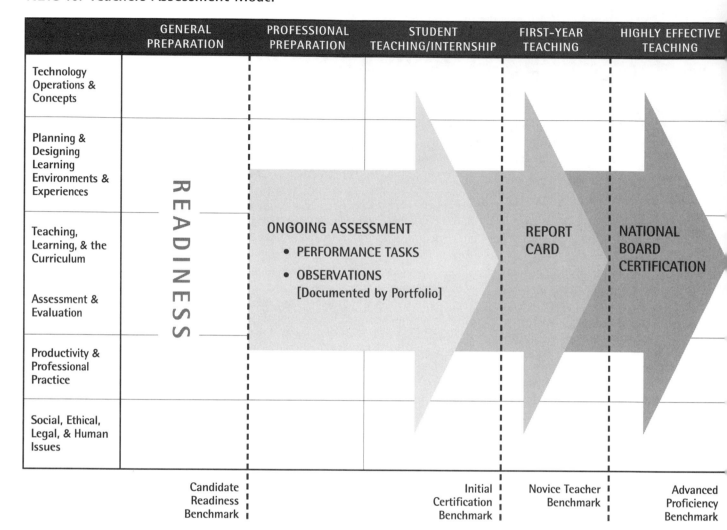

The horizontal rows of the model represent the six NETS for Teachers (ISTE, 2000). The columns of the model represent the four NETS Performance Profiles (General Preparation, Professional Preparation, Student Teaching/Internship, and First-Year Teaching) of a teacher preparation program, as well as Highly Effective Teaching. As candidates advance through their teacher preparation program, each profile designates the minimum level of competence candidates should achieve prior to the subsequent benchmark assessment. The dashed lines designate four benchmark assessments that comprise the NETS assessment system for teacher preparation:

CANDIDATE READINESS BENCHMARK: An initial benchmark assessment measures the applicant's readiness for entry into the teacher education professional coursework component. This entry-level assessment provides information to the candidate about the skills that will be required for the teacher education program, and information to the teacher education program about the technology skills individual candidates still need to develop. It provides diagnostic information regarding the teacher candidate's current technology knowledge, skills, and dispositions. Results can be used to decide on admission to the professional teaching component (i.e., upper division, professional preparation program). The information may also be used to advise the candidates on a course of action for improving in any areas where their performance indicates that they have not yet met the general preparation standards.

INITIAL CERTIFICATION BENCHMARK: This assessment generally occurs at the end of the student teaching/internship and prior to initial licensure. At this point, the faculty in the program determine the readiness of their pending graduates to be successful teachers. After ongoing formative assessment of effective technology use during the teacher education professional coursework and student teaching/internship components, it is essential to apply a summative assessment to determine the candidates' ability to apply technology in their own classroom. The teacher candidate who obtains initial licensure should meet the ISTE NETS for Teachers at least at the Approaching level.

NOVICE TEACHER BENCHMARK: Within the early years of teaching, colleges of education and school districts will assess new teachers' effectiveness in the classroom and continue to support their professional growth. Based on criteria from the Higher Education Act (Title II, Section 207, often known as the Federal Report Card for Teacher Preparation), colleges of education may be required to include data on their graduates in a Title II report submitted annually to the U.S. Department of Education. Additionally, school districts will likely seek to determine the level of technology competencies that new teachers demonstrate and use this information to plan appropriate professional development opportunities. The benchmark assessment will evaluate the performance of teachers on each of the six standards as Initial, Developing, Approaching, Proficient, or Exemplary. The teacher meeting the ISTE NETS for Teachers at the Proficient level has performed at a level at which they are prepared to take an assessment that results in an ISTE NETS Certificate. ISTE is currently working with nonprofit and for-profit groups to develop assessments for those seeking the ISTE NETS Certificate.

ADVANCED PROFICIENCY BENCHMARK: A teacher scoring at the Exemplary level has performed technology integration at a level commensurate with Advanced or National Board Certification. In the future, ISTE will work, possibly in conjunction with the National Board for Professional Teaching Standards (NBPTS), to identify technology performance proficiency at this "accomplished" level. The purpose is to recognize those highly effective teachers who integrate technology into the teaching and learning experiences in their classroom and who provide models for others to emulate.

This chapter will focus on assessments designed for the first two benchmarks as they are within the direct control of teacher education programs. The last two benchmarks will be addressed in a later ISTE publication.

A LITTLE BACKGROUND ON ISTE NETS ASSESSMENT

The NETS for Teachers Project held a focused Assessment Writing Meeting in Tempe, Arizona, in December 2000. Through an exhaustive selection process, an elite group of educators from across the nation were selected to thoughtfully examine the issues of assessment and technology. The contributing team members included teachers, technology coordinators, administrators, teacher educators, college of education administrators, and professionals from the assessment community. Four subcommittees were formed, each of which worked on different strategies to assess the NETS for Teachers. The areas of focus for each subcommittee and their tasks were:

▶ **General Preparation—***Listed specifications for the assessments meeting the tasks described in the profile*

▶ **Performance Assessment Tasks and Rubrics—***Developed a metarubric to address the Professional Preparation and Student Teaching/Internship Performance Profiles*

▶ **Electronic Portfolio—***Outlined the process and content for development of an electronic portfolio for the Professional Preparation and Student Teaching/Internship Performance Profiles with links to the First-Year Teaching Performance Profile*

▶ **Observation and Survey Tools—***Identified a series of options to address the Student Teaching/Internship and First-Year Teaching Performance Profiles*

The outcomes of the Assessment Writing Meeting contributed to the basis of this chapter. Additional specific products and ideas from the meeting will be found in later ISTE publications.

General Preparation—Candidate Readiness Benchmark

Establishing a national assessment instrument designed to determine the technology proficiency of those applying for admission to the teacher education professional coursework component presents several problems. First, institutions of higher education have various program models for the preparation of teachers. Some programs and state-level directives purposefully separate the general preparation from teacher preparation by requiring candidates to hold an initial degree before admission to the teacher preparation; other programs integrate general preparation and teacher preparation within a four-year undergraduate program. Second, many colleges of education have little influence over the content and sequence in the general education component typically offered by the college of arts and sciences. This variability in program and lack of control contribute to the difficulty in establishing a common method of assessment.

Collaboration throughout all aspects of the university is essential. NCATE encourages the collaboration between the college of arts and sciences and teacher education through its accreditation requirements. Several other initiatives have emphasized the importance of essential conversations between the two groups; the Technology Literacy Challenge and Preparing Tomorrow's Teachers to Use Technology grant initiatives, the CEO Forum Star Charts, and ISTE NETS for Teachers including the related essential conditions have each emphasized the shared responsibility for the preparation of new teachers among teacher education, arts and sciences, and the P–12 community. Critical to colleges of education is the institution's readiness to provide opportunities for their candidates to apply technology. This readiness is defined in the ISTE NETS essential conditions (see Section 1, "Establishing National Educational Technology Standards for Teachers"). Without strong support for integration of technology across all phases of the teacher education, successful preparation of candidates to use technology to improve student learning is severely limited.

Developed by the ISTE NETS Writing Team subgroup on General Preparation, the following box provides a preliminary list of tools and experiences teacher candidates should have before admission to the professional program. This list does not include discipline-specific experiences teacher candidates should have as part of their general liberal arts or major course of study.

TOOLS AND EXPERIENCES FOR THE GENERAL PREPARATION PERFORMANCE PROFILE

1. **Operating system**—*Can save and move files, format disks, and perform other maintenance tasks; understands what a network is compared with a stand-alone system; knows what an operating system is and its purpose; can install and use application programs (such as a CAI program that teaches Spanish)*

2. **Trouble-shooting**—*Can solve routine hardware and software problems (e.g., installing software, selecting the correct printer, hooking up the projector)*

3. **Computer purchases**—*Understands basic criteria for purchasing hardware, software, and services*

4. **Word processing**—*Understands word processing capabilities as well as basic desktop publishing, page design, and layout principles*

5. **Spreadsheets**—*Has sufficient knowledge to create a gradebook and make charts*

6. **Multimedia**—*Can use draw and paint programs, digital video, and digital cameras; can import graphics; can use images in presentations and publications*

7. **Database management**—*Can use an existing database (search, sort, and enter data into a template); can organize and develop own database*

8. **Presentation software**—*Will use appropriate design principles in classroom presentations prepared with software*

---

9. **E-mail—**Is able to send and receive messages and attachments, sort and handle e-mails, embed pictures in messages

10. **Devices—**Understands mouse, keyboard, printer, and scanner

11. **Ethics—**Understands copyright law, intellectual property, ethical use, and netiquette (such as inappropriate "spamming")

12. **Health and safety—**Is aware of issues such as ergonomics, predators on the Internet, inappropriate sites, proper use of children's names and pictures, and the dangers of completing surveys and divulging personal information

13. **Web research—**Knows how to evaluate the quality and objectivity of Web sites; employs efficient and effective searching techniques

14. **Web pages—**Is able to create simple Web pages

15. **Diversity, equity, and access—**Is aware of diversity, equity, and access issues

A forthcoming ISTE NETS document will include specifications for test developers to create the entry-level assessment that in many aspects aligns with the NETS for Students.

Professional Preparation and Student Teaching/Internship— Initial Certification Benchmark

For most teacher education programs, assessment of the outcomes of the Professional Preparation and Student Teaching/Internship Performance Profiles represents the core of the assessment system for the program itself. In planning for a total assessment system, colleges of education must pay particular attention to the notion of alignment. "Alignment does not refer to a comparison... [of] one assessment instrument with a curriculum, but extends to a set of assessment instruments or the assessment system" (Webb, 1997). Assessment of meeting the NETS must be interwoven with assessment of meeting other program standards. NCATE has revised its standards on assessment to emphasize an outcomes-based approach. The purpose of presenting the following assessment tools and guidelines is to provide options for programs to consider in developing their overall program assessment system that include technology proficiencies in teaching and learning.

PERFORMANCE ASSESSMENT

Performance assessment techniques particularly lend themselves to systems that are focused on outcomes-based assessment. Performance assessment concentrates on the direct observation of a candidate's performance. Candidates create projects or perform tasks based on predetermined standards, criteria, and indicators, which are evaluated by scoring rubrics. The results or products from the performance tasks may form the contents or artifacts for a portfolio and become part of an overall assessment of teacher candidates' competence in meeting the standards.

The following table is a sample of the type of rubric being developed for the ISTE NETS Assessment initiative. Note that the sample rubric progresses from high to low performance to force the user to look at best peformances first. The document will contain a metarubric for all NETS for Teachers.

Sample of NETS for Teachers Four-Level Rubric

| II. PLANNING AND DESIGNING LEARNING ENVIRONMENTS AND EXPERIENCES | | | |
DISTINGUISHED (4)	PROFICIENT (3)	APPRENTICE (2)	NOVICE (1)
Teachers plan and design effective learning environments and experiences supported by technology. The teacher:			
A. Consistently and creatively attends to developmental needs and student diversity	A. Shows adequate attention to developmental needs and student diversity	A. Shows moderate attention to developmental needs and student diversity	A. Shows weak attention to developmental needs and student diversity
B. Applies current research and theory when planning technology-rich learning activities	B. Mentions current research and theory when planning technology-rich learning activities	B. Gives minimal attention to current research and theory when planning technology-rich learning activities	B. Does not utilize conclusions from current research and theory when planning technology-rich learning activities
C. Consistently demonstrates critical thinking in selecting software	C. Shows some critical thinking in selecting software	C. Shows minimal critical thinking in selecting software	C. Rationale for selecting software is weak, lacking evidence of critical analysis
D. Anticipates technology-related classroom management issues and plans multiple courses of action	D. Anticipates technology-related classroom management issues and plans a course of action	D. Anticipates technology-related classroom management issues but does not plan alternative actions	D. Does not anticipate technology-related classroom management issues and does not plan alternative actions
E. Plans multiple strategies to facilitate students' higher-order thinking, critical thinking about electronic information, ethical sensitivity, and technical skills	E. Plans some strategies to facilitate some of the following: students' higher-order thinking, critical thinking about electronic information, OR technical skills	E. Plans strategies to facilitate only technical skills or is focused on only one aspect of technology use	E. Planning is inconsistent and does not cover any strategy well.

The above four-level rubric sample forces the assessor to make a choice in the continuum, whether completed as a self-assessment or by a supervisor. An odd number of levels, such as three or five, would have allowed the assessor to mark the middle option to indicate "average," much in the same way teachers grade students with A through F, with C denoting average.

The descriptive words for each indicator illustrate a developmental sequence—novice, apprentice, proficient, and distinguished. The rubric is designed to be used repeatedly to help teacher candidates to see movement toward the goal of becoming distinguished in each category.

OBSERVATION TOOLS

Once prospective teachers move into their student teaching/internship experience, there is a need for classroom observation tools to assess appropriate uses of technology in the curriculum. Not only will these tools assist with the assessment of prospective teachers by teacher education faculty and master/cooperating teachers, but the tools will also assist administrators as they evaluate the appropriate use of technology in the classroom. In addition to observational instruments, the use of survey information collected from students, parents, and other stakeholders provides valuable data for assessing the effect of technology in supporting student learning.

Following is a sample rubric for assisting in classroom observation. The sample rubric focuses on the Standard III—Teaching, Learning and the Curriculum. Note that the box to the far left states that technology was not used. This enables the assessor to also note that the situation did not exist for examining the use of technology during the observation.

Observational assessment protocols with associated rubrics are being field tested and will be available in another format through subsequent ISTE NETS publications.

III. B. Teachers use technology to support learner-centered strategies that address the diverse needs of learners.

Observation

Element: Is technology being used to support learner-centered strategies?			
Definition: Learner-centered strategies place the learner in the center of the learning process. It is distinguished from teacher-centered learning or instruction, which is characterized by the transmission of information from a knowledge expert (teacher) to a relatively passive recipient (student/learner) or consumer. Common learner-centered strategies include portfolio construction and assessment, collaborative learning and team projects, and learning contracts. Guiding theories and practices associated with it include constructivism, problem-based learning, resource-based learning, and collaborative/cooperative learning.			
LEVELS OF PERFORMANCE			
	UNACCEPTABLE	APPROACHING	ACCEPTABLE
Technology was not used.	Technology was not used in a way that supported learner-centered strategies.	Technology was used to support one learner-centered strategy.	Technology was used to support more than one learner-centered strategy.

Element: Is technology being used to address diverse needs of students?			
Definition: Students have diverse learning needs such as different styles of learning, multiple intelligences, and special needs due to disabilities. Technology lends itself to addressing these needs.			
LEVELS OF PERFORMANCE			
	UNACCEPTABLE	APPROACHING	ACCEPTABLE
Technology was not used.	Technology was not used in a way that addressed diverse needs of learners.	Technology was used in a way that addressed diverse needs of some learners.	Technology was used in a way that addressed diverse needs of all learners.

USING RUBRICS

A rubric is a set of categories that define and describe the important components of the work being completed, critiqued, or assessed. Each category contains a gradation of levels of completion or competence with a score assigned to each level and a clear description of what criteria need to be met to attain the score at each level. (San Mateo County Office of Education, 1997)

Rubrics to Assess Teacher Candidate Performance

There are many examples of rubrics in the professional preparation activities in Section 2. The format purposefully differs considerably. Some are organized top-to-bottom or left-to-right from highest to lowest level, showing the target level of proficiency first then working down or to the right. Others show progress from the lowest level (minimum or no proficiency) to the highest or target level. There does not appear to be any preference in the rubric development literature for one format over another; the order appears to be determined by the appropriateness to the task or the situation. Some teachers prefer to show the target performance first (high to low) in order to highlight the level of performance expected of students or teacher candidates. Others prefer to show a developmental continuum, from beginning/emergent/novice to expert/fluent/target levels of performance. Perhaps when the performances in the rubric are more developmental, the progression from low to high is preferred. This is used so that the novice does not become discouraged by first seeing the descriptions of high levels of performance.

Another example, the ISTE NETS•T Electronic Portfolio Metarubric, is designed to examine the entire portfolio. It is possible to add the scores, arriving at a single score for the entire portfolio. The descriptions are listed from high to low to cause the teacher candidate to read the exemplary description first before proceeding to the less accomplished levels. Likewise, the assessment team developing the Four-Level Rubric for ISTE NETS, found on the preceding pages, preferred showing the exemplary descriptors first to highlight the desired level of performance.

ISTE NETS•T Electronic Portfolio MetaRubric

	NOVICE 1	DEVELOPING 2	PROFICIENT 3	EXEMPLARY 4
Instructional Units	The unit does not provide adequate detail to guide instruction or does not reflect understanding of student learning. Major elements of the unit are not present. Technology use is in appropriate or underdeveloped.	Some content is inaccurate or out of date. Lessons are not consistently planned according to student abilities, developmental appropriateness, student prior knowledge, experiences, and alignment with standards. Technology use is inconsistent or underdeveloped.	Lesson plans and activities accurately portray content, are appropriate for developmental level of students, in alignment with standards, and focus on developing conceptual understanding. Technology use is appropriate and supports meeting objectives.	Lesson plans and activities accurately portray content and are appropriate for student developmental level. The unit is creative, novel, relevant to learners, in alignment with standards, focuses on developing conceptual understanding, and requires active engagement of learners. Technology use is creative, supports meeting objectives, and increases student technology competence.
Technology in Communication	The plan does not represent consistent communication with families over time.	The plan relies on one strategy for communicating with families.	The plan includes a consistently applied set of strategies for communicating with families.	The plan includes appropriate and creative strategies for communicating with families. Methods used meet the diverse needs of students and families.
Philosophy Statement	The technology section of the philosophy statement is unclear.	The technology section of the philosophy statement focuses on the purposes.	The technology section of the philosophy of education statement is clear and links to the overall statement. Justification is provided for beliefs.	The philosophy statement is clear and comprehensive. Philosophy statements on technology use are clearly described and woven into ideas on teaching and learning. Appropriate references are present to justify beliefs.
Classroom Lesson Plan	The management plan is inconsistent and does not exhibit an understanding of behavior or motivation. Management of technology use is not consistent with the rest of the plan.	The management plan relies heavily on extrinsic motivation sources and is unclear. Management of technology use is not clearly described but shows promise of being part of the overall management plan.	The management plan is clear and relies on one method of appropriately managing student behavior, uses both external and internal motivational theory. Management of technology is an integral	Includes clear management plan that includes multiple methods of managing student behavior and emphasis intrinsic and self motivation. The management of technology use is clear,

	NOVICE 1	DEVELOPING 2	PROFICIENT 3	EXEMPLARY 4
			part of the single dimensional management plan.	integrated into the overall management plans but varied to meet the needs of the students.
Assessment of Technology Use	An attempt at creating an assessment was made. The assessment does not clearly articulate criteria.	The assessment is missing two or three of the following attributes: authenticity, congruence with instructional goals, clear criteria for success, or rubric scoring.	The assessment is missing one of the following: authenticity, congruence with instructional goals, clear criteria for success, or rubric scoring.	The assessment is authentic, congruent with instructional goals, has clear criteria for success, and is scored using a rubric with the results communicated.
Lesson Plan Requiring use of Technology	Lesson plan demonstrates students viewing or having minimal use of the technology.	Technology tools used by the students are not appropriate for the grade or subject. The technology provides minimal support of the learning objectives.	Student use appropriate technology-based tools to support meeting content area standards. Students meet technology standards while addressing content are standards.	Student use appropriate technology tools in meaningful, inquiry-based learning of concepts. Lesson is in alignment with content area and ISTE NETS for Students.
Video Clip	Video clip selected illustrates minimal understanding of how to communicate with students bot verbally and nonverbally.	An authentic teaching experience is illustrated in the video clip, but the producer needs improvement in communications skills.	An authentic teaching experience is illustrated through the video clip. The producer consistently exhibits some characteristics of effective communication skills, but needs some assistance in one or two of the areas.	An authentic teaching experience is illustrated through the video clip. The producer consistently uses a variety of visual communication aids to support student learning and exhibits effective communication skills in the following areas: (1) questioning techniques, (2) explaining ideas, (3) restating ideas, (4) nonverbal cues, or (5) helping students to question, or (6) use of visual communication tools.
Evaluation of Learning Resources	Resources evaluated do not reflect an understanding of what is useful and appropriate for promoting student learning to meet the objectives outlined.	Resources selected are missing several of the major characteristics of exemplary learning resources. The accompanying evaluation is not complete.	Resources selected are inadequate in one or two of the exemplary criteria. Evaluation of the resources is complete.	Resources selected are: (1) grade and subject appropriate, (2) described and critically evaluated, and (3) include interdisciplinary connections.
Reflective Statements	Reflection is more descriptive than reflective or evaluative. Understanding of reflective practice is limited.	Reflections include only one or two of the four exemplary characteristics.	Reflections include two or more of the exemplary characteristics.	Reflections consistently include: (1) justification for selection of artifact, (2) connections between the portfolio artifact and philosophy, (3) evaluation of methods used, and (4) improvements to consider for the future.

Continued on next page.

ISTE NETS•T Electronic Portfolio MetaRubric continued

	NOVICE 1	DEVELOPING 2	PROFICIENT 3	EXEMPLARY 4
Organization	Organization pattern is not clear.	Portfolio is incomplete and hard to follow. All artifacts are labeled according to required component name.	Organization is clear, simple and readily apparent to the reviewer. All artifacts are labeled according to required component name.	Organization is clear, well-thought out, creative, readily apparent, and easy to navigate. All artifacts are labeled according to required component name.
Spelling and Grammar	Errors in grammar, punctuation, word usage, spelling, and format interfere with the reviewer's ability to read the portfolio.	Errors in grammar, punctuation, word usage, spelling, and format are consistent through the portfolio. Most errors would be corrected through spelling/grammar checking documents.	A few inconsistent errors in grammar, punctuation, word usage, spelling, and format are present. The errors do not interfere with the reviewer's ability to read the portfolio.	The portfolio is free of errors in grammar, punctuation, word usage, spelling, and format.

Note: When items are not present, a score of "0" is given.

Some rubrics describe the characteristics of a project and provide simple scoring (5=excellent, 4=good, 3=fair, etc.) without any descriptive language to define the differences between those levels. The rubrics in this book attempt to provide the descriptions or anchors that differentiate levels of performance. For example, see the rubric for the science activity "Bounce Back—The Long and Short of It" in Section 2, "Technology in Middle School Education Programs."

While the simple scoring guides are easier to develop, they often provide little guidance for students as they strive to meet the highest standards. Some simple scoring methods, however, can combine both a description and a general means of separating levels. For example, see the rubric for "Wearing Your Geography," also in Section 2, "Technology in Middle School Education Programs."

Rubrics Developed by Teacher Candidates

An integral part of developing technology-rich lessons is learning how to assess those lessons with students. Many of the rubrics in Section 2 are only partially complete. The incomplete rubrics vary from lacking the assignment criteria to providing only a partially completed table. Within the activities are statements prompting the teacher preparation faculty member to engage in a discussion about the development of the assessment rubric.

As activities are being implemented in the classroom, periodically focusing on the assessment device helps candidates discuss their perceptions of the expectations of the upcoming assignment.

In assisting teacher candidates to develop rubrics, encourage candidates to keep in mind the following characteristics and guiding questions for high-quality rubrics provided by the work of Judith Arter and Jay McTighe (from *Scoring Rubrics in the Classroom*, p. 72, ©2001 by Corwin Press, Inc. Reprinted with permission of Corwin Press, Inc.).

1. Content/Coverage—Does the rubric cover the features that really indicate quality performance?

2. Clarity/Detail—Does the rubric make it clear what you mean with definitions, indicators, and samples of work?

3. Practicality—Do teachers and students find it useful for instruction and assessment?

4. Technical Quality/Soundness/Fairness—Can you get raters to agree on scores? Is the rubric fair to all students?

Considering these characteristics as the discussion takes place will guide candidates into a more substantive discussion of expectations for themselves as teachers and their students as learners.

Below is the video project assessment rubric from the elementary activity "Oral History."

Rubric: Video Project

CRITERIA	LEVELS OF PERFORMANCE				
	1	2	3	4	5
Editing					The editing is respectful of the subject, includes smooth transitions, only the essential footage.
Alignment with Theme					Holistically the information on the video is in alignment with the selected theme.
Quality			TO BE COMPLETED BY CLASS		The video includes a title screen and credits, has good camera angles, and is of high enough resolution to be posted on the Web site and viewed through a browser.
Archived					Video is posted on the class Web site, within the time line, and is fully functional through the browser.

Note: (1) This rubric uses a numerical scoring mechanism with "5" as the highest and "1" as the lowest possible scores. There are no descriptive words associated with each scoring category. (2) The rubric is created with the lowest score on the left to the highest on the right, which is the opposite of the electronic portfolio rubric.

As the classroom conversation proceeds, the faculty member may ask, "How might the editing of the video actually be disrespectful to the subject of the video?" The conversation would then ensue around the elements of respect for subjects, how videographers can demonstrate insensitivity, and how to edit down to the essential elements of the story without jeopardizing the authenticity of the story being told.

As the elements are discussed, levels one through four can be described. Discussing what is meant by each criterion further clarifies the expectation for the production of the project, thus raising the level of achievement for candidates who otherwise may have misinterpreted the expectations. The discussion of the remainder of the criteria progresses in the same manner as the assignment is being made.

An alternative to holding a whole group discussion involves the use of consensus groups. Each element in the table is assigned to a small group for discussion and drafting of the achievement levels on the specific criteria. The groups then share their outcomes, leading a class discussion to edit the results and ensure comprehension by classmates.

Regardless of the organizational structure used to complete the rubric, the exercise of delineating between the levels of the rubric provides additional experience in rubric development and clarifies the process and performance results for candidates.

REFLECTIONS

Reflecting on one's work in a written form has become a staple in teacher preparation. Often teacher preparation programs include in their mission statement the idea of developing reflective practitioners. The act of reflecting on work completed brings the cycle of planning, implementation, and assessment full circle by linking the assessment to self-assessment of teaching and critical planning for instructional improvement.

Burke (1997) writes, "Without written commentaries, explanations and reflections, the portfolio is no more than a notebook of artifacts or a scrapbook of teaching mementos." The attachment of a reflection to each entry in the portfolio provides the context for assessing the artifact as evidence in meeting the standards. The reflection is a glimpse into the thinking of the candidate, providing the faculty member with more information as to the candidate's understanding of the criteria and how the criteria have been addressed.

The format for reflections can vary. The seemingly simplistic question of "How does this entry address the standard?", supplemented with additional space for the meaning and value of the entry in addressing the criteria, provides a forum for candidates to address the criteria in a written form. Candidates can complete the reflection as a cover sheet to each entry in the portfolio. Initially, the reflection should be completed immediately as the entry is placed in the portfolio. This ensures that the initial thinking about the entry has been recorded. As the portfolio is being assembled, reflections can be altered to fit the purpose of the portfolio and the criteria being addressed. The strength of the portfolio as an assessment tool lies in the quality of the reflections included.

Portfolios

Two key purposes of using portfolios with preservice teachers are (1) to advance the pace of teacher development in increasing the level of teacher professionalism, and (2) to improve teacher assessment for licensure and employment decisions (Tierney, 1994). Items selected for inclusion in the portfolio show the candidate's best work (Bloom & Bacon, 1995); growth and competence around a variety of themes (content, pedagogy, management professionalism) (Geiger & Shugarman, 1988); or effort, progress, and achievements (Paulson, Paulson, & Meyer, 1991). These items can be required by the teacher education program or selected by the candidate.

From the learner's perspective, portfolio assessment means, "Let me show you" (Fogarty, 1998, p. 10). This type of assessment focuses on growth and development over time, with learners collecting, selecting, and reflecting on artifacts as evidence of their learning. Portfolio entries can take the form of artifacts (items from previous classroom experiences), reproductions (photographs and videos, often of student work), productions (items specifically produced for the portfolio), and attestations (acknowledgements of candidate accomplishments from others who have observed the candidate's work) (Collins, 1992). Portfolios promote self-analysis and critical reflection in ways that help unpack the complexities of teaching (Costantino & DeLorenzo, 1994). Reflections on and about the entries and the processes of developing and using the strategies outlined in the entries provide insight into candidate knowledge, skills, and dispositions as developing professionals. Figure 4 shows an adaptation of the NETS for Teachers Assessment Model to address the progression of the teacher candidate's portfolio through the stages of the teacher education program, to the classroom teaching experience, and on to advanced certification, possibly through the National Board for Professional Teaching Standards.

Portfolio Development Progression—From Preservice to Advanced Certification

	GENERAL PREPARATION	PROFESSIONAL PREPARATION	STUDENT TEACHING/INTERNSHIP	FIRST-YEAR TEACHING	HIGHLY EFFECTIVE TEACHING
Technology Operations & Concepts					
Planning & Designing Learning Environments & Experiences					
Teaching, Learning, & the Curriculum					
Assessment & Evaluation					
Productivity & Professional Practice					
Social, Ethical, Legal, & Human Issues					

1. LEARNING PORTFOLIO [Formative]
2. ASSESSMENT PORTFOLIO [Summative]
3. EMPLOYMENT PORTFOLIO

PROFESSIONAL DEVELOPMENT PORTFOLIO [Formative]

ADVANCED CERTIFICATION PORTFOLIO [Summative]

Candidate Readiness		Initial Certification	Novice Teacher Benchmark	Advanced Professional Proficiency

To effectively use technology to develop a portfolio, students are encouraged to become "digital packrats" (see Section 2, "Educational Foundations") from the beginning of their teacher education program. From the artifacts they collect and from others that they produce, a teacher candidate can create several types of portfolios.

TEACHER PREPARATION PROGRAM PORTFOLIOS

Learning/Formative Assessment Portfolio

Throughout their teacher education program candidates collect and present artifacts and other evidence demonstrating their journey to becoming an effective teacher. The purpose of this portfolio is to provide evidence of their present competence and might include a plan for professional growth. Evidence might include a philosophy statement, courses taken, course assignments, videos, and evaluations of their work. Ideally each entry would include a reflective component telling how the entry affected their growth toward becoming an effective teacher. Formative feedback takes place periodically by individuals or groups of peers, faculty, practicing teachers, and administrators.

Summative Portfolio

By the end of the student teaching program, the portfolio is used for summative assessment, to demonstrate achievement of any group of standards (i.e., NETS, INTASC). The purpose of this portfolio is to document attainmentt of the standards. Candidates examine their collection of items and select those that best document their journey toward, and describe them as effective teachers. As items are selected, candidates are asked to include the connection to the teacher education program and/or ISTE NETS goals in their caption or reflection about the artifact. An individual item might address one or more standards, and a group of items might address parts of a standard. If all standards are not met through the items collected within a reasonable amount of space, candidates can produce additional items that address the standard.

TEACHING PORTFOLIO

Employment Portfolio

The teacher candidate may use the items collected during the teacher preparation program to develop an employment portfolio. The purpose of this portfolio is to show that he or she is the right person for the job. The configuration of this portfolio is, again, determined by the audience, the potential employer and the particular job. For example, a secondary science teacher's portfolio might include different items if they were applying for a middle level earth/space science position than if they were applying for a secondary chemistry position. Careful selection from the items collected over time and reflection about these items focused on the purpose (getting the job) is required.

Professional Development Portfolio

Once in the teaching profession, the portfolio becomes more like the Learning/Formative Assessment Portfolio created during teacher preparation. Teachers collect items over the course of their teaching career—evidence of their effect on student work, attendance at conferences, completion of courses—to document continued growth. Each year during evaluation the teacher and administrator or teacher and mentor collaboratively evaluate teaching effectiveness and set goals. The portfolio can be used for performance assessment, based on appropriate teaching standards and individually set goals for professional development.

ADVANCED DEGREE OR CERTIFICATION PORTFOLIO

Advanced Degrees

Many masters and doctoral programs also require the use of a portfolio to document accomplishment of knowledge, skills, and dispositions. Candidates add to and select from their ever-increasing collection of items to fit the purpose of the advanced degree portfolio.

National Board for Professional Teaching Standards Certification

According to its Web site, "the National Board's mission is to establish high and rigorous standards for what accomplished teachers should know and be able to do, to develop and operate a national voluntary system to assess and certify teachers who meet these standards, and to advance related education reforms for the purpose of improving student learning in American schools" (NBPTS, 2001a, www.nbpts.org/about/history.html). The process consists of two major parts, the portfolio entries and the assessment center exercises. The NBPTS also indicates that "a good portfolio reflects the standards and provides evidence of a teacher's level of accomplishment" (NBPTS, 2001b, **www.nbpts.org/ nat_board_certification/certification_process.html#portfolio**).

ELECTRONIC PORTFOLIOS TO DEMONSTRATE NETS

The artifacts and reflections from performance activities within a given teacher education program, such as described in other chapters in this book, can be placed into a teacher candidate's electronic portfolio. This electronic evidence can serve to demonstrate the growth in knowledge and skills noted on the NETS for Teachers. When started early, an electronic portfolio can become a tool to organize and present evidence of learning that results from these performance assessment activities over time. Armed with this understanding, the subcommittee from the ISTE NETS Writing Team defined the purpose, audience, process, and various developmental strategies for using technology to maintain authentic samples of a teacher candidates' work, demonstrating achievement of not only the ISTE NETS for Teachers but also the school of education's teaching standards and any other standards that the candidate is responsible for demonstrating. The purpose of an electronic portfolio is to document the prospective teacher's growth and change over time and provides the ideal container in which to organize and document both the teacher education program standards (INTASC and content area standards) and various performance assessments that demonstrate achievement of the ISTE NETS.

Portfolio Entries

Because the portfolio evolves over time and can be repurposed for various uses, many artifacts should be obtained to allow maximum flexibility for the candidate as well as provide evidence for the attainment of the NETS for Teachers. To assist in determining what might go into a portfolio to demonstrate that these standards have been met, Figure 5 provides a list of artifacts that could be included in an electronic portfolio, demonstrating each of the NETS for Teachers performance indicators. One item, such as a comprehensive teaching unit, might address parts of several standards. This list of items is not meant to be exhaustive. Rather, it is designed to provide faculty and programs with a starting point to determine the data that might be collected by both candidates and programs to demonstrate the NETS for Teachers.

NETS for Teachers Electronic Portfolio—Suggested Artifacts by Standard

STANDARD I

TECHNOLOGY OPERATIONS AND CONCEPTS

A. Evidence of proficiency as described in the ISTE NETS for Teachers (General Preparation Performance Profile assessment results)

B. Evidence of professional development in technology plan and action steps

STANDARD II

PLANNING AND DESIGNING LEARNING ENVIRONMENTS AND EXPERIENCES

A. Evidence of instruction that connects appropriate technology resources, curriculum content, and assessments for specific student populations:

- Unit and lesson plans in which the candidate has selected a broad range of technology resources to adapt instruction to different learning needs and ability levels, to enable participation of students with special needs, and to support second language learners.

- Candidate work samples in which a broad range of technologies have been used to adapt instruction to different learning needs and ability levels, to enable participation of students with special needs, and to support second language learners.

B. Evidence of knowledge of current research and the application of current research to designing effective learning environments and experiences including:

- Citations or references to current research on teaching and learning with technology are cited in technology plan or unit plan.

C. Evidence of a rationale for inclusion of specific technology resources in a unit or lesson plan, including how these resources were identified, located, evaluated, and selected. Technology resources may include software, Web-based media, peripherals, video, and so on.

D. Evidence of orchestration of activities to maximize student learning by matching the most appropriate technology setting and resources to instructional and learner needs.

- Classroom technology plan includes how technology resources will be matched to student learning experiences.

- Instructional unit reflects appropriate match between technology resources and student learning experiences.

E. Evidence of adapting to a variety of technology-enhanced learning environments, such as one-computer classrooms, multi-workstations, portable technologies, and computer labs.

- A variety of technology-enhanced environments included in technology plan.

- A variety of technology-enhanced environments used in unit and lesson plans appropriately matched to instructional strategies.

STANDARD III

TEACHING, LEARNING, AND THE CURRICULUM

A. Evidence of unit and lesson plans that specifically reference NETS.

B. Evidence of units and lessons that use technology resources to individualize instruction to address diverse learning needs.

C. Evidence of units and lessons that allow students to explore higher-order thinking and problem solving by using technology to extend and expand (go beyond the classroom) instruction.

D. Evidence of student learning activities that demonstrate adaptation to a variety of technology-enhanced learning environments, such as one-computer classrooms, multi-workstations, portable technologies, computer labs, including:

- Examples of student work produced using a variety of technology resources.
- Observations.
- Reproductions (images, video, audio) of students using a variety of technology resources while learning.

STANDARD IV

ASSESSMENT AND EVALUATION

A. Evidence of using technology to collect and analyze student performance data may include electronic gradebooks, Web-based testing, spreadsheets, databases, student electronic portfolios, and other performance task end products.

B. Evidence of using technology to interpret student assessment information, report results, analyze trends, recognize patterns, and draw conclusions about classroom performance to improve instructional practice, including:

- Technology-supported individual learning reports for parents and students.
- Assessment data across years for individual teaching, across schools, and across students to show long-term gains or effects of changes in teaching pedagogy.
- Reflections including specific references.

STANDARD V

PRODUCTIVITY AND PROFESSIONAL PRACTICE

A. Evidence of participation in continuing education (educational technology conference attendance, curriculum integration workshops, online courses).

B. Evidence of professional development in technology plan and action steps.

C. Evidence of using technology to collaborate, prepare publications, and produce other creative work

D. Evidence of using technology tools for sustained communication, (e.g., e-mail, listservs, shared network folders, Web pages, videoconferences).

STANDARD VI

SOCIAL, ETHICAL, LEGAL, AND HUMAN ISSUES

A. Evidence of:

- Lessons that include copyright policy, and citations.
- Student work that includes appropriate references, and lessons that model intellectual property rights and acceptable use policies.
- Classroom rules that address issues of privacy, security, appropriate access, and implementation of acceptable use policies.

B. Evidence of:

- Selecting and using a broad range of technology resources to adapt instruction to different learning needs and ability levels and support second language learners.
- Arranging equitable access to appropriate technology that enables students to engage successfully in learning activities across subject-content levels.
- Purposeful use of assistive technologies to enable all students, regardless of special needs, to participate in learning.

C. (See A) Evidence that classroom use of technology is organized in ways that

- Are developmentally appropriate,
- Do not put student health at risk (ergonomically sound, time appropriate, etc), and
- Ensure the security of student data and information.

D. Evidence of classroom planning and management, including scheduling, room arrangement, and rules, that ensure all students have access to technology resources (i.e., a classroom technology plan).

Required Entries

For the purposes of program assessment and improvement, the subcommittee identified six required entries for the portfolio that should be expected from all students. *Required Artifacts Correlated to Standards—Recording Sheet* lists these six pieces of evidence to be included, with specifications for each item. The development of each item should become embedded in the teacher preparation program with several opportunities for review and enhancement based on growth and experiences.

When combining the required entries with other artifacts selected by the candidate, an organizing table should be provided to validate how each artifact relates to meeting the standards. *Required Artifacts Correlated to Standards—Recording Sheet* is an example of a candidate recordkeeping chart showing how the candidate perceives each of the required items addressed by ISTE NETS for Teachers. An expansion of this table, providing for more self-selected entries, allows teacher candidates to maintain a record of the types of documents in their portfolios and which standards they address. Because candidates may improve upon previous work, several variations of an entry might be listed with dates and updated reflections showing continued progress moving from novice to distinguished in performance. Teacher education and professional development programs are highly encouraged to use multiple artifacts that address general standards. Additionally, progress toward meeting the standards should be documented with multiple assessment opportunities throughout the program. Therefore, it will not be unusual for the following recording sheet to have several marks in each line and column.

Instructional Unit—Curriculum unit that includes (among other elements) technology goals and objectives, technology management plan, sample lessons, and electronic student work samples.

Classroom Technology Plan—A classroom-wide year-long plan that focuses on systematic curriculum integration to meet student standards and classroom management of student access to technology resources.

Record Keeping—Examples of a comprehensive strategy for maintaining student data, curriculum planning information, electronic examples of student work, and tracking student progress.

Required Artifacts Correlated to Standards—Recording Sheet

NETS FOR TEACHERS E-PORTFOLIO REQUIRED ENTRIES	ISTE NETS FOR TEACHERS																					
	Technology and Operations Concepts		Planning and Designing Learning Environments and Experiences					Teaching, Learning, and the Curriculum				Assessment and Evaluation			Productivity and Professional Practice				Social, Ethical, Legal, and Human Issues				
CANDIDATE:	I A	I B	II A	II B	II C	II D	II E	III A	III B	III C	III D	IV A	IV B	IV C	V A	V B	V C	V D	VI A	VI B	VI C	VI D	VI E
1. Classroom technology plan			●	●	●	●	●																
2. Technology in an instructional unit																							
3. Technology in communication																							
4. Technology for record keeping																							
5. Professional development in applying technology to teaching and learning																							
6. Technology in education vision/philosophy statement or platform																							

Candidate to complete chart based on how each artifact addresses the standards.

Professional Development—A section of an in-depth personal professional development plan including targeted technology goals and an action plan.

Communication—Samples of technology-based ongoing communication that occur among the teacher, family, and student, teacher to teacher and teacher to community.

Education Vision/Philosophy Statement—Part of a larger philosophy statement focusing on the personal beliefs and rationale for technology to improve teaching, learning, and assessment.

Note: A complete description and associated scoring rubric for each suggested required artifact can be found in the ISTE NETS Assessment document.

Assessing the Electronic Portfolio

Many elements are assessed in an electronic portfolio. Not only are the entries and reflections assessed, but, as with a paper portfolio, issues of presentation and design enter into the user's perception of the portfolio's contents. The process of developing an electronic portfolio itself becomes a performance assessment task.

Conclusions

Many strategies can be used to assess whether teacher candidates have achieved the NETS for Teachers. The primary types of assessment measures discussed here include performance tasks, many of which are outlined in this book, along with assessment rubrics. A teacher candidate's evidence of meeting the standards, organized and presented in an electronic portfolio, supports an emerging trend in balanced assessment that provides a richer picture of achievement than can be gained from more traditional, objective forms of assessment. ISTE will be developing a more in-depth resource on assessing the NETS for Teachers to provide further support for teacher educators and school leaders. An electronic portfolio has the potential to become a dynamic celebration of learning that documents a teacher's professional development across his or her career.

References

Angelo, T. A. (1995). *AAHE Bulletin*, November 1995, 7.

Arter, J., & McTighe, J. (2001). *Scoring rubrics in the classroom*. Thousand Oaks, CA: Corwin Press, Inc.

Barrett, H. (2000). Create your own electronic portfolio. *Learning & Leading with Technology, 27*(7), 14–21.

Bloom, L., & Bacon, E. (1995). Professional portfolios: An alternative perspective of the preparation of teachers of students with behavioral disorders. *Behavioral Disorders, 20*(4), 290–300.

Burke, K. (1997). *Designing Professional Portfolios for Change.* Arlington Heights, IL: Skylight Professional Development.

Collins, A. (1992). Portfolios in science education: Issues in purpose, structure, and authenticity. *Science Education, 76*(4), 451–463.

Costantino, P., & DeLorenzo, M. (1994, February). *Developing a professional portfolio: Suggested guidelines for preservice and inservice teachers.* Paper presented at the annual meeting of the Association of Teacher Educators, Atlanta, GA.

Fogarty, R. (1998). *Balanced assessment.* Arlington Heights, IL: Skylight Professional Development.

Geiger, J., & Shugarman, S. (1988). Portfolios and case studies to evaluate teacher education students and programs. *Action in Teacher Education, 10*(3), 31–34.

International Society for Technology Education. (2000). *National educational technology standards for teachers.* Eugene, OR: ISTE.

National Board for Professional Teaching Standards. (2001a). *History of the National Board* [Online]. Available: **www.nbpts.org/about/history.html**.

National Board for Professional Teaching Standards. (2001b). *National Board certification process* [Online]. Available: **www.nbpts.org/nat_board_certification/certification_process.html#portfolio**.

National Council for Accreditation of Teacher Education. (2000). *Principles for performance-based assessment systems in professional education programs.* Washington, DC: NCATE.

Paulson, F. L., Paulson, P. R., & Meyer, C. A. (1991). What makes a portfolio a portfolio? *Educational Leadership, 48*(5), 60–63.

San Mateo County Office of Education. (1997). *Project-based learning with multimedia* [Online]. Available: **http://pblmm.k12.ca.us/PBLGuide/ThoughtPieces/Rubric.html**.

Tierney, D. (1994, April). *Teacher portfolios: Would an assessment by any other name smell as sweet?* Paper presented at the annual meeting of the American Education Research Association, New Orleans, LA.

Webb, N. L. (1997). *Criteria for alignment of expectations and assessments in mathematics and science education.* Washington, DC: National Institute for Science Education.

Helen C. Barrett is an assistant professor at the University of Alaska, Anchorage, and a member of the NETS for Teachers Project Leadership Team.

M. G. (Peggy) Kelly is a professor of education at California State University, San Marcos, and co-director of the ISTE NETS Project.

Lajeane Thomas is a professor of education at Louisiana Tech University, director of the ISTE NETS Project, and chair of the ISTE Standards and Accreditation Committee.

NETS Assessment Writing Team

The following individuals contributed to this chapter.

David Barr
Illinois Mathematics and Science Academy (IL)

Helen Barrett
University of Alaska Anchorage (AK)

Gary Bitter
Arizona State University (AZ)

Christy Blauer
High Plains Regional Technology in Education Consortium (KS)

Roger Carlsen
Wright State University (OH)

Jeri Carroll
Wichita State University (KS)

Leslie Conery
International Society for Technology in Education (OR)

Ed Coughlin
The Metiri Group (CA)

Steven Cowdrey
Cherry Creek School District (CO)

Doug Daniell
International Society for Technology in Education (OR)

Leslie Flanders
Scott County Schools (KY)

Joyce Friske
Jenks Public Schools (OK)

Juanita Guerin
University of Louisiana (LA)

Sharnell Jackson
Chicago Public Schools (IL)

Peggy Kelly
California State University San Marcos (CA)

Walter Kimball
University of Southern Maine (ME)

Don Knezek
National Center of PT3 (TX)

Andy Latham
Educational Testing Service (CA)

Priscilla Lundberg
Tempe Regional Training Center (AZ)

Lynn Nolan
The School District of Greenville County (SC)

Julie O'Brian
The HEAT Center (CO)

Kyle Peck
Pennsylvania State University (PA)

Dianne Porter
Louisiana Tech University (LA)

Pamela Redmond
California Commission for Teacher Credentialing (CA)

Heidi Rogers
University of Idaho (ID)

Meg Ropp
Michigan Virtual University (MI)

Ferdi Serim
Online Internet Institute (NM)

Debbie Silver
Louisiana Tech University (LA)

John T. Spagnolo
Appalachian State University (NC)

Jane Strickland
Idaho State University (ID)

Nancy Thomas
The Chauncey Group International (NJ)

Lajeane Thomas
Louisiana Tech University (LA)

John Vaille
International Society for Technology in Education (OR)

Rosie O'Brien Vojtek
Bristol School District & National Staff Development Council (CT)

James Wiebe
California State University Los Angeles (CA)

Lynne Wyly
National Board for Professional Teacher Standards (VA)

Louise Yarnall
Stanford Research Institute (CA)

Appendices

Appendix A
National Educational Technology Standards
for Teachers

National Educational Technology Standards for Teachers

All classroom teachers should be prepared to meet the following standards and performance indicators.

I. TECHNOLOGY OPERATIONS AND CONCEPTS
Teachers demonstrate a sound understanding of technology operations and concepts. Teachers:

A. demonstrate introductory knowledge, skills, and understanding of concepts related to technology (as described in the ISTE National Educational Technology Standards for Students).

B. demonstrate continual growth in technology knowledge and skills to stay abreast of current and emerging technologies.

II. PLANNING AND DESIGNING LEARNING ENVIRONMENTS AND EXPERIENCES
Teachers plan and design effective learning environments and experiences supported by technology. Teachers:

A. design developmentally appropriate learning opportunities that apply technology-enhanced instructional strategies to support the diverse needs of learners.

B. apply current research on teaching and learning with technology when planning learning environments and experiences.

C. identify and locate technology resources and evaluate them for accuracy and suitability.

D. plan for the management of technology resources within the context of learning activities.

E. plan strategies to manage student learning in a technology-enhanced environment.

III. TEACHING, LEARNING, AND THE CURRICULUM
Teachers implement curriculum plans that include methods and strategies for applying technology to maximize student learning. Teachers:

A. facilitate technology-enhanced experiences that address content standards and student technology standards.

B. use technology to support learner-centered strategies that address the diverse needs of students.

C. apply technology to develop students' higher-order skills and creativity.

D. manage student learning activities in a technology-enhanced environment.

IV. ASSESSMENT AND EVALUATION
Teachers apply technology to facilitate a variety of effective assessment and evaluation strategies. Teachers:

A. apply technology in assessing student learning of subject matter using a variety of assessment techniques.

B. use technology resources to collect and analyze data, interpret results, and communicate findings to improve instructional practice and maximize student learning.

C. apply multiple methods of evaluation to determine students' appropriate use of technology resources for learning, communication, and productivity.

V. PRODUCTIVITY AND PROFESSIONAL PRACTICE
Teachers use technology to enhance their productivity and professional practice. Teachers:

A. use technology resources to engage in ongoing professional development and lifelong learning.

B. continually evaluate and reflect on professional practice to make informed decisions regarding the use of technology in support of student learning.

C. apply technology to increase productivity.

D. use technology to communicate and collaborate with peers, parents, and the larger community in order to nurture student learning.

VI. SOCIAL, ETHICAL, LEGAL, AND HUMAN ISSUES
Teachers understand the social, ethical, legal, and human issues surrounding the use of technology in PK–12 schools and apply that understanding in practice. Teachers:

A. model and teach legal and ethical practice related to technology use.

B. apply technology resources to enable and empower learners with diverse backgrounds, characteristics, and abilities.

C. identify and use technology resources that affirm diversity.

D. promote safe and healthy use of technology resources.

E. facilitate equitable access to technology resources for all students.

Note: For profiles, see "Technology Performance Profiles for Teacher Preparation" in Section 1, "Establishing National Educational Technology Standards for Teachers."

Appendix B
Content Area Standards

- National Educational Technology Standards for Students

- English Language Arts Standards

- Mathematics Standards

- Science Standards

- Social Studies Standards

- Early Childhood Professional Preparation Guidelines

National Educational Technology Standards for Students

1. BASIC OPERATIONS AND CONCEPTS

- Students demonstrate a sound understanding of the nature and operation of technology systems.
- Students are proficient in the use of technology.

2. SOCIAL, ETHICAL, AND HUMAN ISSUES

- Students understand the ethical, cultural, and societal issues related to technology.
- Students practice responsible use of technology systems, information, and software.
- Students develop positive attitudes toward technology uses that support lifelong learning, collaboration, personal pursuits, and productivity.

3. TECHNOLOGY PRODUCTIVITY TOOLS

- Students use technology tools to enhance learning, increase productivity, and promote creativity.
- Students use productivity tools to collaborate in constructing technology-enhanced models, preparing publications, and producing other creative works.

4. TECHNOLOGY COMMUNICATIONS TOOLS

- Students use telecommunications to collaborate, publish, and interact with peers, experts, and other audiences.
- Students use a variety of media and formats to communicate information and ideas effectively to multiple audiences.

5. TECHNOLOGY RESEARCH TOOLS

- Students use technology to locate, evaluate, and collect information from a variety of sources.
- Students use technology tools to process data and report results.
- Students evaluate and select new information resources and technological innovations based on the appropriateness to specific tasks.

6. TECHNOLOGY PROBLEM-SOLVING AND DECISION-MAKING TOOLS

- Students use technology resources for solving problems and making informed decisions.
- Students employ technology in the development of strategies for solving problems in the real world.

Note: For profiles, see "Profiles for Technology-Literate Students' in Section 1, "Establishing National Educational Technology Standards for Teachers."

English Language Arts Standards

The vision guiding these standards is that all students must have the opportunities and resources to develop the language skills they need to pursue life's goals and to participate fully as informed, productive members of society. These standards assume that literacy growth begins before children enter school as they experience and experiment with literacy activities—reading and writing, and associating spoken words with their graphic representations. Recognizing this fact, these standards encourage the development of curriculum and instruction that make productive use of the emerging literacy abilities that children bring to school. Furthermore, the standards provide ample room for the innovation and creativity essential to teaching and learning. They are not prescriptions for particular curricula or instruction.

Although we present these standards as a list, we want to emphasize that they are not distinct and separable; they are, in fact, interrelated and should be considered as a whole.

1. *Students read a wide range of print and nonprint texts to build an understanding of texts, of themselves, and of the cultures of the United States and the world; to acquire new information; to respond to the needs and demands of society and the workplace; and for personal fulfillment. Among these texts are fiction and nonfiction, classic and contemporary works.*

2. *Students read a wide range of literature from many periods in many genres to build an understanding of the many dimensions (e.g., philosophical, ethical, and aesthetic) of human experience.*

3. *Students apply a wide range of strategies to comprehend, interpret, evaluate, and appreciate texts. They draw on their prior experience, their interactions with other readers and writers, their knowledge of word meaning and of other texts, their word identification strategies, and their understanding of textual features (e.g., sound-letter correspondence, sentence structure, context, and graphics).*

4. *Students adjust their use of spoken, written, and visual language (e.g., conventions, style, and vocabulary) to communicate effectively with a variety of audiences and for different purposes.*

5. *Students employ a wide range of strategies as they write and use different writing process elements appropriately to communicate with different audiences for a variety of purposes.*

6. *Students apply knowledge of language structure, language conventions (e.g., spelling and punctuation), media techniques, figurative language, and genre to create, critique, and discuss print and nonprint texts.*

7. *Students conduct research on issues and interests by generating ideas and questions, and by posing problems. They gather, evaluate, and synthesize data from a variety of sources (e.g., print and nonprint texts, artifacts, and people) to communicate their discoveries in ways that suit their purpose and audience.*

8. *Students use a variety of technological and information resources (e.g., libraries, databases, computer networks, and video) to gather and synthesize information and to create and communicate knowledge.*

9. *Students develop an understanding of and respect for diversity in language use, patterns, and dialects across cultures, ethnic groups, geographic regions, and social roles.*

10. *Students whose first language is not English make use of their first language to develop competency in the English language arts and to develop understanding of content across the curriculum.*

11. *Students participate as knowledgeable, reflective, creative, and critical members of a variety of literacy communities.*

12. *Students use spoken, written, and visual language to accomplish their own purposes (e.g., for learning, enjoyment, persuasion, and the exchange of information).*

Mathematics Standards

STANDARD 1: NUMBER AND OPERATIONS
Instructional programs from PK–12 should enable all students to—

- understand numbers, ways of representing numbers, relationships among numbers, and number systems;
- understand meanings of operations and how they relate to one another;
- compute fluently and make reasonable estimates.

STANDARD 2: ALGEBRA
Instructional programs from PK–12 should enable all students to—

- understand patterns, relations, and functions;
- represent and analyze mathematical situations and structures using algebraic symbols;
- use mathematical models to represent and understand quantitative relationships;
- analyze change in various contexts.

STANDARD 3: GEOMETRY
Instructional programs from PK–12 should enable all students to—

- analyze characteristics and properties of two- and three-dimensional geometric shapes and develop mathematical arguments about geometric relationships;
- specify locations and describe spatial relationships using coordinate geometry and other representational systems;
- apply transformations and use symmetry to analyze mathematical situations;
- use visualization, spatial reasoning, and geometric modeling to solve problems.

STANDARD 4: MEASUREMENT
Instructional programs from PK–12 should enable all students to—

- understand measurable attributes of objects and the units, systems, and processes of measurement;
- apply appropriate techniques, tools, and formulas to determine measurements.

STANDARD 5: DATA ANALYSIS AND PROBABILITY
Instructional programs from PK–12 should enable all students to—

- formulate questions that can be addressed with data and collect, organize, and display relevant data to answer them;
- select and use appropriate statistical methods to analyze data;
- develop and evaluate inferences and predictions that are based on data;
- understand and apply basic concepts of probability.

STANDARD 6: PROBLEM SOLVING
Instructional programs from PK–12 should enable all students to—

- build new mathematical knowledge through problem solving;
- solve problems that arise in mathematics and in other contexts;
- apply and adapt a variety of appropriate strategies to solve problems;
- monitor and reflect on the process of mathematical problem solving.

Reprinted with permission from Principles and Standards for School Mathematics. *Copyright 2000 by the National Council of Teachers of Mathematics. Available online: http://standards.nctm.org.*

STANDARD 7: REASONING AND PROOF

Instructional programs from PK–12 should enable all students to—

- recognize reasoning and proof as fundamental aspects of mathematics;
- make and investigate mathematical conjectures;
- develop and evaluate mathematical arguments and proofs;
- select and use various types of reasoning and methods of proof.

STANDARD 8: COMMUNICATION

Instructional programs from PK–12 should enable all students to—

- organize and consolidate their mathematical thinking through communication;
- communicate their mathematical thinking coherently and clearly to peers, teachers, and others;
- analyze and evaluate the mathematical thinking and strategies of others;
- use the language of mathematics to express mathematical ideas precisely.

STANDARD 9: CONNECTIONS

Instructional programs from PK–12 should enable all students to—

- recognize and use connections among mathematical ideas;
- understand how mathematical ideas interconnect and build on one another to produce a coherent whole;
- recognize and apply mathematics in contexts outside of mathematics.

STANDARD 10: REPRESENTATION

Instructional programs from PK–12 should enable all students to—

- create and use representations to organize, record, and communicate mathematical ideas;
- select, apply, and translate among mathematical representations to solve problems;
- use representations to model and interpret physical, social, and mathematical phenomena.

Science Standards

Grades K–12

CONTENT STANDARD: UNIFYING CONCEPTS AND PROCESSES
As a result of activities in Grades K–12, all students should develop understanding and abilities aligned with the following concepts and processes:

- Systems, order, and organization
- Evidence, models, and explanation
- Constancy, change, and measurement
- Evolution and equilibrium
- Form and function

Grades K–4 Standards

CONTENT STANDARD A: SCIENCE AS INQUIRY

A1. Abilities necessary to do scientific inquiry:

- Ask a question about objects, organisms, and events in the environment.
- Plan and conduct a simple investigation.
- Employ simple equipment and tools to gather data and extend the senses.
- Use data to construct a reasonable explanation.
- Communicate investigations and explanations.

A2. Understanding about scientific inquiry:

- Scientific investigations involve asking and answering a question and comparing the answer with what scientists already know about the world.
- Scientists use different kinds of investigations depending on the questions they are trying to answer.
- Simple instruments provide more information than scientists obtain using only their senses.
- Scientists develop explanations using observations (evidence) and what they already know about the world (scientific knowledge).
- Scientists make the results of their investigations public; they describe the investigations in ways that enable others to repeat the investigations.
- Scientists review and ask questions about the results of other scientists' work.

CONTENT STANDARD B: PHYSICAL SCIENCE
B1. Properties of objects and materials
B2. Position and motion of objects
B3. Light, heat, electricity, and magnetism

CONTENT STANDARD C: LIFE SCIENCE
C1. The characteristics of organisms
C2. Life cycles of organisms
C3. Organisms and environments

CONTENT STANDARD D: EARTH AND SPACE SCIENCE
D1. Properties of earth materials
D2. Objects in the sky
D3. Changes in earth and sky

Reprinted with permission from National Science Education Standards. *Copyright 1996 by the National Academy of Sciences. Courtesy of the National Academy Press, Washington, D.C.*

CONTENT STANDARD E: SCIENCE AND TECHNOLOGY

E1. Abilities of technological design

E2. Understanding about science and technology

E3. Abilities to distinguish between natural objects and objects made by humans

CONTENT STANDARD F: SCIENCE IN PERSONAL AND SOCIAL PERSPECTIVES

F1. Personal health

F2. Characteristics and changes in populations

F3. Types of resources

F4. Changes in environments

F5. Science and technology in local challenges

CONTENT STANDARD G: HISTORY AND NATURE OF SCIENCE

G1. Science as a human endeavor:

- Science and technology have been practiced by people for a long time.
- Men and women have made a variety of contributions throughout the history of science and technology.
- Science will never be finished.
- Many people choose science as a career.

Grades 5–8 Standards

CONTENT STANDARD A: SCIENCE AS INQUIRY

A1. Abilities necessary to do scientific inquiry:

- Identify questions that can be answered through scientific investigations.
- Design and conduct a scientific investigation.
- Use appropriate tools and techniques to gather, analyze, and interpret data.
- Develop descriptions, explanations, predictions, and models using evidence and explanations.
- Recognize and analyze alternative explanations and predictions.
- Communicate scientific procedures and explanations.
- Use mathematics in all aspects of scientific inquiry.

A2. Understanding about scientific inquiry:

- Different kinds of questions suggest different kinds of scientific investigations.
- Current scientific knowledge and understanding guide scientific investigations.
- Mathematics is important in all aspects of scientific inquiry.
- Technology used to gather data enhances accuracy and allows scientists to analyze and quantify results of investigations.
- Scientific explanations emphasize evidence, have logically consistent arguments, and use scientific principles, models, and theories.
- Science advances through legitimate skepticism.
- Scientific investigations sometimes result in new ideas and phenomena.

CONTENT STANDARD B: PHYSICAL SCIENCE

B1. Properties and changes of properties in matter

B2. Motion and forces

B3. Transfer of energy

CONTENT STANDARD C: LIFE SCIENCE

C1. Structure and function in living systems

C2. Reproduction and heredity

C3. Regulation and behavior

C4. Populations and ecosystems

C5. Diversity and adaptations of organisms

CONTENT STANDARD D: EARTH AND SPACE SCIENCE

D1. Structure of the earth system

D2. Earth's history

D3. Earth in the solar system

CONTENT STANDARD E: SCIENCE AND TECHNOLOGY

E1. Abilities of technological design:

- Identify appropriate problems for technological design.
- Design a solution or product.
- Implement a proposed design.
- Evaluate completed technological designs or products.
- Communicate the process of technological design.

E2. Understanding about science and technology:

- Scientific inquiry and technological design have similarities and differences.
- Many different people in different cultures have made and continue to make contributions to science and technology.
- Science and technology are reciprocal.
- Perfectly designed solutions do not exist.
- Technological designs have constraints.
- Technological solutions have intended benefits and unintended consequences.

CONTENT STANDARD F: SCIENCE IN PERSONAL AND SOCIAL PERSPECTIVES

F1. Personal health

F2. Populations, resources, and environments

F3. Natural hazards

F4. Risks and benefits

F5. Science and technology in society

CONTENT STANDARD G: HISTORY AND NATURE OF SCIENCE

G1. Science as a human endeavor:

- Women and men of various social and ethnic backgrounds engage in the activities of science, engineering, and related fields.
- Science requires different abilities.

G2. Nature of science:

- Scientists formulate and test their explanations of nature using observation, experiments, and theoretical and mathematical models.
- It is normal for scientists to differ with one another about the interpretation of the evidence or theory being considered.
- It is part of scientific inquiry to evaluate ideas proposed by other scientists.

G3. History of science:

- Many individuals have contributed to the traditions of science.
- In historical perspective, science has been practiced by different individuals in different cultures.
- Tracing the history of science can show how difficult it was for scientific innovators to break through the accepted ideas of their time to reach the conclusions that we currently take for granted.

Grades 9–12 Standards

CONTENT STANDARD A: SCIENCE AS INQUIRY

A1. Abilities necessary to do scientific inquiry:

- Identify questions and concepts that guide scientific investigations.
- Design and conduct a scientific investigation.
- Use technology and mathematics to improve investigations and communications.
- Formulate and revise scientific explanations and models using logic and evidence.
- Recognize and analyze alternative explanations and models.
- Communicate and defend a scientific argument.

A2. Understanding about scientific inquiry:

- Scientists usually inquire about how physical, living, or designed systems function.
- Scientists conduct investigations for a wide variety of reasons.
- Scientists rely on technology to enhance the gathering and manipulation of data.
- Mathematics is essential in scientific inquiry.
- Scientific explanations must adhere to criteria such as: a proposed explanation must be logically consistent; it must abide by the rules of evidence; it must be open to questions and possible modification; and it must be based on historical and current scientific knowledge.
- Results of scientific inquiry emerge from different types of investigations and public communication among scientists.

CONTENT STANDARD B: PHYSICAL SCIENCE

B1. Structure of atoms

B2. Structure and properties of matter

B3. Chemical reactions

B4. Motions and forces

B5. Conservation of energy and increase in disorder

B6. Interactions of energy and matter

CONTENT STANDARD C: LIFE SCIENCE

C1. The cell

C2. Molecular basis of heredity

C3. Biological evolution

C4. Interdependence of organisms

C5. Matter, energy, and organization in living systems

C6. Behavior of organisms

CONTENT STANDARD D: EARTH AND SPACE SCIENCE

D1. Energy in the earth system

D2. Geochemical cycles

D3. Origin and evolution of the earth system

D4. Origin and evolution of the universe

CONTENT STANDARD E: SCIENCE AND TECHNOLOGY

E1. Abilities of technological design:

- Identify a problem or design an opportunity.
- Propose designs and choose between alternative solutions.
- Implement a proposed design.
- Evaluate the solution and its consequences.

- Communicate the problem, process, and solution.

E2. Understanding about science and technology:

- Scientists in different disciplines ask different questions, use different methods of investigation, and accept different types of evidence to support their explanations.
- Science often advances with the introduction of new technologies.
- Creativity, imagination, and a good knowledge base are all required in the work of science and engineering.
- Science and technology are pursued for different purposes.
- Technological knowledge is often not made public because of patents and the financial potential of the idea or invention. Scientific knowledge is made public.

CONTENT STANDARD F: SCIENCE IN PERSONAL AND SOCIAL PERSPECTIVES

F1. Personal and community health

F2. Population growth

F3. Natural resources

F4. Environmental quality

F5. Natural and human-induced hazards

F6. Science and technology in local, national, and global challenges

CONTENT STANDARD G: HISTORY AND NATURE OF SCIENCE

G1. Science as a human endeavor:

- Individuals and teams have contributed and will continue to contribute to the scientific enterprise.
- Scientists have ethical traditions.
- Scientists are influenced by societal, cultural, and personal beliefs and ways of viewing the world.

G2. Nature of scientific knowledge:

- Science distinguishes itself from other ways of knowing and from other bodies of knowledge.
- Scientific explanations must meet certain criteria.
- Because all scientific ideas depend on experimental and observational confirmation, all scientific knowledge is, in principle, subject to change as new evidence becomes available.

G3. Historical perspectives:

- In history, diverse cultures have contributed scientific knowledge and technologic inventions.
- Usually, changes in science occur as small modifications in extant knowledge.
- Occasionally, there are advances in science and technology that have important and long-lasting effects on science and society.
- The historical perspective of scientific explanations demonstrates how scientific knowledge changes by evolving over time, almost always building on earlier knowledge.

Social Studies Standards

Performance Expectations

I. CULTURE

Social studies programs should include experiences that provide for the study of culture and cultural diversity, so that the learner can:

Early Grades

a. explore and describe similarities and differences in the ways groups, societies, and cultures address similar human needs and concerns;

b. give examples of how experiences may be interpreted differently by people from diverse cultural perspectives and frames of reference;

c. describe ways in which language, stories, folktales, music, and artistic creations serve as expressions of culture and influence behavior of people living in a particular culture;

d. compare ways in which people from different cultures think about and deal with their physical environment and social conditions;

e. give examples and describe the importance of cultural unity and diversity within and across groups.

Middle Grades

a. compare similarities and differences in the ways groups, societies, and cultures meet human needs and concerns;

b. explain how information and experiences may be interpreted by people from diverse cultural perspectives and frames of reference;

c. explain and give examples of how language, literature, the arts, architecture, other artifacts, traditions, beliefs, values, and behaviors contribute to the development and transmission of culture;

d. explain why individuals and groups respond differently to their physical and social environments and/or changes to them on the basis of shared assumptions, values, and beliefs;

e. articulate the implications of cultural diversity, as well as cohesion, within and across groups.

High School

a. analyze and explain the ways groups, societies, and cultures address human needs and concerns;

b. predict how data and experiences may be interpreted by people from diverse cultural perspectives and frames of reference;

c. apply an understanding of culture as an integrated whole that explains the functions and interactions of language, literature, the arts, traditions, beliefs and values, and behavior patterns;

d. compare and analyze societal patterns for preserving and transmitting culture while adapting to environmental or social change;

e. demonstrate the value of cultural diversity, as well as cohesion, within and across groups;

f. interpret patterns of behavior reflecting values and attitudes that contribute or pose obstacles to cross-cultural understanding;

g. construct reasoned judgments about specific cultural responses to persistent human issues;

h. explain and apply ideas, theories, and modes of inquiry drawn from anthropology and sociology in the examination of persistent issues and social problems.

Reprinted with permission from Expectations of Excellence—Curriculum Standards for Social Studies, *published by National Council for the Social Studies, 1994, p. 33–45.*

II. TIME, CONTINUITY, AND CHANGE

Social studies programs should include experiences that provide for the study of the ways human beings view themselves in and over time, so that the learner can:

Early Grades

a. demonstrate an understanding that different people may describe the same event or situation in diverse ways, citing reasons for the differences in views;

b. demonstrate an ability to use correctly vocabulary associated with time such as past, present, future, and long ago; read and construct simple timelines; identify examples of change; and recognize examples of cause and effect relationships;

c. compare and contrast different stories or accounts about past events, people, places, or situations, identifying how they contribute to our understanding of the past;

d. identify and use various sources for reconstructing the past, such as documents, letters, diaries, maps, textbooks, photos, and others;

e. demonstrate an understanding that people in different times and places view the world differently;

f. use knowledge of facts and concepts drawn from history, along with elements of historical inquiry, to inform decision making about and action-taking on public issues.

Middle Grades

a. demonstrate an understanding that different scholars may describe the same event or situation in different ways but must provide reasons or evidence for their views;

b. identify and use key concepts such as chronology, causality, change, conflict, and complexity to explain, analyze, and show connections among patterns of historical change and continuity;

c. identify and describe selected historical periods and patterns of change within and across cultures, such as the rise of civilizations, the development of transportation systems, the growth and breakdown of colonial systems, and others;

d. identify and use processes important to reconstructing and reinterpreting the past, such as using a variety of sources, providing, validating, and weighing evidence for claims, checking credibility of sources, and searching for causality;

e. develop critical sensitivities such as empathy and skepticism regarding attitudes, values, and behaviors of people in different historical contexts;

f. use knowledge of facts and concepts drawn from history, along with methods of historical inquiry, to inform decision making about and action-taking on public issues.

High School

a. demonstrate that historical knowledge and the concept of time are socially influenced constructions that lead historians to be selective in the questions they seek to answer and the evidence they use;

b. apply key concepts such as time, chronology, causality, change, conflict, and complexity to explain, analyze, and show connections among patterns of historical change and continuity;

c. identify and describe significant historical periods and patterns of change within and across cultures, such as the development of ancient cultures and civilizations, the rise of nation-states, and social, economic, and political revolutions;

d. systematically employ processes of critical historical inquiry to reconstruct and reinterpret the past, such as using a variety of sources and checking their credibility, validating and weighing evidence for claims, and searching for causality;

e. investigate, interpret, and analyze multiple historical and contemporary viewpoints within and across cultures related to important events, recurring dilemmas, and persistent issues, while employing empathy, skepticism, and critical judgement;

f. apply ideas, theories, and modes of historical inquiry to analyze historical and contemporary developments, and to inform and evaluate actions concerning public policy issues.

III. PEOPLE, PLACES, AND ENVIRONMENTS

Social studies programs should include experiences that provide for the study of people, places, and environments, so that the learner can:

Early Grades

a. construct and use mental maps of locales, regions, and the world that demonstrate understanding of relative location, direction, size, and shape;

b. interpret, use, and distinguish various representations of the earth, such as maps, globes, and photographs;

c. use appropriate resources, data sources, and geographic tools such as atlases, databases, grid systems, charts, graphs, and maps to generate, manipulate, and interpret information;

d. estimate distances and calculate scale;

e. locate and distinguish among varying landforms and geographic features, such as mountains, plateaus, islands, and oceans;

f. describe and speculate about physical system changes, such as seasons, climate and weather, and the water cycle;

g. describe how people create places that reflect ideas, personality, culture, and wants and needs as they design homes, playgrounds, classrooms, and the like;

h. examine the interaction of human beings and their physical environment, the use of land, building of cities, and ecosystem changes in selected locales and regions;

i. explore ways that the earth's physical features have changed over time in the local region and beyond and how these changes may be connected to one another;

j. observe and speculate about social and economic effects of environmental changes and crises resulting from phenomena such as floods, storms, and drought;

Middle Grades

a. elaborate mental maps of locales, regions, and the world that demonstrate understanding of relative location, direction, size, and shape;

b. create, interpret, use, and distinguish various representations of the earth, such as maps, globes, and photographs;

c. use appropriate resources, data, sources, and geographic tools such as aerial photographs, satellite images, geographic information systems (GIS), map projections, and cartography to generate, manipulate, and interpret information such as atlases, databases, grid systems, charts, graphs, and maps;

d. estimate distance, calculate scale, and distinguish other geographic relationships such as population density and spatial distribution patterns;

e. locate and describe varying landforms and geographic features, such as mountains, plateaus, islands, rain forests, deserts, and oceans, and explain their relationships within the ecosystem;

f. describe physical system changes such as seasons, climate and weather, and the water cycle and identify geographic patterns associated with them;

g. describe how people create places that reflect cultural values and ideals as they build neighborhoods, parks, shopping centers, and the like;

h. examine, interpret, and analyze physical and cultural patterns and their interactions, such as land use, settlement patterns, cultural transmission of customs and ideas, and ecosystem changes;

High School

a. refine mental maps of locales, regions, and the world that demonstrates understanding of relative location, direction, size, and shape;

b. create, interpret, use, and synthesize information from various representations of the earth, such as maps, globes, and photographs;

c. use appropriate resources, data sources, and geographic tools such as aerial photographs, satellite images, geographic information systems (GIS), map projections, and cartography to generate, manipulate, and interpret information such as atlases, databases, grid systems, charts, graphs, and maps;

d. calculate distance, scale, area, and density, and distinguish spatial distribution patterns;

e. describe, differentiate, and explain the relationships among various regional and global patterns of geographic phenomena such as landforms, soils, climate, vegetation, natural resources, and population;

f. use knowledge of physical system changes such as seasons, climate and weather, and the water cycle to explain geographic phenomena;

g. describe and compare how people create places that reflect culture, human needs, government policy, and current values and ideals as they design and build specialized buildings, neighborhoods, shopping centers, urban centers, industrial parks, and the like;

h. examine, interpret, and analyze physical and cultural patterns and their interactions, such as land use, settlement patterns, cultural transmission of customs and ideas, and ecosystem changes;

III. PEOPLE, PLACES, AND ENVIRONMENTS (CONTINUED)

Early Grades

k. consider existing uses and propose and evaluate alternative uses of resources and land in home, school, community, the region, and beyond.

Middle Grades

i. describe ways that historical events have been influenced by, and have influenced, physical and human geographic factors in local, regional, national, and global settings;

j. observe and speculate about social and economic effects of environmental changes and crises resulting from phenomena such as floods, storms, and drought;

k. propose, compare, and evaluate alternative uses of land and resources in communities, regions, nations, and the world.

High School

i. describe and assess ways that historical events have been influenced by, and have influenced, physical and human geographic factors in local, regional, national, and global settings;

j. analyze and evaluate social and economic effects of environmental changes and crises resulting from phenomena such as floods, storms, and drought;

k. propose, compare, and evaluate alternative policies for the use of land and other resources in communities, regions, nations, and the world.

IV. INDIVIDUAL DEVELOPMENT AND IDENTITY

Social studies programs should include experiences that provide for the study of individual development and identity, so that the learner can:

Early Grades

a. describe personal changes over time, such as those related to physical development and personal interests;

b. describe personal connections to place—especially place as associated with immediate surroundings;

c. describe the unique features of one's nuclear and extended families;

d. show how learning and physical development affect behavior;

e. identify and describe ways family, groups, and community influence the individual's daily life and personal choices;

f. explore factors that contribute to one's personal identity such as interests, capabilities, and perceptions;

g. analyze a particular event to identify reasons individuals might respond to it in different ways;

h. work independently and cooperatively to accomplish goals.

Middle Grades

a. relate personal changes to social, cultural, and historical contexts;

b. describe personal connections to place—as associated with community, nation, and world;

c. describe the ways family, gender, ethnicity, nationality, and institutional affiliations contribute to personal identity;

d. relate such factors as physical endowment and capabilities, learning, motivation, personality, perception, and behavior to individual development;

e. identify and describe ways regional, ethnic, and national cultures influence individuals' daily lives;

f. identify and describe the influence of perception, attitudes, values, and beliefs on personal identity;

g. identify and interpret examples of stereotyping, conformity, and altruism;

h. work independently and cooperatively to accomplish goals.

High School

a. articulate personal connections to time, place, and social/cultural systems;

b. identify, describe, and express appreciation for the influences of various historical and contemporary cultures on an individual's daily life;

c. describe the ways family, religion, gender, ethnicity, nationality, socioeconomic status, and other group and cultural influences contribute to the development of a sense of self;

d. apply concepts, methods, and theories about the study of human growth and development, such as physical endowment, learning, motivation, behavior, perception, and personality;

e. examine the interactions of ethnic, national, or cultural influences in specific situations or events;

f. analyze the role of perceptions, attitudes, values, and beliefs in the development of personal identity;

g. compare and evaluate the impact of stereotyping, conformity, acts of altruism, and other behaviors on individuals and groups;

h. work independently and cooperatively within groups and institutions to accomplish goals;

i. examine factors that contribute to and damage one's mental health and analyze issues related to mental health and behavioral disorders in contemporary society.

V. INDIVIDUALS, GROUPS, AND INSTITUTIONS
Social studies programs should include experiences that provide for the study of interactions among individuals, groups, and institutions, so that the learner can:

Early Grades

a. identify roles as learned behavior patterns in group situations such as student, family member, peer play group member, or club member;

b. give examples of and explain group and institutional influences such as religious beliefs, laws, and peer pressure, on people, events, and elements of culture;

c. identify examples of institutions and describe the interactions of people with institutions;

d. identify and describe examples of tensions between and among individuals, groups, or institutions, and how belonging to more than one group can cause internal conflicts;

e. identify and describe examples of tension between an individual's beliefs and government policies and laws;

f. give examples of the role of institutions in furthering both continuity and change;

g. show how groups and institutions work to meet individual needs and promote the common good, and identify examples of where they fail to do so.

Middle Grades

a. demonstrate an understanding of concepts such as role, status, and social class in describing the interactions of individuals and social groups;

b. analyze group and institutional influences on people, events, and elements of culture;

c. describe the various forms institutions take and the interactions of people with institutions;

d. identify and analyze examples of tensions between expressions of individuality and group or institutional efforts to promote social conformity;

e. identify and describe examples of tensions between belief systems and government policies and laws;

f. describe the role of institutions in furthering both continuity and change;

g. apply knowledge of how groups and institutions work to meet individual needs and promote the common good.

High School

a. apply concepts such as role, status, and social class in describing the connections and interactions of individuals, groups, and institutions in society;

b. analyze group and institutional influences on people, events, and elements of culture in both historical and contemporary settings;

c. describe the various forms institutions take, and explain how they develop and change over time;

d. identify and analyze examples of tensions between expressions of individuality and efforts used to promote social conformity by groups and institutions;

e. describe and examine belief systems basic to specific traditions and laws in contemporary and historical movements;

f. evaluate the role of institutions in furthering both continuity and change;

g. analyze the extent to which groups and institutions meet individual needs and promote the common good in contemporary and historical settings;

h. explain and apply ideas and modes of inquiry drawn from behavioral science and social theory in the examination of persistent issues and social problems.

VI. POWER, AUTHORITY, AND GOVERNANCE

Social studies programs should include experiences that provide for the study of how people create and change structures of power, authority, and governance, so that the learner can:

Early Grades

a. examine the rights and responsibilities of the individual in relation to his or her social group, such as family, peer group, and school class;

b. explain the purpose of government;

c. give examples of how government does or does not provide for needs and wants of people, establish order and security, and manage conflict;

d. recognize how groups and organizations encourage unity and deal with diversity to maintain order and security;

e. distinguish among local, state, and national government and identify representative leaders at these levels such as mayor, governor, and president;

f. identify and describe factors that contribute to cooperation and cause disputes within and among groups and nations;

g. explore the role of technology in communications, transportation, information-processing, weapons development, or other areas as it contributes to or helps resolve conflicts;

h. recognize and give examples of the tensions between the wants and needs of individuals and groups, and concepts such as fairness, equity, and justice.

Middle Grades

a. examine persistent issues involving the rights, roles, and status of the individual in relation to the general welfare;

b. describe the purpose of government and how its powers are acquired, used, and justified;

c. analyze and explain ideas and governmental mechanisms to meet needs and wants of citizens, regulate territory, manage conflict, and establish order and security;

d. describe the ways nations and organizations respond to forces of unity and diversity affecting order and security;

e. identify and describe the basic features of the political system in the United States, and identify representative leaders from various levels and branches of government;

f. explain conditions, actions, and motivations that contribute to conflict and cooperation within and among nations;

g. describe and analyze the role of technology in communications, transportation, information-processing, weapons development, or other areas as it contributes to or helps resolve conflicts;

h. explain and apply concepts such as power, role, status, justice, and influence to the examination of persistent issues and social problems;

i. give examples and explain how governments attempt to achieve their stated ideals at home and abroad.

High School

a. examine persistent issues involving the rights, roles, and status of the individual in relation to the general welfare;

b. explain the purpose of government and analyze how its powers are acquired, used, and justified;

c. analyze and explain ideas and mechanisms to meet needs and wants of citizens, regulate territory, manage conflict, establish order and security, and balance competing conceptions of a just society;

d. compare and analyze the ways nations and organizations respond to conflicts between forces of unity and forces of diversity;

e. compare different political systems (their ideologies, structure, and institutions, processes, and political cultures) with that of the United States, and identify representative political leaders from selected historical and contemporary settings;

f. analyze and evaluate conditions, actions, and motivations that contribute to conflict and cooperation within and among nations;

g. evaluate the role of technology in communications, transportation, information-processing, weapons development, or other areas as it contributes to or helps resolve conflicts;

h. explain and apply ideas, theories, and modes of inquiry drawn from political science to the examination of persistent issues and social problems;

i. evaluate the extent to which governments achieve their stated ideals and policies at home and abroad;

j. prepare a public policy paper and present and defend it before an appropriate forum in school or community.

VII. PRODUCTION, DISTRIBUTION, AND CONSUMPTION

Social studies programs should include experiences that provide for the study of how people organize for the production, distribution, and consumption of goods and services, so that the learner can:

Early Grades

a. give examples that show how scarcity and choice govern our economic decisions;

b. distinguish between needs and wants;

c. identify examples of private and public goods and services;

d. give examples of the various institutions that make up economic systems such as families, workers, banks, labor unions, government agencies, small businesses, and large corporations;

e. describe how we depend upon workers with specialized jobs and the ways in which they contribute to the production and exchange of goods and services;

f. describe the influence of incentives, values, traditions, and habits on economic decisions;

g. explain and demonstrate the role of money in everyday life;

h. describe the relationship of price to supply and demand;

i. use economic concepts such as supply, demand, and price to help explain events in the community and nation;

j. apply knowledge of economic concepts in developing a response to a current local economic issue, such as how to reduce the flow of trash into a rapidly filling landfill.

Middle Grades

a. give and explain examples of ways that economic systems structure choices about how goods and services are to be produced and distributed;

b. describe the role that supply and demand, prices, incentives, and profits play in determining what is produced and distributed in a competitive market system;

c. explain the difference between private and public goods and services;

d. describe a range of examples of the various institutions that make up economic systems such as households, business firms, banks, government agencies, labor unions, and corporations;

e. describe the role of specialization and exchange in the economic process;

f. explain and illustrate how values and beliefs influence different economic decisions;

g. differentiate among various forms of exchange and money;

h. compare basic economic systems according to who determines what is produced, distributed, and consumed;

i. use economic concepts to help explain historical and current developments and issues in local, national, or global contexts;

j. use economic reasoning to compare different proposals for dealing with a contemporary social issue such as unemployment, acid rain, or high quality education.

High School

a. explain how the scarcity of productive resources (human, capital, technological, and natural) requires the development of economic systems to make decisions about how goods and services are to be produced and distributed;

b. analyze the role that supply and demand, prices, incentives, and profits play in determining what is produced and distributed in a competitive market system;

c. consider the costs and benefits to society of allocating goods and services through private and public sectors;

d. describe relationships among the various economic institutions that make up economic systems such as households, business firms, banks, government agencies, labor unions, and corporations;

e. analyze the role of specialization and exchange in economic processes;

f. compare how values and beliefs influence economic decisions in different societies;

g. compare basic economic systems according to how rules and procedures deal with demand, supply, prices, the role of government, banks, labor and labor unions, savings and investments, and capital;

h. apply economic concepts and reasoning when evaluating historical and contemporary social developments and issues;

i. distinguish between the domestic and global economic systems, and explain how the two interact;

j. apply knowledge of production, distribution, and consumption in the analysis of a public issue such as the allocation of health care or the consumption of energy, and devise an economic plan for accomplishing a socially desirable outcome related to that issue;

k. distinguish between economics as a field of inquiry and the economy.

VIII. SCIENCE, TECHNOLOGY, AND SOCIETY

Social studies programs should include experiences that provide for the study of relationships among science, technology, and society, so that the learner can:

Early Grades

a. identify and describe examples in which science and technology have changed the lives of people, such as in homemaking, childcare, work, transportation, and communication;

b. identify and describe examples in which science and technology have led to changes in the physical environment, such as the building of dams and levees, offshore oil drilling, medicine from rain forests, and loss of rain forests due to extraction of resources or alternative uses;

c. describe instances in which changes in values, beliefs, and attitudes have resulted from new scientific and technological knowledge, such as conservation of resources and awareness of chemicals harmful to life and the environment;

d. identify examples of laws and policies that govern scientific and technological applications, such as the Endangered Species Act and environmental protection policies;

e. suggest ways to monitor science and technology in order to protect the physical environment, individual rights, and the common good.

Middle Grades

a. examine and describe the influence of culture on scientific and technological choices and advancement, such as in transportation, medicine, and warfare;

b. show through specific examples how science and technology have changed people's perceptions of the social and natural world, such as in their relationship to the land, animal life, family life, and economic needs, wants, and security;

c. describe examples in which values, beliefs, and attitudes have been influenced by new scientific and technological knowledge, such as the invention of the printing press, conceptions of the universe, applications of atomic energy, and genetic discoveries;

d. explain the need for laws and policies to govern scientific and technological applications, such as in the safety and well-being of workers and consumers and the regulation of utilities, radio, and television;

e. seek reasonable and ethical solutions to problems that arise when scientific advancements and social norms or values come into conflict.

High School

a. identify and describe both current and historical examples of the interaction and interdependence of science, technology, and society in a variety of cultural settings;

b. make judgements about how science and technology have transformed the physical world and human society and our understanding of time, space, place, and human-environment interactions;

c. analyze how science and technology influence the core values, beliefs, and attitudes of society, and how core values, beliefs, and attitudes of society shape scientific and technological change;

d. evaluate various policies that have been proposed as ways of dealing with social changes resulting from new technologies, such as genetically engineered plants and animals;

e. recognize and interpret varied perspectives about human societies and the physical world using scientific knowledge, ethical standards, and technologies from diverse world cultures;

f. formulate strategies and develop policies for influencing public discussions associated with technology-society issues, such as the greenhouse effect.

IX. GLOBAL CONNECTIONS

Social studies programs should include experiences that provide for the study of global connections and interdependence, so that the learner can:

Early Grades

a. explore ways that language, art, music, belief systems, and other cultural elements may facilitate global understanding or lead to misunderstanding;

b. give examples of conflict, cooperation, and interdependence among individuals, groups, and nations;

c. examine the effects of changing technologies on the global community;

d. explore causes, consequences, and possible solutions to persistent, contemporary, and emerging global issues, such as pollution and endangered species;

e. examine the relationships and tensions between personal wants and needs and various global concerns, such as use of imported oil, land use, and environmental protection;

f. investigate concerns, issues, standards, and conflicts related to universal human rights, such as the treatment of children, religious groups, and effects of war.

Middle Grades

a. describe instances in which language, art, music, belief systems, and other cultural elements can facilitate global understanding or cause misunderstanding;

b. analyze examples of conflict, cooperation, and interdependence among groups, societies, and nations;

c. describe and analyze the effects of changing technologies on the global community;

d. explore the causes, consequences, and possible solutions to persistent, contemporary, and emerging global issues, such as health, security, resource allocation, economic development, and environmental quality;

e. describe and explain the relationships and tensions between national sovereignty and global interests, in such matters as territory, natural resources, trade, use of technology, and welfare of people;

f. demonstrate understanding of concerns, standards, issues, and conflicts related to universal human rights;

g. identify and describe the roles of international and multinational organizations.

High School

a. explain how language, art, music, belief systems, and other cultural elements can facilitate global understanding or misunderstanding;

b. explain conditions and motivations that contribute to conflict, cooperation, and interdependence among groups, societies, and nations;

c. analyze and evaluate the effects of changing technologies on the global community;

d. analyze the causes, consequences, and possible solutions to persistent, contemporary, and emerging global issues, such as health, security, resource allocation, economic development, and environmental quality;

e. analyze the relationships and tensions between national sovereignty and global interests, in such matters as territory, economic development, nuclear and other weapons, use of natural resources, and human rights concerns;

f. analyze or formulate policy statements demonstrating an understanding of concerns, standards, issues, and conflicts related to universal human rights;

g. describe and evaluate the role of international and multinational organizations in the global arena;

h. illustrate how individual behaviors and decisions connect with global systems.

X. CIVIC IDEALS AND PRACTICES

Social studies programs should include experiences that provide for the study of the ideals, principles, and practices of citizenship in a democratic republic, so that the learner can:

Early Grades

a. identify key ideals of the United States' democratic republican form of government, such as individual human dignity, liberty, justice, equality, and the rule of law, and discuss their application in specific situations;

b. identify examples of rights and responsibilities of citizens;

c. locate, access, organize, and apply information about an issue of public concern from multiple points of view;

d. identify and practice selected forms of civic discussion and participation consistent with the ideals of citizens in a democratic republic;

e. explain actions citizens can take to influence public policy decisions;

f. recognize that a variety of formal and informal actors influence and shape public policy;

g. examine the influence of public opinion on personal decision making and government policy on public issues;

h. explain how public policies and citizen behaviors may or may not reflect the stated ideals of a democratic republican form of government;

i. describe how public policies are used to address issues of public concern;

j. recognize and interpret how the "common good" can be strengthened through various forms of citizen action.

Middle Grades

a. examine the origins and continuing influence of key ideals of the democratic republican form of government, such as individual human dignity, liberty, justice, equality, and the rule of law;

b. identify and interpret sources and examples of the rights and responsibilities of citizens;

c. locate, access, analyze, organize, and apply information about selected public issues—recognizing and explaining multiple points of view;

d. practice forms of civic discussion and participation consistent with the ideals of citizens in a democratic republic;

e. explain and analyze various forms of citizen action that influence public policy decisions;

f. identify and explain the roles of formal and informal political actors in influencing and shaping public policy and decision making;

g. analyze the influence of diverse forms of public opinion on the development of public policy and decision making;

h. analyze the effectiveness of selected public policies and citizen behaviors in realizing the stated ideals of a democratic republican form of government;

i. explain the relationship between policy statements and action plans used to address issues of public concern;

j. examine strategies designed to strengthen the "common good," which consider a range of options for citizen action.

High School

a. explain the origins and interpret the continuing influence of key ideals of the democratic republican form of government, such as individual human dignity, liberty, justice, equality, and the rule of law;

b. identify, analyze, interpret, and evaluate sources and examples of citizens' rights and responsibilities;

c. locate, access, analyze, organize, synthesize, evaluate, and apply information about selected public issues—identifying, describing, and evaluating multiple points of view;

d. practice forms of civic discussion and participation consistent with the ideals of citizens in a democratic republic;

e. analyze and evaluate the influence of various forms of citizen action on public policy;

f. analyze a variety of public policies and issues from the perspective of formal and informal political actors;

g. evaluate the effectiveness of public opinion in influencing and shaping public policy development and decision making;

h. evaluate the degree to which public policies and citizen behaviors reflect or foster the stated ideals of a democratic republican form of government;

i. construct a policy statement and an action plan to achieve one or more goals related to an issue of public concern;

j. participate in activities to strengthen the "common good," based upon careful evaluation of possible options for citizen action.

Early Childhood Professional Preparation Guidelines

1.0 CHILD DEVELOPMENT AND LEARNING

Programs prepare early childhood professionals who:

1.1 Use knowledge of how children develop and learn to provide opportunities that support the physical, social, emotional, language, cognitive, and aesthetic development of all young children from birth through age eight.

1.2 Use knowledge of how young children differ in their development and approaches to learning to support the development and learning of individual children.

    1.2.1 Demonstrate understanding of the conditions that affect children's development and learning, including risk factors, developmental variations, and developmental patterns of specific disabilities.

    1.2.2 Create and modify environments and experiences to meet the individual needs of all children, including children with disabilities, developmental delays, and special abilities.

1.3 Apply knowledge of cultural and linguistic diversity and the significance of socio-cultural and political contexts for development and learning, and recognize that children are best understood in the contexts of family, culture, and society.

    1.3.1 Demonstrate understanding of the interrelationships among culture, language, and thought and the function of the home language in the development of young children.

    1.3.2 Affirm and respect culturally and linguistically diverse children, support home language preservation, and promote anti-bias approaches through the creation of learning environments and experiences.

2.0 CURRICULUM DEVELOPMENT AND IMPLEMENTATION

Programs prepare early childhood professionals who:

2.1 Plan and implement developmentally appropriate curriculum and instructional practices based on knowledge of individual children, the community, and curriculum goals and content.

    2.1.1 Use and explain the rationale for developmentally appropriate methods that include play, small group projects, open-ended questioning, group discussion, problem solving, cooperative learning, and inquiry experiences to help young children develop intellectual curiosity, solve problems, and make decisions.

    2.1.2 Use a variety of strategies to encourage children's physical, social, emotional, aesthetic, and cognitive development.

    2.1.3 Demonstrate current knowledge of and ability to develop and implement meaningful, integrated learning experiences, using the central concepts and tools of inquiry in curriculum content areas including language and literacy, mathematics, science, health, safety, nutrition, social studies, art, music, drama, and movement.

    2.1.4 Develop and implement an integrated curriculum that focuses on children's needs and interests and takes into account culturally valued content and children's home experiences.

    2.1.5 Create, evaluate, and select developmentally appropriate materials, equipment, and environments.

2.1.6 Evaluate and demonstrate appropriate use of technology with young children, including assistive technologies for children with disabilities.

2.1.7 Develop and evaluate topics of study in terms of conceptual soundness, significance, and intellectual integrity.

2.1.8 Adapt strategies and environments to meet the specific needs of all children, including those with disabilities, developmental delays, or special abilities.

2.2 Use individual and group guidance and problem-solving techniques to develop positive and supportive relationships with children, to encourage positive social interaction among children, to promote positive strategies of conflict resolution, and to develop personal self-control, self-motivation, and self-esteem.

2.3 Incorporate knowledge and strategies from multiple disciplines (for example, health, social services) into the design of intervention strategies and integrate goals from Individual Education Plans (IEPs) and Individual Family Service Plans (IFSPSs) into daily activities and routines.

2.4 Establish and maintain physically and psychologically safe and healthy learning environments for children.

2.4.1 Demonstrate understanding of the influence of the physical setting, schedule, routines, and transitions on children and use these experiences to promote children's development and learning.

2.4.2 Demonstrate understanding of the developmental consequences of stress and trauma, protective factors and resilience, and the development of mental health, and the importance of supportive relationships.

2.4.3 Implement basic health, nutrition, and safety management practices for young children, including specific procedures for infants and toddlers and procedures regarding childhood illness and communicable diseases.

2.4.4 Use appropriate health appraisal procedures and recommend referral to appropriate community health and social services when necessary.

2.4.5 Recognize signs of emotional distress, child abuse, and neglect in young children and know responsibility and procedures for reporting known or suspected abuse or neglect to appropriate authorities.

3.0 FAMILY AND COMMUNITY RELATIONSHIPS

Programs prepare early childhood professionals who:

3.1 Establish and maintain positive, collaborative relationships with families.

3.1.1 Respect parents' choices and goals for children and communicate effectively with parents about curriculum and children's progress.

3.1.2 Involve families in assessing and planning for individual children, including children with disabilities, developmental delays, or special abilities.

3.1.3 Support parents in making decisions related to their child's development and parenting.

3.2 Demonstrate sensitivity to differences in family structures and social and cultural backgrounds.

3.3 Apply family systems theory, knowledge of the dynamics, roles, and relationships within families and communities.

3.4 Link families with a range of family-oriented services based on identified resources, priorities, and concerns.

3.5 Communicate effectively with other professionals concerned with children and with agencies in the larger community to support children's development, learning, and well being.

4.0 ASSESSMENT AND EVALUATION

Programs prepare early childhood professionals who:

4.1 Use informal and formal assessment strategies to plan and individualize curriculum and teaching practices.

    4.1.1 Observe, record, and assess young children's development and learning and engage children in self-assessment for the purpose of planning appropriate programs, environments, and interactions, and adapting for individual differences.

    4.1.2 Develop and use authentic, performance-based assessments of children's learning to assist in planning and to communicate with children and parents.

    4.1.3 Participate and assist other professionals in conducting family-centered assessments.

    4.1.4 Select, evaluate, and interpret formal, standardized assessment instruments and information used in the assessment of children, and integrate authentic classroom assessment data with formal assessment information.

    4.1.5 Communicate assessment results and integrate assessment results from others as an active participant in the development and implementation of IEP and IFSP goals for children with special developmental and learning needs.

4.2 Develop and use formative and summative program evaluation to ensure comprehensive quality of the total environment for children, families, and the community.

5.0 PROFESSIONALISM

Programs prepare early childhood professionals who:

5.1 Reflect on their practices, articulate a philosophy and rationale for decisions, continually self-assess and evaluate the effects of their choices and actions on others (young children, parents, and other professionals) as a basis for program planning and modification, and continuing professional development.

5.2 Demonstrate an understanding of conditions of children, families, and professionals; current issues and trends; legal issues; and legislation and other public policies affecting children, families, and programs for young children and the early childhood profession.

5.3 Demonstrate an understanding of the early childhood profession, its multiple historical, philosophical, and social foundations, and how these foundations influence current thought and practice.

5.4 Demonstrate awareness of and commitment to the profession's code of ethical conduct.

5.5 Actively seek out opportunities to grow professionally by locating and using appropriate professional literature, organizations, resources, and experiences to inform and improve practice.

5.6 Establish and maintain positive, collaborative relationships with colleagues, other professionals and families, and work effectively as a member of a professional team.

5.7 Serve as advocates on behalf of young children and their families, improved quality of programs and services for young children, and enhanced professional status and working conditions for early childhood educators.

5.8 Demonstrate an understanding of basic principles of administration, organization, and operation of early childhood programs, including supervision of staff and volunteers and program evaluation.

6.0 FIELD EXPERIENCES

Programs prepare early childhood professionals who:

6.1 Observe and participate under supervision of qualified professionals in a variety of settings in which young children, from birth through age eight, are served (such as public and private; centers, schools, and community agencies).

6.2 Work effectively over time with children of diverse ages (infants, toddlers, pre-schoolers, or primary school-age), with children with diverse abilities, with children reflecting culturally and linguistically diverse family systems.

6.3 Demonstrate ability to work effectively during full-time (totally at least 300 clock hours) supervised student teaching and/or practica experiences in at least two different settings, serving children of two different age groups (infant/toddler, preprimary, or primary age) and with varying abilities.

6.4 Analyze and evaluate field experience, including supervised experience in working with parents, and supervised experience in working with interdisciplinary teams of professionals.

Appendix C
Sample Rubrics

- Lesson Presentation

- Multimedia Presentation or Project

- Written Reflection

- Focus on Technology (Holistic Format)

- Nonspecific Content Lesson Plan
  (Specific Criteria Format)

- Assessment of Technology Integration in
  a Lesson

- Lesson Plan Integrating Technology

- Cooperation/Responsibility

- Mini-Lesson

Rubric: Lesson Presentation

The assessment rubric below is one in which a generic scoring scale is applied to the specific criteria for the lesson. In this model of assessment, teacher candidates are familiar with the scoring statements as they are applied to multiple assignments and settings. The criteria for the specific project are created to guide candidates in the development of their project and specify the important elements of the project.

CRITERIA	PERFORMANCE INDICATORS
Lesson Plan	The lesson plan is in the approved format following the tenets of a well-designed lesson. The lesson is presented in a manner appropriate to the age level of the students, contains vocabulary development techniques to enhance the comprehension by second language learners, and attends to the unique requirements of special needs students.
Technology	The lesson uses appropriate electronic media to enhance the understanding of the diverse perspectives presented. The technology is embedded in the lesson as a natural part of the instruction.
Resources	Multiple resources were accessed and are appropriately cited. Resources include information obtained from the Internet. Primary source information is included.
Questioning	The lesson incorporates high-level questioning strategies that cause students to think about the diverse perspectives on the event presented. Questions challenge students to confront their perceptions of people different from themselves and genuinely consider alternative points of view.
Unit Context	The lesson is preceded by a synopsis of the unit. The brief synopsis describes a unit of instruction that is in alignment with the curriculum for the target grade level. The lesson is an appropriate introduction to the unit described.
Oral Presentation	The oral presentation is well organized, interesting, informative, and stays within the time frame requirements. All members of the group participate in the oral presentation. The group interacts with the class and is able to respond knowledgeably to questions.
Web Posting	The lesson plan and supporting material including resource citations are posted on the class Web site in a timely manner and in a format that is accessible to classmates. Any suggested modifications have been made prior to posting. The posting is free of grammatical errors and is of high quality to be shared with anyone who accesses the Web site.
Reflection	Reflection follows general guidelines on reflections. All three questions have been answered in an insightful and thoughtful way. Reflection includes personal reactions that show growth in understanding the need to expose elementary students to diverse perspectives on historical events. The reflection shows a positive disposition toward including teaching that attends to diverse perspectives.

Scoring Scale

5	The work exceeds all expectations and shows an exceptionally high level of creativity, and sophisticated application of knowledge and skills. It contains elements that were not considered or discussed in class, thus setting it in a category all of its own. (Very rarely given score.)
4	The work exceeds the standard and shows very strong applications of the knowledge and skills.
3	Work meets the standard and demonstrates appropriate application of knowledge and skills. It contains minor errors that do not diminish the quality.
2	The work does not quite meet the standard. It shows inconsistent application of knowledge and skills. The minor errors are significant enough to detract from the overall quality. Additional work is required.
1	The work does not meet the standard and shows limited understanding of the knowledge and skills. The work lacks depth and/or is incomplete with significant errors and/or omissions.
0	No work is presented.

Rubric: Multimedia Presentation or Project

This rubric is adapted from the Multimedia Mania 2000 Rubric. Multimedia Mania is an award sponsored by ISTE's HyperSIG (**www.iste.org/hypersig/**), SAS inSchool (**www.SASinSchool.com**), and North Carolina State University (**www.ncsu.edu**). The original rubric may be downloaded from **www.ncsu.edu/midlink/mmania.how.html**.

CRITERIA	BEGINNER	NOVICE	INTERMEDIATE	EXPERT
Curriculum Alignment	Relationship to target curriculum is unclear; users or audience is likely to be confused.	Some evidence of connection to target curriculum; a few references to facts with some supporting documentation. Users or audience may learn something from experience.	Adequate evidence of connection to target curriculum; clear references to facts and properly documented resources. Users or audience can learn from experience.	Clear evidence of connection to target curriculum, frequent reference to facts, concepts, and properly documented resources. Users or audience is likely to learn from experiences.
Organization of Content	No logical sequence of information; menus and/or paths to information are not evident.	Some logical sequence of information, but menus or paths are confusing or flawed.	Logical sequence of information is evident; menus and/or paths to additional information are clear.	Logical, intuitive sequence of information is clear; menus and/or paths to all information are clear and direct.
Subject Matter Knowledge	Subject matter knowledge is not evident. Information is confusing, incorrect, or flawed.	Some subject matter knowledge is evident. Some information is confusing, incorrect, or flawed.	Subject matter knowledge is evident in much of the presentation/project. Information is clear, appropriate, and correct.	Subject matter knowledge is evident throughout (more than required). All information is clear, appropriate, and correct.
Copyright and Documentation	Sources have not been cited properly and permissions have not been obtained.	Some sources have not been cited and all permissions have not been obtained.	Most sources are properly cited according to MLA style. Permissions to use any graphics from commercial Web pages or other sources have been received, saved, and printed for future reference.	All sources are properly cited according to MLA style. Permissions to use any graphics from commercial Web pages or other sources have been received, printed, and saved for future reference.
Graphical Design	Exaggerated emphasis on graphics and special effects weakens the message and interferes with the communication of content and ideas.	Graphical and multimedia elements accompany content but there is little evidence of mutual reinforcement. No attention to visual design. There is some tendency toward random use of graphical elements.	Design elements and content combine effectively to deliver a high-impact message with the graphics and the words reinforcing each other.	The combination of multimedia elements with words and ideas takes communication and persuasion to a very high level, superior to what could be accomplished alone.
Enhancements	No video, audio, or 3-D enhancements are present or use of these tools is inappropriate.	Limited video, audio, or 3-D enhancements are present. In most instances, use of these tools is appropriate.	Some video, audio, or 3-D enhancements are used appropriately to entice users/audience to learn and to enrich the experience. In some cases, clips are too long or too short to be meaningful.	Appropriate amounts of video, audio, or 3-D enhancements are used effectively to entice users/audience and to enrich the experience. Clips are long enough to convey meaning without being too lengthy.
Presentation	Difficult to maintain interest of audience. Presenters read from screens.	Presenters read from the screens, interacted with audience a few times on low level points.	Presenters referred to multimedia presentation as a tool to clarify or amplify learning, using it as a tool to provide experiences that the live presentation could not do otherwise. The presenters engaged with the audience to ensure understanding.	Presenters used multimedia presentation as a tool for learning subject matter, engaged with the audience in an interesting, high energy, and yet thoughtful way, causing the learners to think critically and check their own understanding of the content.

Rubric: Written Reflection

This rubric is used for general reflections on a teaching or learning experience related to teaching. When reflections are targeted, as in using a writing prompt, additional criteria should be added to the assessment to address the objective of the writing prompt.

RATING	DESCRIPTION
3	Clear evidence that the candidate can critically assess his or her own beliefs and actions and has considered salient issues in examining classroom practices.
2	Some evidence that the candidate is able to assess the educational implications and consequences of teaching decisions and actions.
1	Focus is on personal feelings about the experience. Little questioning of teaching objectives.

Rubric: Focus on Technology (Holistic Format)

This rubric is used as a holistic assessment of a lesson created by a teacher candidate. This rubric is designed for lessons that target the use of technology within the context of teaching content area standards. The criteria used in the rubric are in alignment with fostering the development of new learning environments as opposed to traditional teaching methods. Additional phrases may be added to the description to fit the given situation.

LEVELS OF PERFORMANCE			
NOVICE 1	DEVELOPING 2	APPROACHING 3	PROFICIENT 4
• Student-centered project-based learning with no information resources	• Student-centered project-based learning with few information resources	• Student-centered authentic project-based learning with some information resources	• Student-centered authentic project-based learning with effective use of information resources
• No opportunity is available for collaborative learning allowing students to develop teamwork, communication, and problem-solving skills	• Collaborative learning allows only a few students to develop teamwork, communication, and problem-solving skills	• Collaborative learning allows some students to develop teamwork, communication, and problem-solving skills	• Collaborative learning allows all students to develop teamwork, communication, problem-solving skills, and reflection
• Lack of higher-order critical thinking with no access to multimedia content	• Minimal higher-order critical thinking evident with limited access to multimedia content	• Somewhat improves higher-order critical thinking with some access to multimedia content	• Improves higher-order critical thinking with equal and appropriate access to multimedia content
• No evidence of communication with experts, community members and educators	• Minimal communication with experts, community members, and educators	• Embedded communication with experts, community members, and educators.	• Communication for all students with experts, community members, and educators as appropriate
• Lesson not developed and does not support the content knowledge and technology standards	• Lesson partially developed and does not support the content knowledge and technology standards	• Lesson somewhat developed and supports the content knowledge and technology standards	• Lesson fully developed and supports the content knowledge, standards performance indicators, and technology
• No use of technology for measurement and accountability	• Minimal use of technology for measurement and accountability	• Experimenting with technology for measurement and accountability	• Use of technology for measurement and accountability

Rubric: Nonspecific Content Lesson Plan (Specific Criteria Format)

This rubric is designed to be used with lesson plans developed in the context of meeting content area standards. The descriptions of the levels of performance can be applied across disciplines or modified to fit a specific situation.

CRITERIA	LEVELS OF PERFORMANCE			
	DEVELOPING 1	PROMISING 2	ACCEPTABLE 3	ACCOMPLISHED 4
Type of Activities	Uses only one type of activity that is questionable in its appropriateness for the developmental level of the students.	Uses some developmentally appropriate activities that are a mixture of hands on and technology based.	Uses mostly activities that are developmentally appropriate and are a mixture of hands on and technology based.	Uses developmentally appropriate activities that are both hands on and technology based.
Identification of Standards	Lists only one set of standards.	Lists both sets of standards but is incomplete.	Lists both sets of standards with only minor omissions or over-statements.	Lists appropriate standards from NCTM and NETS for students in developing knowledge and skills.
Uses of Technology	Uses technology but does not enrich conceptual understanding of student.	Uses technology to communicate knowledge of mathematical concepts "discovered" in the lesson activities, but method of use is not necessarily engaging for students.	Uses generally appropriate technology that enhances concept development. Effectively utilizes tool developed.	Uses developmentally appropriate technology that enhances concept development. Effectively utilizes tool developed as an integral part of the lesson.
Reflection	Reflection does not include all elements: strength, weaknesses, modifications, and evaluation of technologies employed.	Reflection includes a surface level analysis of the strengths and weaknesses of the lesson taught, explanation of what should be done differently and why, and assessment of the technologies used.	Reflection includes a reasonable analysis of the strengths and weaknesses of the lesson, explanations of what should be done differently and why, and an assessment of the technologies used.	Reflection includes a thoughtful analysis of the strengths and weaknesses of the lesson, clear explanations of what should be done differently and why, and a critical assessment of the technologies used.

Rubric: Assessment of Technology Integration in a Lesson

CRITERIA	LEVELS OF PERFORMANCE		
	APPROACHING STAGE	NOVICE STAGE	DISTINGUISHED STAGE
Planning	Plans and designs the management of learning environment experiences.	Plans and designs the management of learning environment experiences supported by appropriate technology resources.	Plans and designs the management of collaborative learning environment experiences supported by appropriate technology resources.
Implementation	Curriculum plan includes methods and strategies that address content standards and student technology standards.	Curriculum plan includes methods and strategies that address content standards and student technology standards, maximizing use of technology resources.	Curriculum plan includes methods and strategies that address content standards and student technology standards, maximizing collaborative use of technology resources and tools.
Assessment	Use of technology provides no evidence that students use a variety of assessment and evaluation strategies to assess acquisition of knowledge.	Use of technology provides evidence that students use a variety of assessment and evaluation strategies to assess acquisition of knowledge.	Use of technology provides evidence that students use a variety of assessment and evaluation strategies to assess acquisition of knowledge to produce and publish.
Productivity	Technology is used to enhance communication, collaboration, and productivity.	Technology is used to enhance communication, collaboration, productivity, and presentation skills.	Technology is used to enhance communication, collaboration, productivity, presentation skills, and reflection of professional practice development.

Rubric: Lesson Plan Integrating Technology

RATING	CRITERIA
1	The lesson does not provide for any technology-connected activities or technology is mentioned only superficially.
2	Technology-connected learning activities are contrived or limited to enrichment or extension activities.
3	Technology is integrated into the lesson to improve the quality of student work and/or presentation.
4	A variety of technology is integrated appropriately throughout the lesson in a manner that enhances the effectiveness of the lesson and the learning of the student.

Modified from www.lcet.doe.state.la.us/connections.

Rubric: Cooperation/Responsibility

CRITERIA	LEVELS OF PERFORMANCE			
	0	1	2	3
Fulfill Team Role's Duties	Does not perform any duties of assigned team role	Performs very few of the duties	Performs nearly all duties	Performs nearly all duties of assigned team role
Shares Equally	Always relies on others to do the work	Rarely does the assigned work—often needs reminding	Usually does the assigned work—rarely needs reminding	Always does the assigned work without having to be reminded

Modified from http://projects.edtech.sandi.net/morse/oceanhealth/rubrics/collrubric.html.

Rubric: Mini-Lesson

CRITERIA	LEVELS OF PERFORMANCE		
	NEEDS IMPROVEMENT	ACCEPTABLE	TARGET
Objectives	Vague in focus	Clearly stated	Clearly stated and aligned with state and national standards
Teaching Strategies	Teaching strategies weak in focus, appropriateness, and structure	Cloze procedure and choral reading method structured with clear connection to lesson purpose	Excellent use of cloze technique, choral reading, sequenced well with subject integration
Technology Integration	No, ineffective, or inappropriate use of technology	Appropriate use of technology	Presentation and materials visually motivating with technology infused throughout lesson in an appropriate and effective manner
Assessment	Performance-based project did not correlate to objectives	Performance-based project was similar to objectives	Performance-based project clearly met all objectives
Reflection (See reflection rubric above.)			

Appendix D

Sample Software and Web Site Evaluation Forms

- Educational Software Evaluation Form

  Using the Educational Software
  Evaluation Form

- Educational Web Sites You Discover

- Educational Web Sites Recommended
  by Others

- Rubric: Evaluating Web Resources for
  Reliability and Credibility

Educational Software Evaluation Form

Title: _____

Publisher: _____

Copyright: _____ Version: _____

Platform/version: __ Mac   __ Windows

Media: __ Diskette   __ CD-ROM   __ DVD

Also Needs: __ Internet   __ Microphone   __ Other _____

Cost: _____

Classroom

SUBJECT AREAS—*Please circle all that apply*

ASSESS	IT	MC	SW
AT	IN	MM	SC
CC	KB	PS	SS
EC	LA	PRO DEV	SN
HPER	MA	RL	TE
WL			

Topic: _____

GRADES/ABILITY LEVELS—*Circle the range*

PK K 1 2 3 4 5 6 7 8 9 10 11 12

_____Teacher also   _____Teacher only

READABILITY LEVEL—*Circle one*

Easier	Consistent with grade	More difficult

STUDENT GROUPING

_____Individuals   _____Groups of 3 or 4

_____Pairs   _____Whole group

Teacher Support

DOCUMENTATION: __Binder __Booklet __Included on media __on Internet

INSTRUCTION MANUAL HAS:

____Objectives   ____Lesson plans   ____Sample screens

____Resource information   ____Reproducible student pages

____Student booklets

____Other _____

Content

Material is presented impartially and without bias or distortion: ___Yes ___No

Compared to the standards from: _____

Meets these standards: (Mark only one)

___Inadequately   ___Minimally   ___Appropriately   ___Exceeds Them

DESCRIBE THE CONTENT:

Content is current.	__No	__Some	__Mostly	__Yes
Content is thorough.	__No	__Some	__Mostly	__Yes
Content is age appropriate.	__No	__Some	__Mostly	__Yes
Content is reliable.	__No	__Some	__Mostly	__Yes
Content is clear.	__No	__Some	__Mostly	__Yes
Content is fully referenced.	__No	__Some	__Mostly	__Yes

Assessment

Has pretest.	__Yes	__No
Has posttest.	__Yes	__No
Has record keeping by student.	__Yes	__No
Has record keeping by group.	__Yes	__No
Has assessment guidelines.	__Yes	__No

PROVIDES

Student journal	__Yes __No
E-mail option	__Yes __No
Spreadsheet	__Yes __No
Calculator	__Yes __No
Print options	__Yes __No
Other	_____

Technical Quality

Installation and Setup:	__Difficult	__Time consuming	__Simple
Sound is: __Essential	__High quality	__Supplemental	
Videos: __Run jerkily	__Run smoothly	__Are essential	__Not essential

FINAL REPORT CARD

Teacher support	A	B	C	D	F
Content	A	B	C	D	F
Assessment	A	B	C	D	F
Technical quality	A	B	C	D	F
Instructional design	A	B	C	D	F

Reviewer's Name: _____

Contact Information: _____

_____

YOUR OVERALL RATING _____

Dated: _____

Instructional Design

CIRCLE THE MODES THAT APPLY

AC   AU   BL   CA   CP   DE   DP   EG   EX   GP   IN   LEP   MM   PS   RF   SI   TE   TL   TU

PROMOTES

___ Creativity   ___ Collaboration   ___ Discovery
___ Higher-order thinking   ___ Problem solving   ___ Memorization

MOTIVATIONAL

___ Student controls pacing   ___Stimulates curiosity   ___Challenging   ___Real-world connections

STRENGTHS:

WEAKNESSES:

DESCRIBE THE LEARNING STRATEGY INCORPORATED IN THE DESIGN: (Either here or on another page)

RECOMMENDATIONS:

Using the Educational Software Evaluation Form

The goal of this form is to provide teachers with an evaluation guide that focuses on the educational use of a technology resource. This form can be used for software, an Internet site, a laserdisc, or any other technology-based resource to be used with students.

The abbreviations and classifications used throughout the form are consistent with those in the 2002 Educational Software Preview Guide published by ISTE.

This form is not the final word on evaluation. You are encouraged to modify the criteria so they address your school's or district's needs. For example, cost is often crucial in determining whether a resource can be recommended for purchase. So, in addition to a rating, you might add another category— "Recommend for Purchase"—with grades or just a "yes/no" option.

USING THE FORM

1. Schedule enough time to examine materials, install any programs, explore the level of interactivity, and set up any management components.

2. Write your name and contact information in the lower left of the form. This information is only for the person collecting the information—someone who may need to clarify your comments— not for general distribution. If this review is to be viewed in a public place, then the reviewer box could contain only an identification code.

3. Use the publisher's materials to supply the publisher, copyright, version, and cost. You may also want to list the company's Web site. Circle all the hardware platforms that apply to the resource you are evaluating. List further needs under "Also needs," for example, "at least 8 MB of RAM."

4. Look through the documentation and note what is contained under the section titled "Teacher Support." Instead of checking any of the items listed there, you may want to insert a qualifier or quantifier to indicate the quality of support material in the documentation. Many publishers now include manuals on CD-ROM or at their Internet sites; record that information, too. If the publisher provides documentation only in an electronic form, then reduce the grade for teacher support. The documentation should have all the information needed to make any necessary installations.

5. You might want to use pencil to fill in the "Classroom" section. Publishers may provide information that accurately describes their materials in relation to subject area, topic, grade level, readability, and special-needs provisions.

If you examine the material and still feel a different set of selections is more appropriate, then use your ink pen. The subjects are:

ASSESS   Assessment (Includes tests and testing)

AT   Fine Arts, such as music, performing arts, and visual arts

CC   Cross Curricular

EC   Early Childhood

HPER   Health/Physical Education/Recreation

IT   Instructional Tools

IN   Internet/World Wide Web

KB   Keyboarding

LA   Language Arts, English literature, and appropriate tools

MA   Mathematics; filling in the specific area will narrow down this topic

MC	Multicultural
MM	Multimedia Production
PS	Problem Solving/Logic
PRO DEV	Professional Development
RL	Reference Library
SW	School to Work; skills taught in school that directly translate into jobs
SC	Science; filling in the specific topic will narrow down this subject
SS	Social Studies; filling in the specific topic will narrow down this subject
SN	Special Needs
TE	Tests and Testing
WL	World Languages (includes foreign language, American sign language, and ESL)

The grades are the standard grade levels; PK stands for prekindergarten.

6. Start using the technology resource. Examine it from the student's point of view, making mistakes and hitting wrong keys. Examine it from a teacher's perspective, and compare what it offers with what is needed in the classroom. Examine it as a supportive colleague and identify how else the resource might be used (e.g., which other grades, topics, etc.).

7. You might want to begin with the "Technical Quality" section. This section is quite short. If the program is not accessible, installable, or operational, then the evaluation is over. Be fair. If the resource did not perform well because of limiting hardware, then note that exception. If you used at least the minimum resources recommended by the publisher and the program still did not perform well, then grade accordingly. In your grading on technical quality, indicate the way it leaves your equipment when you're done. Does your computer monitor suddenly show a new color or a different resolution? Does the resource alter any settings without returning them to normal?

8. Under "Content," list the objective set of guidelines you are using for comparison. If you are using a curriculum guide that is in print, please state that information. For example, when examining a math program you might be comparing the content to the NCTM Standards or your state framework. List both and how well the software meets each.

9. Under "Assessment," answer the questions: Did the resource provide guidelines or rubrics for assessing student success? Are there pretests and posttests? Does the resource have built-in features for students to express what they learn, such as a presentation component? If the software allows students to print a report that could be used for assessment in a student portfolio, include that information here.

10. The very first entry under the "Instructional Design" section is the most cryptic on the form. Mode describes how the student uses the resource.

AC	Accessibility: The software was written to provide access for students with special needs. For example, it might provide a connection to an alternative input device.
AU	Authoring System: These use a code of commands that enables a nonexpert to write interactive programs. This mode also includes shell programs in which teachers insert their own problems or data.
BL	Bilingual: Verbal and/or written information or directions are available in more than one language.
CA	Creative Activity: Programs with this designation have some structure or activity that encourages students to exercise imagination and creativity.

CP   Computer Programming: This denotes a computer language or software-based activity for teaching computer science or computer literacy classes.

DE   Demonstration and Presentation: This is software used to present some aspect of the curriculum or used to create a presentation of material, for example, to create slides using a slideshow option.

DP   Drill and Practice: These programs offer students unlimited practice on concepts they presumably have already learned. A good drill and practice program provides feedback to students, explains how to get the correct answer, and contains a management system to keep track of student progress.

EG   Educational Game: Usually these introduce drill and practice in a game format with a winner or scoring system.

EX   Exploration: Students can maneuver through a predesigned environment, testing and trying various components of the environment.

GP   Guided Practice: These offer students hints, assistance, and even reteaching as they practice a concept.

IN   Internet: The program directly connects to the Internet or World Wide Web. Some programs function fully without currently being connected to the Internet but can be connected for additional resources or interaction.

LEP   Limited English Proficiency: This is software that can be used by students who have limited English-speaking skills.

MM   Multimedia: This software facilitates the development of multimedia presentations.

PS   Problem Solving: These require student strategy and input. Most simulations (SI) and educational games (EG) require some problem solving on the students' part but may not have PS in their mode listing.

RF   Reference: These include electronic forms of traditional references, such as dictionaries, thesauri, and encyclopedias, as well as extensive references on particular subjects.

SI   Simulation: These programs create a world on the screen where realistic conditions apply and students can see cause and effect, test hypotheses, and fix variables one by one.

TE   Testing: Program tests students on subjects already taught, records their scores, and provides the correct answer.

TL   Tool: These include word processing, desktop publishing, database management, spreadsheets, graphics, and telecommunications programs, and any software that students use to perform a task.

TU   Tutorial: The computer presents new concepts and skills through interactive text, illustrations, descriptions, questions, and problems.

11. Under the list of items the resource promotes, add your own criteria. Or change the beginning term from promotes to provides and fill in your descriptors, such as remediation, practice, reinforcement, new information, application, and so on.

12. Identify all of the four classic "Motivational" features that apply to this resource.

13. Complete the "Strengths" and "Weaknesses" sections.

14. Complete the section that begins "Describe the learning strategy incorporated in the design" with a description of the resource in educational terms.

15. Complete your recommendation. Publishers tend to lump everyone under the word "user" when describing how a resource can be used in the classroom. Please use educational terms; specify if you are referring to students, teachers, or a group of students, for instance.

16. After all of the sections have been filled in and additional comments supplied, grade the resource. The final rating should not be an average of the grades but a combined grade based on both the scores and the importance of the criteria. For examples, if a resource scores an F on technical quality, then even the best instructional design may not be deliverable to the student, thus the overall rating of F. Or a resource might be excellent in every category but based on flawed content or outdated premises, thus rendering it useless in the classroom.

17. Now for the acid test of both the resource and the report. Take both into the classroom. Use the technology resource with students and modify the report based on your observations and interviews with students.

Educational Web Sites You Discover

Use this form to record complete information on educational Web sites you discover as you explore the World Wide Web. The information can be used to help you evaluate the site's usefulness in terms of your own particular needs.

Site Name: _____ Site Address/URL: _____

Brief Description: _____

_____

Approximate time necessary to access and download desired information:

CHECK ALL THE CATEGORIES THAT DESCRIBE THE SITE:

❏ Student Reference   ❏ Question/Answer   ❏ Newsgroup

❏ Data Source   ❏ Access to an Expert   ❏ Professional Information

❏ Student Projects   ❏ Interactive   ❏ Other _____

❏ Connections to Other Projects   ❏ Teacher Reference

EDUCATIONAL SETTING—MARK ALL THAT APPLY: K   1   2   3   4   5   6   7   8   9   10   11   12   T

❏ Individual Students   ❏ Downloadable Content   ❏ Completely Interactive

❏ Student Groups   ❏ Interactive Time Necessary

SUBJECT AREAS—CHECK ALL THAT APPLY:

❏ Language Arts   ❏ Social Studies   ❏ Science

❏ Mathematics   ❏ Arts   ❏ Foreign Language

❏ Careers   ❏ Business   ❏ Cross-Curricular

RATE THE SITE PERFORMANCE FOR EACH CRITERION LISTED

	Exemplary	Adequate	Unacceptable
CONTENT			
1. Is it correct, accurate?	❏	❏	❏
2. Is it from an authoritative source?	❏	❏	❏
3. Is it free from stereotypes and bias?	❏	❏	❏
4. Is this the best medium for this information?	❏	❏	❏
5. Do the images enhance the content?	❏	❏	❏
EDUCATIONAL VALUE			
1. Is the information useful?	❏	❏	❏
2. Is the information readable by students?	❏	❏	❏
3. Is the information available elsewhere?	❏	❏	❏
4. Can students collaborate with other sites?	❏	❏	❏
5. Can teachers share results?	❏	❏	❏
6. Does the site respond to student questions?	❏	❏	❏
TECHNICAL QUALITY			
1. Does the site work the way it is intended to work?	❏	❏	❏
2. Are all the links current?	❏	❏	❏
3. Is the home page concise and quick to view?	❏	❏	❏
4. Are lengthy pictures files saved for later pages?	❏	❏	❏
5. Is the menu clear, informative, and current?	❏	❏	❏
6. Is the navigation for the site obvious?	❏	❏	❏
OVERALL RATING	❏	❏	❏

Educational Web Sites Recommended by Others

Use this form to record and supplement information on educational Web sites recommended to you by others.

Site Name: _____ Site Address/URL: _____

Brief Description: _____

_____

This site was recommended by: _____

For: _____

I COULD USE THIS SITE FOR THE FOLLOWING:
- ❏ Reference source for my students (appropriate reading level and content)
- ❏ Source of up-to-date data for analysis by my students
- ❏ Source of project(s) for my classes to join
- ❏ Source of connections to other projects at other sites
- ❏ Question/answer site where students can have their questions answered
- ❏ Ask-an-Expert sessions (special sessions to interact with a writer or other expert)
- ❏ Interactive sessions (students interact with the site's learning activity while online)
- ❏ Reference for myself (content for my subject area, lesson plans, etc.)
- ❏ Newsgroup site where I can share and get information
- ❏ Professional information site (educational research or other relevant material)
- ❏ Other: _____

EDUCATIONAL SETTING—MARK ALL THAT APPLY: K   1   2   3   4   5   6   7   8   9   10   11   12   T
- ❏ Individual Students
- ❏ Student Groups
- ❏ Downloadable Content
- ❏ Interactive Time Necessary
- ❏ Completely Interactive

SUBJECT AREAS—CHECK ALL THAT APPLY:
- ❏ Language Arts
- ❏ Mathematics
- ❏ Careers
- ❏ Social Studies
- ❏ Arts
- ❏ Business
- ❏ Science
- ❏ Foreign Language
- ❏ Cross-Curricular

RATE THE SITE PERFORMANCE FOR EACH CRITERION LISTED.

	Exemplary	Adequate	Unacceptable
CONTENT			
Does the content meet my needs?	❏	❏	❏
EDUCATIONAL VALUE			
Can students collaborate with other sites?	❏	❏	❏
Can teachers share results?	❏	❏	❏
Does the site respond to student questions?	❏	❏	❏
TECHNICAL QUALITY			
Is the site easy for my students to navigate?	❏	❏	❏
OVERALL RATING	❏	❏	❏

Rubric: Evaluating Web Resources for Reliability and Credibility

CRITERIA	NO INFORMATION	SOME INFORMATION	RICH AND RELEVANT INFORMATION
1. Determine the author's expertise on the topic.			Information includes the author's occupation, experience, educational background, and reputation among others in the field.
2. Learn more about the site where the page appears.			Information includes who supports the Web site (an individual's page, an educational site, a commercial site, an organization—the mission of the group) and contact information.
3. Check out the links from the author's page to other pages.			These facts/pictures/videos/ audio can be substantiated at other sites.
4. Find out which Web pages have links pointing to the author's page or to the sponsoring organization's site.			Information from sites that link to the author's page is legitimate and provides documentation for the author's page.
5. Look for "pages on the Web" rather than "Web pages" about the author or organization.			Information is triangulated—available from more than one source, preferably three—from traditional sources such as newspapers, magazines, encyclopedias, or library resources on the Web.
6. Determine how recently the page was published or updated.			Information is included about the date of publication, its effect on the reliability and accuracy of the information.
7. Assess the accuracy of the information in the document.			Information is included about the accuracy of the content and its presentation (grammar, spelling, punctuation, layout).
8. Look for bias in the presentation of the Web page.			Information includes an examination of the language of the document (extreme, appeal, limited perspective).
9. Assess the evidence presented to support opinions or conclusions expressed in the document.			Information includes evidence to support opinions and conclusions expressed in the document (data driven, either qualitative or quantitative, references provided, author contact information).
10. Contact someone with expertise on the topic to comment on the information presented in the document.			Information is included about experts in the area contacted to confirm the authenticity of the site.

Adapted from Illinois Math and Science Academy Internet Toolkit. Available online: http://toolkit.imsa.edu/evaluate.

Appendix E
Resources

- Software Listed by Type

- Software Publishers

- National Educational
  Software Distributors

- Web Sites with Links

Software Listed by Type

These software categories or specific titles are listed in the lessons in Section 2. The titles are organized by type of software. The titles under each category do not necessarily represent all the software of that particular type. The category Instructional or Reference Software includes various educational packages that do not fall under the other categories.

Application (Productivity Software, Integrated Packages)
AppleWorks (formerly ClarisWorks), by Apple

ClarisWorks for Kids, by Apple

Kid Works Deluxe, by Knowledge Adventure

Microsoft Office, by Microsoft Corporation (This product is a suite of several products rather than an integrated package.)

Atlas
Children's Atlas of the United States, by Rand McNally Educational Publishing

Children's World Atlas, by Rand McNally Educational Publishing

My First Amazing World Explorer: School Version, by DK Publishing

New Millennium World Atlas Deluxe Education Edition, by Rand McNally Educational Publishing

SchoolHouse Rock: America Rock, by The Learning Company

See Multimedia Encyclopedias

Big Book (This software prints in poster or big book format.)
EasyBook Deluxe, by Sunburst Technology

SuperPrint Deluxe, by Scholastic

CAD or Home Design
3D Home, by Brøderbund

AutoCAD, by AutoDesk

Diorama Designer, by Tom Snyder Productions

Home Plan (shareware available at www.homeplansoftware.com/homeplan.htm)

Concept Mapping or Webbing
Inspiration, by Inspiration Software

Kidspiration, by Inspiration Software

Database
AppleWorks (formerly ClarisWorks), by Apple

ClarisWorks for Kids, by Apple

Filemaker Pro, by Filemaker, Inc.

Microsoft Access (part of Microsoft Office), by Microsoft Corporation

Tabletop (includes Tabletop Jr.), by The Learning Company

Desktop Publishing
Adobe PageMaker, by Adobe

EasyBook Deluxe, by Sunburst Technology

Print Shop, by Brøderbund

QuarkXpress, by Quark

Student Writing Center, by The Learning Company

Digital Art (Graphics, Drawing or Painting, Rendering or Illustration)
Adobe Illustrator, by Adobe

Adobe Photoshop, by Adobe

Kid Pix Studio Deluxe, by Brøderbund

Kid Works Deluxe, by Knowledge Adventure

SuperPrint Deluxe, by Scholastic

See Application

Document Sharing
Adobe Acrobat by Adobe (uses Adobe's Portable Document Format—PDF)

Drawing or Painting
See Digital Art

Electronic Publishing
See Desktop Publishing, Multimedia Authoring, and Presentation

E-mail Programs
Eudora Light 3.1 (available at http://eudora.qualcomm.com/eudoralight)

Eudora Pro, by Qualcomm

Outlook and Outlook Express, by Microsoft Corporation

Geometry (Geometry Representation)

Cabri Geometry, by Texas Instruments

Geometer's Sketchpad, by Key Curriculum Press

Shape Up, by Sunburst Technology

Graphics
See Digital Arts

Graphing
Graph Club, by Tom Snyder Productions
GraphPower, by Ventura
See Application

Image Manipulating (Photo Manipulation)
Adobe PhotoDeluxe, by Adobe
Adobe Photoshop, by Adobe
Picture It! 99 by Microsoft Corporation

Instructional or Reference
Community Construction Kit, by Tom Snyder Productions
Decisions, Decisions series, by Tom Snyder Productions
National Inspirer, by Tom Snyder Productions
Timeliner, by Tom Snyder Productions

Integrated Packages
See Application

Interactive Dictionaries
American Heritage Children's Dictionary, by Houghton Mifflin Interactive (Sunburst Technology)
Merriam-Webster's Collegiate Dictionary, by Merriam-Webster, Inc.
My First Incredible Amazing Dictionary, by DK Publishing

Internet/Web Browser
Microsoft Internet Explorer, by Microsoft Corporation
Netscape Communicator, by Netscape Communications

LEGO®
LEGO dacta Control Lab Starter Pack
Lego Mindstorms Robotics Invention System
Lego Mindstorms

Logo/Turtle Geometry
MicroWorlds, by Logo Computer Systems, Inc.

Mapping
MapMaker Toolkit, by Tom Snyder Productions
Neighborhood Map Machine, by Tom Snyder Productions
Rand McNally TripMaker Deluxe, by Rand McNally New Media

Multimedia-Authoring
HyperStudio, by Knowledge Adventure
Macromedia Director Academic, by Macromedia
mPower, by Tom Snyder
Stagecast Creator, by Stagecast Software, Inc.

Multimedia Encyclopedias
Children's Encyclopedia: School Version, by DK Publishing
Encyclopædia Britannica (www.eb.com)
Grolier Multimedia Encyclopedia, by Grolier Interactive
Microsoft Encarta Encyclopedia, by Microsoft Corporation
World Book (www.worldbook.com)

Photo Manipulation
See Image Manipulating

Presentation
AppleWorks (formerly ClarisWorks), by Apple
ClarisWorks for Kids, by Apple
Kid Pix Studio Deluxe, by Brøderbund
PowerPoint, by Microsoft Corporation (also part of Microsoft Office)
See Multimedia Authoring

Probeware Software
See the following companies for probeware and sensors:
Vernier Software & Technology
Texas Instruments

Productivity
See Application

Spreadsheet
AppleWorks (formerly ClarisWorks), by Apple
ClarisWorks for Kids, by Apple

Cruncher, by Knowledge Adventure

Microsoft Excel, by Microsoft Corporation (also part of Microsoft Office)

Video Production/Editing

Adobe Premiere, by Adobe

Avid Videoshop, by Strata

Imovie, by Apple

QuickTime, by Apple. (available at www.apple.com/quicktime)

QuickTime Virtual Reality (QTVR), by Apple (available at www.apple.com)

Web Page Creation

FrontPage, by Microsoft Corporation

Home Page (formerly Claris Home Page), by Filemaker, Inc.

Netscape Composer, by Netscape Communications (part of Netscape Communicator)

Web Workshop, by Sunburst Technology

Word Processing/Writing

AppleWorks (formerly ClarisWorks), by Apple

ClarisWorks for Kids, by Apple

Aspects (collaborative electronic writing program), by Group Logic

Kid Works Deluxe, by Knowledge Adventure

Microsoft Word, by Microsoft Corporation (also part of Microsoft Office)

Software Publishers

Many software companies have been purchased by other companies. Another company name in parentheses after the company name indicates the purchasing company. Many software distributors offer educational discounts. A separate listing of educational software distributors follows this list.

Adobe Systems, Inc.

Contact Douglas Stewart for reseller referrals

800.279.2795

Fax: 608.221.5217

www.adobe.com

Apple

1 Infinite Loop

Cupertino, CA 95014

408.996.1010 • 800.795.1000

www.apple.com

Apple Education

408.987.3022 • 800.747.7483

Fax: 408.987.7105

www.apple.com/education

Autodesk, Inc.

Order from an authorized distributor

www.autodesk.com

Brøderbund Software

Order through Riverdeep Interactive Learning

DK Publishing

95 Madison Ave.

New York, NY 10016

212.213.4800

Fax: 212.213.5240

www.dk.com

Encyclopædia Britannica

310 S. Michigan Ave.

Chicago, IL 60604

312.347.7309 • 800.747.8503

www.eb.com

FileMaker, Inc.

5201 Patrick Henry Dr.

Santa Clara, CA 95054

408.987.7000 • 800.725.2747

Fax: 408.987.7563

www.filemaker.com

Grolier Interactive

90 Sherman Turnpike

Danbury, CT 06816

203.797.3530 • 800.217.1495

Fax: 203.797.3835

www.gi.grolier.com

Group Logic
4350 North Fairfax Drive, Suite 900
Arlington, VA 22203
703.528.1555 • 800.476.8781
Fax: 703.528.3296

Houghton Mifflin Interactive
Order from Sunburst Technology

Inspiration Software, Inc.
7412 SW Beaverton Hillsdale Hwy., Suite 102
Portland, OR 97225-2167
503.297.3004 • 800.877.4292
Fax: 503.297.4676
www.inspiration.com

Key Curriculum Press, Inc.
1150 65th St.
Emeryville, CA 94608
510.548.2304 • 800.995.6284
Fax: 510.548.0755 or 800.541.2446
www.keypress.com

Knowledge Adventure
6060 Center Drive
Los Angeles, CA 90045
310.431.4000 • 800.545.7677
Fax: 310.410.2244
www.KnowledgeAdventure.com

Learning Company, The
500 Redwood Blvd.
Novato, CA 94947
415.382.4400 • 800.825.4420
Fax: 415.382.4419
www.learningcompanyschool.com

LEGO Dacta (Pitsco LEGO Data)
915 E. Jefferson
PO Box 1707
Pittsburg, KS 66762
800.362.4308
Fax: 888.534.6784
www.lego.com/dacta/

Logo Computer Systems, Inc.
PO Box 162
Highgate Springs, VT 05460
514.331.7090 • 800.321.5646
Fax: 514.331.1380
www.lcsi.ca

Macromedia
Order from a national educational software
distributor
www.macromedia.com

Merriam-Webster, Inc.
47 Federal St., PO Box 281
Springfield, MA 01102
413.734.3134 • 800.828.1880
Fax: 413.731.5979
www.m-w.com

Microsoft Corporation
Order from a national educational software
distributor
www.microsoft.com

Netscape Communications
Download from Web site
www.netscape.com

Qualcomm, Inc.
510.490.4750
800.238.3672
http://store.qualcomm.com

Quark, Inc.
1800 Grant St.
Denver, CO 80203
307.772.7100 • 800.676.4575
Fax: 307.772.7123
www.quark.com

Rand McNally New Media
8255 North Central Park Ave.
Skokie, IL 60076
847.329.6576 • 800.671.5006
Fax: 847.674.4496
www.randmcnally.com

Riverdeep Interactive Learning
125 Cambridge Park Drive
Cambridge, Massachusetts, 02140
800.564.2587
www.riverdeep.net

Scholastic, Inc.
2931 E. McCarty St.
Jefferson City, MO 65101
212.505.3130 • 800.724.6527
Fax: 573.635.5881
www.scholastic.com

Stagecast Software, Inc.
580 College Ave.
Palo Alto, CA 94306
650.354.0735
Fax: 650.354.0739
www.stagecast.com

Strata
Order from a national educational software
distributor

Sunburst Technology
101 Castleton St.
Pleasantville, NY 10570
914.747.3310 • 800.321.7511
Fax: 914.747.4109
www.sunburstonline.com

Tom Snyder Productions
80 Coolidge Hill Rd.
Watertown, MA 02472
617.926.6000 • 800.342.0236
Fax: 617.926.6222
www.teachtsp.com

Ventura Educational Systems
910 Ramona Ave., Suite E
Grover City, CA 93433
805.473.7380 • 800.336.1022
Fax: 805.473.7382
www.venturaES.com

Vernier Software & Technology
13979 SW Millikan Way
Beaverton, OR 97005-2886
503.277.2299 • 503.277.2440
www.vernier.com

World Book
525 West Monroe
Chicago, IL 60661
800.975.3250
Fax: 312.258.3950
www.worldbook.com

A Plus Computing
PO Box 26496

National Educational Software Distributors

Prescott Valley, AZ 86312
520.772.8282 • 800.878.1354
Fax: 520.772.5929
www.a-plus-computing.com

Academic Distributing, Inc.
12180-1 E. Turquoise Circle
Dewey, AZ 86327
520.772.7111 • 800.531.3227
Fax: 520.772.8855
www.academic-wholesale.com

Cambridge Development Laboratory, Inc.
86 West St.
Waltham, MA 02154
781.890.4640 • 800.637.0047
Fax: 781.890.2894
http://cdl-cambridge.com

Campus Technology
751 Miller Dr.
Leesburg, VA 20175
703.777.9110 • 800.543.8188
Fax: 703.777.3871
www.campustech.com

Educational Resources
1550 Executive Dr.
PO Box 1900
Elgin, IL 60121-1900
847.888.8300 • 800.624.2926
Fax: 847.888.8499
www.edresources.com

Educational Software Institute (ESI)
4213 South 94th St.
Omaha, NE 68127
402.592.3300 • 800.955.5570
Fax: 402.592.2017
www.edsoft.com

Laser Learning Technologies
120 Lakeside Ave., Suite 240
Seattle, WA 98122
206.322.3085 • 800.722.3505
Fax: 206.322.7421
www.llt.com

Learning Services
3895 E. 19th Ave.
PO Box 10636
Eugene, OR 97403
541.744.0883 • 800.877.9378
Fax: 541.744.2056
www.learnserv.com

Scantron Quality Computers
20200 Nine Mile Rd.
PO Box 349
St. Clair Shores, MI 48080
810.774.7200 • 800.777.3642
Fax: 800.947.1121
http://catalog.sqc.com

Web Sites with Links

Many Web sites were given as resources in the lessons in Section 2. Here are additional Web sites that link to valuable educational Web sites or offer lessons and projects that make use of technology. These sites evaluate educational Web sites, organize them by subject area, and provide information and links to the positively evaluated sites.

BLUE WEB'N
www.kn.pacbell.com/wired/bluewebn/

Busy Teacher's Web Site
www.ceismc.gatech.edu/busyT/

Education World—The Educator's Best Friend
www.education-world.com/

The Educator's Toolkit
www.eagle.ca/~malink/

Kathy Schrock's Guide for Educators
http:// school.discovery.com/schrockguide/

The Learning Space
By Ann McGlone
www.learningspace.org

Ron MacKinnon's Educational Bookmarks
http://juliet.stfx.ca/people/stu/x94emj/bookmark.html

Scholastic Network
www.teacher.scholastic.com/index.htm

Teacher/Pathfinder
http://teacherpathfinder.org/

The Teacher Resource Page
www.atlantic.net/~klesyk/

Web Sites and Resources for Teachers
By Vicki Sharp and Richard Sharp
www.csun.edu/~vceed009/

Appendix F
Glossary of Educational Terms

Glossary of Educational Terms

ACCEPTABLE USE POLICY (AUP)
The written agreement of a school or university that provides guidelines and/or specifies the permissible actions for students and faculty using the educational unit's local area and wide area networks.

ADAPTIVE/ASSISTIVE HARDWARE
Hardware (external and internal devices) to adapt the computer's capability for input, processing, and output for students of different needs (e.g., touch screen, voice-recognition devices).

AUTHORING TOOL
Software that allows an individual to develop or program an application to meet specific objectives (e.g., HyperStudio).

BROWSER
Tool used to access and manipulate information on the Web (e.g., Netscape Navigator, Internet Explorer).

BULLETIN BOARD SYSTEM (BBS)
A computer network with special software that allows users to post information and communications for a particular interest group.

CLASSROOM CLUSTER
Small groups of workstations or learners in a classroom setting.

COMPUTER-ASSISTED DRAFTING (CAD) SOFTWARE
Software designed to facilitate computer-generated drawings or schematics.

COMPUTING ENVIRONMENTS
Particular combinations of hardware and software that determine how a user works with a computer system. Single-user and networked computers are examples of computing environments, as are Windows and Macintosh operating systems and the machines they run on.

CONCEPT-MAPPING SOFTWARE
Software that can graphically represent the relationships among ideas (e.g., Inspiration).

CONSTRUCTIVISM
A theory and teaching strategy holding that learners actively acquire or "construct" new knowledge by relating new information to prior experience. It contrasts with strategies that rely primarily on passive reception of teacher-presented information.

DIGITAL ARCHIVE
Information stored in digital format.

DIGITAL OR ELECTRONIC PORTFOLIO
A digital or electronic archive of student work. The work may be digital to begin with or scanned into electronic form and can include digital video.

DIGITAL STORAGE SYSTEM
Information management system that holds information in digital format.

DRAWING SOFTWARE
A computer program that allows the user to simulate drawing. Image elements created with a draw program are stored as mathematical formulas, and each element can be changed or moved independently (e.g., Adobe Illustrator, Macromedia FreeHand).

E-COMMERCE (ELECTRONIC COMMERCE)
Commerce conducted through electronic transactions. May refer to online transactions between humans or accounting systems.

EDUCATIONAL COMPUTING AND TECHNOLOGY
Educational computing and technology encompasses knowledge about and use of computers and related technologies in (1) delivery, development, prescription, and assessment of instruction; (2) effective uses of computers as an aid to problem solving; (3) school and classroom administration; (4) educational research; (5) electronic information access and exchange; (6) personal and professional productivity; and (7) computer science education.

EDUCATIONAL COMPUTING AND TECHNOLOGY LITERACY
This area includes (1) issues of technology use in society; (2) fundamental vocabulary and operations of computer/technology-based systems; (3) use of tool applications for personal, academic, and instructional productivity; and (4) use of the computer as a tool for problem solving.

ELECTRONIC JOURNAL
Journal created electronically, as with word-processing software, and stored in digital format.

ELECTRONIC OR DIGITAL PORTFOLIO
A digital or electronic archive of student work. The work may be digital to begin with or scanned into electronic form and can include digital video.

ELECTRONIC (REFERENCE) RESOURCES
Collections of reference materials in electronic format (e.g., Encarta, ERIC—Educational Resources Information Centers).

EQUITY ISSUES
Issues of equal distribution and use of computers and related technologies and resources across subpopulations of students and educators.

ETHICAL ISSUES
Those issues that deal with the ethical use of software and computers and related technologies by students and educators (e.g., privacy, piracy, integrity of information, responsibility for content, and use of recreational applications).

FAIR USE
A legal principle that allows portions of a copyrighted work to be used for educational purposes without permission from the copyright holder (e.g., use of portions of a copyrighted work with students by educators to illustrate a concept).

FAQ (FREQUENTLY ASKED QUESTIONS)
A technique for disseminating information through publication of a group of commonly asked questions and answers about a particular subject.

GRAPHICS PROGRAM (GRAPHICS SOFTWARE, GRAPHICS UTILITIES)
One of a number of types of computer software that enable the user to create or manipulate illustrations, graphs, drafting products, and a variety of other images.

GRAPHING CALCULATORS
A hand-held calculator that, in addition to performing calculations and functional operations, can graph functions and relations.

HUMAN ISSUES
Those issues that deal with the societal and humanistic effect of information, computer, and related technologies.

HYPERMEDIA
Hypermedia refers to interactive, nonlinear presentation of information in which more than one medium may be used (e.g., print, video, and computer), and in which users select their own paths through the material.

INFORMATION ACCESS AND DELIVERY TOOLS
Hardware and software used to access electronically archived information and computer- or satellite-based telecommunications networks (e.g., FTP, search engines, satellite downlink and receivers, Web browsers).

INTEGRATED SOFTWARE PACKAGE
A program that combines several software applications with a common interface and data sharing among the tools in the collection. Typically, packages include word processing, database management, telecommunications, spreadsheet, and business graphics (e.g., AppleWorks).

JAVA
A Sun Microsystems programming language for intranet and Internet (World Wide Web) applications. Java is designed to occupy small amounts of memory to run, and it does its own memory management. Java may be run stand-alone or launched from within HTML pages. Modern Web browsers support Java.

JAVA APPLET
A small program in the Java language that is embedded in an HTML Web page.

JIGSAW
A cooperative learning strategy in which each member of a group leaves the home base group to become part of another group that specializes in becoming an expert in some aspect of a topic.

KNOWLEDGE NAVIGATOR
An intelligent search agent that identifies and retrieves "best" information for the user based on parameters specified for each search.

KWHL CHART
A KWHL chart has four columns with the following headings: What I KNOW, What I WANT to know, HOW I am going to learn what I want to know, and what I LEARNED as a result. Students usually begin study of a topic by filling out the K or K and W part of the chart and fill in the rest as they progress through the activities of the lesson. Graphic Organizers, http://graphic.org/kwhl.html, provides information on how to create KWHL charts.

LEGAL ISSUES
Those issues that deal with the legal use of information, software, and technology by students and educators.

LOGO
A programming language especially good for students because of its ease of use and graphics capability.

MAILING LIST
Software that manages electronic discussion groups or computer conference distribution lists from one person to many. The messages are sent directly to the participants' e-mail addresses. Listserv and majordomo are commonly used programs of this type.

MANIPULATIVE MATERIALS
Materials that support tactile learning and reinforcement of concepts (e.g., blocks, rods).

MEDIA LITERACY
The ability to assess the purpose, legitimacy, and appropriateness of information received, particularly mass media messages.

MULTIMEDIA-AUTHORING SOFTWARE
Computer software used to prepare a multimedia presentation or interactive session or products (e.g., HyperStudio, Macromedia Director).

MULTIMEDIA COMPUTER
A personal computer workstation capable of supporting multimedia, including high-quality audio, video, still images, and text. Usually indicates having a CD-ROM drive.

MULTIMEDIA-PRESENTATION SOFTWARE
Computer software designed to support presentations involving multimedia (e.g., PowerPoint).

ONLINE SERVICES
Computer-based telecommunications networks that allow users to access, retrieve, and communicate information; broadcast messages; send electronic mail; and participate in user forums (e.g., America Online).

PAINTING SOFTWARE
A graphics program that enables the user to simulate painting and to manipulate image colors. Paint images are stored as patterns of dots called bitmaps. Individual image elements cannot be moved independently (e.g., Photoshop, PhotoDeluxe). (See drawing software.)

PDA (PERSONAL DIGITAL ASSISTANT)
A handheld computer that often includes pen-based entry and wireless transmission to a cellular service or desktop system.

PERFORMANCE INDICATORS
Descriptions of behaviors that demonstrate acquisition of desired knowledge, attitudes, or skills.

PRINT/GRAPHIC UTILITIES
Tools that can be used to make picture-related documents such as banners, signs, certificates, and cards (e.g., PrintShop, SuperPrint).

PROBEWARE
Computer peripherals that measure and report data directly to a computer program where it is stored.

PRODUCTIVITY TOOLS
Productivity tools refer to any type of software associated with computers and related technologies that can be used as tools for personal, professional, or classroom productivity (e.g., Microsoft Office, AppleWorks).

PROFILE
A collection of performance indicators that, when taken together, define expected characteristics or behaviors.

PROJECT BASED
Undertaken in the context of progress toward completion of a project.

REAL-TIME VIDEOCONFERENCING
An online conference using video in which all sites participate simultaneously.

SEARCH ENGINES
Software that allows retrieval of information from electronic databases (library catalogs, CD-ROMs, the Web) by locating user-defined characteristics of data such as word patterns, dates, or file formats.

SIMULATION PROGRAM
A computer program that simulates an authentic system (city, pond, company, organism) and responds to choices made by program users (e.g., Oregon Trail II, SimCity).

SSR (SILENT SUSTAINED READING)
Specific time allocated in the day or week during which everyone in a school or class stops what they are doing and reads silently.

STORYBOARD
A sketch of the components of a frame or slide in a multimedia presentation.

TECHNOLOGY-BASED INSTRUCTION
Instructional applications that involve some aspect of computers or related technologies (e.g., use of a teacher-constructed database in a social studies unit; using a graphing utility to teach relationships between two measures in economics, science, or mathematics).

TECHNOLOGY RESOURCE PERSON
A person designated to provide knowledge, information, and support for hardware, software, networks, and staff development within an educational institution (e.g., school district technology coordinator).

URL
The Uniform Resource Locator is the address on the World Wide Web used to access a particular Web server, site, or page (e.g., www.iste.org).

VIDEOCONFERENCING
Video and audio transmitted live through telecommunications that allow people at remote locations to see and hear each other. Examples of videoconferencing systems used in education include VTEL and CU-SeeMe.

VIRTUAL REALITY (VR) SOFTWARE
Computer software that allows the creation of realistic depictions of physical space. Users appear to move through and manipulate objects in this artificial environment (e.g., QuickTime Virtual Reality).

WEB PAGE
Site on the Web representing an individual's, organization's, or institution's Web presence.

WEB PAGE CREATION SOFTWARE
Editing tools that generate and display files in hypertext markup language (World Wide Web) format (e.g., PageMill, Home Page, FrontPage).

WEB SEARCH
Invoking one of the many search engines available for locating information on the Web related to specific key words.

WEB SITE
See Web page.

WORLD WIDE WEB (WEB)
(1) The worldwide array of hypertext transfer protocol (http) servers allowing access to text, graphics, sound files, and more to be mixed together and accessed through the Internet. (2) Used loosely to refer to the whole universe of resources available using Gopher, FTP, http, Telnet, USENET, WAIS, and some other tools.

Appendix G
Credits

- The NETS Project and Partners
- Writing Team
- About ISTE

The NETS Project and Partners

The NETS Project was initiated by ISTE's Accreditation and Standards Committee. ISTE has emerged as a recognized leader among professional organizations for educators involved with technology. ISTE's mission is to promote appropriate uses of technology to support and improve learning, teaching, and education administration. Its members are leaders in educational technology, including teachers, technology coordinators, education administrators, and teacher educators.

The primary goal of the NETS Project is to facilitate a series of activities and events enabling stakeholders in P–12 education to develop and apply national standards for the educational uses of technology that facilitate school improvement in the United States. The NETS Project has also developed guidelines for educational leaders to use in recognizing and addressing the essential conditions necessary for the effective use of technology to support P–12 education and teacher preparation (see Section 1, "Setting the Stage for Technology Use.")

NETS Project Goals

Goals for the NETS Project include development, review, and dissemination of standards and resources in the following areas:

- National Educational Technology Standards for Students
- P–12 learning activities modeling integration of both curriculum and technology standards
- Educational technology support standards, including standards for infrastructure, teacher preparation, administrators, and other essential conditions
- Learning activities modeling integration of both curriculum and technology standards for teacher preparation
- Assessment and evaluation of technology use
- ISTE/NCATE accreditation standards for programs specializing in educational technology

NETS STANDARDS AND RESOURCES

The following standards and resources have been or are in the process of being developed:

National Educational Technology Standards for Students (©1998)

Describes what students should know about technology and be able to do with technology.

NETS for Students—Connecting Curriculum and Technology (©2000)

Describes how technology can be used throughout the curriculum for teaching, learning, and instructional management applying both the NETS for Students and subject matter standards.

National Educational Technology Standards for Teachers (©2000)

Describes what teachers should know about and be able to do with technology and provides performance profiles and essential conditions for effective use of technology in four environments supporting the teacher preparation process.

NETS for Teachers—Preparing Teachers to Use Technology (©2002)

Describes how technology can be used throughout preparation programs for new teachers by providing model learning activities that integrate the NETS for Teachers with subject matter and teacher preparation content.

National Educational Technology Standards for Administrators (©2002)

Describes what administrators should know about technology and be able to do with technology.

NETS for Teachers—Assessment

Describes how teacher education and professional development can assess teachers' attainment of the NETS for Teachers.

TECHNOLOGY STANDARDS FOR ACCREDITATION

The ISTE Accreditation and Professional Standards Committee has developed accreditation standards for teacher preparation programs that prepare preservice and inservice teachers for specialization in educational computing and technology. The educational technology specialization guidelines have been adopted by the National Council for Accreditation of Teacher Education (NCATE) and are currently being used in evaluation of teacher preparation programs for accreditation.

ISTE/NCATE accreditation standards for programs in educational computing and technology include:

- **ISTE/NCATE Educational Computing and Technology Facilitation Standards**—initial endorsement program to prepare teachers of technology literacy and those campus leaders who support teachers' integration of technology in the classrooms;
- **ISTE/NCATE Educational Computing and Technology Leadership Standards**—advanced program to prepare district, state, or regional educational technology coordinators; and
- **ISTE/NCATE Educational Computing and Technology Secondary Computer Science Education Standards**—initial endorsement or degree programs to prepare secondary teachers of computer science.

For more information, see **www.ncate.org** or **www.iste.org**.

NETS FOR TEACHERS PT^3 PROJECT

ISTE's NETS Project has been funded by the U.S. Department of Education's Preparing Tomorrow's Teachers to Use Technology (PT^3) Program with matching support from a consortium of distinguished partners and contributors. The project is designed to address the following objectives:

1. Develop for all teachers a comprehensive set of performance-based technology standards reflecting fundamental concepts and skills for using technology to support teaching and learning.
2. Define essential conditions for teacher preparation and school learning environments necessary for effective use of technology to support teaching, learning, and instructional management.
3. Develop standards-based performance assessment tools to measure achievement of the technology standards and to serve as a basis for certification, licensing, and accreditation.
4. Disseminate models of teacher preparation in which candidates receive experiences that prepare them to effectively apply technology to student learning.
5. Establish the National Center for Preparing Tomorrow's Teachers to Use Technology (NCPT^3), which will provide coordination, leadership, and support for the PT^3 initiative and dissemination of program results.

These objectives have directed the planning and development of standards and resources designed to guide America's educational system in applying technology effectively to improve student learning.

PT³ Project Partners

Karen (Jordan) Cator
(jordan2@apple.com)
Jennifer Sayre (sayre1@apple.com)
Apple Computer, Inc.
www.apple.com

M. G. (Peggy) Kelly
(pkelly@csusm.edu)
California State University, San Marcos
www.csusm.edu

Nitin Naik (nitin@cet.edu)
NASA Classroom of the Future
www.cotf.edu

Art Wise (art@ncate.org)
William Freund (bill@ncate.org)
National Council for the Accreditation
of Teacher Education (NCATE)
www.ncate.org

Glenn Olson (glenn.olson@intel.com)
Intel Corporation
education.intel.com

PT³ Project Contributors

Cathleen Barton
(cathleen.a.barton@intel.com)
Semiconductor Industry Association
www.semichips.org

Mark Clark
(mark.clark@learningco.com)
The Learning Company
www.learningcompany.com

Stephan Knobloch
(sknobloch@pbs.org)
Public Broadcasting Service
www.pbs.org

Marcia Kuszmaul
(marciak@microsoft.com)
Microsoft Corporation
www.Microsoft.com

Scott Noon (snoon@classroom.com)
Classroom Connect, Inc.
www.classroom.com

PT³ Project Evaluators

Saul Rockman (saul@rockman.com)
Rockman et Al.
San Francisco, CA
www.rockman.com

Valerie Knight-Williams
(Valerie@rockman.com)
Rockman et Al.
San Francisco, CA
www.rockman.com

NETS Partners

Julie Walker (jwalker@ala.org)
American Association of School
Librarians (AASL), a division of the
American Library Association (ALA)
www.ala.org/aasl/

Tim Stroud (tstroud@aft.org)
American Federation of Teachers (AFT)
www.aft.org

Vicki Hancock (vhancock@ascd.org)
Association for Supervision and
Curriculum Development (ASCD)
www.ascd.org

Christine Mason
(chrism@cec.sped.org)
The Council for Exceptional Children
(CEC)
www.cec.sped.org

Art Sheekey (arthurs@ccsso.org)
Council of Chief State School Officers
(CCSSO)
www.ccsso.org

Heidi Rogers (hrogers@uidaho.edu)
International Society for Technology in
Education (ISTE)
www.iste.org

Fred Brown (fbrown@naesp.org)
National Association of Elementary
School Principals (NAESP)
www.naesp.org

Gerald Tirozzi (tirozzig@principals.org)
National Association of Secondary
School Principals (NASSP)
www.nassp.org

Barbara Stein (bstein@nea.org)
Marilyn Schlief (mschlief@nea.org)
National Education Association (NEA)
www.nea.org

Carol Edwards (CEdwards00@aol.com)
NEA Foundation for the Improvement
of Education
www.nfie.org

Ismat Abdal-Haqq
(iabdal-haqq@nsba.org)
National School Boards Association's
(NSBA) ITTE: Education Technology
Programs

Abby S. Greene (agreene@nsba.org)
www.nsba.org/itte

Melinda George (mgeorge@siia.net)
Software Information Industry
Association (SIIA)
www.siia.net

NETS Co-sponsors

Karen (Jordan) Cator
(jordan2@apple.com)
Jennifer Sayer (sayre1@apple.com)
Apple Inc.
www.apple.com

Nitin Naik (nitin@cet.edu)
NASA Classroom of the Future
www.cotf.edu

Tom Carroll (tom_carroll@ed.gov)
Lavona Grow (lavona_grow@ed.gov)
U.S. Department of Education,
Preparing Tomorrow's Teachers to Use
Technology
www.ed.gov/Technology/

ISTE Accreditation and Standards Committee

Lajeane Thomas, Chair
(lthomas@latech.edu)
Louisiana Tech University
Ruston, Louisiana

Amy Massey Vessel, Program Review
Coordinator (avessel@latech.edu)
Louisiana Tech University
Ruston, Louisiana

Joyce Friske
(friskej@jenksusa.k12.ok.us)
Jenks Public Schools
Jenks, Oklahoma

M. G. (Peggy) Kelly
(pkelly@csusm.edu)
California State University, San Marcos
San Marcos, California

Don Knezek (dknezek@iste.org)
University of North Texas
San Antonio, Texas

Heidi Rogers (hrogers@uidaho.edu)
University of Idaho, Coeur d'Alene
Coeur d'Alene, Idaho
www.uidaho.edu

Harriet Taylor (hgtaylor@att.net)
Louisiana State University
Baton Rouge, Louisiana

James Wiebe (jwiebe@calstatela.edu)
California State University, Los Angeles
Los Angeles, California

NETS for Teachers Project Leadership Team

Lajeane Thomas, Project Director
(lthomas@latech.edu)
Louisiana Tech University

M. G. (Peggy) Kelly, Co-Director
(pkelly@csusm.edu)
California State University, San Marcos

Don Knezek, Co-Director
(dknezek@iste.org)
University of North Texas

Gary Bitter, Coordinator of Administration and Evaluation
(bitter@asu.edu)
Arizona State University

David Barr (barr@imsa.edu)
Illinois Math and Science Academy

Helen Barrett (afhcb@uaa.alaska.edu)
University of Alaska Anchorage

Leslie Conery (lconer@iste.org)
International Society for Technology in Education

Joyce Friske
(friskej@jenksusa.k12.ok.la)
Jenks Public Schools

Heidi Rogers (hrogers@uidaho.edu)
University of Idaho, Coeur d'Alene

Meg Ropp (megropp@mivu.org)
Michigan Virtual University

Harriet Taylor (hgtaylor@att.net)
Louisiana State University

Amy Massey Vessel
(avessel@latech.edu)
Louisiana Tech University

James Wiebe (jwiebe@calstatela.edu)
California State University, Los Angeles

Writing Team

The following individuals contributed to this publication.

Writers Representing Curriculum Organizations

Dale Allender (dallender@ncte.org)
National Council of Teachers of English
(NCTE)
Urbana, Illinois
www.ncte.org

Erma Anderson (eanderson@nsta.org
or ermaa@aol.com)
National Science Teachers Association
(NSTA)
Needmore, Pennsylvania
www.nsta.org

Jerry Aschermann
(ascher@griffon.mwsc.edu)
National Council for the Social Studies
(NCSS)
Missouri Western State College
St. Joseph, Missouri
www.socialstudies.org

Ward Cockrum
(ward.cockrum@nau.edu)
International Reading Association (IRA)
Northern Arizona University
Sedona, Arizona
www.nau.edu

Tom Schroeder (TLS7@Buffalo.edu)
National Council of Teachers of
Mathematics (NCTM)
University of Buffalo
Buffalo, New York
www.nctm.org

Al Smith (asmith@cc.usu.edu)
American Council on the Teaching of
Foreign Language (ACTFL)
Logan, Utah

Writers Representing NETS Partners

Lola Franks (lfranks@bright.net)
NEA/Wooster City Schools
Wooster, Ohio
www.nea.org

Carole Hruskocy (carolehrus@aol.com)
Formerly with NASA Classroom of the
Future
Denver, Colorado
www.cotf.edu

Walter Kimball
(wkimball@usm.maine.edu)
CEC/University of Southern Maine
Gorham, Maine
www.cec.sped.org/

Nitin Naik (nitin@cet.edu)
NASA Classroom of the Future
Wheeling, West Virginia
www.cotf.edu

Carol Shields (carols@tenet.edu)
Intel Teach to the Future
Fort Worth, Texas
www.learningspace.org/itf/

Writing Team Members

Valeria Amburgey
(amburgey@nku.edu)
Northern Kentucky University
Highland Heights, Kentucky
www.nku.edu

David Barr (barr@imsa.edu)
Illinois Mathematics and Science
Academy
Warrenville, Illinois

Helen Barrett (afncb@uaa.alaska.edu)
University of Alaska
Anchorage, Alaska

Mary Bird (bird@pegasus.cc.ucf.edu)
ITRC at University of Central Florida
Orlando, Florida

Marylee Boarman
(mlboarman@aol.com)
Bishop Dunne Catholic School
Dallas, Texas

Pamela Burish (pjburish@usa.net)
Metropolitan Nashville Public Schools
Nashville, Tennessee

Arlene Cain (ACvid53@aol.com)
Sam Houston High School
Lake Charles, Louisiana

Jeri Carroll (jericar@twsu.edu)
Wichita State University
Wichita, Kansas

Leslie Conery (lconery@iste.org)
International Society for Technology in
Education
Eugene, Oregon

Marcia Cushall
(mcushall@frostburg.edu)
Frostburg State University
Frostburg, Maryland

Dara Feldman
(darafeldman@hotmail.com)
The Literacy Through Technology
Initiative
Kensington, Maryland

Joyce Friske
(friskej@jenksusa.k12.ok.us)
Jenks Public School System
Jenks, Oklahoma

Lynn Hines (lhines@kde.state.ky.us)
Kentucky Department of Education
Bowling Green, Kentucky

Elizabeth (Beth) Holmes
(holmes_elizabeth@colstate.edu)
Columbus State University
Columbus, Georgia

Sharnell Jackson (sharnellj@aol.com)
Chicago Public Schools
Barrington, Illinois

Judi Mathis Johnson (judimj@iste.org)
International Society for Technology in
Education
Powhatan, Virginia

Michael Jordan
(michaelj@csufresno.edu)
California State University, Fresno
Fresno, California

Virginia (Ginny) Keen
(gkeen@bgnet.bgsu.edu)
Bowling Green State University
Bowling Green, Ohio

M. G. (Peggy) Kelly
(pkelly@csusm.edu)
California State University, San Marcos
San Marcos, California

Kim Kimbell-Lopez
(kklopez@latech.edu)
Louisiana Tech University
Ruston, Louisiana

Scott Kirst (sctkirst@aol.com)
Oconto Falls High School
Abrams, Wisconsin

Don Knezek, Director
(dknezek@iste.org)
ISTE's NCPT3
ISTE/University of North Texas
San Antonio, Texas

Anita McAnear (amcanear@iste.org)
International Society for Technology in
Education
Eugene, Oregon

Bonnie Mathies
(bonnie.mathies@wright.edu)
Wright State University
Dayton, Ohio

Mark Meyers (meyers@rowan.edu)
Rowan University
Glassboro, New Jersey

Janet Miller (jamille7@earthlink.net)
Huntington Park High School, Los
Angeles Unified School District
Santa Monica, California

Bryan Miyagishima
(bmiyagishima@stcloudstate.edu)
St. Cloud State University
St. Cloud, Minnesota

Kathy Norman (knorman@csusm.edu)
California State University, San Marcos
San Marcos, California

Nancy Patterson (patter@voyager.net)
Portland Middle School
Portland, Michigan

Pamela Redmond (redmond@cnd.edu)
College of Notre Dame
Belmont, California

Virginia Reid (vreid@osd.wednet.edu)
Thurgood Marshall Middle School
Olympia, Washington

Paul Reinhart
(preinhart@bgcs.k12.oh.us)
Bowling Green City Schools
Bowling Green, Ohio

Meg Ropp (megropp@mivu.org)
Michigan Virtual University
Lansing, Michigan

Sally Shumard (sshumard@vcu.edu)
Virginia Commonwealth University
Richmond, Virginia

Lucy Carpenter Snead
(lsnead@gandalf.colacoll.edu)
Columbia College
Columbia, South Carolina

John Spagnolo
(spagnolojt@appstate.edu)
Appalachian State University
Boone, North Carolina

Barbara Slater Stern
(sternbs@jmu.edu)
James Madison University
Winchester, Virginia

Candy Stocker
(candy_stocker@ceo.cudenver.edu)
Denver Public Schools
Lakewood, Colorado

Gib Stuvé (gibstuve@home.com)
Lake Elsinore Unified School District
Lake Elsinore, California

Lajeane Thomas (lthomas@latech.edu)
Louisiana Tech University
Ruston, Louisiana

John Vaille (jvaille@cenic.org)
Digital California Project
Eugene, Oregon

Amy Massey Vessel
(avessel@latech.edu)
Louisiana Tech University
Ruston, Louisiana

Rosie O'Brien Vojtek
(rvojtek@home.com)
Bristol School District and National
Staff Development Council
Bristol, Connecticut

Laura Wendling (wendling@csusm.edu)
California State University San Marcos
San Marcos, California

David Whitehorse
(davidw@csucm.edu)
California State University San Marcos
San Marcos, California

Karin Wiburg (kwiburg@nmsu.edu)
New Mexico State University
Las Cruces, New Mexico

James Wiebe (jwiebe@calstatela.edu)
California State University, Los Angeles
San Gabriel, California

About ISTE

ISTE is a nonprofit professional organization with a worldwide membership of technology-using educators. We are dedicated to the improvement of education through the integration of computer-based technology into the curriculum. ISTE's role is leadership—we provide our members with information, networking opportunities, and guidance as they face the challenge of incorporating computers, the Internet, and other new technologies into their schools.

ISTE directs the National Educational Technology Standards for Teachers Project and further supports it through:

- curriculum ideas for the classroom in *Learning & Leading with Technology* (*L&L*).
- its Special Interest Group for Teacher Educators (SIGTE).
- research in teacher education, and models and curriculum for teacher preparation in SIGTE's journal—*Journal of Computers in Teacher Education* (*JCTE*).
- research on teacher educational models and curriculum through ISTE's Research and Evaluation Department.
- books about educational technology and its use in the classroom.
- symposia and other special events addressing current topics, resources, and trends in teacher education and teacher professional development.
- collaboration with the National Educational Computing Conference (NECC) to ensure an exemplary strand on teacher education for the annual conference.
- workshops for teachers and teacher educators based on NETS•S and NETS•T.

ISTE Board of Directors

INTERIM CHIEF EXECUTIVE OFFICER

Leslie Conery
International Society for Technology in Education

EXECUTIVE BOARD

Cheryl Williams, President
Corporation for Public Broadcasting (D.C.)

Heidi Rogers, Past President
University of Idaho at Coeur d'Alene (Idaho)

Sally Brewer, Secretary
University of Montana (Montana)

Jan Van Dam, Treasurer
Oakland Schools (Michigan)

Leslie Flanders
Scott County Board of Education (Kentucky)

Kathleen (Kathy) Hurley
NetSchools Corporation (Georgia)

BOARD

Affiliate Representatives

Frada Boxer
Nichols Middle School (Illinois)

Amy Perry
Wayne Finger Lakes BOCES, NYSC, &
TE (New York)

Special Interest Group Representative

Jan Van Dam
Oakland Schools (Michigan)

K–12 Representatives

Marilyn Piper
Washington Middle School (Washington)

Susan (Sue) Waalkes
Upper Dublin School District (Retired)
(Pennsylvania)

College/University Representatives

Sally Brewer
University of Montana (Montana)

Toni Stokes Jones
Eastern Michigan University (Michigan)

Policy, Leadership and Coordination

Leslie Flanders
Scott County Board of Education (Kentucky)

Kurt Steinhaus
Los Alamos National Laboratory (New Mexico)

ISTE 100 Representatives

Jennifer House
Classroom Connect, Inc. (California)

Kathleen (Kathy) Hurley
NetSchools Corporation (Georgia)

Information Resource Management

Steve Cowdrey
Cherry Creek Schools (Retired) (Colorado)

At-Large

Jiang (JoAnne) Lan
Southern Methodist University (Texas)

Al Rogers
Global SchoolNet Foundation (California)

International Representative

Michelle Williams
Australia Council for Computers in Education
(Queensland)

ISTE Contact Information

480 Charnelton Street
Eugene, OR 97401-2626
Phone: 800.336.5191 or 541.302.3777
Fax: 541.302.3778
E-Mail: iste@iste.org
Web: www.iste.org

Complete your library of
Technology Standards books!

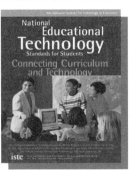

National Educational Technology Standards for Students—Connecting Curriculum and Technology

National Educational Technology Standards for Students

NETS for Teachers— Preparing Teachers to Use Technology

National Educational Technology Standards for Teachers

ne: _____   Membership #: _____

ool/Business: _____

rcss: _____   City: _____   State: _____

Postal Code: _____   Country: _____

ne: _____   E-Mail: _____

Code NETS1101

Join ISTE and its members as we lead the way in preparing students and teachers for the future.

ISTE members receive a subscription to either *Learning & Leading with Technology* or the *Journal of Research on Technology in Education*. Choose your periodical:

☐ U.S. ($58)   ☐ International ($78)

☐ L&L   ☐ JRTE (Formerly JRCE)

			Quantity	Membership Order
			x 1	=

			Quantity	NETS Order
Preparing Teachers to Use Technology	☐ Member Price $44.95	☐ Nonmember Price $49.95	x	=
Connecting Curriculum and Technology	☐ Member Price $26.95	☐ Nonmember Price $29.95	x	=
National Educational Technology Standards for Students	☐ Member Price $5.00	☐ Nonmember Price $5.00	x	=
National Educational Technology Standards for Teachers	☐ Member Price $13.50	☐ Nonmember Price $15.00	x	=

Payment enclosed. Make checks payable to ISTE—
international orders must be prepaid with U.S. funds or credit card.

VISA   ☐ MasterCard   ☐ Discover Card

☐☐☐☐ ☐☐☐☐☐ ☐☐☐☐☐ ☐☐☐☐

iration date _____   Signature _____

Purchase Order enclosed. Please add $4.00 for order processing—P.O. not including $4.00 fee will be returned.
Airmail. International orders are sent surface mail—
ISTE will bill you the additional shipping charge for airmail.
Send me ISTE membership and subscription information.

Deduct 13% if ordering quantities of 10 or more of the same title	–
SUBTOTAL	=
*Shipping and Handling (see box above)	+
*Add additional 7% of SUBTOTAL if shipped to a PO Box, AK, HI	+
*Add 12% of SUBTOTAL if shipped outside the U.S.	+
Add 7% of SUBTOTAL for GST if shipped to Canada	+
If billed with purchase order, add $4.00	+
NETS ORDER TOTAL	=
MEMBERSHIP ORDER TOTAL	+
TOTAL	=

Order by
Mail: Send this order form to:
International Society for Technology in Education
480 Charnelton Street • Eugene, OR 97401-2626 USA
Phone: 800.336.5191 (U.S. & Canada) • 541.302.3777 (International)
Fax: 541.302.3778 • E-mail: iste@iste.org • Web: www.iste.org

Photocopy this form for additional memberships.
*If actual shipping cost exceeds this amount, we will bill you for the difference.